Empirical Le
Research

A Guidance Book for Lawyers,
and Regulators

Frans L. Leeuw

Professor of Law, Public Policy and Social Science Research, Maastricht University; Faculty of Law and Director, Security and Justice Research Center (WODC), the Hague, the Netherlands

with

Hans Schmeets

Professor in Social Statistics, Maastricht University and Senior Researcher, Statistics Netherlands, the Netherlands

EE Edward Elgar
PUBLISHING

Cheltenham, UK • Northampton, MA, USA

Published by
Edward Elgar Publishing Limited
The Lypiatts
15 Lansdown Road
Cheltenham
Glos GL50 2JA
UK

Edward Elgar Publishing, Inc.
William Pratt House
9 Dewey Court
Northampton
Massachusetts 01060
USA

Paperback edition 2017

A catalogue record for this book
is available from the British Library

Library of Congress Control Number: 2015957856

This book is available electronically in the **Elgar**online
Law subject collection
DOI 10.4337/9781782549413

ISBN 978 1 78254 939 0 (cased)
ISBN 978 1 78254 941 3 (eBook)
ISBN 978 1 78254 940 6 (paperback)

Typeset by Servis Filmsetting Ltd, Stockport, Cheshire
Printed on FSC approved paper
Printed and bound in Great Britain by Marston Book Services Ltd, Oxfordshire

Contents

Figures

Tables

1. Introducing empirical legal research and structure of the book*

1.1 AN APPETIZER

Characterizing empirical legal research (abbreviated as: ELR) for lawyers, legislators and regulators is not that easy. One reason is the difference between the way lawyers and 'empiricists' *think*.

> While both modes of thinking are grounded in rigorous analysis, lawyers and empiricists often have different goals and approaches. Legal analysis places a premium on argumentation and appeals to authority, is frequently geared toward proving a particular view, is often focused on the particulars of an individual case, and is directed at reaching a definitive conclusion. In contrast, empirical analysis places a premium on observation, challenges assumptions, is oriented toward the testing of hypotheses, is usually focused on describing patterns that operate in the aggregate, and is a continuing enterprise in which new work builds on that which came before and generates even more questions for further investigation. (Lawless, Robbennolt and Ulen, 2010:10)

Although this contrast is exaggerated, there are notable differences between the two types of work.

A second reason why a characterization is difficult is that ELR makes it necessary to consider topics that students, scholars and practitioners of law are often not *acquainted* with. When you hear about empirical legal research, you probably think about data and how the data was collected. You will wonder how the (legal or societal) problem at hand was 'translated' into a research(able) problem. One of your colleagues may ponder the design of the study and the relationship between the 'legal' (normative) part and the 'social sciences' part. Can they be bridged? It would not be bad guesswork to think that discussions were held on what the 'units of analysis' are (offenders, victims, business contract partners, judges, civil servants, courts, asylum seekers, or internet service providers) and whether or not 'we will work with a sample and use statistics'. The same goes for the researcher-jurist who is given the task to find relevant research evidence from the past. Finally, on a dog's day afternoon, there is that young assistant visiting Wikipedia, trying to understand the role of 'theories' in the current project, probably wondering what is meant by the word. Purely by accident she stumbles upon 'legal Big Data' and 'disruptive legal technologies' (and sends a message to her colleagues that she's a bit lost).

These topics are all relevant and 'in-need-of-being-known' for anyone planning to *do* ELR, to *commission* ELR and/or to *use* (and *evaluate*) it. However, they are also fragmented and miss an overarching characterization of what *empirical legal research* basically is.

This guidance book is dedicated to prepare and present such an overarching perspective. Its goal is to give guidance to students, scholars and practitioners, be they lawyers, legislators, regulators, policy makers, commissioners of research, prosecutors or judges. A complete 'menu' of what empirical legal research entails will therefore be offered.

Good dinners start, according to the norms of *haute cuisine*, with an *amuse bouche*. Several of these are now served as well as the concept of the 'empirical cycle'.

1.1.1 'Law in the Books versus Law in Action'

Empirical legal research (ELR) covers all major fields of law, as the *Oxford Handbook of Empirical Legal Research* (Cane and Kritzer, 2010) shows. The chapters include family law and penal law, access to (civil) justice, evidence law, contract law and international law, but also police activities, naming and shaming, regulatory impact assessments, the role of law and regulation with regard to topics such as bankruptcy and financial markets and consumer protection.

Empirical legal research, however, is *not* primarily or only interested in *laws* (or any other legal arrangement) *in the books*, but in *law(s) in action*, to quote Pound:

> If we look closely, distinctions between law in the books and law in action, between the rules that purport to govern the relations of man and man and those that in fact govern them, will appear and it will be found that today also the distinction between legal theory and judicial administration is often a very real and a very deep one. (Pound, 1910: 15)

Llewellyn (1930), a few decades later, distinguished between 'paper rules' and 'real rules' or 'working rules'. Laws and rules can exist everywhere, although they are often 'seen as a body of rules that . . . are determined and enforced by the state' (Shavell, 2002: 227).

In this book we broaden this concept in two ways. First, because there are more organizations than states producing rules, regulations and related interventions like 'private regulatory regimes' (Aviram, 2003), 'legislative Marktinterventionen' (Hosemann, 2014: 45), publicly declared (corporate) codes (as binding promises) (Beckers, 2015) and international treaties and protocols. Second, because as Howarth (2013) highlights, the legal world designs 'social structures and devices [like] contracts, companies, trusts, constitutions, and statutes . . . A successful contract is one that gets the job done of facilitating a deal between the parties. A contract that results in litigation is unsuccessful – it has failed to do its job'.[1]

In this book we use different terms to describe the object of empirical legal research: *(legal) arrangements*, *devices*, *interventions*, but we will also refer to *laws*, *legislation* and *regulation*. All these 'legal arrangements' aim at influencing individuals and organizations, codify and/or regulate (to some extent) their functioning, create restrictions and opportunities for them and can be enforced with various degrees of involvement of the state.[2] Westerman (2011: 106–107) adds that 'many rules nowadays prescribe in a fairly direct manner the goals that should be attained' and calls this the 'ongoing instrumentalisation [that] has led to different demands on both the legislator and judge'. Verbruggen (2014: 79) sees 'commercial contracts [becoming] increasingly important vehicles for the implementation and enforcement of safety, social and sustainability standards in transnational supply chains'.

ELR thus addresses developments and actions in the 'real (social) world'[3] as relating to legal arrangements, either to influence this world, to facilitate it, or to legalize what has been the 'usual' practice.

One of the backgrounds of ELR has been the critique, articulated decades ago, on legal formalism; some even referred to the construction of a 'heaven of legal concepts' far removed from social reality, and disregarded the ways in which law is produced by and operates within society (Cohen, 1935). Although this statement is an exaggeration and causes unnecessary skepticism about *any* role formal laws and rules play in reality, differences between the 'legal reality' and the 'social (empirical) reality' cannot be denied.[4] The distinction between doctrinal (legal) research and non-doctrinal studies is related to this point.

Doctrinal research asks what the law is on a particular issue. It is concerned with an analysis of the legal doctrine and how it has been developed and applied (McConville and Chui, 2007). This approach, according to Hutchinson (2013: 9) 'lies at the heart of any lawyer's task because it is the research process used to identify, analyze and synthesize the content of the law . . . Doctrine has been defined as a synthesis of rules, principles, norms, interpretative guidelines and values, which explains, makes coherent or justifies a segment of the law as part of a larger system of law'. McCrudden (2006: 634) adds that 'doctrinal analysis takes [the] form, in which the writer attempts to argue that this or that is the "best" solution to a particular problem, "best" meaning having the best fit with which already exists'. Non-doctrinal research is legal research that employs methods taken from other disciplines to generate empirical data to answer other research questions. It can focus on a problem, its causes and consequences, a policy, a law or any other legal arrangement while institutions and organizations can also be studied.

ELR focuses on 'empirical'. In line with the editors of *The Oxford Handbook on Empirical Legal Research*, this 'involves the systematic collection of information ("data") and its analysis according to some generally accepted method. Of central importance is the systematic nature of the process, both of collecting and analysing the information' (Cane and Kritzer, 2010: 4 5). Epstein and Martin (2014: 3) usc a morc informal terminology: data is 'just a term for facts about the world', sometimes numerical (or quantitative), sometimes non-numerical (or qualitative).

How does empirical legal research work look in practice? A few examples: Smits (2011) studied mandatory rights of withdrawal in *consumer contract law* and what consumers think about these rights. Withdrawal rights allow the consumer to terminate the contract within a set 'cooling-off period'. Smits made a comparison between statutory withdrawal rights in Europe and in the United States. He presented results of a 'modest survey' of the voluntary use of withdrawal rights in general conditions of retailers. He also studied the usefulness of mandatory withdrawal rights.

Ruiter et al (2011: 135) investigated the *(penal) sentencing preferences* of the general public versus those of judges in the Netherlands. 'Given the opportunity, how would the Dutch public sentence perpetrators of different types of crime? To what extent are these verdicts related to characteristics of the criminal act (e.g. offender characteristics, type of crime, victim characteristics)? Does the verdict depend on characteristics of the citizen who issues a sentence (e.g. young/old, male/female)? And does information about sentencing options (i.e. the costs involved and rates of recidivism) affect verdicts decided by members of the general population?'

Increasingly the impact of regulation and other (legal) arrangements is studied from an experimental or quasi-experimental perspective: individuals, groups or organizations are compared, over a certain period, while some get a 'treatment' (the (legal) intervention, program, sanction, piece of legislation, contract) and others do not. Interventions like Hot Spots Policing (Braga et al, 2012) are studied along these lines, but there are many other examples in the field of private and administrative law.

ELR also covers studies of a different nature: studies describing, analysing and comparing ways in which – as an example – nation states safeguard the *rule of law* or *freedom rights*. The 'World of Justice' project (Agrast et al, 2014: 2) presents a set of empirical indicators on the rule of law from the perspective of the 'ordinary person'. It examines practical situations in which a rule of law deficit may affect the daily lives of those interviewed. The project provides data on 10 dimensions, such as order and security, absence of corruption, regulatory enforcement and access to justice. McMahon (2012) is one of the authors behind the *index of human freedom* which combines country data on the freedom of movement, freedom of expression, and freedom of relationships. It also covers data on government's threat to freedom (the occurrence of political imprisonment) and society's threat to freedom (like human trafficking, homicide and female genital mutilation).

1.1.2 The Functioning of Organizations and Institutions in the Legal Field

ELR is not only focused on *laws and regulations (in action)*, but also on the *functioning of organizations and institutions in the legal field.* What they do, how they do it, what the consequences are of their work and what they cost are topics of interest. The legal field is characterized by large numbers of organizations and institutions. National and international courts, prosecutors, prisons and probation services, but also ombudsman institutions, human rights organizations, bailiffs and notaries, and their professional organizations, including what Jansen and Michaels (2007) call private law beyond the state (multinational companies creating systems of rules and imposing them on their suppliers and customers; examples are standardization and accreditation organizations and transnational governance networks).

Van Dijk et al (2009) studied one such institution, the *Netherlands Ombudsman.* They used the *Ombudsman's complaints database*, which contains information from over 140,000 dossiers covering 25 years. They applied a mix of conventional database techniques and a data mining algorithm to scan and map this database and were able to detect paths in the handling of complaints that were not known before.

Posner and de Figueiredo (2004) present a second, rather different example. They studied the International Court of Justice (ICJ) which has jurisdiction over disputes between nations. Its defenders argue that the ICJ decides cases impartially and confers legitimacy on the international legal system. Its critics argue that the members of the ICJ vote in the interests of the states that appoint them. Prior empirical scholarship is 'ambiguous', as Posner and de Figueiredo (2004) showed, which urged them to undertake a new empirical investigation. They studied theories on judging behavior and tested the charge of bias using statistical methods on voting behavior of Court members.

1.1.3 Evaluating Laws, Regulations and Other Legal Arrangements like Interventions and Sanctions

Doing ELR often implies asking and answering *evaluative questions*. Cummings (20135: 186) refers to the 'challenges of evaluation' that empirical legal researchers face. 'How to study the impact of law is a question that has confronted scholars since the 1960s. There are questions about which types of impacts to study and the proper methodology for doing so'. Hage (2010: 6) refers to 'evaluative legal science which can take the shape of passing value judgments on actual or hypothetical (proposed) regulations or of the selection of the "best" regulation from a set of alternatives'.

Evaluation is the more so important because, as Howarth (2013: 15; 17; 67ff) argued, lawyers in fact are (transaction-costs-) engineers: they make devices for others that try to reduce or prevent transaction costs, conflicts and other problems (Gilson, 1984).[5] Devices are 'contracts, conveyances, wills, trusts, regulations, statutes and constitutions, and companies' (i.e. their legal structure).[6] However, between ambition and reality can be discrepancies, and evaluators are 'designed' to monitor and explain them.

Evaluators also study the predictions (of public and semi-public organizations) about the consequences of policies, rules, legislation and other 'tools of governments' (like information campaigns and incentives), sometimes before they are even implemented. This is known as *ex ante evaluation* or 'prospective evaluation'. The European Union refers to these activities as *regulatory impact assessments*.[7] A US GAO (1996) study trying to find out what the impact on teenage pregnancy would be if law A or law B would be implemented, is a (classic) example.

Evaluations also address the way in which legal arrangements are implemented and what difficulties are experienced during this process (*process evaluations* or *implementation evaluations*). A related approach is known as *compliance (or regularity) auditing*. Here the empirical investigation describes the extent to which natural and corporate actors behave in compliance with protocols, rules and regulations.

And there are studies (often ex post) on the *effects, consequences or impacts* of legal arrangements and interventions on the behavior of persons and organizations (*impact* or *effectiveness evaluations*). A rather old example is Aubert's study done in the early 1950s. He wanted to find out the 'extent to which behavior (of housemaids) conformed to the rules laid down in the (Norwegian) Law on Housemaids of 1948'. The purpose of this law was to protect the interests of domestic help. Aubert used a sample of some 200 housewives and 200 housemaids in Oslo and interviewed them about their conduct, level of knowledge, and attitudes and motives, in so far as these related to the law. 'It has to be concluded that the law was, at least for some years, ineffective in the sense that actual conditions of work remained at variance with the norms laid down' (Aubert, 1969:121).[8]

Interventions in the world of penal law not only refer to regulations and sanctions (for example with regard to the role they play in reducing recidivism), but also include (cognitive-behavioral) programs used by prisons and probation organizations to alter attitudes and behavior of (re)offenders. Examples are ETS ('Enhanced Thinking Skills') and ART ('Aggression Regulation/Replacement Training'), which are regularly evaluated (Cornet et al, 2014).

Since the introduction of the internet, laws, regulations and (other) policies are confronted with and directed at the digital world. Evaluating the impact of (digital) sanctions to help prevent or reduce digital piracy (illegal copying of music, movies, 3-D printing designs and e-books) is only one example; others deal with evaluating the governance (structure) of the internet, e-law enforcement, circumvention policies and digital surveillance activities (Leeuw and Leeuw, 2012).

Evidence-based regulation, wherein results from social science research including behavioral economics are used to help law makers draft regulations that have a (fair) chance of realizing their set goals, is a blossoming field. Sunstein (2013: 1) states:

> In recent years, social scientists have been incorporating empirical findings about human behavior into economic models. These findings offer important insights for thinking about regulation and its likely consequences. They also offer some suggestions about the appropriate design of effective, low-cost, choice-preserving approaches to regulatory problems, including disclosure requirements, default rules, and simplification.

Parts of this approach are the so-called design studies and pilots. Alternative dispute resolution activities, for example, are developed and tested before being implemented at a broader scale. The Hague Institute for the Internationalization of Law[9] shares examples of how research is related to modernizing justice.

Throughout this book, examples of legal evaluations are on the menu, including the designs that are used and why, what the role of 'intervention theories' are, how data is collected and analyzed and how evidence from legal evaluations can be visualized in a modern way.

1.1.4 Big Data, Technology and the Law: Legal Predictions, Machine Learning and Computational Legal Studies[10]

Big Data and *technology* (artificial intelligence, machine learning and the internet) are strongly related. Big Data consist of (call) logs, mobile-banking transactions, online user-generated content such as blog posts, social media, sensor apps, online (Google) searches, satellite images and the data one holds in emails, blogs, intranets, extranets etc.[11] The *Internet of Things* refers to the ability of everyday objects to connect to the internet, allowing these devices to gather, send and receive data. Examples include wearable technology, such as watches and fitness bands or smartphones but also thermostats that know when we are home and cars that monitor our driving habits (O'Neill, 2015). The more (historical) paper documents like wills, contracts, treaties and other legal case materials, as well as books and newspapers, become digitized, the larger 'legal Big Data' becomes.

Susskind (2008; 2013) refers to these and other technological developments as *disruptive* (for the legal world). Examples are *automated document assembly* (disruptive, because widespread use can greatly reduce the time that lawyers expend on document drafting and production); *relentless connectivity* (he uses this term to describe how the use of hand-held devices with wireless broadband access, powerful video, high processing speed and nearly endless storage capacity will create expectations among clients for 24/7 lawyer availability) and *online legal guidance* (systems that provide legal diagnoses, generate legal documents, assist in legal audits and provide legal updates).[12] With regard to Big Data, Süsskind (2013: 48–9) suggests that 'in due course they will be of profound significance for legal practice and scholarship'. A question like 'what legal issues are troubling communities can very easily be answered, while by collecting and analyzing huge bodies of commercial contracts and exchanges of emails, we might gain insight into the greatest legal risks that specific sectors face'. Online dispute resolution (ODR) is materializing[13] while social media can help in finding out which public perceptions exist about magistrates.

Also for ELR Big Data are important. One reason is that (a new form of) *legal analytics*, including *legal prediction* is possible. McGinnis and Pearce (2014: 3052) put it as follows:

> Law, with its massive amounts of data from case law, briefs, and other documents, is conducive to machine data mining (machine learning)[14] that is the foundation of legal analytics. Legal data include fact patterns, precedents, and case outcomes. For instance, one form of legal analytics would use fact patterns and precedents to predict a case's outcome, thereby better equipping lawyers to assess the likely result of litigation.

Nelson and Simek (2013:1) refer to 'using Big Data to *evaluate* (law) firms'. Another application is that Big Data will stimulate *transparency* of the legal world. Katz and Bommarito (2013: 3–4) studied how complex legal rules are (in the USA). Big Data may also facilitate *legal practice/legal aid*. Empirical researchers doing pattern recognition in legal advice, complaints and electronic transcripts of court procedures and know-how can play an important role in aid processes. In criminal investigations, tax fraud detection and detecting money laundering already play such a role. Finally, Big Data can deliver *new evidence* in court. Several American examples indicate that big data collected and analyzed from public data sets can be admitted as evidence. Although the legal sector has always been a 'data-driven industry', until recently all that data stayed offline (i.e. on paper).

Some of these examples come from the USA, and indeed, the Big Data movement in law seems to be more developed than in Europe. However, it can be expected that, as has happened in other fields (marketing and business analytics), the European legal world will soon catch up. One reason is that digitization does not stop at the frontier. Another reason is that while in the justice domain many organizations, such as the police, public prosecution, courts and prisons have their *own* data and information systems, society expects empirical insights *throughout this domain* on *overarching* items like judiciary efficiency, case load, elapsed time and privacy risks.[15] These insights can only be produced when judicial data space systems are available, covering the diverse organizations' own data and making domain-wide analysis of the 'enterprise of law', including legal logistics possible.

1.1.5 Explaining what is Happening: the Role of Theories

Observing that legal arrangements make a difference (or do not) is something; to explain what has happened is something else. *Explanatory questions* have to be asked, like what are the underlying causes that lead some legal arrangements to trigger behavior(al changes), while others are falling dead on the ground? An example is MaCaulay's (1963) study on (non-) contractual relations in businesses. He found that in the USA, contract law is often ignored in transactions, which he tried to explain by using insights from sociological and behavioral theory. Since this path-breaking study, a research program has developed, investigating under which conditions 'contractual behavior' occurs (see Chapter 10).

Explaining why wrongful convictions occur is a second example. Technical mistakes during police investigations and incorrect eyewitnesses are one aspect of such an explanation, but cognitive biases of officials like tunnel vision, yeah-yeah-saying, hindsight bias, and the fundamental attribution error[16] also help explain the occurrence of erroneous convictions.[17]

A third example has to do with explaining a (lack of) compliance with rules and regulations. It is known that some people and organizations are more focused on compliance than others. A Dutch study showed that with regard to the introduction of cognitive-behavioral interventions like

Enhanced Thinking Skills (ETS) into the Dutch penitentiary system, around half of the interventions were not implemented in accordance with procedures and protocols agreed upon (Nas et al, 2011). Insights from *public choice theory* help to explain this. One such insight is that there is competition inside bureaucracies about (the number of) clients to be 'treated' ('by me'). In particular, when numbers of clients are small (or decreasing), bureau-politics and bureaucratic firefighting pop up as factors causing implementation problems[18] (while the bill is paid by taxpayers).

To explain why individuals differ in levels of compliance with the law, *rational choice theory*, sometimes in connection with *biosocial theories*, is used.

Bio-social theories – in this example – point to differences in cognitive and emotional capacity ('agency') of persons to perceive and experience threats of being caught. Fearlessness theory, low arousal theory and other theories from endocrinology, neurosciences and genetics are important points of reference (Raine, 2013). These insights are also used to explain what the impact of behavior modification programs is on (re)offenders (Cornet et al, 2014).

We have outlined five important characteristics of ELR, and used the word 'empirical' rather often. What is it and what is the empirical cycle?

1.2 THE EMPIRICAL CYCLE

What is 'empirical'? The editors of the *Oxford Handbook on Empirical Legal Research* describe 'empirical' as 'the systematic collection of information ("data") and its analysis according to some generally accepted method' (Cane and Kritzer, 2010: 4–5; Lawless, Robbennolt and Ulen, 2010: 7). 'Systematic data-collection and analysis' and 'accepted methods' are important elements. What this entails will be discussed in the following chapters. However, we emphasize that ELR is much more than data-collection and analysis. It includes research problems, theories, systematic literature reviews, research designs and knowledge transfer.

A *second characteristic* is that the empirical cycle *includes both quantitative research and qualitative research*. This may seem an entirely superfluous remark, but it is not. Some of you remember or have heard about 'paradigm wars'[19] between approaches (in the latter part of the twentieth century). Although these times are behind us, there remain epistemological and methodological differences. While quantitative research often employs experimental designs and quantitative measures to test hypotheses and emphasizes the measurement and analysis of causal relationships between variables, qualitative research uses a more naturalistic approach that seeks to understand phenomena in 'real world settings'. Unlike quantitative researchers who seek causal determination, prediction and generalization of findings, qualitative researchers seek illumination, understanding and extrapolation to similar situations (Golafshani, 2003). Computer-assisted qualitative research methods have reduced the differences between 'quali' and 'quanti', while the introduction of Big Data, including sensor data, will further reduce 'paradigmatic firefighting'.[20]

A third characteristic is the *cyclical nature* of empirical research. Empirical research starts with a question ('research problem'), passes through several stages of activities like data collection and analysis, formulating an answer to the problem and often starts again in another cycle addressing a related research question.

The cycle starts with → (research) problems: In every discipline and specialty, research starts with *(research) problems* (Popper, 1972; Ultee, 1976; 2001; Bunge, 1997). The same is true for ELR. These problems find their origin in different things:

- in prior research ('unsolved scientific problems');
- in scientific debates (contradictions between findings and theories, mixed results, different interpretations, known unknowns and unknown unknowns);
- in trends, developments and problems in the physical, social, legal and virtual world.

Examples of research problems addressed in the *Oxford Handbook on Empirical Legal Research* and in recent empirical legal research are the following:[21]

- What are the possible reasons for not holding executives and oversight officials internally liable for the damage caused by the improper performance of duties by agencies in cases where there is sufficient ground to do so?[22]
- How can claiming behavior be explained and what are findings from empirical research on naming, blaming and claiming?
- To what extent is Automatic Number Plate Recognition (ANPR) technology an efficient instrument to improve investigations by police and prosecutors? What are (unintended) side effects of implementing this technology in the Netherlands?
- What are assumptions about human behavior underlying the decisions made in refugee status determinations by judges in the UK?
- Has federal antidiscrimination law in the USA been effective in moving women and minorities into management?

After the research problem(s) have been articulated → 'theory' marches in (most of the time): A theory 'is simply a reasonable and precise answer to the research question' (Epstein and Martin, 2010: 906). Although there are several types of theories, in this book we discuss two of them: *formal, aka explanatory theories* and *intervention, aka program theories*. Formal (explanatory) theories often have been developed by the academic community and have a label or a name. Examples are public choice theory (on decision-making mechanisms in publicly financed organizations), cognitive dissonance theory (on balancing cognitions, attitudes and behavior) and incentive theory (on different types of incentives and prompts). Intervention or program theories are sets of assumptions underlying (public/private) interventions like laws and other regulations, contracts, covenants, verdicts, levies, subsidies, awareness raising campaigns and naming and shaming strategies. Often these assumptions are not (fully) articulated by practitioners, policy makers and other users and producers. The assumptions imply the answer to the question why they believe that their interventions, operations or verdicts are capable of reaching certain goals or at least contributing to them.

Related to the theoretical work, researchers want to find, systematize and synthesize results from earlier research → research reviews and synthesis marches in: Researchers want to know what has already been published on 'their' problem. In earlier times, surveys of the literature were based on suggestions from friends, colleagues, librarians and journals ('snowball sampling'). Over the last two to three decades a more rigorous type of literature study has been developed, known as the *systematic research review* (and *synthesis*).[23] Based on a broad (on-line) coverage of literature through search engines like Web of Science, other (meta-)search engines and websites from publishers, the field is scanned and mapped, while inclusion and exclusion criteria (which studies will be used and which not) are applied (based on protocols). One of the goals is to distinguish between empirical and non-empirical studies, and to take into account the robustness of the research designs and (data collection and analysis) methods (including statistics). These '[systematic review] techniques have been developed to weigh studies against each other in terms of the confidence with which their findings can be accepted and to combine data from different studies to reach overall judgments' (Gomm, 2008: 345; see also Gough et al, 2012).

Often this review work addresses the research problem directly; if the problem concerns the impacts of a restorative justice program in Canada, then a systematic review of empirical studies of (similar and other) restorative justice programs is very probably available. Another approach is to carry out a systematic search and review of earlier work focusing on the *mechanisms* underlying legal arrangements, interventions and policies (Farnsworth, 2007). If the research problem is to find out what the impact is of legal interventions to curb digital piracy, and there is a theory specifying which behavioral mechanisms may explain (and change) this behavior, information from empirical studies about *these mechanisms* can be retrieved (Leeuw and Leeuw, 2012). However, research reviews may not be available, or the results may be contradictory or apply to fundamentally different contexts.

Then: the decision is to continue the project by doing new (primary) research which necessitates that the research design appears on the agenda: To collect *empirical information* in a methodologically robust way, decisions have to be made on the *research design*. The function of such a design is to ensure that the evidence obtained enables us to answer the initial question as unambiguously as possible. Research designs structure the way in which a study is constructed. Examples of designs are the experiment, the quasi-experiment, the case study and the longitudinal observational study. Designs are *not* the same as methods to collect data like interviews, focus groups or questionnaires.

Next → the choice of data collection methods marches in: There is wide variety of data collection methods available: questionnaires, item lists (for interviews), observation schemes and 'reading lenses' to categorize and summarize documents (like reports, contracts, proceedings of meetings, e-mails, blogs, websites), but also videos (YouTube) and pictures, psychological, physiological and neuro-scientific tests, sensors and digital 'apps'. Both quantitative and qualitative methods are part of this toolkit as well as multi-method approaches (Nielsen, 2010). Deciding about who the units of analysis are is important too.

Sometimes data are already structured and stored and (almost) 'ready for use': databases and data warehouses are the places to be. Stanford University's Faculty of Law has the Intellectual Property Litigation Clearinghouse, which provides real-time data on intellectual property litigation. The Research Institute of the Dutch Ministry of Security and Justice (http://www.wodc.nl) has databases covering penal law, administrative law and civil law.

Collecting data is one thing, analyzing them is another thing → now data analysis is on the menu:

> How do empirical legal scholars perform this task? The answer depends in no small part on their goals. If the goal is to summarize the data they have collected, then some simple statistical measures might suffice. For the vast majority of ELR projects, however, making inferences (using facts we know to learn about facts we do not know) is the goal. (Epstein and Martin, 2010: 912–13)

Then more complex statistical (descriptive and causal) activities, with the help of software, are carried out. However, not every ELR study is quantitative in nature. More qualitative data can be collected through interviews, focus groups or participatory observation. Also, documents like wills, contracts, verdicts, jurisprudence and policy papers can be analyzed. Special methods including software to analyze this kind of data are available.

The penultimate step → presenting the results of ELR and answering the research question(s): This was usually done through a book or report, a paper or a fact sheet. Nowadays, in order to transfer findings to relevant audiences in a more modern way, use is made of seminars and webinars, blogs, apps and round table meetings with stakeholders, colleagues and commissioners. Data-visualization has become important too. What is also at stake is 'the problem of adding normative value to facts: no legal obligation follows from empirical facts' (Lepsius, 2005). This topic is known as the fact-value-dichotomy or the gap problem (between empirics and normativity). ELR folks should not only be capable of understanding this problem but also detecting and handling it. The same is true for normative-doctrinal researchers (Leeuw, 2015).

Then the process may start again → a new (related) research problem is formulated and a new research cycle starts . . . [24]: It may start again because the investigators have not been able to answer the research problem (in full) due to (methodological) difficulties, data restrictions or other causes. The research cycle can also start again (on a 'higher' level) when the research problem is answered, but leads to *new* questions.

Graphically speaking this is the *empirical research cycle* as presented in Figure 1.1.[25]

As the examples presented show, ELR has breadth, depth and width. *Breadth*, because it covers all legal fields and specialties. *Depth*, because it studies these fields by combining what is happening with laws and regulations 'in the books', and 'in action', by applying different approaches, designs and methods of empirical research. And *width*, because it does not look into research topics from one perspective (like compliance audits do) but addresses them *side to side*, i.e. at its full extent.

Before we move on, a few words of caution. Is this circle, with its six steps, a 'mechanical process from which the analyst can never deviate' (Epstein and Martin 2014: 19)? They compare the analyst/researcher who strictly follows such an approach with a 'baker who must follow every step in the recipe or else the cake will fall'.[26] For them, researchers 'should have the flexibility of mind to deviate, to overturn old ways of looking at the world, revise their blueprints as necessary and collect more (or different) data than they might have intended'. We agree with the idea that researchers have the intellectual and professional freedom to deviate, *but at the same time research is not an 'anything goes' process, a free floating 'pick and choose-thing'*. Formulating low-quality research problems, leaving theory outside the investigation, not knowing right from wrong when discussing

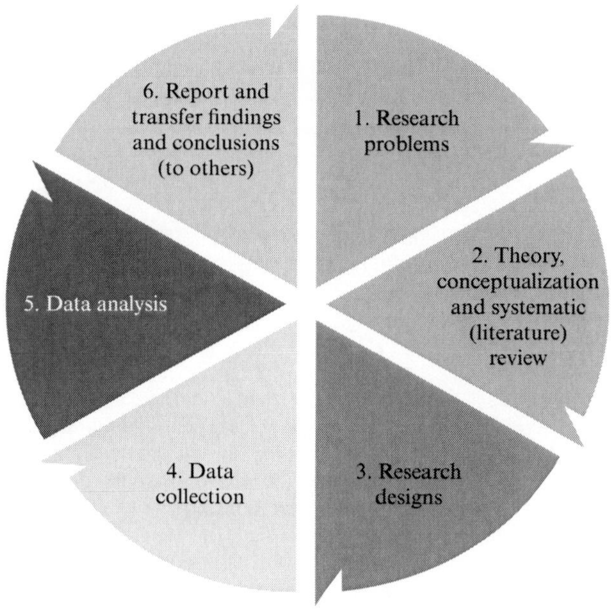

Figure 1.1 The empirical cycle

and implementing research designs, forgetting about validity when collecting and working with data and neglecting the fact-value dichotomy, is *not* the way to go.[27]

Although Ramsey and Keller's (2006) list of 11 tips is designed for judges and lawyers when *using* empirical research, insights as to what is commendable when *doing* empirical work in a legal environment can easily be deduced from it. The authors stress the relevance of an adequate research problem and hypotheses, the importance of how concepts are operationalized and measured, the causality problem (and which research designs are capable of addressing it) and several others.

My suggestion to the reader is: use and follow the different steps, the related methodological 'rules of thumbs' and criteria, but do so *in a smart way, preventing it from becoming a tick & flick-box or iron cage.*

1.3 STRUCTURE OF THE BOOK

Chapter 2 starts with looking back. It gives a *concise contemporary history* of ELR and discusses its 'intellectual roots'.

BOX 1.1 ON THE QUALITY OF EMPIRICAL LEGAL RESEARCH

For the USA, Epstein and King (2002) studied the problem of (methodological) quality of (US) empirical legal research. Initially they read and analyzed all 231 articles published in American law reviews between 1990 and 2000 that had the word 'empirical' in their title. Their purpose was to establish what current practices in the US law reviews were and what were the (methodological) problems. Later they added all empirical papers from six (top) US law reviews (Chicago, Columbia, Harvard, NYU, Stanford and Yale) published between 1995 and 2000, the 50 most-cited articles (according to the Legal Scholarship Network) that were written by legal academics and appeared in the law reviews and studies in four peer-reviewed law journals (like the *Journal of Law & Economics* and the *Journal of Legal Studies*). Finally, they used 'a much more informal approach; namely, by reading widely through law reviews, following citations, and reading further'. The results were 'discouraging', which led them to formulate guidelines on how to do empirical legal research. Most of them directly boil down to the dimensions of our empirical cycle outlined above, while a few are broader in nature.

In the Netherlands, Smits (2009) has criticized the state of the art of (empirical) legal research, as did the Report of the Evaluatiecommissie Rechtswetenschappelijk Onderzoek. Tijssen (2009: 197, 206) analyzed some 100 PhDs in legal research: 'The (Phd) research offered an evaluative test of the methodological justification of the legal research presented against general methodological norms'. His conclusion was that 'in terms of verifiability, legal doctoral theses do little in the way of explaining and justifying the sources selected and the methods used, yet an increasing number of doctoral theses include an explanation and justification of the research problem'. For the field of human rights research, Coomans, Grunfeld and Kamminga (2008) are of the opinion that 'in academic human rights research, especially legal human rights research, little attention tends to be devoted to questions of methodology'.

Next, the focus shifts to describing the *different aspects (steps or dimensions)* of the empirical cycle.

Chapter 3 focuses on (typologies of) *research problems*, including *suggestions on how to develop adequate formulations of problems.*

In Chapter 4 the role of *theories* is highlighted. *Two types* of theories are discussed (explanatory and intervention theories), what their *ingredients* are (mechanisms), how theories can be found and/or articulated, including examples.

Systematic research reviews and synthesis studies as ways to capture *earlier research* are discussed in Chapter 5. Types of systematic reviews are presented as well as information how to find them and how to do them.

Chapter 6 brings types of *research designs* to the menu. Criteria are presented for selecting and assessing design(s) that fit the type of research problems, including methodological characteristics of designs as well as examples.

Chapter 7 summarizes *data collection methods and instruments*, both *quantitative and qualitative, including ethical considerations*. Three types of data are discussed: *register-based (and stored) data, data collected through primary research and Big Data*. Reliability and validity of data (collection) are discussed as well as other criteria, including ethical.

Chapter 8 gives information, suggestions and examples on *quantitative and qualitative data-analysis, including statistics, Big Data analysis and mixed methods*. A large part of this chapter is structured around several empirical investigations dealing with elections in OSCE regions. The chapter also describes data-visualization, including some of its tools.

Chapter 9 discusses two issues on how to handle the transfer and dissemination of findings from empirical research. The *first* is how to help the *diffusion/transfer of the evidence to diverse audiences*, in such a way that the results are known. The *second* issue discusses the (complex) relationship between empirical legal research and normative aspects, including legal practice and scholarship.

Chapter 10 asks two final questions. *Is an empirical revolution in law taking place?* And: *is there growth of knowledge in the ELR field?*

ENDNOTES

* Thanks to Jaap Hage, Miet Vanderhallen, Willemien de Jongste, Frank Willemsen, Cor Hermans, Jack Tomlin, Katja Zimmerman, Honours Track master students from Maastricht University and members of the Maastricht Law and Philosophy Platform for their comments and suggestions.

1. Howarth compares the work of lawyers with engineering. He was not the first, as Pound (1942: 64) saw law as 'social engineering designed to eliminate friction and waste in the satisfaction of unlimited human interests and demands out of a limited store of goods in existence'. See also McManaman (1958: 16ff).
2. Hadfield (2001), Schwarcz (2002) and Ellickson (1991) point to the lengthy historical precedence of this type of legal arrangements. Hadfield (2001: 40, 41) shows that 'from the middle ages to infant digital age, there are examples of law developed and administrated by private entities with various degrees of state involvement'.
3. This includes virtual reality, augmented reality and, in the not too distant future, inter-reality (where virtual and off-line reality merge).
4. Schauer (2013) presented a balanced view on differences between 'law in books/ in action', including types of rules. Social and behavioral researchers are well-versed in understanding the role formal rules/legislation play, as they influence incentives and other mechanisms that underlie behavioral choices and outcomes.
5. Susskind (2008) sees lawyers as 'knowledge engineers', who work as knowledge brokers together with expert systems. See also Howarth (2013: 20–21).
6. In the 1950s (in the USA) a new discipline: 'eunomics was suggested, the study of good order and workable arrangements' (Fuller, 1953: 477). See also Polish sociologists Podgorecki and Petrazycki, who worked in line with social engineering.

7. In the evaluation literature 'impact assessment' is usually done *ex post*, to find out what the effects ('impact') of policies and programs have been.
8. Seen from a contemporary perspective, the design that was used can be criticized. See Chapter 6 for more on research designs.
9. http://www.hiil.org/search?form=search&q=trends, accessed 4 July 2015, describes the many 'modernizing' activities of this institute, including trend and future studies.
10. Sometimes the concept of money-ball legislation/regulation is mentioned. It goes back to Michael Lewis' 2003 book *Moneyball*. 'Lewis tells the story of Billy Beane, the general manager of the Oakland Athletics baseball team. With the help of his statistics-obsessed assistant, Paul DePodesta, Beane brought the once lowly Athletics into the top tier of baseball teams, and wound up transforming professional baseball, by substituting empirical data for long-standing dogmas, intuition, and anecdote-driven judgments' (Glaeser and Sunstein, 2014: 1). As Moneyball legislation largely uses statistical data and findings from cost-benefit studies and policy analysis, and – as far as we know – has not yet worked with 'Big Data', we do not discuss it here (although the underlying idea, that data are important when designing and implementing regulation, is the same).
11. Nelson and Simek (2013: 2) give examples ranging from search and rescue persons and law enforcement agencies working with drones to 'the Occupy Wall Street protesters (who also) had their own drone' (The Occucopter).
12. See a selection of the results from the 2010 American Bar Association (ABA) Legal Technology Survey Report, http://www.americanbar.org/groups/departments_offices/legal_technology_resources/resources/articles/youraba0610.html, accessed 17 July 2015. During European Law and Technology conferences disruptive technologies are also discussed (http://www.prweb.com/releases/2012/8/prweb9779900.htm, accessed 16 July 2015).
13. To give an example: LetsGetDivorced.com is an online self-directed legal document assembly service for people looking to file a simple uncontested divorce, where both spouses agree on all issues of their divorce, such as equitable distribution of their marital property and marital debts, spousal support, child custody, visitation and child support.
14. Machine learning is a type of artificial intelligence that provides computers with the ability to learn without being explicitly programmed. Machine learning programs detect patterns in data and adjust program actions accordingly. Examples range from speech recognition, to web searches, the understanding of the human genome and robot control.
15. The elapsed time of a case is the period that is required to handle a case that pertains to a suspect or convict. Long elapsed times may be interpreted as delays in a criminal justice system, which in turn may lead to 'justice delayed, justice denied'.
16. Other examples are confirmation bias (searching for confirmation and verification), the Texas sharpshooter fallacy (perceiving patterns in random events that do not exist) and the Lake Wobegon mechanism (observed among drivers, CEO's, coaches, radio show hosts and others). It was dubbed the (fictional) 'Lake Wobegon Effect' in tribute to the fictional radio comedy community of Lake Wobegon, where all the children are above average.
17. Lawless, Robbennolt and Ulen (2010: 14) use this phenomenon to stress the importance that ELR focuses on aggregate data, while lawyers often deal with individual cases. They also show that research on estimator variables when dealing with eyewitnesses (like stress, lighting levels and the presence of a weapon) and system variables ('the features of the identification that are under the control of the legal system') can shed light on individual cases, although the primary goal is to find evidence 'about factors that affect the ability of eyewitnesses *generally* to make accurate identifications'.
18. In medical studies Lasagna's law is well-known, basically saying that researchers have a tendency to overestimate the pool of available patients who meet the inclusion criteria and would be willing to enroll into the study.
19. A well-known statement by Guba (1987: 31) was that 'the one (paradigm) precludes the

other just as surely as belief in a round world precludes believing in a flat one'. Howe (1988: 10) labeled these thinkers as 'advocates of the "incompatibility thesis" – the belief that the compatibility between quantitative and qualitative methods is merely apparent'.

20. See Greiffenhagen et al (2011) for a methodographic study on differences between the two 'paradigms' in practice and Onwuegbuzie et al (2012) for innovations in qualitative research methods that bridge the gap between 'Quant'and 'Qual'.
21. Those that are not referred to in footnotes can be found in Cane and Kritzer (2010).
22. See Eshuis et al (2012) and Eshuis and Leeuw (2014).
23. It started in the world of medicine with the Cochrane Collaboration/Library, now covering hundreds of thousands (experimental and other types) of studies in medicine and public health. See Chapter 5.
24. Lawless, Robbenholt and Ulen (2010: 15) say that empirical research is 'an incremental and ongoing process'.
25. Addressing empirical legal research in a professional way necessitates that attention is paid to *all* aspects of this cycle. Unfortunately, that is not always the case. Brems (2008) studied what 65 (human rights) legal scholars 'from her address book' thought about the importance of methodology for human rights research, how they used methodology, whether or not they were trained in it etc. Unfortunately, the idea of an empirical cycle, including types of research problems, the role of theories and research designs and data analysis, were *not* even mentioned by this author.
26. The comparison between researchers and bakers is largely incorrect. Many bakers combine the art and craft when making (truffle) cakes, Cote d 'Ivory chocolate cookies and bio-bread, which is not an easy, mechanical activity.
27. An example of an unprofessional approach to ELR is given by Heise (2002: 821): 'When I speak of empirical legal scholarship I refer only to the subset of empirical legal scholarship that uses statistical techniques and analyses'. Crucial characteristics are missed, as will be clear for the readers of this book (and a few others).

2. Roots of empirical legal research: a concise history in $20^{1/4}$ pages[1]

This chapter sketches the history of ELR. As contemporary textbooks sometimes make mistakes as to its ancestry,[2] we deemed it necessary to discuss this item. We sketch – by leaps and bounds – the most important contributing (sub)disciplines and research traditions: i.e. legal realism, criminology, sociology, psychology and anthropology of law, law and economics, civilology, law and political sciences, and evaluation studies.[3]

2.1 THE ROOTS

2.1.1 (American) Legal Realism and New Legal Realism[4]

Kritzer's (2009: 1) essay on the contemporary history of ELR in the USA not only paid attention to studies conducted in the 1950s and early 1960s (like the American jury project, the commercial arbitration study and the court delay study), but took us further back into history:

> In the 1920s and 1930s, and in a few cases even earlier, one can find a wide range of empirically-oriented research on law. The specific topics of this early research include: appellate courts and appellate decision making, automobile accident compensation and litigation, bankruptcy, criminal courts, divorce, judicial staffing and judicial selection, juries and legal needs and legal aid. A significant portion of the early work was linked one way or another to the American legal realist movement.

American Legal Realism[5] is indeed related to the work Kritzer described (Fisher III, Horwitz and Reed, 1993: xiv). Core actors were Llewellyn, Underhill Moore, Pound (who – as was mentioned – emphasized the importance of 'laws in books' versus 'laws in action') and Cardozo.[6]

Leiter (2002: 1) characterized Legal Realism as follows:

> The Realists were lawyers (plus a few social scientists) [and] they were reacting against the dominant 'mechanical jurisprudence' or 'formalism' of their day. 'Formalism . . . held that judges decide cases on the basis of distinctively legal

BOX 2.1 THE METAPHYSICAL CLUB

Though not brought under the umbrella of American Legal Realism, the Metaphysical Club established in Cambridge, USA in 1871 also contributed to the development of ELR. This Club was an informal discussion group of scholarly friends, close from their associations with Harvard University, which started in 1871 and continued until spring 1879. Legal scholar Oliver Wendell Holmes, Jr, philosopher and psychologist William James and philosopher Charles Sanders Peirce were among the founding fathers. In their view, the law was not to be interpreted (only) as a formal, logical set of rules but also as an instrument to realize certain societal goals. They were interested in empirical research and social change.

> rules and reasons, which justify a unique result in most cases (perhaps every case). The Realists argued, instead, that careful empirical consideration of how courts really decide cases reveals that they decide not primarily because of law, but based (roughly speaking) on their sense of what would be 'fair' on the facts of the case.[7]

Guthrie, Rachlinski and Wistrich (2007: 2) are sharper in their wording.

> According to the formalists, judges apply the governing law to the facts of a case in a logical, mechanical, and deliberative way . . . For the realists [on the other hand], the judge 'decides by feeling and not by judgment'; by 'hunching' and 'not by ratiocination' and later uses deliberative faculties not only to justify that intuition to himself, but to make it pass muster.

These and similar pronunciations have led to serious critique by Tamanaha (2008: 2):

> Much of [this] conventional account is misleading. Legal Realism is largely misunderstood because the work of the realists is interpreted within a false set of historical and theoretical assumptions . . . The term realism . . . has two integrally conjoined aspects – a skeptical aspect and a rule-bound aspect. 'Realism' refers to an awareness of the flaws, limitations, and openness of law, an awareness that judges must sometimes make choices, that they can manipulate legal rules and precedents, and that they can be influenced by their political and moral views and by their personal biases (the skeptical aspect); but 'realism' about law and judging also conditions this more skeptical awareness with the understanding that legal rules nonetheless can work, that judges can abide by and apply the law, that there are practice-related, social, and institutional factors that constrain judges, and that judges can render generally predictable, legally based decisions (the rule-bound aspect). A realistic view holds that the rule-bound aspect of judging can function reliably notwithstanding the challenges presented by the skepticism-inducing side, although this is an achievement that must be earned, is never perfectly achieved, and is never guaranteed.[8]

BOX 2.2 THE INSTITUTIONAL METHOD OF AMERICAN LEGAL REALISM

An example of the approach of American Legal Realists is what Underhill Moore and Hope (1929) called 'the institutional method'. Underhill Moore and Hope's idea was to identify the normal behavior for any 'institution' (e.g. commercial banking); then identify and demarcate deviations from this norm quantitatively, and try to identify the point at which deviation from the norm will cause a judicial decision that corrects the deviation from the norm (e.g. how far must a bank depart from normal check-cashing practice before a court will decide against the bank in a suit brought by the customer?). The goal is a predictive formula: deviation of degree X from 'institutional behavior (i.e. behavior which frequently, repeatedly, usually occurs) will cause courts to act' (Underhill Moore and Hope, 1929: 707). Sociological and psychological studies were used to understand (and predict) legal decisions, as Underhill Moore and Callahan (1943) show in their work on the relationship between how to organize 'legal control' (now known as law enforcement) by using insights from psychological learning theory.

What this discussion tells us is that there are two core elements in the work of Legal Realists. The first is 'the method of empirical testing: hypotheses had to be tested against observations of the world. . . [American] Realists frequently claimed that existing articulations of the "law" were not, in fact, "confirmed" by actual observation of what the courts were really doing' (Leiter, 2002: 2). The second is that formal rules per se and on their own often will not be able to explain and predict behavioral outcomes (completely), though sometimes they will.

'*Sociological jurisprudence*' was also part of this movement. White (1972) articulated the background of sociological jurisprudence,[9] while Gardner (1961: 9–10) described it:

> Sociological jurisprudence is . . . a method which attempts to use the various social sciences to study the role of the law as a living force in society and seeks to control this force for the social betterment . . . Law is an instrument of social control, backed by the authority of the state, and the ends towards which it is directed and the methods for achieving these ends may be enlarged and improved through a consciously deliberate effort. The sanction of law lies in social ends which law is designed to serve. The sociological jurist has no preference for any particular type of precept but only for that which will do the most effective job.[10]

In 1931, Llewellyn attempted to capture the empirical goals of the legal realist tradition by referring to early 'efforts to capitalize the wealth of our reported cases to make large-scale quantitative studies of facts and outcome'. Llewellyn emphasized the 'hope that these might develop lines of prediction more sure, or at least capable of adding further certainty to the predictions based as hitherto on intensive study of smaller bodies of cases'. However, he also added: 'I know of no published results' (Miles and Sunstein, 2008). Posner (1995) also criticized the contribution Legal Realism made: 'The empirical projects of the legal realists, which not only failed but in failing gave empirical research rather a bad name among legal academics, illustrate the futility of empirical investigation severed from a theoretical framework'. Schlegel (1995) sees the lack of a 'conceptual schema that could explain the results of the Realist's research' as a cause of its demise.

Decades after Llewellyn in 1931 made his point on the lack of results, Miles and Sunstein (2008:1–2) published a paper on 'New Legal Realism',[11] while also launching a website.[12] It is 'an effort to understand the sources of judicial decisions on the basis of testable hypotheses and large data sets. [New legal realists] are in the midst of a flowering of large-scale quantitative studies of facts and outcome, with numerous results. The relevant studies have produced a New Legal Realism'. They refer to the increased appetite for empirical work among American law professors, and make the point that this work within law schools 'has become so prevalent as to constitute its own subgenre of legal scholarship'. Suchman and Mertz (2010) make comparisons with other approaches like the Law and Society movement (in the USA), originating in the 1960s and the 'ELS-brand', which is characterized by doing 'legally sophisticated empirical analysis' and 'using quantitative methods and hypothesis testing' (Suchman and Mertz, 2010: 557).

Miles and Sunstein (2008: 3) see the strongly reduced costs of data-gathering, computing and 'the prevailing sense in certain interdisciplinary fields, particularly economic analysis of law, that empirical work rather than abstract theory now presents the greatest opportunities for contributions' as one of the reasons for this development. Howarth (2013: 6) takes this a step further when he, in line with Pound, thought it commendable to 'think of [law and] jurisprudence as a science of *social engineering*' (White, 1972: 1010 ff; McManaman, 1958).

When we discuss (legal) Big Data (Chapters 7 and 8), it will become clear that there is a relation between conceptualizing law (and jurisprudence) as a form of social engineering and the world of Big Data, including machine learning, algorithms and experiments.

2.1.2 Criminology

Criminology also is an important pillar (or *root*) of ELR. It is the scientific study of the nature, extent, causes and control of criminal behavior in both the individual and in society.[13] It is an interdisciplinary field, drawing upon research of sociologists and psychologists, psychiatrists and biologists, economists and social anthropologists, as well as lawyers. Areas of research include the incidences, forms, causes and consequences of crime, as well as social and governmental regulations and their impact on criminals, victims and others, including their reactions to crime. For studying the distribution and causes of crime, criminology often relies upon quantitative and qualitative methods.

Over time, several schools of thought have existed. Fijnaut (2014), alongside many others, describes some of them, ranging from what he called the 'classical school' with founding fathers like Beccaria, Bentham and Quetelet's 'social physics' to biological approaches, like the Italian School (with Lombroso, Feri and Garofalo) and frenology. In response to the biological and evolutionary schools, French sociologists like Tarde, Lacassagne and Durkheim presented an alternative program in which social behavior, imitation and other sociological factors played a prominent role in explaining (trends in) crime. Fijnaut (2014: 276ff) describes the paradigmatic 'war(s)' between the French and the Italian approaches. In the USA the Chicago school created by sociologists Park and Burgess prospered between the late 1920s until the late 1940s, but – as Fijnaut (2014: Ch. 10) shows – bio-criminology also played a major role between the latter part of the nineteenth century and the 1950s. Scholars like Macdonald ('a transatlantic missionary of criminal bio-anthropology'), Hooton, the Gluecks and James Q Wilson were active and well-known. However, starting in the late 1960s and ending around the mid/late 1990s, attention paid to biological factors to understand and help reduce criminal behavior was (extremely) limited.

Nowadays, criminology offers interesting examples of ELR work, addressing the causes of delinquent behavior, trends in crime and costs of crimes, the impact of incarceration on recidivism, how digital piracy and other cybercrimes can be prevented or reduced and what biosocial causes of persistent antisocial and callous-unemotional behavior are (Raine, 2013).

2.1.3 Sociology of Law[14]

In 1937 Timasheff wrote a paper with the title: 'What is sociology of law?' It started as follows:

> Since olden times, law has been the object of a science called 'jurisprudence'. This science has had a glorious record, numbering in its annals many famous names and immortal treatises. It is a many-branched science, which has developed into a network of numerous special sciences called 'civil law,' 'criminal law,' 'constitutional law,' and so forth. Is there room in this field for still another science, that of 'sociology of law'? Or is 'sociology of law' only a new name for a science known for centuries? Yes, there is room. No, it is not a new name for

> an old science . . . Human behavior in society, in so far as it is related to law, is the object of the new science, called 'sociology of law.' Causal investigation is its chief method (Timasheff, 1937: 225, 227).

He discussed demarcations with other (sub)disciplines like criminology and suggested research methods that sociologists of law could (or should) use, while he ended his paper as follows: 'There is room for a new science of the sociology of law; there are sufficient materials and methods to help us gain new knowledge; and there exist already brilliant attempts to solve the problem of the sociology of law' (ibid., p. 235).

Contemporary sociology of law did not move very far away from the core of Timasheff's article. Sociologists of law examine the interaction between the law, legal and non-legal institutions and social factors. Areas of investigation include the social development of legal institutions, forms of social control, regulation, the interaction between legal cultures, the social construction of legal issues, legal professions, and the relation between law and social change. The roots of sociology of law can be traced back to the works of sociologists and jurists of the turn of the twentieth century like Weber, Durkheim, Petrazycki, Gurvitch and Ehrlich. Weber interpreted regulations and laws in terms of a rational-legal authority. He investigated to what extent a coherent and calculable law formed a precondition for modern political developments, the bureaucratic state and the growth of capitalism. Central to the development of modern law is the formal rationalization of law on the basis of general procedures that are applied equally and fairly to all. Modern rationalized law is also codified and impersonal in its application to specific cases, according to Weber.

Durkheim's contributions to the development of sociology of law can be partly subsumed under what is known as his science of morals and rights. He studied different types of rules (e.g. technical and normative) and what the sanctions were that society, including the legal system, used (Schluchter, 2003: 539). Durkheim not only studied the repressive function of the legal system, but also its contribution to different types of solidarity. In 'The Division of Labour in Society' Durkheim saw that as society becomes more complex, the body of law will primarily be concerned with restitution and compensation (civil law) and less with criminal law and penal sanctions. Over time, law has undergone a transformation from repressive law to restitutive law, according to Durkheim. Restitutive law operates in societies in which there is a high degree of individual variation and emphasis on personal rights and responsibilities. For Durkheim, law is an indicator of the mode of integration of a society, which can be mechanical, among identical parts, or organic, among differentiated parts such as in industrialized societies.

Schluchter (2003: 544–5) reconstructed the sociology of law research programs on which Durkheim and Weber worked.

Other (European) scholars, several of them jurists, also employed social scientific approaches and methods in an attempt to develop sociological theories of law. Notably among these were Petrazycki, Gurvitch and Ehrlich. Petrazycki distinguished between forms of 'official law', supported by the state, and 'intuitive law', consisting of legal experiences that, in turn, consist of a complex of psychic processes in the mind of the individual. As Kojder (2006: 335–6) describes:

> For Petrazycki, law is able to shape strong social habits over centuries because it prescribes a common 'pattern of conduct' for all of its addressees. This 'capital of habits' . . . is stored up over centuries, and guarded by legal-criminal means and other institutions of legal control. [He] further emphasized the educative value of law, which is due to the fact that it continually stimulates certain motives of action, while repressing others.

In the post-World War II period, the sociology of law grew to become a sociological specialty. Early overviews of that period are given by Davis (1957), Gibbs (1966) and Aubert (1969). Deflem (2011) sees 'law and institutions', 'the legal profession' and 'law, punishment and social control' as the central themes of research over the past few decades.

Specialties closely related to the sociology of law are *socio-legal research*, *law and social science* and the *law & society movement* (LSS) (Galanter, 2006: 1; Suchman and Mertz, 2010):

> *Law and social science* is only one of several intersecting knowledges about law and its relation to society. By law I refer not to a discipline of inquiry, but to a set of practices, roles, and ideas embodied in distinctive institutions and reflected in general culture . . . LSS . . . seeks explanation rather than justification. It emphasizes social structures and processes rather than rules. It rejects the notion of law as an autonomous self-contained realm; it appreciates the dynamics of law as part of more inclusive patterns of social life.

In a report on the state of the art in *socio-legal studies* in the UK, Hazel Genn et al (2006) showed that although a clear definition of this concept is lacking, sociology of law, 'law and society studies' and 'empirical legal studies' are part of an extended '*socio-legal studies-family*'.[15] Banakar and Travers (2005) argue that 'socio-legal researchers increasingly recognize the need to employ a wide variety of methods and that this needs to be informed by an understanding of debates about theory and method in mainstream social science'. Socio-legal scholars study 'a range of topics, including EU law, ombudsmen, judges, lawyers, Shariah Councils, and the quality assurance industry'. Travers (2001: 26, 27) however made an interesting distinction: 'Sociology of law was a scientific attempt to understand the place of law in society. Socio-legal research, by contrast, was a-theoretical or empiricist research commissioned by, or intended to influence, the government agencies responsible for the legal system'. And: 'socio-legal research in Britain is mainly concerned with influencing or serving government policy in the provision of legal services. It first developed in the 1960s as a political movement concerned with fairness and justice'.[16]

Ferrari (2015) studied the recent editorial policy of three influential sociology of law journals in France, Germany and Italy and found that middle range socio-legal theory has successfully dealt with some relevant aspects of legal change of the last decades, in such fields as criminal justice, migrations or family law. Yet, it has left aside other and no less important aspects, such as commerce and property laws, common goods, environment and other crucial questions of our times.

2.1.4 Law and Anthropology[17]

Although its origins are much older, the point of departure for the recently established Law and Anthropology Department (2012) of the Max Planck Institute for social anthropology functions rather well as an introduction:

> Its point of departure is the observation that values and norms today are circulating ever more vigorously among diverse societies and cultures. With this intensification of exchanges and encounters comes an increasing demand for translation between different legal orders at various levels of decision making all over the world. This demand engages, among others, the disciplines of social anthropology and law.

One of the central research topics is the comparison and comparability of concepts, procedures, institutions and practices within and across normative orders. Another is to promote 'the integration of anthropological research and legal practice. This priority encourages greater collaboration between anthropologists and legal practitioners, giving equal weight both to an anthropologically informed understanding of the diversity of normative orders and to the practical, hands-on experience and concerns of judges, lawyers, legal services representatives, and others who, in their daily practice, confront the phenomenon of 'inter-normativity' – situations where different normative orders and logics (often existing side-by-side within a single state system) come into contact (and often conflict) with one another – and the resulting need for state legal systems to accommodate this diversity'.

Pirie (2013: 217) sees as the central argument of *The Anthropology of Law* that:

> we should take law seriously as a class of social phenomena, one that is defined by its form, rather than its functions . . . Anthropology pays close attention to the detail of empirical examples, embracing variety and inconsistency, exploring the boundaries of concepts we routinely employ to make sense of the world and questioning the ways in which we normally use them to simplify and categorize.

Broadly speaking, legal anthropology goes back more than two centuries. Henry Maine is generally seen as the founder of legal anthropology. Maine was a former colonial legal official who became a lecturer in jurisprudence at Cambridge and Oxford, publishing *Ancient Law* in 1861. In this book a theory of the development of law within an evolutionary framework was developed. Malinowski's *Crime and the Savage Society* (1926) is of a later period and is critical of Maine's approach; he proposed an ethnographic approach to the study of legal issues, calling for extended fieldwork in order to 'study by direct observation the rules of custom as they function in actual life' (1926: 126). Llewellyn and Hoebel's *The Cheyenne Way* (1941) is also regarded as a classic text in legal anthropology. The authors articulate their 'theory of investigation' ('a case method procedure of going in the first instance after cases of trouble and how they were handled' (Llewellyn and Hoebel, 1941: viii).[18] They also refer to the concept of 'law jobs', indicating that society has a need to fulfill certain legal functions like 'the disposition of trouble-cases, the preventive channeling and reorientation of conduct and expectations and the allocation of authority and the arrangement of procedures which legitimize action as being authoritative' (ibid., p. 292; Witteveen, 2013: 52–3).

During the 1950s and 1960s, legal anthropologists in the USA were largely concerned with law as an aspect of social control through the imposition of sanctions, and saw legal procedures as the means of enforcing social rules. A debate emerged about the relationship between legal and anthropological methods, and particularly over the question whether legal anthropologists should apply Anglo-American legal categories to the study of non-Western societies.

In the 1970s, another debate centered on the question whether the focus of study should be on rules or processes. An increasing number of legal anthropologists critiqued the long-standing emphasis on the rules of adjudication, and argued instead to study the processes by which disputes are resolved and norms elaborated. In the 1980s, a discourse and postmodernist critique began to emerge that questioned traditional categories of legal anthropologists. Around the same time, 'Clifford Geertz suggested a cultural approach to law, arguing that law is not just a bounded set of norms, rules and principles, but a frame that elucidates the world' (Engle Merry, 2012: 106). The same author charted several 'areas [within anthropology and law] of a particularly rapid and significant growth since the 1980s'. We mention three of them:

> The first is the development of concepts of legal culture, legal consciousness, and law in everyday life. As legal anthropology expanded from an analysis of legal institutions such as courts, moots, or dispute processing centers to the study of how ordinary people use law in their natural lives, it raised questions about how people think about law outside these institutions and why they do or do not comply with the law . . . A second area of growth is the expansion of the legal pluralism concept from colonial contexts to global ones. Human Rights and transitional justice are a third area of increasing anthropological attention . . . Recent ethnographic work explored how transitional justice works in practice in various locales. (Engle Merry, 2012: 105)

2.1.5 Psychology and Law

In his textbook *Psychology and Law*, Kadardis (2003: 2) addresses the question how to define the psychology of law, aka 'legal psychology' (and sometimes even as 'forensic psychology') (*Observer*, 2011). While there is no generally acceptable definition, one put forward by Ogloff (2000: 467) is sufficiently broad and parsimonious:

> Legal psychology is the scientific study of the effects of law on people; and the effects people have on the law. Legal psychology also includes the application of the study and practice of psychology to legal institutions and people who come into contact with the law. In essence, psycho-legal scholars apply psychology's methodologies and knowledge to studying jurisprudence, substantive law, legal processes and law breaking.

Topics covered by law and psychology studies are jury decision making and judging, eyewitness testimonies, interrogation techniques, false confessions, forensic psychopathology, offender treatment, malingering, boardroom behavior and the behavior of oversight agencies and inspectorates. Wells, Memon and Penrod (2006) for example discuss reasons why 'innocent people are wrongfully convicted [and point to] faulty eyewitness evidence – roughly 75 percent of DNA-exonerated individuals had been convicted because eyewitnesses made a wrong identification'. Psychological 'offender profiling' is another major activity of legal and in particular, forensic psychologists. This field of research has also examined the cognitive and motivational dimensions of judging, i.e. heuristics, motivation, biases, schemas, attitudes and motivated cognition (Quintanilla, 2012: 613). Experimental psychologists investigate how implicit theories of human nature and moral character affect legal decision-making. Dweck and colleagues[19] provided participants with summary transcripts of a murder trial, and experimentally manipulated impressions about the defendant's respectability. These implicit theories may shape how judges find facts in particular disputes, the inferences they draw, and the punishments they impose.

Law and psychology has a long tradition exemplified since the beginning of the twentieth century by the work of pioneers like Binet, Gross, Jung, Münsterberg and Wertheimer. Ogloff (2000: 461) reminds us that a number of well-known psychologists expressed an interest in applying psychology's findings to law as early as the 1890s. The field of legal psychology:

> has been expanding at an impressive rate since the mid-1960s, especially in North America, since the late 1970s in the UK and in Australia since the early 1980s. In fact, on both sides of the Atlantic, research and teaching in legal psychology has grown enormously since the mid-1970s . . . More recently, the field of psychology and law has also been expanding in Europe, especially in the Netherlands, Germany and Spain. Also in these countries professional societies have been established.

Petrila (2009: 387, 391) adds that:

> the best science in the field of forensic psychology has emerged in response to specific questions posed in specific legal cases: is the defendant competent? Is this eyewitness' testimony reliable? Is the defendant likely to pose a future risk to third parties? . . . .One of the most salutary developments in this field has been the creation of research-based assessment tools.

A recent development is neuro-law, where neuroscientists, psychologists and legal scholars collaborate. As neuro-scientific evidence is increasingly being offered in court cases (Jones et al, 2013 for the USA; de Kogel et al, 2014 for the Netherlands), 'new' challenges appear on the agenda. One is to distinguish between neuro-facts and neuro-myths, where a neuro-myth is defined as a common misconception about brain mechanisms, which are taken for granted in today's society (like 'there is a visual, auditive and a haptic type of learning' or 'we only use 10% of our brains').[20] Another is the bias-ability of neuro-scientific measurements.

2.1.6 Law and Economics

Law and economics, including behavioral economics, has as one of its founding fathers Adam Smith, who studied the economic effects of legislation (i.e. mercantilist laws) on society. Hoseman (2014: 48) considers as the pioneers of this tradition:

> zwei unabhängig voneinander entstandene Aufsätze von Ronald Coase und Guido Calabresi aus den Jahren 1960 bzw. 1961; ihr eigentlicher Durchbruch

> erfolgte freilich erst in den frühen 1970er Jahren, etwa zeitgleich mit dem Erscheinen der Erstauflage von Richard Posners Lehrbuch 'Economic Analysis of Law', welches zum Standardwerk avancierte [two independently developed essays by Ronald Coase and Guido Calabresi from 1960 or 1961; their real breakthrough took place during the early 1970s, around the time when Richard Posner published the first edition of his textbook 'Economic Analysis of Law', which later became a standard work.]

Posner's book addresses 'the application of the theories and empirical methods of economics to the central institutions of the legal system'. Law and economics offers a general theory of law as well as conceptual tools for the clarification and improvement of its practices. The general theory is that law is best viewed as a social tool that promotes economic efficiency, and economic analysis and efficiency as an ideal that can guide legal practice.[21] Next to this general theory, other theories play an important role. One of them is the 'legal origins' theory which draws on institutional and evolutionary economics to provide an account of how legal systems have shaped the development of market economies (La Porta et al, 2008). Another field of study is that of 'legal evolution'; law is seen as a complex system with adaptive properties, where game-theoretic studies of strategic behavior are as pivotal, as are insights from evolutionary biology. In combination they can help to understand the origins and evolution of legal institutions (Deakin, 2011).

Jolls (2006: 3) shows that:

> many topics within economics relate to law. A large body of work in public economics, for instance, examines the effects of legally-mandated government programs such as disability and unemployment insurance; work on the labor market examines the effects of many types of antidiscrimination laws and recent corporate governance research studies the consequences of corporate and securities law on stock returns and volatility.

Jolls (2006) suggests several distinctive features that help to demarcate work that is typically regarded as falling within the law and economics 'family'. One is that much of this work focuses on various areas of law that were sparsely studied by economists prior to the advent of law and economics; they include tort law, contract law, property law, and rules governing the litigation process. Another is the sustained interest in explaining and predicting the content, rather than the effects, of legal rules.

A recent development in this field is:

> behavioral economics and law, involving both the development and the incorporation within law and economics of behavioral insights drawn from various

> fields of psychology. As has been widely recognized . . . some of the foundational assumptions of traditional economic analysis may reflect an unrealistic picture of human behavior. Not surprisingly, models based on these assumptions sometimes yield erroneous predictions. Behavioral law and economics attempts to improve the predictive power of law and economics by building in more realistic accounts of actors' behavior. (Jolls, 2006: 3)

Game theory is also studied by law and economics scholars; it analyzes decision-making by agents under conditions of strategic interaction, which means that the outcomes of their (behavioral) choices depend on what other agents do. According to Deakin (2014: 1) game theory research 'can be used to generate formal models of the workings of markets and other economic institutions, and of the role of the law in shaping economic behavior'. It is useful to view human actors as departing from traditional economic assumptions in three distinct ways: human actors exhibit bounded rationality, bounded willpower and bounded self-interest. Examples of empirical studies using this approach are easy to find.[22] Tor (2011: i) cites studies showing that 'the behavioral analysis of law has become increasingly popular in legal scholarship in recent years'.

2.1.7 Law and Politics

Mills and Sunstein (2007: 3) are of the opinion that:

> an entire subfield of political science, known as *law and politics* has contributed a large and illuminating empirical literature . . . Some early contributions cast the influence of law (the legal model) as a competing hypothesis to the influence of judicial ideology (the attitudinal model). More recently, political scientists have given greater attention to the institutional context of judicial decision making by positing and testing models of strategic behavior.

This statement is backed by the contents of the *Oxford Handbook of Law and Politics* (Whittington, Kelemen and Caldeira, 2008a). One of the opening questions concerns why political science is interested in 'law'. The answer is that 'law is one of the central products of politics and the prize over which many political struggles are waged . . . It is the principal instrument by which government exerts its will on society, and as such it might be thought to lie (at least indirectly) close to the heart of the study of politics' (p. 3). The magnitude of topics covered in this handbook (from 'judicial behavior', the rule of law and courts in democratizing regimes and constitutionalism to comparative judicial politics and the political and policy environment of courts) shows the breadth of this specialty. The study of law and politics is a 'varied and multidisciplinary enterprise. The starting point in political science was 'that politics matters and that considerable analytical and empirical leverage over our understanding of law and legal institutions can be gained by placing politics in the foreground' (ibid., p. 4). 'The field soon added courts, lawyers and related legal actors to its purview' (ibid., p. 3).

In the USA it was John Burgess who was amongst the founding fathers of this specialty. He helped develop and teach 'a science of jurisprudence that would provide better preparation for the new federal civil service' (around 1880). Constitutional and public scholars in the twentieth century like Charles Grove Haines, Edward Corwin and Robert Cushman led this discussion. Between 1917 and 1961 the 'flagship journal of the American Political Science Association (the American Political Science Review) published an annual overview of the constitutional decisions of the US Supreme Court, written by Cushman' (ibid., p. 5). Slowly but steadily the study of law and politics in the USA shifted away from constitutional law and towards judicial politics (including statistical studies). More recently, law and politics scholars study criminal justice systems, the operation of trial courts, juries, dispute resolution, the behavior of lawyers, tribunals and other aspects of international law. 'Game theoretic accounts of political strategy have come forth and provided new perspectives on judicial behavior and new approaches linking courts with other political institutions' (ibid., p. 7).

In particular with regard to administrative law and public administration, the use of experiments slowly increased. As Van de Walle and Van Ryzin (2011) show, this field still lags behind neighboring fields such as psychology or economics. Experiments not only shed light on the impact of new legal arrangements and institutions but also provide 'robust answers to old questions that are of theoretical importance, such as the test of an extended version of Niskanen's budget maximization model' (Moynihan, 2013) or the effect of governmental performance information and transparency on citizen's voting behavior and trust (Grimmelikhuijsen and Meyer, 2014). A similar line of thought can be found in McGinnis' (2012) study how to accelerate democracy by conducting experiments with legal arrangements, while applying machine-learning to analyze Big Data.

2.1.8 Civilology

The less well known field of civilology, with De la Grasserie[23] as the (European) inventor of this label, is a combination of civil law and behavioral studies.[24] Van Boom, Giesen and Verheij (2013:1) define civilology as follows: 'the collection of disciplines studying behavioral assumptions used by civil law, the effects of civil law on behavior of individuals and organizations and the relevance of these assumptions for civil law policies, civil law regulation and implementation'. Rather than analyzing private law from a strictly legal doctrinal perspective, civilology encompasses the combined use of insights from social sciences – ranging from economics to psychology and sociology – in order to analyze the behavioral assumptions underlying private law, to understand the effects it has on individuals, organizations and businesses and to appreciate the impact of both assumptions and effects on policy makers, legislatures and courts. One of the starting points of this field is that civil law can be analyzed by surfacing and analyzing its behavioral presumptions (i.e. implicit theories) and behavioral effects, by doing empirical research and/or using findings from behavioral research that already exist in the literature. These 'presumptions' not only relate to actors in civil processes themselves but also to governments as rule-makers. Presumptions bear a strong resemblance to what evaluators call 'intervention or program theories' (i.e. the sets of assumptions underlying policies, programs and interventions) (see Chapter 4). Behavioral effects are defined as the consequences (intended or unintended) of the interaction between parties after rules by governments and courts have been implemented (ibid., p. 4).

Topics civilologists cover include the impact that regulation has (like the 'Common European Sales Law'), tort law including damages, insurance law, corporate governance, and corporate and securities law. The authors of the *Civilology Handbook* present a sample of disciplines forming the building blocks upon which civilology elaborated (psychology, economics, sociology, organizational sciences, marketing sciences and public administration).

Historically, civilology does not have many roots. As mentioned earlier, the Metaphysical Club established around 1871 in Cambridge, USA (see Box 2.1) was an informal group of jurists and some behavioral scientists. Their empirical research related to what we now call civilology. In the Netherlands, several civil law professors like Meijers, Sinzheimer, Hamaker and Hijmans (active in the first decades of the twentieth century) more or less adopted these ideas and undertook empirical legal research regarding civil law (Croes and Leeuw, 2012). Hazel Genn, Partington and Wheeler (2006: 4–5) are of the opinion that 'there is no "civilology" equivalent to criminology. The sheer breadth and diversity of civil justice issues – spanning family, administrative justice, commercial, employment, property, contract etc. – may inhibit the creation of a critical mass of researchers in any one subject area, which in turn slows down the development'.

However, Van Boom (2011: 5) suggests that the ultimate goal of civilology:

is to do for private law what criminology has been doing for criminal law for decades; that is, to reflect on its function on the basis of facts rather than plausible arguments. What we will not do, however, is neglect, ignore or substitute the arts and languages sides to legal teaching and research. Legal research has direct relevance for society and lawyers may only continue to play their societal roles when they *combine* the strengths of the arts and languages with the social sciences. Lawyers should be able to construe, interpret and analyze legislation and case law, but they should also be able to appreciate both empirical and normative questions, such as: does the law actually work in accordance with its design? At what cost? Can it do better? How can it do better?

2.1.9 Evaluation Studies

Evaluation studies is a combination of social sciences research, including sociology and psychology and – to a lesser extent – economics, policy sciences and administrative sciences[25] with a particular focus on what (governmental) interventions 'do' to society. Scriven (1996: 395) noted that 'evaluation is a very young discipline – although it is a very old practice'. One of the earliest (registered) evaluation studies (taking place in the 1700s) is mentioned by Rossi et al (2003: 4). They describe what happened:

> when a British naval captain observed the lack of scurvy among sailors serving on the ships of Mediterranean countries where citrus fruit was part of the rations. Thereupon he made half his crew consume limes while the other half continued with their regular diet. The good captain probably did not know that he was evaluating a demonstration project nor did he likely have an explicit 'program theory' (see chapter 4), namely, that scurvy is a consequence of a vitamin C deficiency and that limes are rich in vitamin C. Nevertheless, the intervention worked and British seamen eventually were compelled to consume citrus fruit regularly, a practice that gave rise to the still-popular label *limeys*. Incidentally, it took about 50 years before the captain's 'social program' was widely adopted.

In the beginning of the twentieth century American sociologist Stuart Chapin was doing experimental sociology. One evaluation looked into the effects of rehousing on the living conditions of slum families in Minneapolis, while a second study evaluated the impact on social adjustment of encouraging university students to engage in extra-curricular activities. During World War II social-psychological evaluations were carried out in the USA, some of them referred to as the Hovland experiments (Yale University). Hovland contributed to several areas of psychology, such as the efficiency of different methods of learning. One of the most widely cited of these experimental evaluations was on opinion change, and involved testing the effects of a one-sided versus a two-sided presentation of a controversial issue. The results contradicted contentions that claimed that a communication that presents only one side of the issue would generally be more successful than one that mentions the opposing side of the argument. Mark et al (2011) summarized the relevance that psychological studies had and have for the development of evaluation studies (in the USA) and vice versa.

This process not only took place in the USA but also in the UK, where since the late 1950s, experimental evaluations in the field of crime and justice occurred. Examples were effectiveness studies of social work in prisons, probation programs and a therapeutic community in a residential school for delinquent children (Nuttal, 2003: 273ff). These studies 'mark both the beginning and the end of random allocation experiments in Home Office research' (ibid., p. 274). Problems that the evaluators had in doing these studies, the mixed bag of results and the problem that 'the experiment[s] might have been able to say what had happened but [it] could not answer how or why' (ibid., p. 277) were behind this development.

As Leeuw (2009a) has written elsewhere, in the Netherlands the tradition of social policy research (going back to the early years of the twentieth century) played a role in getting evaluation going, together with activities by the Netherlands National Audit Office and debates on how to realize a more efficient and effective government in the 1970s and 1980s.

The first wave of booming business years for evaluation started in the 1960s and late 1970s in the USA (Leeuw, 2009b). President Lyndon Johnson's Great Society Program and the War on Poverty were game changers and caused a boom in legislation which stimulated and urged evaluations. That period is known as the Golden Years of Evaluation. In Europe, the expansion of the welfare state and its first noticeable flaws (like unintended side effects and governmental budget problems) made evaluation studies blossom a bit later (Derlien, 1999). The 'Evaluation Atlas' by Furubo et al (2002) and its recent update (covering 2002–2012) by Jacob et al (2015) describe the development of evaluation studies in some 20 countries in detail.

2.2 CONCLUSIONS

Empirical legal research is rooted in diverse disciplines, sub-disciplines and specialties, some going back for centuries. Its tool box of research-approaches, methods and techniques is rather broad. Examples are:

- the 'sociological jurisprudence' of American Legal Realism, where law and sociology were to some extent combined;
- insights from and experiences with experimental studies in criminology, economics and sociology and psychology of law are combined

with legal research on the societal impact of penal sanctions, dispute resolution and other arrangements;

- insights from survey methods in sociology to satisfy the need for evidence on the 'dark number' in criminology and to know the perceptions of victims of crime, are combined with ethnographic interviews, case-studies and 'thick descriptions' from legal anthropology and with register data (from the policy and the public prosecutor);
- work by psychology and law researchers on 'judicial mindsets', which includes articulating implicit theories of legal actors, is related to 'theory-driven evaluations', in which assumptions underlying (legal) interventions and policies are reconstructed (into intervention theories) and tested; and:
- experiences from working with repositories, systematic reviews, rapid reviews and realist syntheses from medicine, public health research and behavioral and economic research are related to the need to understand the social acceptance and behavioral impacts of legal arrangements.

By way of conclusion, Figure 2.1 presents a graphic impression of what we see as the cognitive ('scientific') roots of empirical legal research. In itself,

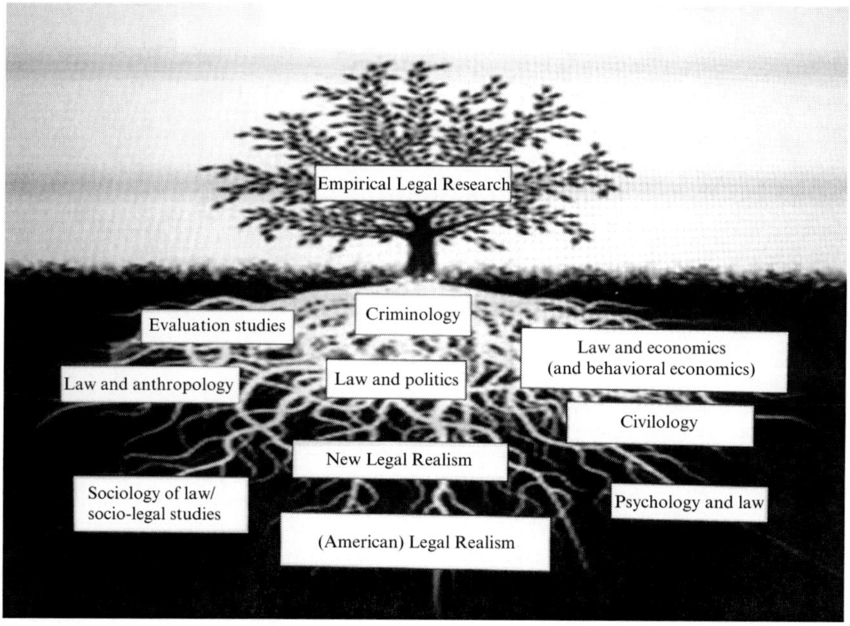

Figure 2.1 The roots of empirical legal research

ELR combines combinations of (sub)disciplines and specialties that can be found within these roots.

ENDNOTES

1. Thanks to the example from Pawson and Tilley (1997) when they labelled one of their chapters 'A History of Evaluation in 28½ pages'.
2. McConville and Chui (2007: 5) tell us that it was in the '60s and 70s [that] legal realists and socio-legal researchers started the law and society movement'. This information is wrong. It was at least four to five decades earlier, if we neglect work in the nineteenth century by well-known sociologists (of law).
3. Next to the literature referred to, also 'the Bridge' was used (essays on Legal Realism, the Law and Society movement and several others, including Critical Legal Analysis (that we do not discuss in this book). See http://cyber.law.harvard.edu/bridge/index.htm, accessed 16 July 2015.
4. Instead of trying to cover 'the' legal sciences, we only discuss the legal realism-tradition.
5. Coleman (1960: 152–3) refers to Axel Hägerström who is seen as the founder of the realist movement in Scandinavia, with his 'successors, particularly Lundstedt and Ross, [who] devoted themselves to the propagation and elaboration of the new "scientific" method of Legal Realism by which they hoped our obsolete structure of society could be transformed into that more perfect society which social science would rationally elaborate by using methods of the same kind as those by which science had brought about the great achievements of modern medicine and technology'. Schauer (2013: 752) adds that 'on some topics the two Realisms are compatible, but their agendas diverge sufficiently that distinguishing them from each other is more important than seeing them as different branches of the same perspective'.
6. Leiter (2003) sees Oliver Wendell Holmes as the 'forebear' of this movement, though Witteveen (2013: 50) has a different viewpoint. One of Holmes's well-known statements is that 'the life of the law has not been logic, it has been experience'. Holmes was so well known in the USA that a Hollywood movie was produced about him in 1950: *The Magnificent Yankee*.
7. Galanter (2006: 3) refers to social-institutional factors to explain the development of law and society studies and adds that 'if the Realists supplied or carried the intellectual seed, the fertile soil on which it alighted was the [US] New Deal's expansive improvisation of legal regulation to stimulate the economy and weave a net of protections for ordinary citizens, a process that gave social science an enlarged role in the functioning of government'. Fisher III et al (1993: xiv) also discuss the relationship between the New Deal policy and Legal Realism: 'a large group of Realists, including Berle, Dowlin, Arnold, Douglas, Frankfurter, and Frank served in the federal government during the New Deal, helping to shape most of the major administrative agencies (and important systems of rules like the Uniform Commercial Code)'. Witteveen (2013: 50) makes the same point. In the decades after World War II this development expanded by bringing new actors in, like the black civil rights movement, consumer, environmental, and women's movements. 'LSS flourished at the intersection of legal optimism, academic expansion, and interdisciplinary enterprise' (Galanter, 2006: 3). He ends in a somewhat dialectical tone, saying that 'LSS [now, 2008) faces perils that its founders could hardly have anticipated because they are the perils of success in a setting very different from the one in which LSS arose'. In particular he is concerned about 'the first traces of production of LSS knowledge as part of corporate campaigns in the legal arena' (ibid. p. 13).
8. In his book *The Nature of the Judicial Process*, Benjamin N. Cardozo (1921: 128-9) describes the core of Legal Realism. See also Schauer (2013: 779) for an analysis of Legal Realism.

9. 'In a long article in the 1911 and 1912 issues of the *Harvard Law Review*, Pound announced the emergence of sociological jurisprudence as a discrete and definable philosophy of law. Among its common elements were a realization of 'the backwardness of law in meeting social ends'; discontent with prevailing modes of juristic thought and juridical method; an insistence upon study of the actual social effects of legal doctrines; and a belief in 'the equitable application of law', by which judges eschewed the illusory certainty of legal rules for 'reasonable and just solutions of individual causes'. Pound (1911: 594) added: 'The rising and still formative school to which we may look chiefly henceforth for advance in juristic thought, may be styled the Sociological School'.
10. Hoseman (2014: 43), who sees Oliver Wendell Holmes 'als Vorreiter dieser später als, 'revolt against formalism' glorifizierten Gegenbewegung' [as a pioneer of this later, as a 'revolt against formalism' glorified countermovement], also shows that Holmes *Harvard Law Review* paper ('The Path of the Law' 1897) '[auch] ein Plädoyer enthält für ein instrumentelles, sozialwissenschaftlich fundiertes Rechtsverständnis' [holds a plea for an instrumental, social science-based understanding of the law].
11. According to Howarth (2013: 12ff) an earlier successor of Legal Realism is the Law, Science and Policy (LSP) approach pioneered at Yale University by Lasswel and Myres.
12. http://www.newlegalrealism.org/about.html, accessed 17 July 2015.
13. See also Bruinsma and Weisburd (2014), 10 volumes.
14. See also Deflem (2011) and http://en.wikipedia.org/wiki/Sociology_of_law, accessed June 30 2015.
15. However friendly this may look, families are not always cohesive and warm. Suchman (2006: 1) returning from a conference on ELS in the USA, presented a bit of a different story: 'No one, however, [at the conference] seemed quite as confident of what, exactly, ELS is. People who merely parsed ELS's self-proclaimed moniker wondered aloud whether ELS might simply be the sociology of law in new clothing. Or more menacingly, law and economics in sociologists' clothing. Or more cynically, the legal professoriate in the emperor's new clothing'. Tamanaha (1997: Ch. 1) summarized (paradigmatic) 'fights' between socio-legal scholars (postmodernist, Marxists, 'positivists') and referred to 'the problematic state of socio-legal studies'.
16. Travers's (2001: 30) argument was 'that what often passes for sociology of law these days is not really sociology at all, in the sense that it is mainly pursued through textual analysis (a critical version of traditional legal scholarship) or philosophical reflection about law. . . .The nearest thing to sociology of law in British law schools is critical jurisprudence, which draws on various Marxist and post-Marxist theories in addressing legal topics. This has been one of the big growth areas in legal scholarship in recent years'. See also Wheeler (2008).
17. Largely based on Pirie (2013), Engle-Merry (2012) at http://www.indiana.edu/~wanthro/theory_pages/LEGAL.htm), accessed 17 July 2015 and http://www.anthro.illinois.edu/faculty/cfennell/syllabus/anth560/anthlawbib.htm; http://allegralaboratory.net/publications/ (a virtual lab on legal anthropology), accessed 19 July 2015. See Max Plank Institute website at http://www.eth.mpg.de/2951631/department_foblets, accessed 25 November 2015.
18. They add an interesting insight. 'Each legal concept becomes a candle to illumine the working of society. It became a (legal) concept because some type of problem has occurred often enough, has required to be wrestled with often enough, to be not only felt, but seen, as a type of problem. Every legal concept represents then in first instance an effort at diagnosis of a recurrent social trouble of some particular kind. It represents what W.I. Thomas might call an effort to define a situation of perplexity' (Llellewyn and Hoebel, 1941: 42–3).
19. See Dweck et al (1995) and Gervey et al (1999).
20. http://www.oecd.org/edu/ceri/neuromyths.htm, accessed 19 July 2015.
21. http://www.iep.utm.edu/law-econ/, accessed 25 November 2015.
22. For other examples see the *Encyclopedia of Law and Economics* (Bouckaert and De Geest, 2001).

23. De La Grasserie published books on civilology in 1904 and 1906 (Croes and Leeuw, 2011). 'La civilologie offre une partie interne sociologique qui concerne ce qui a été introduit dans le droit lorsque les citoyens non personnellement liés sont en conflit et une partie externe qui étudie l'influence que telle législation a exercée sur l'état sociale.' Now, a century (plus a few years) later civilologists are doing experiments, systematic research reviews, case studies and observational investigations.
24. In the USA Isaiah C. Wears used this concept for the first time in his *unpublished history of the 15th Amendment* (the amendment forbidding discrimination in electoral law in the late nineteenth century) in the subtitle (http://lcweb2.loc.gov/rbc/lcrbmrp/t0b/t0b23.sgm).
25. The political sciences and anthropology could be added to this list.

3. Research problems

3.1 INTRODUCTION: SOCIETAL PROBLEMS AND RESEARCH PROBLEMS[1]

Legal, organizational or economic problems can create a *need* for empirical research, but often need to be 'translated' into research(able) problems. Take the issue of differences between geographic regions in a country when dealing with adopting and implementing forensic-technological innovations by law enforcement agencies. When these differences exist, they can lead not only to inequalities in terms of crime detection (or clearance) rates between regions, but also to inefficiencies in the operational activities of law enforcement agencies. That, in turn, can contribute to debates about how innovative certain regions are, who are the 'early adopters' and who the 'laggards', and why that is. Such a situation can lead to the following *research problem*:

> *What are the indicators of differences in the adoption (rate) of technological-forensic innovations like the 'lab on a chip' and 'automatic number plate recognition' (ANPR), how do regions in country X differ in adoption (rates), how can these differences be explained and what will be the consequences for law enforcement in this country?*

A second example concerns the problem that some public sector organizations are confronted with more fraud and corruption than others. Fraud and corruption are societal problems that have (strong) moral and legal connotations. But before embarking on a research project, such a problem needs to be translated to make it researchable. Fraud and corruption are too broad, so focus is needed. That could be realized by looking into the prevalence of fraud and corruption in agencies over a number of years and into the role (internal) audit departments played (or did not play) in detecting, preventing and reducing fraud. Such a focus would make a research project more do-able. The goal could be to produce evidence for lawyers that help them design and implement regulations and operations in the 'war against fraud' (like empowering (internal) audit departments). The research problem could then be something like this:

> *Can the existence (or lack) of internal audit departments within agencies explain why these organizations run more risks with regard to fraud and corruption than others, to what extent is this the case and how can the findings be explained and be used to establish (more effective) ways to detect, prevent and reduce fraud and corruption?*

If the transformation from a societal problem to a research problem in both examples is relatively simple, in the third example it is more complicated. Here the societal problem is 'rule-jungling'. Barendrecht et al (2012: 3) describe this phenomenon as follows:

> For most of the 20th century, the power to set rules was concentrated in the nation state. This changed when international organizations started to appear on the scene; it changed even more dramatically in the age of globalization, where private, informal and international rulemaking is becoming more and more prevalent. Now, all you need to create rules is a well-organized group of people and a website. Such a body can set rules for others and try to gain legitimacy, often with rather minimal control by national lawmakers . . . At this point in time, are there no tools to evaluate the vast worldwide rulemaking activity in any comprehensive way? Are rule of law values guaranteed? Do the new forms of rulemaking decrease or increase the probability of what economists call regulatory failure and regulatory capture? And what can we say about impacts and fairness of outcomes?

In order to formulate an *(empirical) research problem*, it is necessary to spell out what is meant by concepts like 'international organization', 'globalization', 'control by national lawmakers', 'private law making', 'values' and 'regulatory failure and capture'. Another challenge is to check if the background against which this problem is formulated ('in earlier times largely only nation states produced regulations') is correct. And it must be articulated when the number (and complexity) of rules in societies can be labelled as a 'jungle'. Finally, not only is the specification of concepts needed, but also which countries/nation states are involved, over which years – the inclusion criteria. Transforming the rule-jungling problem into a research problem is almost a small research project on its own.

In this chapter we distinguish between different types of research problems, how to formulate them, and to prevent failures when drafting them. First, we ask where research problems usually come from.

White (2009: 9ff) provides a number of sources. Newspapers, magazines, TV programs and earlier studies (leading to contradictory findings or only partial answers to earlier research questions) regarding (socio-)legal issues, blogs, talking to colleagues, *monologues interieur* and websites are sources. Looking, learning and browsing are routes to follow. As the number of topics of a legal or semi-legal nature in society are overwhelming,

Graziano and Raulin's (2004: 57) idea that 'questions are everywhere; all you have to do is observe and be curious', is halfway to the truth. It is also wise to create a 'stopping rule' or 'exit option'. Otherwise, the interior monologues, the browsing, the talking and the learning can go on for such a long time that you will never even start the research itself.

Once a particular topic has been identified, the process of specification starts. Suppose that the topic is 'gender and crime'. This is too broad to make a serious empirical investigation possible. Specification and focus are needed. What helps is, again, browsing, looking, learning and combining. It is also important to think about the objective(s) of the study. Objectives 'identify the outcomes (or "goals") that are desired and point to the kind of questions that would need to be asked in order to achieve these outcomes' (White, 2009: 34). He gives the following example:

- *Objective:* To find out why certain individuals and groups adopt new technologies 'xyz' before others.
- *Research questions:* What are the patterns of consumption of new technologies amongst different groups of adults in the UK? What reasons do different individuals provide for adopting or not adopting new technologies?

Bunge (1997: 190) suggests several injunctions on how to find research topics and problems:

- *criticize* known solutions to (existing) problems, i.e. look for flaws in them;
- *apply* known solutions to new situations and see whether they still hold;
- *generalize* old problems: try new variables and/or new domains;
- *look outside*: search for relationships to problems belonging to different fields.

3.2 TYPOLOGIES OF RESEARCH QUESTIONS

Until now we may have made the impression that there is *a-one-size-fits-all type* of research problem. In reality this is not the case: *several types of problems do exist. And they have to be distinguished.* Why is that? *Because how you design your empirical research project* (see Chapter 6) *is partly dependent upon the type of research problem you're working on.* It is not *the* single most important determinant of empirical work, but its role should not be underestimated.

Trochim and Donnelly (2007) make a distinction between *descriptive problems* and *explanatory problems*.

- ***Descriptive questions:*** Here the focus is to describe what is going on in a certain field, society or organization (over a certain period). Public opinion polls answering the question, what is the proportion of people holding certain opinions about legal topics?, is an example. Questioning relationships between variables are often part of such a problem. A public opinion poll that compares what proportion of males and females is in favor of a (new) euthanasia law in their country, and what their social characteristics are, is addressing a descriptive question. Sometimes, *comparative* research problems are part of this 'problem family'. Descriptive research questions can also be *exploratory*, trying to understand a (new, unknown) topic. Lakhani (2013) explored the consequences of the 'infiltration' of iPhone, Blackberry and Android into the profession of law and dispute resolution and looked at how this trend affects laws and the legal profession, what issues it presents to lawyers and judges, whether new laws are necessary to take into account the impact of social networking sites (on the legal profession) and what the benefits of such technology in fostering access to justice could be.
- ***Explanatory (causal) questions:***[2] If we conducted a public opinion poll to determine whether an awareness campaign in Belgium on a new (im)migration law changed peoples' preferences on the number of asylum seekers that are deemed acceptable for the country, we would be studying whether the campaign (cause) changed the

BOX 3.1 W AND H RESEARCH QUESTIONS

Descriptive W questions: what, who, when, where? What is happening in the field of family law with regard to divorce? Who is involved? Which time period will be looked at and in which countries?

Explanatory W(hy) questions: why are the developments X and Y in family law with regard to divorce taking place in country Q?

Explanatory H(ow) questions: how do these X and Y developments influence the legal system and the behavior of people P and organizations O?

All other questions[1]

[1] Knight (2009: 1546) refers to the first three and to 'how-questions'. Van Thiel (2010: 23–4) mentions exploratory and diagnostic research problems. However, exploratory problems often are descriptive problems while her definition of diagnostic problems ('what are bottlenecks, and what factors contribute to them?') also points to description (and to some extent 'explanation').

proportion of people that are positive or negative about immigration. Causal questions are also known as 'explanatory' or 'why' questions. These question types can be viewed as cumulative. One cannot address an explanatory question if the descriptive question has *not* been answered correctly first (Trochim and Donnelly, 2007). Formulated in more epistemological terms: the *explanandum* has to be known before the *explanans* can be developed (see also Chapter 4).

A second typology is based on Bunge (1997) and White (2009). It distinguishes between descriptive W questions, explanatory W questions and other questions.

Another typology is partly based on Van Thiel (2010). As empirical research covers more than just descriptive and explanatory questions,[3] this typology also addresses normative and design questions.

Denscombe (2002: 26) suggested a fourth typology, covering a few new focuses.

BOX 3.2 VAN THIEL'S (2010) TYPOLOGY OF RESEARCH QUESTIONS

Descriptive questions: how do individuals and small and medium businesses handle their (legal) conflicts? How many people are illegally downloading music, movies and books? How does a sample of countries score on indicators A, B and C of the rule of law and human rights?

Causal (or explanatory) questions: do increasing court fees lead to less legal conflicts brought to courts and why? Are web-based information campaigns trying to reduce digital piracy, changing consumer choice behavior (i.e. preventing and/or reducing illegal downloading) and if so, how does this work? How can differences in countries X and Z between the scores on rule of law- and human rights-indicators be explained?

Normative questions: Should governments encourage conflicts between members of society to be settled outside the legal system, not through courts?

Design questions:[1] how can common property regimes/common pool resources be organized in such a way that they contribute in an efficient and effective way to the sustainability of natural resources? How can a digital oversight authority be best organized and managed so that cybercrime and cyber insecurity will be prevented or reduced?

[1] Sometimes design-oriented research questions can be related to 'action research'. Action research is 'a participatory, democratic process concerned with developing practical knowing in the pursuit of worthwhile human purposes, grounded in a participatory worldview. . . . It seeks to bring together action and reflection, theory and practice, in participation with others, in the pursuit of practical solutions to issues of pressing concern to people, and more generally the flourishing of individual persons and their communities'. See Reason and Bradbury (2001) for more information.

BOX 3.3 DENSCOMBE (2002) TYPOLOGY RESEARCH QUESTIONS

Research problems focusing on forecasting and predictions: will the law on preventing commercialization of surrogacy be effective in terms of realizing its goals?

Research problems focusing on explaining causes and/or consequences: how is it to be explained that the social acceptance of penal sanctions S 1–S 3 has increased in country Y since 2000?

Evaluative research problems: what are the effects and side effects of the teenage pregnancy reduction law implemented in 2015 in country Y? When does disclosure and 'naming and shaming' in the medical world work (for whom and with which impact)?

Descriptive research problems: how do people and small and medium businesses handle their (legal) conflicts?

Developing good practice problems: how can oversight organizations (like inspectorates) be stimulated to reduce the administrative burden of their inspections for inspectees without jeopardizing the independent execution of their tasks?

Research problems addressing empowerment: are implementing European-wide withdrawal rights empowering the position of consumers in the EU?

What these typologies first tell us is that despite different labels, there is *overlap between the types of problems*. *Design problems* and *problems focusing on developing good practices* are overlapping. To design a (legal) policy or another intervention or organization is similar to trying to develop a '(good) practice', or as Howarth (2013) calls it, a legal device. *Descriptive and explanatory problems* include *comparative* questions,[4] while *normative problems* and *problems addressing empowerment* also overlap.[5] The same is to some extent true for problems focusing on *forecasting and predicting* and problems addressing *evaluations*,[6] as ex ante evaluations often try to predict the impact on human behavior of interventions. A related point is that *causal problems* in empirical legal research resemble '*evaluative/evaluation-oriented*' problems. 'Legal research often concerns topics [like]: will it work? Is it going to be implemented (or executed) in a way which is compliant with what was agreed upon? And: has it worked?' (Leeuw, 2011: 64). However, be aware of the fact that not *all* evaluations are ex ante and impact (or effectiveness) evaluations. Processes of *implementation* are also the object of (legal) evaluations.

However, these typologies also share information on *differences* between (types of) research problems. In particular, the difference between *normative problems* and *other problems* is crucial. White (2010: 43ff) puts it as follows:

> Normative questions . . . are often concerned with what 'ought to be' or 'should be', what is 'desirable' or 'undesirable', what is 'right' or 'wrong', or what

> is ‘good’ or ‘bad’. In philosophy, normative statements are contrasted with descriptive statements, which can in principle be tested through observation . . . A simple example of a normative question is: ‘should corporal punishment be re-introduced in the UK in secondary schools?’ The main problem with this question is the inclusion of the term ‘should’. This is not a question about the effect that corporal punishment has on a particular facet of students’ schooling, rather, it is a question seeking an opinion about an ethical issue . . . It cannot be solved empirically because there is no one correct answer.

One can be a supporter or opponent of corporal punishment, regardless of the results of empirical studies on causes and consequences of this behavior. In Chapter 9 we will discuss this gap between empirical evidence and (legal) normativity more in depth.

In this book we will work with the following (integrated) typology of *five types and subtypes of research problems.*

As said before, understanding the types of research problems is crucial, because of the relationship between what the research problem entails and the design of the empirical investigation. Studying a descriptive problem on attitudes of high school pupils on immigration allows more freedom when designing the study than when an ex post evaluation of the impact of anti-rape laws on violence is carried out. In Chapter 6 we will discuss this aspect of ELR more in depth.

3.3 HOW TO DISTINGUISH ADEQUATE FROM LESS ADEQUATE RESEARCH PROBLEMS?

It is a fact of life that research problems are not always formulated in an adequate way. The field of study called ‘theory and methodology of problems’ discusses deficiencies in problem formulations (Ultee, 2001). One deficiency is that researchers work on ‘ill-formulated’ problems (Ultee, 1976; Bunge, 1997). Another is that problem formulations sometimes lack brevity, clarity and precision (White, 2010: 66ff). A third deficiency is that the background of problems is incorrect. Ultee (2001) calls these ‘erroneous problems’. It is necessary to prevent these and a few other failures before embarking on the research itself.[7]

Failure 1: studying ill-formulated and sub-optimally formulated research problems: Waddington et al (2012: 361) give an interesting example. ‘A good answer needs a good question. The main issue in setting the question is the breadth of the question. We would all like to know the answer to the question ‘how do we end global poverty and achieve world peace?’, but it is rather too broad for a research project’. In line with this, asking the question ‘how is the situation in France with regard to cyber-crime?’ is

BOX 3.4 AN INTEGRATED TYPOLOGY OF RESEARCH PROBLEMS

Type 1: Descriptive research problems:
Type 1.1 Research problems focusing on exploring and describing the state of affairs of (legal) phenomena: How do people and small and medium businesses in Scandinavia and the Netherlands handle their (legal) conflicts? How many people in Europe are illegally downloading music, movies and books?

Type 1.2 Research problems focusing on exploring or making comparisons: How does a sample of countries score on indicators a–k of the rule of law and human rights over the last five years?[1] How is judicial independence established and maintained in practice in Y countries?

Type 2: Causal (or explanatory) research problems:
When increasing court fees in country P lead to less legal conflicts brought to courts, how can this be explained? Do government-sponsored web-based information campaigns on digital piracy change consumer choice behavior (i.e. prevent and/or reduce illegal downloading of – e.g. – books/music/movies) in country Z and how can this be explained?

Type 3: Normative research problems:
Should European governments encourage conflicts between members of society to be settled outside the legal system, and not through courts?

Type 4: Evaluative research questions:
Type 4.1 Evaluative research problems of an ex ante character: Will the law on preventing commercialization of surrogacy in country M be effective in terms of realizing its goals?

Type 4.2 Evaluative research problems focusing on implementation processes: To what extent are behavioral modification programs X, Y and Z implemented in prisons P and Q according to plan?

Type 4.3 Evaluative research problems of an ex post character: What are the effects and side effects of the teenage pregnancy reduction law implemented in 2010 in country Q? What are the effects of liberalizing the use of cannabis for leisure reasons on health and crime (rates)?

Type 5: Design-oriented research questions:
Type 5.1 Research problems regarding the development of designs: How can common property regimes/common pool resources (CPR) be organized in such a way that they contribute in an efficient and effective way to the sustainability of natural resources?

Type 5.2 Research problems regarding the piloting of designs: How can a CPR-design focused on preventing deterioration of fish stock in the Mediterranean be tested and what are the results?

[1] Sometimes known as trend problems.

another example of an ill-formulated problem, because only a very broad topic (the 'object variable') is formulated. *Which aspects of cyber-crime* (the modus operandi or the fields covered), *over which period* (last month, last year, last decade) and *regarding whom* (companies, individuals, victims, offenders) are not defined. This failure can be prevented by specifying at least two other variables, next to the 'object variable': the independent and the dependent variable. An example will help. Take this 'research problem': *how is the situation in the Netherlands with regard to dispute solution?* This problem is ill-formulated. A more precise problem is: *will the introduction of a no-cure, no-pay arrangement for lawyers in the Netherlands influence the ways in which citizens solve their disputes and their satisfaction levels with regard to dispute resolution?* Now the central topic (dispute resolution [object variable]), the 'independent' (or assumed causal) variable (the no cure, no fee arrangement) and the assumed consequences (or 'dependent' variables) (solving disputes and satisfaction levels) are articulated.[8] This makes the problem 'smaller', but that is the price one has to pay to prevent working on low or bad quality problems.

A second example is a bit more complex. Small commercial disputes in the Dutch court system are handled by canton judges. Over the last decade, the jurisdiction of these judges has increased. On 1 July 2011, commercial civil disputes with a financial value between 5,000 and 25,000 euros were added to the competence of canton judges. Under the jurisdiction of canton judges, the cases are expected to be handled less formally. Important changes for the parties included that hiring a lawyer is no longer compulsory (parties are allowed go to court unrepresented, or to be represented by anyone they choose) and that it is possible to present their case orally. Together with the implementation of this change, another part of the legislation was altered: court duties were increased, in particular for corporate actors. Eshuis et al (2014) investigated the changes, measuring what, in a sample of cases, happened during the processes of implementation, how satisfied parties were with the handling process, and what the relationship was between these (and several other) changes[9] in rules and the number of civil law cases handled by the judges. Statistical information showed that after a period of almost 20 years in which the number of civil cases increased, around 2011 there was a sudden decrease. Figure 3.1 shows the data.

Eshuis et al (2014) asked the question *if and to what extent the decline in numbers of court cases is related (or can be attributed) to – in particular – two changes in legislation: the higher court duties and the change in the court's competence levels*. The authors restricted their research to 2009–2012, and did not take into consideration the 17 years prior to this change (when there was a strong *increase* in numbers of cases). Although this may appear

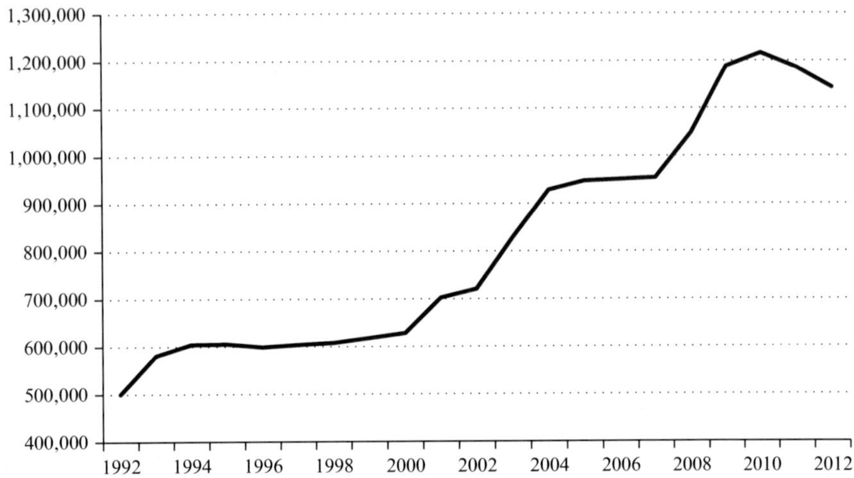

Source: Eshuis et al, 2014.

Figure 3.1 Development of civil cases in the Netherlands in total numbers (1992–2012)

an adequate approach, the authors worked on a *sub-optimally formulated problem*. First, because they did not pay attention to the discrepancy between 17 years of growth and two to three years of decline in numbers of civil law cases. Second, due to their focus on the last few years, the role the two policy changes played (higher court duties and changes in court competence) was probably overstressed. A broader formulation of the problem ('which factors have caused the *increase* in numbers of civil law cases *since 1992*, has there been a change in these factors over the last few years, which role did the two policy changes play in explaining the recent developments and what other factors (may) contribute to this development?') would have been commendable.[10]

Failure 2: studying erroneous research problems: These are problems that are formulated against a background consisting of at least one incorrect statement. The background 'is constituted by the antecedent knowledge and, in particular, by the presuppositions of the problem. The presuppositions of the problem are the statements that are somehow involved but not questioned in the statement of the problem and in the inquiry prompted by it' (Bunge, 1997: 194). Two examples will help. To ask the question why women who voted for conservative party X in country Y over the last 10 years have a lower fertility rate than women who voted for socialist party P (in the same country during the same period), is an erroneous research problem, *if* the statement included in the background of the problem is empirically *incorrect* (i.e. women voting for the socialist party did *not* have a lower fertility rate than women voting for the conservative party).[11] The second example comes from White (2010): 'Take the question "At what age do boys stop underachieving in schools?" It looks like a "clear" question but in fact it is a *double question*: do boys underachieve in schools? And: at what age?' The assumption that boys *do underachieve* has first to be tested (and corroborated) *before* the age question can be asked.

Failure 3: studying problems lacking clarity: Defining key terms is central to realizing clarity of a research question (Nachmias and Nachmias, 1976). However, clarity does not only concern definitions. Although the suggestion by Kane (1984) that all research problems should be posed as a single sentence is an exaggeration, the German proverb that '*in der Beschränkung zeigt sich erst der Meister*' is applicable, as the structure of a research problem can indeed be unclear. When a single research problem includes some 20 (or more) sub-questions and sub-sub-questions, not specifying how they relate to each other, this will reduce the guidance emanating from the research problem. Such a failure can also occur in the opposite direction. Epstein and Martin (2014: 23) give as an example the problem, 'what leads people to obey the law?' An interesting overarching problem, but if it is not broken down into one or more specific sub-questions (like, in their case, 'do gun control laws reduce violent crime?'), it will be difficult to answer.

Failure 4: studying problems characterized by a wrong level of abstraction: Van Thiel (2010: 29) gives two examples. The first is when a researcher formulates a problem of too abstract and general a nature (for example regarding the impact of key performance indicators on the efficiency of public tasks carried out by municipalities), when in fact the study will be dedicated to only *one particular municipality*. The other example is selecting too low a level of abstraction. This takes place when the research problem is basically nothing more than one or two very concrete and direct questions that respondents in a (web) survey have to answer. Then a link with a more general ('overarching') problem, under which these 'respondent questions' reside, is missing. As Yeager (2008: 45) puts it: a research problem 'is the focal question a research project is intended to answer. It is *not* a question developed for a survey or an interview protocol'.

Failure 5: studying tautological research problems:

> Tautological problems are problematic because they are true by definition and because they ask the same question twice. An example of a tautological research question is: why are the working classes over-represented in some types of occupation? . . . At first sight this may appear to be a perfectly reasonable question . . . The difficulty with [it] is that the type of work a person is employed in is central to most definitions of social or occupational class. People are

defined as 'working class' at least partly because of the kind of occupations in which they are employed. The question is therefore redundant as it already supplies the answer: *the working class are over-represented in certain types of occupation because working in these occupations lead people to be defined as working class*. (White, 2010: 41)[12]

3.4 SOME GUIDANCE[13]

- Understand the types of research problems; 'they can help you think about what type of question(s) *you* are asking' (White, 2009: 52).
- Know and check background knowledge against which you formulate the research problem and pay attention to what 'is already known about the issue' (Yeager, 2008).
- Understand the (other) failures with regard to problem formulation.
- Be precise in terms of the scope of your problem; the definitions of concepts; the time frame for the study; the geographical location(s); the level of abstraction of the problem and the unit(s) of analysis (natural persons, corporate actors, periods, places, and others).
- And: ask the following questions to evaluate the quality of your research problem (and the ease with which you are able to answer it):[14]
  - Does the question deal with a topic or issue that interests you enough to spark your own thoughts, opinions and 'energy'?
  - Is it relevant for others and will the answer(s) have potential implications (for the legal sciences, practice, society, etc.)?
  - Does it seek to engage the existing literature (to prevent reinventing the wheel)?
  - Can it be understood by relevant others?
  - What sources will have the type of information that I need to answer the research question?
  - Can I access these sources?

ENDNOTES

1. We will use the words 'research problem' and 'research question' interchangeably. However, in this book research questions are not the same as questions used in a questionnaire/survey or an interview.
2. Sometimes this type of question is also called 'theoretical'.
3. There are several other typologies. One is from Cormack and Benton (1996) who distinguish between interrogative and declarative research problems (Draper, 2004: 74ff). However, the problem statement of an 'interrogation' (investigation) is confused with the declaration of what the purpose of a study is. Yeager (2008: 54) distinguishes

between descriptive and normative questions and questions about relationships (but relationships can be described).

4. White (2009: 51) adds that although many research problems in one way or another deal with making comparisons, 'it can be argued that comparison is part of the descriptive stage of research' (and of descriptive research problems).
5. Research that strives to enhance empowerment has a strong normative connotation. White (2009: 50–51) links empowerment with political motives 'that can interfere with the research process and jeopardize the integrity and rigor of a study'.
6. Evaluators do this by unraveling the behavioral, social and institutional assumptions that underlie the policy, law or program. And by looking into the 'operational logic' of prospective interventions: who has to do what, when, for how long, under which (legal) constraints and opportunities to make the implementation a success? See also Chapter 4 and Chapter 9, section 9.3; Astbury and Leeuw (2010) and Leeuw (2012).
7. White (2010: 42) refers to another danger, i.e. that empirical researchers are confronted with metaphysical questions that by their very nature are 'related to debates that cannot be resolved through empirical inquiry'.
8. Ultee (1976:8) describes a research problem as 'a statement with a question mark, with regard to which it is possible that not all variables of the statement have been mentioned or addressed'. In line with Bunge (1997) he distinguished three variables that are part of research problems.
9. See Eshuis et al (2014) for a description of these changes in the legal system.
10. In a seminar organized by the Raad voor de Rechtspraak and WODC, held in The Hague in May 2014, this critique was discussed. One of the counter-arguments was that the authors checked for *alternative explanations* (i.e. (other) societal developments) regarding the decline in number of cases (Eshuis and van Tulder, 2014).
11. It is interesting to see that Plakhotnik and Rocco (2009) while discussing the background of problems ('situating the study in a broader context, for example, historical, national, or international') and suggesting that 'it should also 'hook the reader', do not discuss the problem of working with an *incorrect* background knowledge.
12. In philosophy, the principle of charity requires interpreting a speaker's statements to be rational and, in the case of any argument, considering its best, i.e. strongest, possible interpretation. If one would have followed that principle, one could have said that if the researcher would no longer define and operationalize 'occupations' in terms of class(es), this research problem would *not* have been labeled as tautological (Baillargeon, 2007: 78).
13. See also http://dissertation.laerd.com/how-to-structure-quantitative-research-questions-p2.php, accessed 25 November 2015; and Anna Beckers, 'How to draft a research question and how to solve it methodologically (and avoid having to read V.A. Morozow, Methods for solving incorrectly posed problems, New York, 1984)', powerpoint presentation Universiteit Maastricht, 5 March 2015.
14. Based on http://www8.esc.edu/htmlpages/writerold/menus.htm, accessed 25 November 2015. See also: Epstein and Martin (2014: 27–9).

4. Theories and empirical legal research

Theory is not just theoretical; it is useful.
(Richard Lempert, 2010: 893)

4.1 INTRODUCTION

In policy circles, including in the world of law making and justice, one of the '*opinions chique*' is that theories are for academics and in particular for rainy Friday afternoons. It is even more popular to say that arguments need not to be taken seriously 'because they are only theoretically relevant'. Unfortunately, also in serious publications on ELR, 'theories' are not high in the pecking order. In Epstein and Martin's (2014) recent book, several chapters are dedicated to quantitative data-analysis but hardly a word is written about 'theories'.

We attach a more prominent role to theories in this book. In line with Kurt Lewin the adage is that 'theory without practice is sterile, but practice without theory is blind'. This also applies to empirical legal research.[1] Theories are conjectures that give a reasonable answer to a (research) problem. When policies, legal arrangements and institutions are developed by lawyers, politicians or others, assumptions (about cognitions, behavior and society) play a role. Legal psychologists refer to these assumptions as *implicit theories* (Quintanilla, 2012) while evaluators coined the concept of *intervention theories*. Intervention theories usually look into (cognitive, behavioral and institutional) *mechanisms* making interventions 'work'. Elster (2007: 36) calls them the 'cogs and wheels' that bring the relationship between legal arrangements, policies and institutions on the one hand and the outcomes or consequences of these interventions on the other hand into existence (see section 4.3 where mechanisms will be discussed). Detecting and understanding *intervention theories* is crucial for ELR. Why? Because lawyers, regulators, legislators and policy makers do not always articulate their assumptions (about these mechanisms), let alone put them to test. That is one of the tasks of the empirical legal researcher.

In line with Lempert (2010), we call implicit or intervention theories

theories-with-a-small-t. They are one side of the coin. The other side are *theories-with-a-capital-T*, i.e. *scientific (explanatory or middle-range*[2]*) theories*,[3] usually produced and tested by (academic) researchers and comprised of statements about legal interventions, arrangements and institutions, mechanisms and intended and unintended consequences.

There is no guarantee that theories, *with or without capital T's*, are true ('valid') and produce correct predictions. In fact a theory is a *provisional answer* to a question, waiting for an (empirical) test. Popper (1963) refers to conjectures and refutations. In critical rationalism – the epistemological framework that guides this book – articulating and testing theories are leading principles.[4] White (2009), whose epistemological background is grounded in the same tradition,[5] argues that for empirical researchers 'the most important characteristics of a theory are that it is an idea (or couple of ideas) that is abstract, explanatory and testable'.

To discuss theories and their role in empirical legal research in a chapter of some 28 pages implies that important topics cannot be covered. We will not discuss epistemological aspects of what '*explanation*' means, which *types* of explanations exist, and what its *building blocks* are.[6] We also leave out '*Grand Theories*', i.e. broad, general frameworks, claiming to speak about almost everything. Think of Habermas' Critical Theory, Berger and Luckman's Social Construction of Reality-theory, Black's theory of the Behavior of Law or Wallerstein's World Systems Theory (Reeves et al, 2008; Lempert, 2010). Their relevance for ELR is limited. That is also true for their testability and actual testing. As Lempert (2010: 882) notes: 'it was hard to draw from these and similar [Grand Theories] hypotheses that made it possible to conduct rigorous empirical testing. Even operationalizing core theoretical concepts was difficult and open to dispute'. *Theoretical orientations* like symbolic interactionism or hermeneutics will not be discussed. They can be seen as 'heuristics' more than as theories (Homans, 1984: 318). We also refrain from discussing *approaches* like feminism, Marxism and what Reeves et al (2008: 340) call 'the post-modernist family of theories'.

This chapter discusses the following questions:

- Are explanatory and intervention theories relevant for all types of research problems and in which ways?
- What are 'mechanisms' and why are they important?
- What are explanatory theories and how can we find or articulate them?
- What are intervention theories and how can we find them?[7]
- What are links between explanatory theories and intervention theories?

> **BOX 4.1 LEGAL THEORY**
>
> Somewhat related to Grand Theory and theoretical orientations is '*legal theory*'. According to Galligan (2010: 978ff) 'legal theory includes more than legal philosophy: its perspective can be disciplinary, based on anthropology, sociology, or other social sciences; it can be inspired by ideology, such as Marxism and its offspring critical legal studies, or by a normative standard, as in the case of race theory, or gender theory; and finally, legal theory may reflect an epistemology, as illustrated by postmodernism'.
>
> The subject matter of legal theory is, for Hart (1961), 'the general framework of legal thought' and for Morawetz, echoing Hans Kelsen, the presuppositions 'that go unquestioned by practitioners and are implicit in their activity' (Morawetz, 1980; Kelsen, 1967). Law often means state law in whose making, interpretation, and implementation state officials play a prominent part. The aim is to formulate a theory 'true of all legal systems whose features must of necessity be general and abstract' (Raz, 1979: 104). Galligan (2012) describes relationships between legal theory and empirical legal research. We refer to this paper for more information.

- How to test theories?
- Which are the criteria to assess the quality of theories?

4.2 THE RELEVANCE OF EXPLANATORY (CAPITAL 'T') AND INTERVENTION (SMALL 'T') THEORIES

Let's go back to Chapter 3, on research problems. We distinguished five types of problems. What can be said about the relationship between (types of) problems and theories?

- When handling *descriptive research problems*, theories give guidance to the selection of variables. Take the phenomenon of 'access to justice'. There are numerous variables that may play a role in restricting or opening up access to justice. Investigating 'everything' is inefficient and practically impossible. When the research problem is specified (for example if and to what extent female asylum seekers in Western European countries experience more resistance to accessing justice than male asylum seekers), it can be linked to theories about dispute resolution and the role of gender and will lead to a relevant set of variables about which data have to be collected.
- In research on *exploratory problems*, the very fact that much is unknown makes it difficult to deduce insights from existing theories that clarify what is yet to be clarified. However, when exploration is

underway and the researcher has an 'educated guess' on the problem and the mechanisms that seem to play a role, it is commendable to link these insights with existing theories. If, as an example, a research project explores financial relationships between central government, local government and executive agencies with the goal of detecting which type of financial transaction is most prone to fraud and corruption, and it is found that most of these financial flows are subsidies (e.g. cash grants), then it is smart to deduce from theories about incentives, subsidies and prompts, insights that can steer the investigation.[8]

- For *explanatory research problems*, theories are crucial as they disclose information about what is known about causal factors (mechanisms). Addressing causality is a striking feature of most scientific theories.
- For *evaluative research questions*, studying intervention theories is indispensable. When ex ante evaluations are done, usually the only source documents available are those that deal with the why question: why is this legal device, intervention or policy developed and why is it believed that it will make a difference (which sometimes means reducing a certain problem)? From these documents the underlying intervention theory can be extracted (see below for rules of thumb how to do that). Explanatory theories are also relevant when working on evaluative questions as they function as mirrors, comparing and contrasting assumptions of policy makers, lawyers and regulators with scientific insights.
- For *design-oriented research questions* more or less the same applies, with one important difference. When designing 'something' new, like a new governance model for accreditation of higher education programs or new sentencing guidelines incorporating how to 'deal' with neuro-scientific evidence in court, the empirical legal researcher is not only charged with research, but also with assisting during the implementation of the new governance model or sentencing guidelines. Theories on designing procedures, communication, persuasion and learning will then play a role and the same is true for 'design theory', developed in the world of information systems. As 'the enterprise of law' is pre-eminently an information-processing business, these insights are relevant (Howarth, 2013).

4.3 MECHANISMS: CRUCIAL ELEMENTS OF THEORIES

One of the earliest explicit uses of the term '*mechanism*' in social science research can be found in Merton's (1968) essay 'On Sociological Theories of the Middle Range', first published in 1949. He discussed the 'self-fulfilling prophecy', which was illustrated by means of the example of a run on a bank. It describes 'a false definition of the situation evoking a new behavior which makes the originally false conception come true' (Merton 1968: 477). Mayntz (2004: 239) is, in line with Merton, of the opinion that 'statements about social mechanisms are often considered to be the building blocks of middle-range theories'.

4.3.1 What are Mechanisms?[9]

A number of scholars have compiled 'running lists' of definitions of mechanism (Gerring, 2007; Hedstrom, 2005). Rather than provide another list, we will first tell you what mechanisms are *not*. A common mistake (made by practitioners and researchers) is to conflate the term 'mechanism' with the intervention or legal arrangement *itself*. Mechanisms are not just another label for an intervention or device. If a study looks into the how and why of introducing 'sentencing protocols/guidelines', it is incorrect to see the *guidelines themselves* as mechanisms.[10] As a definition of the mechanism concept that prevents this and other misinterpretation(s),[11] Mayntz's (2004: 241) proposal is adequate. Mechanisms are 'sequences of causally linked events that occur repeatedly in reality if certain conditions are given. Substantively speaking, mechanisms state how and by what intermediate steps a certain outcome follows from a set of initial conditions. A mechanism provides a clear causal chain'. Astbury and Leeuw (2010: 368) stress that mechanisms operate at a deeper level than the intervention itself: 'We must go below the surface level descriptions of constant conjunctions and statistical correlations to identify the underlying mechanisms that account for regularities in the joint-occurrence of events'.

4.3.2 Are there Types of Mechanisms?

The answer is yes. Coleman (1990), Hedstrom (2005) and Elster (2007) point to three types of mechanisms: situational, action-formation and transformational. *Situational mechanisms* show how specific social, legal and/or economic or physical situations or events (occurring at the macro-level of a society) help to shape the beliefs, desires, opportunities and choices of (individual) actors. The *self-fulfilling prophecy mechanism* described by Merton is an example. Another example is the *opportunity structure* a community, village or city is characterized by; the more there are opportunities (for crime, for the unemployed), the larger the chance that crimes will be carried out and jobs will be found.[12]

Action-formation mechanisms operate at what Coleman (1990) calls the micro-level. This type of mechanism looks at how individual choices and actions are made and how these choices are influenced by (specific combinations of) desires, beliefs, opportunities (and increasingly bio-social factors). Festinger's (1957) *cognitive dissonance mechanism* is an example; it shows how individuals reduce psychological distress that arises when a person holds two contradictory ideas or attitudes simultaneously. Smokers, for example, often use techniques of rationalization to avoid quitting despite strong evidence that smoking reduces life expectancy (e.g. 'lung cancer only happens to heavy smokers'). The '*shadow of the future-mechanism*' is another example, sometimes referred to as the behavioral drive to do things differently, *because* the law (and its enforcement powers) functions as a shadow of the future (showing what can happen if ones engages in, say, fiscal non-compliance). *Framing* (how something is presented and influences the choices people make) and *incentives* are other action-formation mechanisms, as are *prisoner's dilemma's*, the *endowment mechanism* (people ascribe more value to things merely because they own them) and some 20–30 (other) cognitive-behavioral mechanisms like *hindsight bias* and *the fundamental attribution error*. Increasingly, researchers also search for bio-social processes underlying these mechanisms.[13]

Transformational mechanisms operate at the micro-to-macro level and show how a number of individuals, through their actions and interactions, can generate macro-level outcomes. An example is *cascading*, by which people influence one another so much that they largely ignore their private knowledge and rely instead on the publicly stated judgments of others. The *bandwagon phenomenon* – the tendency to do (or believe) things because many other people do (or believe) – is related to this, as is *group think* (Elster, 2007). *Tipping points* is another transformational mechanism.

4.3.3 What is the Relationship between the Three Mechanisms?

Coleman (1990), Hedstrom (2005), Hedstrom and Baerman (2009) and Raub, Buskens and van Assen (2011)[14] formulated an answer. It is known as the *Coleman's Boat* (see Figure 4.1).

In this schematic representation, 'nodes A and D represent propositions describing macro-conditions and macro-outcomes, respectively. Arrow 4 represents propositions about an empirical regularity at the macro-level, for example, an association between macro-conditions and macro-outcomes . . . Node B represents (descriptions of) micro-conditions, that is, independent variables assumed to be about regularities of individual behavior or, more ambitiously, in a theory of individual behavior'. Arrow 1 represents assumptions on how social conditions through situational mechanisms affect these variables. For example, networks and institutions

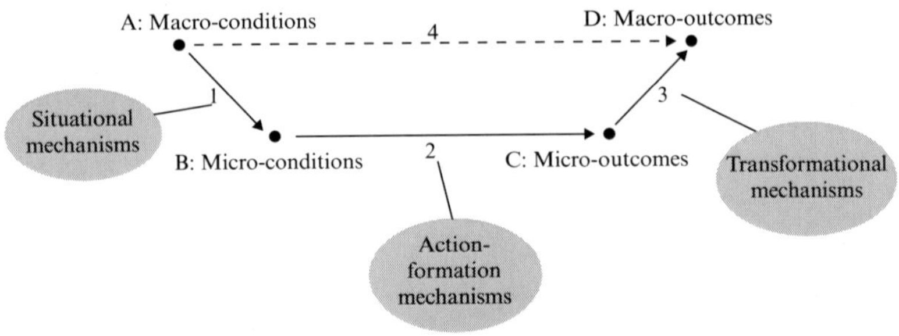

Source: This figure is partly based on Raub et al (2011).

Figure 4.1 Coleman's Boat: a model linking micro and macro-conditions and mechanisms

as well as prices can be conceived as opportunities or, conversely, constraints that affect the feasible alternatives of which actors can choose between.

Therefore, the '*opportunity structure*' of a given situation (as mentioned above) is seen as a *situational mechanism*. Social conditions likewise shape the incentives associated with various feasible alternatives and shape actors' information. Node C represents micro-outcomes, that is, descriptions of individual behavior. Assumptions about regularities of individual behavior or a theory of individual behavior are represented by arrow 2 and to so called '*action-formation mechanisms*'. Examples are *cognitive dissonance*, *social judgment*, and *attachment*. Finally, arrow 3 represents assumptions on how actors' behavior generates macro-level outcomes, here labeled '*transformational mechanisms*' such as *tipping points*.

Which (types of) mechanisms play a role in empirical legal research is *to some extent* dependent upon the type of legal arrangement, device or institution studied. A penal sanction to reduce reoffending is quite different from a program on reducing the case load for the 'enterprise of law'. And so may the mechanisms be. Mechanisms underlying governance approaches are to some extent different from coping mechanisms guiding the behavior of first responders of the police or the fire brigade, after a (terrorist) attack. We use '*to some extent*', because there are, next to context- and situation-specific mechanisms, also generic ones. They 'operate' in a similar way in different situations and can be seen as belonging to 'human nature'. Sometimes they are called *demi-regularities* (Lawson, 1997).[15] Lempert (2013: 25) urges legal researchers to look into mechanisms, because 'a failure to understand mechanism(s) can lead to mistaken conclusions about reasons for behavior, and the result can be poor policy decisions'.

4.4 EXPLANATORY THEORIES AND HOW TO FIND THEM?

4.4.1 Examples

Explanatory theories can be found in textbooks and handbooks of the social and behavioral sciences, including economics; usually they are 'produced' by academic researchers. They often have a 'name' or a 'label' and have been tested in different situations. How do these theories 'look' *in practice*?

A first example is *deterrence theory* (well-known in criminology). It says that, when the certainty, severity and celerity of criminal sanctions are high in a population, criminal behavior will be low. Deterrence theory can be subsumed under the more general *rational choice theory*, saying that people (informally, i.e. without using 'calculation machines') weigh costs and benefits (including emotions) before and during their activities and opt for 'satisfying' outcomes.

Theories of contract analyzed by Posner (2006) 'purport to show that contract law has an internal logic and that the logic is normatively attractive or grounded in historical contingency or struggles for power among competing groups. The first group of theories divides into welfarist and non-welfarist approaches. The welfarist approach understands only one theory: the law and economics theory. The non-welfarist approaches come in many flavors, but can be conveniently divided into 'liberal' or 'promissory' theories, and 'corrective justice' or 'reliance' theories' (Posner, 2006: 138). The law and economics theory assumes that individuals conform to the rationality assumptions of economic theory and that contract law promotes efficiency. Posner outlines the core of these theories too; they refer to both situational and action-formation mechanisms.

Cognitive theories focus on the cognitive dissonance mechanism, the fundamental attribution error mechanism and other mechanisms.

Rogers' (1995) *diffusion of innovation theory* studies the change process within *populations and organizations*. It was originally developed to explain an individual's adoption of technological innovations, but later, organizational change was included. Although the concept of innovation diffusion goes back to the French sociologist Gabriel Tarde, the theory itself was developed by Rogers with Schoemaker in 1962, based on the results of some 2000 empirical diffusion studies.[16] This theory defines several characteristics of innovations that influence an individual's and organization's decision to adopt or reject an innovation (like the 'relative advantage' of an innovation, its 'compatibility' with current operations and approaches; 'complexity' or 'simplicity', 'trialability' and 'observability').

Landes and Posner's (1975) *interest group theory* of the independent judiciary also considers macro-level characteristics of society. Vanberg (2008:100) used this theory to explain the establishment of judicial independence and how it is maintained in practice. Seen from an institutional perspective, his paper deals with the existence of constitutional courts and constitutional review:[17]

> Landes and Posner argue that the expected durability of legislation (the time period for which a statute is expected to be in force) poses a central concern as to interactions between legislators and interest groups. If interest groups expect that legislation they are able to secure to promote their interests is easily undone by subsequent legislative or judicial action, the value of legislation for interest groups declines – and along with it the 'payments' that groups are willing to make to legislators in order to secure it. To increase the value of legislation, legislators therefore have an interest in 'tying their own hands' in ways that increase the durability of legislation. Delegation to an independent judiciary is one way of doing this, because it diminishes the influence of legislative majorities over the interpretation and enforcement of past legislative deals. (Vanberg, 2008:107)

Galanter's *repeat players versus one shotters-theory* (1974: 95) helps to understand what the 'different kinds of parties (during litigation) are and [what] the effect these differences might have on the way the [legal] system works' (ibid., p. 97). He divided 'actors into those claimants who have only occasional recourse to the courts (one-shotters [OS]) and repeat players (RP) who are engaged in many similar litigations over time. The spouse in a divorce case, the auto-injury claimant, the criminal accused are OS; the insurance company, the prosecutor, the finance company are RP'. For Galanter, the 'RP is an individual or entity that participates or contemplates participating actively in the legal system, has low stakes in the outcome of any one case, and . . . has the resources to pursue its long-run interests' (ibid., p. 98). He juxtaposes RP against OS and outlines the advantages that the RP typically has over the OS. We refer to Chapter 10 for a discussion on the research program that, since the 1974 article, has been studying Galanter's theory.

Shepherd (2011: 1754) studied the influence of judicial self-interest on judicial behavior and used *public choice theory*. 'The basic assumption of public choice theory is that self-interest rules behavior in public as well as private transactions.' Thus, the public choice model of judicial decision-making takes a '[c]andid look at judicial motivation' and assumes that judges may be influenced by the 'day-to-day pressures and temptations' of their positions.

In the *Oxford Handbook of Empirical Legal Research* (Cane and Kritzer, 2010) a range of explanatory theories can also be found. Table 4.1 is a snapshot covering a part of the *Handbook* (mechanisms are printed in *bold* and *light italics*).

Table 4.1 Label, core content and references of theories referred to in the Handbook of Empirical Legal Research (Cane and Kritzer, 2010)

Label	Core	Reference[1]
Theory of contract behavior	Gaps between formal contracts and the 'real deal'; seeing contracts as social behavior rooted in *cooperation* and *relational contracting*.	Wheeler (2010); Macaulay (1963)
Transaction costs theory	A transaction cost is a *cost incurred in making an exchange*. These play an important role in decision-making. *Search and information costs* (incurred in determining that the required good or case or information is available, which has the lowest price); *bargaining costs* (required to come to an acceptable agreement with the other party to the transaction) and *enforcement costs* (the costs of making sure the other party sticks to the terms of the contract, and taking appropriate action (often through the legal system) if this turns out not to be the case).	Wheeler (2010); Williamson (1966)
The LLSV hypothesis[2]	The degree to which shareholders and creditors are protected by the legal system can explain why there are such different patterns in the use of debt and equity (shares) respectively, to finance companies in different countries. It was found that the rights of minority shareholders as well as shareholders in general were much better *protected* in countries with legal systems that belong to the common law tradition than to the civil law tradition. 'It is also found that common law is associated with low formalism of judicial procedures and greater judicial independence. These indicators in turn are associated with better contract enforcement and greater security of property rights. The legal origins literature adopts a broad conception of legal origin as a style of social control of economic life' (Swedberg, 2000).	Black (2010); La Porta et al, (1998); Swedberg (2000); Ferguson (2014)
Theory on procedural fairness	Disputants attach at least as much importance to the *fairness of a given adjudicative procedure* as to its outcome.	Meili (2009); Thibaut and Walker (1975)

Table 4.1 (continued)

Label	Core	Reference[1]
The regulatory pyramid theory	Focusing on the different steps in regulation, starting with getting engaged in dialogue and encouraging the 'regulands' into *self-regulation*, but also making sure that a 'big stick' is carried when *escalating* up the regulatory pyramid to more mandatory intervention and *coercion* by the regulator is needed.	Haller (2010); Ayres and Braithwaithe (2005)
The naming, blaming and claiming theory of solving disputes	According to this theory, 'disputes come into being through a process in which, first, *some "injurious experience" is recognized* by the injured party or her agent ("naming"), and hence becomes a "*perceived injurious experience*". The injured party then attributes responsibility to another party ("*blaming*"), thus producing a grievance which, under certain conditions, will lead to communicating a claim ("*claiming*").'	Kritzer (2010: 261)
Theory related to international norms and socialization of human rights	This theory focuses on the role of transnational or international socialization to drive the creation of and commitment to international human rights treaties. It emphasizes the transformative *power* of international normative *discourse* on human rights and the role of activism by transnational actors.	Camp Keith (2010)

Notes:
1 Most of the references can be found in Cane and Kritzer (2010).
2 Herlihy published 'The Use and Abuse of Comparative Law in "Legal Origins" Theory – A Cautionary Tale' (http://www.law.georgetown.edu/library/about/125/symposium/biographies.cfm) in which he criticized the work by LLSV. See also Ferguson (2014) for a critique on this theory.

These and other *explanatory theories* focus on natural persons (criminals, persons engaged in disputes, entrepreneurs, refugees, etc.), corporate actors like organizations and institutions, and on how social systems, including the justice system operate.

4.4.2 How to Find Explanatory Theories?

Knowing *that* these theories are important when doing research is one thing. *Knowing where to find them* is step two. There are several routes to tackle this challenge. The *first* is simple. Look for theories that (often in their title) refer directly to the topic of the research problem. If a research question is to measure the impact of alternative dispute resolution (ADR) on solving conflicts between parties, the role higher court duties play in decisions made by civilians whether or not to go court, or how decision-making of asylum seekers to stay in a country illegally or not is at stake, then finding a relevant theory is do-able. Theories on ADR exist and have been tested; there are (economic) theories on price effects of changes in court duties, and there is theoretical work on 'when and why to go illegal'. From these theories, insights can be deduced that help guide the empirical investigations (which variables to study, what is the role of contexts etc.). Van Erp (2010) studied the impact of the disclosure of offending companies (by the Dutch Financial Management Authority) in the Dutch financial market on the behavior of these (and other) companies, and on the level of trust in the market. She used rational choice theory to predict what the consequences of naming and shaming would be. In this example a well-developed explanatory theory, which has been tested before in different situations, together with a specification of this theory into the 'naming & shaming' mechanism *regarding the financial sector in the Netherlands*, was used and tested.

Explanatory (middle-range) theories are not always that easy to find, so we need a plan B. Then one first searches for mechanisms underlying the specific arrangement under investigation and uses these concepts later to find relevant explanatory theories. A few examples will help.

Example 1: explaining why there are wrongful legal decisions. Psychology of law scholars point to cognitive mechanisms that play a role in legal decision-making, like 'tunnel vision' and the 'fundamental attribution error'. They also take into account what is happening with prosecutors and judges in decision-making processes under stress (caused by media exposure or the danger of damaging one's own reputation). Theories spelling out the consequences of stress on decision-making can also be used and the same goes for Kahneman's 'dual-process theory of the brain', with its two fundamentally different modes of thought: System 1 and System 2: 'System 1 is fast; it is intuitive, associative, metaphorical, automatic, impressionistic, and it can't be switched off . . . System 2 is slow, deliberate, effortful. Its operations require attention. System 2 is slothful, and tires easily (a process called "ego depletion")' (Strawson, 2011).

Example 2: evaluating the impact of the fight against illegal downloading ('digital piracy'). If the research question is which effective ways exist to reduce digital piracy, a scan of the literature will tell you that there are a few basic mechanisms that underlie diverse interventions: sticks, carrots, sermons and pillaries (HBM Leeuw, in press).[18] Sticks refer to law enforcement (like the 'graduated response-intervention'), carrots to offering non-illegal download options for a low(er) price to consumers and sermons are information and persuasion activities and campaigns, implemented by governments and/or corporate actors, trying to persuade consumers that it is 'bad' for artists and industries to download illegally. The pillary (the naming and shaming mechanism) influences reputations of persons and organizations which will incentivize them to change their downloading behavior. The next step is to apply theories *about these mechanisms* and, through this process, enrich the empirical study.

Example 3: how to study the impact of laws on health-related behavior. Did mandatory safety-belt laws influence health (related behavior) in the USA between 1990 and 2010? Burris and Anderson (2013: 6) studied this question:

> A change in safety-belt use after the passage of a law could be conceptualized as the result of deterrence: the causal diagram begins with the law, proceeds through rational choices by drivers, to compliance or non-compliance based on the likelihood and cost of detection. This theory would direct researchers toward an inquiry into drivers' risk aversion, or their perceptions of the likelihood and cost of detection. It is also plausible, however, that the law works by signaling the official adoption of an existing social norm of safety-belt use. . . . This theory would highlight variables related to drivers' beliefs about the legitimacy of government authority or their beliefs about what people whose regard they value would expect them to do. A researcher could then test multiple theories, by, for example, surveying drivers about both their perceptions of punishment risk and their beliefs. . . . Or the researcher may make a reasoned choice about which theory to investigate further. For example, if the researcher is aware that the law has a trivial fine and is not being enforced, she may elect not to prioritize deterrence as a subject of investigation. In this way, theory makes it possible to systematically generate and test explanations of how law is working.

Example 4: do prosecutorial guidelines on drunk driving contribute to greater consistency in imposing community service penalties across the Netherlands' court districts?[19] To address this problem it is wise to find theories about guidelines and protocols in which attention is paid to the (behavioral) consequences of working with them (the protocols).[20] It is known that guidelines and protocols sometimes bear the risk of developing 'tick and flick-behavior', 'teaching to the test' and 'crowding out'.[21] The organizational efficiency theory suggests that judges and other courtroom actors, such as public prosecutors, have a desire to share the goal of realizing an effective case management and effective case disposition. However, this could also lead to developing informal norms and the desire to dispose of cases with minimal effort (Dixon, 1995). From this theory (and public choice theory) it could be deduced that judges and public prosecutors follow guidelines more easily, because it will cost less effort and time. If they all operate in this way, it will lead to a consistent application of the guidelines and to (greater) consistency in imposing community service penalties across court districts. Whether or not this behavior also causes (unintended) side effects is not addressed by the theory.

In these examples the empirical legal researcher links the legal interventions or arrangements to more *general mechanisms* that are believed to be 'at work'. Instead of (only) searching for theories about the intervention or arrangement *itself*, he embarks on a trip to find theories about these mechanisms. They are the inputs for the empirical investigation, allowing the presentation of explanations and predictions. Epistemologically, this procedure is called *subsumation* (Leeuw, 2012).

4.4.3 Where to Find Explanatory Theories?

The *first answer* is: use Web of Science (http://www.webofknowledge.com) and other (meta) databases, including ProQuest (http://www.proquest.com/), JSTOR (http://www.jstor.org) and general search engines (e.g. Google Scholar (http://scholar.google.nl/)). Web of Science connects publications and researchers through citations and controlled indexing in curated databases, spanning very probably (almost) every discipline. It is an important tool to track prior research and monitor current developments. Most university libraries have these and other search engines.

A *second answer* is to go for *evidence libraries or evidence repositories* where systematic reviews and syntheses studies can be found. Many are of direct relevance for ELR. Dedicated organizations are sometimes called 'second-order knowledge production institutes' (Hansen and Rieper, 2011): Campbell Collaboration, Cochrane Library, EPPI, 3ie and clearinghouses (for education, labor markets, etc.). In Chapter 5 we will discuss them in more depth.

Third, go for specialized journals and scan them on the topic under investigation or on the mechanisms believed to be working.

Finally (although with hesitation), there are specialized websites[22] containing social and behavioral theories.[23] The reason for hesitation is that these sites can be useful for a trained researcher, but for persons new in a field they might easily lead to 'picking and choosing' irrelevant theories that are not tested or have already been falsified.

4.5 INTERVENTION THEORIES AND HOW TO FIND THEM

While explanatory theories usually come from academia (both from fundamental and applied studies), intervention theories are the (often implicit) assumptions of policy makers, practitioners, lawyers and legislators. These assumptions underlie laws and regulation, contracts, behavior modification programs, alternative dispute resolution systems, legal harmonization, inspections and oversight activities. Every time such an arrangement or device is conceived *and* implemented, assumptions about why it will do what it is supposed to do (i.e. realize set goals), for whom and for how long, play a crucial role. Quintanilla (2012) labels these assumptions as 'implicit theories'. Oliver Holmes's characterization ('unstated major premises') is also applicable (Homans, 1984: 345).

When the (sets of) assumptions are brought together in a structured way, they are called *intervention theories*. Intervention theories comprise an expectation that the introduction of a program, (legal) intervention or device will help realize 'something' (ameliorate a problem, prevent the development of a problem, reinforce existing behavior, channel actions, etc.). They also contain assumptions about the mechanisms that will bring about the change for the better. Farnsworth (2007) gives examples of mechanisms that are behind legal arrangements. Sometimes the mechanism is an incentive, sometimes a cascade or a slippery slope, sometimes a cognitive process and sometimes trust. The intervention theory specifies what the role of these (and other) mechanisms is, which outcomes the intervention or arrangement will probably generate under which conditions and in which contexts. However, as policy actors, legislators, regulators and other (legal) practitioners do not always make their assumptions explicit, researchers have to do this job (Astbury and Leeuw, 2010: 364). Methods how to undertake this are available and will be discussed in section 4.5.2.

4.5.1 Examples: Intervention Theories Underlying Megan's Law, a World Bank Anticorruption Program and Asylum Judgments

Evaluating Megan's law

The *first example concerns Megan's Law* (Pawson, 2002; 2002a). This law was enacted in 1996 in the USA following the rape and murder of Megan Kanka. Her killer was a released sex offender who, unbeknownst to her parents, was living in their neighborhood. News of the case sparked a large public outcry, which resulted in the swift introduction of legislation allowing for a mandatory community notification system for convicted sex offenders (Pawson, 2002). In several other countries such as England,

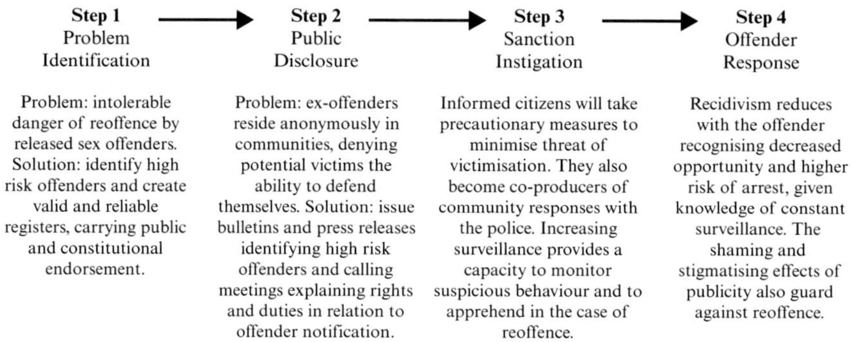

Figure 4.2 The basics of Megan's Law's program theory

Scotland, the Netherlands, and Australia 'look-alike' initiatives are discussed and sometimes implemented (van der Horst et al, 2012).

What are the (behavioral/institutional) assumptions underlying this law? See Figure 4.2.

By digging deeper into the basics (and following Coleman's Boat approach), the result is a more fully reconstructed program theory (see Figure 4.3). It identifies situational mechanisms, which can affect how sex offender naming and shaming policies work. *Agenda setting* describes the processes by which widespread and extensive media coverage can

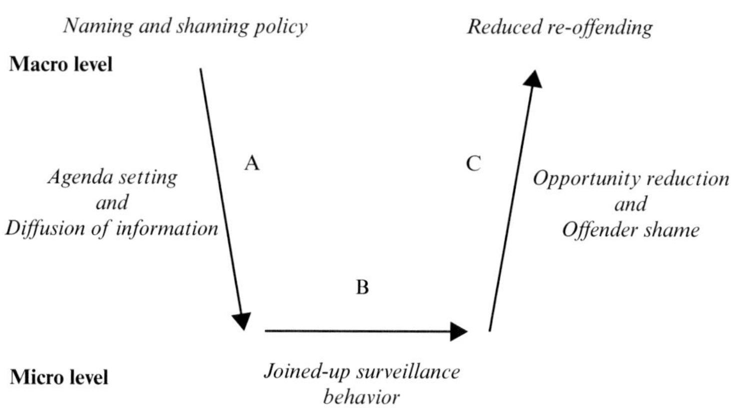

Source: Adapted from Coleman (1986), Hedstrom and Swedberg (1998) and Pawson (2002).

Figure 4.3 A model of mechanisms underlying 'naming and shaming' of sex offenders. A = situational mechanism; B = action-formation mechanism and C = transformational mechanism

influence public opinion on how to respond to the issue of released sex offenders living in the community. Heightened *salience and framing* are likely to determine the way in which naming and shaming policy is put into practice. In a context of strong social pressure to 'do something' about the problem, policy makers and law enforcement officials typically decide that investment in sex offender registration and information management systems are appropriate ways to enact policy.

It is also assumed that these activities will lead to a *diffusion process*, whereby appropriate persons will receive accurate and timely information about registered sex offenders who are residing in their local neighborhood. It describes how information about registered sex offenders spreads through particular communication channels over time among the members of a social system. In practice, the dissemination of information can occur in a variety of ways: for example, mass media outlets such as the internet as well as interpersonal communication channels such as police-community consultative groups and informal meetings of concerned local citizens. However, this is not enough to make naming and shaming work. The next link in the chain involves individual actors responding appropriately (or not) to information once it is received. According to the basic intervention theory of naming and shaming, police officers, members of the community, heads of schools and teachers, sports mentors and others will accept information about registered sex offenders, assume that is valid, and start *to act upon* it. 'Acting upon' implies an increased *joined-up surveillance behavior*, which also implies that the framing of what suspicious behavior constitutes is more or less similar among different stakeholders in different contexts. It also implies that the results of surveillance activities are fed back into information management systems.

Transformational mechanisms aggregate the individual joint (surveillance) actions to such a level that they are believed to make a difference to the behavioral choices of registered sex offenders. Aggregated surveillance increases the (perceived) likelihood of being caught, leading to the possible activation of an *opportunity reduction mechanism*. It also has the potential to trigger a *shame-inducing mechanism* among potential re-offenders. Finally, the *joining up* of the different mechanisms, so the theory goes, will lead to a reduction in re-offending.

What is the contribution of this analysis to the evaluation of Megan's Law and similar legal interventions? First, it stimulates the empirical investigator to think about how to test this theory. For example, situational mechanisms, such as diffusion processes, are identified as an important channel for delivering information to local residents. One way of systematically investigating diffusion would be through a survey that considered the extent to which information is actually getting to individuals and community groups in a timely fashion. A local case study of communication networks might also be useful. If this is not the case, then unintended side effects such as vigilantism may occur.

Second, tapping into existing social science theory on mechanisms is useful as it may provide important insights into the likely functioning of these mechanisms. Again, consider the example of situational mechanisms, such as diffusion, about which a serious body of scholarly research is available (Rogers, 2003). One important finding is that the type of interpersonal network structure can greatly influence information exchange. Radial personal networks comprise a set of individuals linked to a focal individual but not interacting with each other, while interlocking personal networks consist of individuals who interact mainly with each other. The former would seem to be much more effective in ensuring that information about local sex offenders is exchanged with a wider environment, thereby increasing surveillance behavior.

Evaluating a World Bank anticorruption program

The second example comes from a mid-term evaluation of the impact of an anticorruption program developed by (at the time) the World Bank's Economic Development Institute (EDI) (Leeuw et al, 1999). Central in the EDI's approach was helping to develop and/or reinvigorate a country's National Integrity System (NIS). Integrity pillars are administrative reforms, watchdog agencies, parliament, civil society, public awareness, the judiciary, free media and political will.

Langseth et al (1997) have described the EDI/World Bank approach, which emphasizes a NIS as a comprehensive method of fighting corruption. It is a central goal of EDI to help develop:

- awareness-raising within civil society;
- institution building;
- prevention of corrupt practices; and
- prosecution of corrupt officials.

The evaluation focused on two African countries. It described goals and instruments of the World Bank, and put these in an institutional context. The underlying theory was reconstructed. The program consisted of several policy strands of which we only discuss the *integrity and media workshops strand*. It consisted of eight social and behavioral presumptions underlying the idea that workshops can be an effective tool to help curb (and prevent) corruption. The workshops were organized through local organizations together with the World Bank, while VIPs from diverse organizations (parliament, government, churches, companies, etc.)

participated. Exchanging information on what to do in practice, signing pledges to help fight corruption and developing a communication strategy to reach society at large, were among the topics discussed. See Figure 4.4 for a graphic representation of this intervention theory.

This intervention theory was next confronted with findings from a literature study, document analysis and on-site interviews in two countries, Uganda and Tanzania. The (mid-term) evaluation was published at the end of 1990s while in 2005 the ex post evaluation was published of the complete program (Klein Haarhuis and Leeuw, 2004).

Analyzing assumptions about human behavior underlying asylum judgments in the UK

Herlihy et al (2010) studied assumptions in judgments made by UK immigration judges on decision-making, regarding who is to be recognized as a refugee and who not. In the UK, potential refugees must give a 'plausible' account of persecution during the decision-making process. Decision-makers must decide on the truthfulness of the account, and whether the person fits the legal definition of a refugee. Decision-makers often have little corroborating evidence, and must make an assessment of credibility involving a reliance on assumptions about human behavior, judgments, attitudes, and how a truthful account is presented. Through a qualitative process, the authors produced themes, representative of each of the categories of assumptions from 30 UK determinations.

One category dealt with judgments about 'likely' behavior. Stereotyping, common sense and 'the danger of applying the question 'what would I have done in this situation' in order to make a judgment about others' actions', are discussed (ibid., p. 363). A second category of assumptions concerns 'the judgments that have to be made about the quality of expert evidence to the court'. The 'nature of a truthful account' appears to be guided by 'a strong lay belief that "keeping the story straight" is the hallmark of [such] an account'. This is contrary to a growing empirical literature emphasizing that memory for traumatic events is often inconsistent and ill-recalled (ibid., pp. 364–5). Several other categories of assumptions are also discussed. The study concluded that (ibid., p. 365):

> we use assumptions and stereotypes as heuristics to help us make decisions when we lack the time to gather more idiosyncratic information about the situation on which we must decide. [But] what these findings do not tell us is which of these assumptions are consistent with current knowledge on human behavior, particularly during and following situations of danger, and the process of remembering and presenting an account of possibly traumatic situations in the context of a legal process.

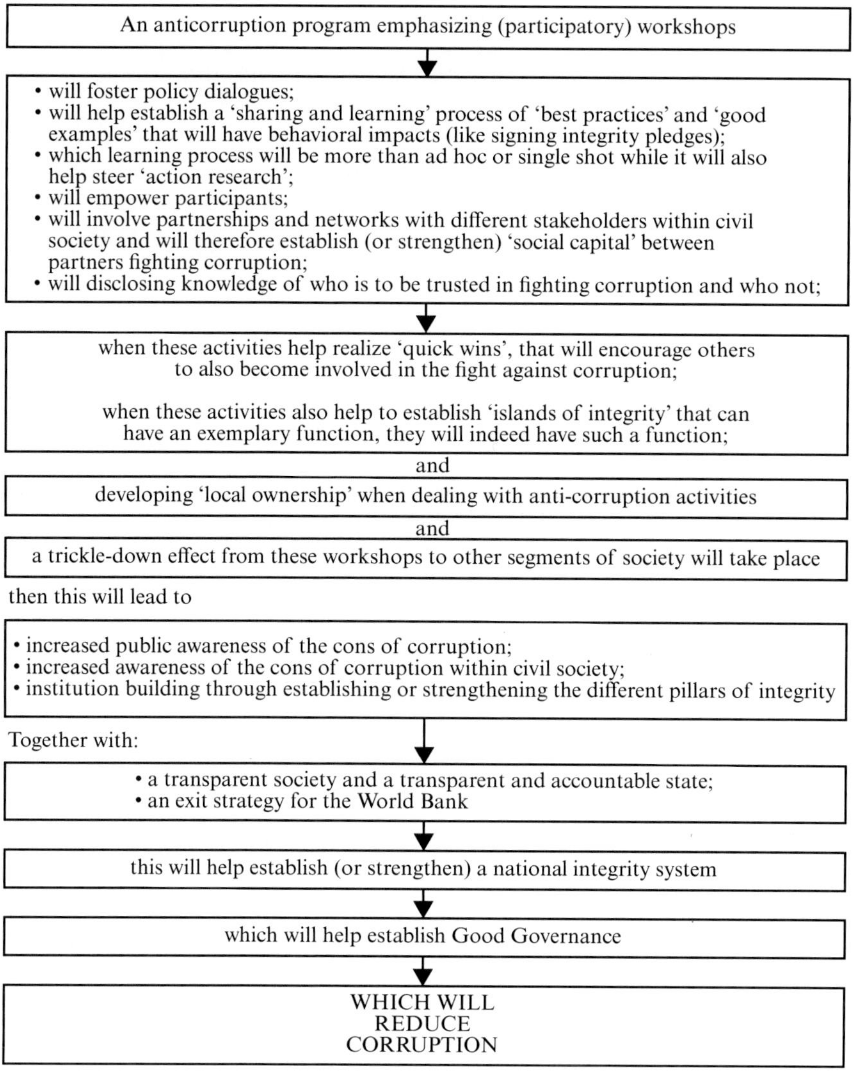

Figure 4.4 Reconstruction of the underlying intervention theory of the anticorruption World Bank Institute program on workshops

Methodologically, the study by Herlihy et al (2010) is different from the two other examples. In the authors' words, '[it] is data-driven, not theory driven, [while] an opportunistic sampling of determinations was made'.[24]

4.5.2 How to Find Intervention Theories?

Policy makers, politicians, lawyers, regulators and legislators are not (always) transparent about their assumptions. Therefore, methods have been developed to search for and detect implicit assumptions and reconstruct them. Here we present two of them, based on an earlier inventory of several other approaches (Leeuw, 2003; 2012; Vanderweele and Staudt, 2011): the policy scientific approach and the strategic assessment approach.

Policy Scientific Approach[25]

The 'policy scientific approach' covers the following six steps:

Step 1: Identify behavioral mechanisms expected to address a/the problem

Searching formal and informal documents and interview transcripts can elicit statements that indicate why it is believed necessary to address a (societal or policy) problem by developing (legal) arrangements or policies and what their goals are. These statements can point to mechanisms.

Step 2: Statements that have the following form are especially relevant for detecting mechanisms:

'It is evident that *X*. . . will work'
'In our opinion, the best way to go about this problem is to. . . '
'The only way to solve this problem is to. . .'
'Our institution's *X* years of experience tells us that. . .'

Step 3: Compile a survey of these statements and link the mechanisms with the goals of the arrangement or policy under review

Step 4: Reformulate these statements in conditional 'if–then' propositions or propositions of a similar structure ('the more X, the less Y').

Step 5: Search for 'warrants' to identify missing links in or between different propositions through argumentation analysis.

Argumentation analysis is a standard tool in logic and philosophy. It describes a model for analyzing chains of arguments and it helps to reconstruct and fill in argumentations. A central concept is the 'warrant', the 'because' part of an argument: it says that B follows from A because of a (generally) accepted principle. For example, 'the organization's performance will not improve next year' follows from 'the performance of this organization has not improved over the last five years', because of the principle, 'past performance is the best predictor of future performance'. The 'because of' part of arguments often is not made explicit. Consequently, these warrants must be inferred by the analyst performing the analysis. Visualization (mapping) software can help in this work. See http://www.criticalthinking.eu/ (accessed 19 July 2015) for examples of software.

Step 6: Reformulate these 'warrants' in terms of conditional 'if–then' (or similar) propositions and draw a chart of the (mostly causal) links.

Step 7: Evaluate the validity of the propositions by looking into:

- the logical consistency of the set of propositions;
- their empirical content, that is, the extent to which the theory and, in particular, the assumed impact of the behavioral mechanisms correspond with the state of the art within the social/behavioral/economic sciences on these mechanisms.

Evaluating the (reconstructed) intervention theory can be done in different ways. One is to confront (or juxtapose) the theory with other theories. Another is to empirically test the theory. A third possibility is to organize an iterative process of continuous refinement using stakeholder feedback and multiple data collection techniques and sources, while a fourth approach is to make use of already published reviews and synthesis studies to test the theory.

Strategic Assessment Approach

There are four major stages central to the Strategic Assessment Approach: (1) group formation; (2) assumption surfacing; (3) dialectical debate; and (4) synthesis (Mason and Mitrof, 1980).

Stage 1 – Group Formation: The aim is to structure groups so that the productive operation of the later stages of the methodology is facilitated. A wide cross-section of individuals with an interest in the relevant question should be involved. They are divided into groups, care being taken to maximize convergence of viewpoints within groups and to maximize divergence of perspectives between groups.

Stage 2 – Assumption Surfacing: The different groups separately unearth the most significant assumptions that underpin the arrangements or interventions and policies. Two techniques assume importance in assisting this process.

The first, stakeholder analysis, asks each group to identify the key individuals or groups upon whom the success or failure of their (preferred) arrangement or intervention would depend. This involves asking questions such as: Who is affected by the arrangement? Who has an interest in it? Who can affect its adoption, execution, or implementation? And who cares about it? For the stakeholders identified, each group then lists what assumptions it is making about each of these when believing that its preferred strategy will succeed.

The second technique is assumption rating. Initially, one should find and list the assumptions. This involves searching for statements about symptoms of the problem (that have to be solved, distinguishing them from statements about causes of the problem). For each of the listed assumptions, each group asks itself two questions: (1) How important is this assumption in terms of its influence on the success or failure of the intervention/arrangement? And (2) how certain are we that the assumption is justified? Here, in fact, the evaluation of the listed assumptions takes place, usually by using research reviews and similar documents. The results are recorded. Each group then is able to identify a number of key assumptions upon which the success of its strategy rests. Techniques like concept mapping or worldle for generating 'word clouds' can help.

Stage 3 – Dialectical debate: The groups are brought back together and each group makes the best possible case to the others for its preferred arrangement or intervention, while identifying its key assumptions. Only points of information are allowed from other groups at this time. There is then an open debate focusing on which assumptions are different between groups, which are rated differently, and which of the other groups' assumptions each group finds most troubling. Each group should develop a full understanding of the preferred interventions or arrangements of the others and their key assumptions.

Stage 4 – Synthesis: An attempt to synthesize is then made. Assumptions are negotiated and modifications to key assumptions are crafted. Agreed assumptions are noted; they can form the basis for consensus around a new (type of) legal arrangement that bridges the gap between the 'old' arrangement and goes beyond them. If no synthesis can be achieved, points of disagreement are noted and the question of what research might be done to resolve these differences is discussed.

These approaches can be seen as *rules of thumb* when entering the world of grasping with underlying theories and judicial mindsets. Using them increases the transparency of what a researcher is doing when trying to detect these 'mindsets'.

4.6 LINKS BETWEEN EXPLANATORY AND INTERVENTION THEORIES

We may have made the impression that explanatory and intervention theories are *not* related. Reality is different. First, mechanisms that are part of the intervention theories and scientific theories can be related. Second, when designing and implementing policies and regulations, actors make use of and learn from (explanatory) theories. An example is social capital theory, which stresses the importance of 'weak ties' versus 'strong ties' in finding jobs, partners or information in general (Granovetter, 1983). The strength of personal ties is usually measured by the degree of emotional intensity, intimacy and reciprocal services. Over the years Granovetter's theory has become part of policy makers' *repertoire*. There are also combinations of intervention and scientific theories that go together well. Ayres and Braithwaite's (1992: 35) theory on the enforcement pyramid (also known as the 'Responsive Regulation theory') has merged with assumptions that governmental inspectorates and oversight authorities work with (sometimes in an implicit way) (Willemsen, Leeuw and Leeuw, 2008). The core of this Responsive Regulation theory is the enforcement pyramid. Most regulatory action occurs at the base of the pyramid, where attempts are initially made to coax compliance by persuasion. The next phase of enforcement escalation is a warning letter; if this fails to secure compliance, imposition of civil monetary penalties [is on the agenda]; if this fails, criminal prosecution; if this fails, plan shutdown or temporary suspension of a license to operate; if this fails, permanent revocation of license.[26]

4.7 CRITERIA FOR TESTING AND USING THEORIES

Theories can be used in different ways. They shed light on variables to be studied, they produce background knowledge, they explain findings, and they contribute to the growth of knowledge in a field (see also Chapter 10).[27] However, as there is no evidence that explanatory or intervention theories are a priori *valid (or true), theories have to be tested. They are conjectures.*

'*Informative content*' of a theory is a first criterion. In more popular terms, this is the ability of a theory to be tested and disproved. It is 'the set of statements that are incompatible with the theory. This formulation sometimes surprises people . . . but it becomes easier to understand when one recalls the slogan that "the more a theory forbids, the more it says"'. A statement like 'wenn der Hahn kraeth auf dem Mist, dann aendert sich das Wetter oder es bleibt wie es ist' ['when the cock crows on the dung, then the weather changes or it remains as it is'] has no or negligible informative content, because the statement is *always* true. The opposite are theories with 'excess content' (over others). When theory A can explain two phenomena but is not capable of explaining a third and theory B can explain all three phenomena, theory B has excess content over theory A (Pawson, 2013: 101). Or, to put it simply: theory B is 'better' than theory A.

Empirical content, also known as 'truth' or 'validity' of a theory is a second criterion. Testing theories can be done through a process consisting of the following steps (Epstein and Martin, 2010: 908; 2014: 32ff):

- deduce observable implications from the theory;
- address and answer the question which research design fits the problem best;
- operationalize, i.e. delineate how the implications can be observed in reality;
- develop (or borrow) measurement instruments to do this work;
- do the measurements and compare the results with the theory;
- look for rival explanations;
- report (and disseminate the findings).

When doing this work, sometimes reference is made to a *null hypothesis*. Such a hypothesis is a general statement or default position that there is no relationship between certain phenomena (while a theory usually argues the opposite, i.e. that there is a relationship between A and B). Rejecting or disproving the null hypothesis – and thus concluding that there are grounds for believing that there is a relationship between these phenomena (for example that a potential behavioral intervention has a measurable effect on a certain outcome variable, like recidivism) – is a central task of scientific research.

Apart from the list's *first step (deduction)*, we will discuss the others in Chapters 7 and 8. *Deducing observable implications* from a theory can take place in a formal way, but also when 'researchers simply think through their theory' (Epstein and Martin, 2014: 34). When the formal route is followed,

BOX 4.2 THEORIES AND THE NULL HYPOTHESIS

A null hypothesis asserts that the samples being compared or contrasted are drawn from the same population with regard to the outcome variable. This means that:

- any observed differences in the dependent variable (outcome) like recidivism must be due to sampling error (=chance) while
- the independent variable (for example a behavioral intervention activity or a legal action) does NOT make a difference.

The symbol 'H0' is the abbreviation for the null hypothesis, the zero stands for null.[1]

The research hypothesis (or hypotheses – there may be more than one) is a working hypothesis – our prediction, or what we expect to happen. Hypotheses can be deduced from theories, though sometimes hypothesis/es are called theories.

[1] http://psychology.ucdavis.edu/faculty_sites/sommerb/sommerdemo/stat_inf/null.htm.

argumentation logic is important. The Hempel-Oppenheim model, also known as the covering law model or the Deductive-Nomological model, is often used. Such an explanation is 'a deductive derivation of the occurrence of the event to be explained from a set of true propositions including at least one statement of a scientific law. The event to be explained is called the *explanandum*; the set of explaining statements is sometimes called the *explanans*' (Strevens, 2006: 2). A well-known example is: 'All human beings are mortal. Socrates is a human being. So, Socrates is mortal'.

The empirical content of a theory comprises the results of studies against which the theory has been tested, how many times that has happened, and how robust the studies used were. However, and in line with critical rationalism, the finding that a theory has been corroborated does not guarantee its 'truth', as it can always be refuted by new empirical tests. Nevertheless, some theories are 'stronger' (i.e. more backed by evidence) than others, which communicates an important message (Lakatos, 1970; see also Chapter 10).

Parsimony (the ability to explain in relatively few terms and statements) is a third criterion, while number four is the *usefulness* (also known as '*usability*') of a theory: does a theory present suggestions that are relevant for practice?[28]

4.8 SOME GUIDANCE

- Theories are important. And not only for rainy Friday afternoons. We have distinguished two types, explanatory and intervention theories. Explanatory theories can often be found in academic papers and books, quite a number of them have names or labels and they have (often) been 'tested' in empirical research. Intervention theories are the (reconstructed sets of) assumptions underlying policy and legal arrangements, like laws, regulations, contracts and treaties. It is the politician, policy maker, judge or legislator that 'signs' them; intervention theories are *their* answers to the question why these interventions and arrangements, 'will' [probably; hopefully] have an impact.
- Sometimes intervention and explanatory theories diverge, sometimes they converge. An important element that links them is their joint focus on (behavioral, institutional and social) *mechanisms*.
- We have also discussed where to find explanatory theories and how to find them. Rules of thumb how to detect and reconstruct intervention theories were presented.

- Finally, try not to get frustrated or confused if you see different concepts being used in different disciplines (when 'theories' are discussed). *It is what they are: conjectures.*

ENDNOTES

1. Underhill Moore, an American Legal Realist, gave an early example in a paper on 'law and learning theory', applying this theory to a legal control phenomenon (Underhill Moore and Callahan, 1943).
2. Merton (1968: 39) coined the concept of middle range theories: 'theories that lie between the minor but necessary working hypotheses that evolve in abundance during day-to-day research and the all-inclusive systematic efforts to develop a unified theory that will explain all the observed uniformities of social behavior, social organization and social change'. Formally defined, a middle range (scientific) theory is a set of systematically interrelated concepts and propositions intended to explain and predict a phenomenon or behavior of interest, within certain boundary conditions (Bhattacherjee, 2012; Bacharach, 1989).
3. See for discussions on what is meant by 'explanation', Bhattacherjee (2012: 25–6) who distinguishes, as was done many times before, between idiographic and nomothetic explanations. Nomothetic explanations 'seek to explain a class of situations or events rather than a specific situation or event. . . . Because theories are . . . intended to serve as generalized explanations for patterns of events, behaviors, or phenomena, theoretical explanations are generally nomothetic in nature'. In this book we restrict ourselves to *this type* of explanation. See Hempel and Oppenheim (1948) and Popper (1935).
4. Tests may lead to refutations ('falsifications') of theories or to verifications.
5. In evaluation studies this tradition is referred to as 'realist evaluation' (Pawson, 2013).
6. See Hempel and Oppenheim (1948) for the covering law model (aka the deductive-nomological type of explanation).
7. There is no need to check for the 'problem relevance' of intervention theories as they are, *eo ipso*, relevant, given that they underlie the intervention, program or legal arrangement to be used (or in use). This does not imply that they are *a priori* valid.
8. Glaser and Strauss (1967) suggested the 'Grounded Theory' approach to develop theoretically comprehensive descriptions and explanations about a particular phenomenon. Strauss and Corbin (1990: 23) state: '[A grounded theory is] one that is inductively derived from the study of the phenomenon it represents . . . One does not begin with a theory, and then prove it. Rather, one begins with an area of study and what is relevant to that area is allowed to emerge'. See Chapter 8 for a discussion on this type of theory.
9. Largely based on Astbury and Leeuw (2010: 367ff). Epistemologically, this way of thinking is related to 'methodological individualism' (Watkins, 1959; Agassi, 1960).
10. Weiss (1997:46) made clear that 'the mechanism of change is not the program service per se, but the response that the activities generate'.
11. See Astbury and Leeuw (2010).
12. A relevant other institutional mechanism pointed at in the literature is a societal belief system (e.g. 'the protestant ethic').
13. See Stuphorn (2005) for neurobiological aspects of the 'shadow of the future' mechanism.
14. See also Ostrom (2010: 6) who distinguished between 'external variables' like attributes of community and rules in use, 'action situations', interactions and outcomes.
15. A 'demi-regularity suggests that human choice or agency manifests itself in a *semi-predictable manner* – "semi", because *variations* in reoccurring, predictable patterns of behavior can be attributed to differences in the contextual dimension from one setting to another' (Jagosh et al, 2011: 7).

16. Rogers (1991: 28) describes the birth of this book (published as the 1962 edition which covered some 300 studies).
17. Ginsburg (2008: 81) presents empirical evidence on constitutional courts: 'Seventy-nine written constitutions [out of 158 constitutional systems] had designated called constitutional courts or councils, whereas before WW II only a handful of constitutions contained provisions for constitutional review'.
18. Hood and Margetts (2007) developed an alternative typology. *Nodality* denotes the property of being 'nodal' to information and social networks and having the capacity to disseminate and collect information. *Authority* denotes the possession of legal or official power to demand, forbid, guarantee or adjudicate. *Treasure* is the possession of money or that which can be freely exchanged. And *organizational capacity* denotes the possession of a stock of people and skills, land, buildings, materials, computers and equipment, somehow arranged.
19. Based on a paper which a group of Honours track Master students of Law produced during Leeuw's course on research methods (2012–13).
20. See Atul Gawande (2007). There is also an interesting video on what happened when a – then – complex plane was steered by a very experienced pilot but without having a protocol/guidelines: see http://fly.historicwings.com/2012/10/from-the-ashes-of-the-model-299/, accessed 25 November 2015.
21. Teaching to the test means to do exactly what is minimally needed, while crowding out is a concept describing that increased public sector spending replaces, or drives down, private sector spending or activities. For example, the higher taxes required for governments to fund social welfare programs leave less discretionary income for individuals and businesses to make charitable donations. Further, when government funds certain activities, there is little incentive for businesses and individuals to spend money on those same things (http://www.investopedia.com/terms/c/crowdingouteffect.asp).
22. There are websites taking you by the hand with regard to the relevance and use of theories (http://www.esourceresearch.org/, accessed 25 November 2015).
23. http://changingminds.org/explanations/theories/theories.htm and http://asgriffith.com/Research_Theories.html, accessed 25 November 2015.
24. Herhily et al (2010: 355–6) describe this process as follows: 'Two firms of solicitors were recruited to the study. Consent for the use of their files was obtained from clients who had received at least one appeal determination . . . By accessing determinations through law firms, a sample of decisions from different immigration judges at different times and in different locations was obtained'. In our opinion this study has serious limitations: 'the analysis was performed by psychologists with no legal training. Thus it may be that some of the legal aspects of the determinations were misunderstood' (p. 366). Another critique is the lack of structure with regard to assumptions and the informative content of the assumptions themselves.
25. Realist evaluators like Pawson (2013) have developed the VICTORE approach to unravel underlying assumptions. It is a conceptual tool helping to answer the question: what makes a program (i.e. law, regulation, other type of intervention) complex? VICTORE stands for searching for (information on) Volitions, Implementation, Contexts, Time, Outcomes, Rivalry and Emergence of interventions.
26. This theory goes back to the work of John Braithwaite and colleagues.
27. There is more to say about this, as a research project can also try to build or create a theory.
28. A theory is useful/ usable when it tells you when relationships between factors can be expected to be observed and when not; when it tells you how or why a relationship occurs; when it has 'surplus meaning' (i.e. when it leads to new ideas that you would not have had without it). For us the 'debunking capacity' of theories (telling you things that are not 'received wisdoms' but in fact challenge them) is an important aspect too, as is the 'knittability' of a theory (whether it can be integrated with other theories, to create excess content; Leeuw and Donaldson, 2015).

5. Research reviews and syntheses

> A proposition of law is nothing more than a sensible object which may arouse a drive and cue a response.
> (Underhill Moore and Callahan, 1943: 3)

5.1 FROM TRADITIONAL LITERATURE STUDIES TO SYSTEMATIC REVIEWS

For a considerable time, scientists have been doing *literature studies* summarizing the existing (empirical) evidence in a field. They wanted to know and understand the results of earlier studies, to test their theories or for other reasons. And rightly so. Progress in science is largely produced through standing on the shoulders of others. However, over the last decades it became clear that the way in which this work was done was often not systematic. Gough, Oliver and Thomas (2011: 5) put it as follows:

> [Literature] reviewers did not necessarily attempt to identify all the relevant research, check that it was reliable or write up their results in an accountable manner. Traditional literature reviews typically present research findings relating to a topic of interest. They summarize what is known on a topic. They tend to provide details on the studies that they consider without explaining the criteria used to identify and include those studies or why certain studies are described and discussed while others are not. Potentially relevant studies may not have been included, because the review author was unaware of them or, being aware of them, decided for reasons unspecified not to include them. If the process of identifying and including studies is not explicit, it is not possible to assess the appropriateness of such decisions or whether they were applied in a consistent and rigorous manner. It is thus also not possible to interpret the meaning of the review findings.[1]

Cochrane was an important *change agent* starting the movement that is now known as the *Cochrane Library/Cochrane Collaboration*.[2] In 1972 he introduced the concept of evidence-based medicine. Cochrane's criticism was that medicine had not organized its knowledge in any systematic, reliable and cumulative way. He encouraged health practitioners to practice evidence-based medicine. A few years later, in 1975, Gene V. Glass of the

Laboratory of Educational Research at the University of Colorado introduced a method that became crucial for the evidence-based movement: *meta-analysis*. He used this term to describe the 'analysis of analyzes' or the statistical analysis of a larger collection of analysis results from individual studies for the purpose of integrating the findings. More or less at the same time, meta-evaluation was introduced, describing the process whereby researchers evaluate the methodological (and procedural) quality of evaluations (and other studies).

In the 1990s the Campbell Collaboration started to do similar work to Cochrane, but now for the social and behavioral sciences. With regard to criminology, the request by the US Congress in 1996 to the Attorney General to provide a 'comprehensive evaluation of the effectiveness' of the Department of Justice grants (annually about US$3 million) to assist state and local law enforcement and communities in preventing crime, also stimulated the development of what came to be known as 'systematic research reviews'. A year later the Sherman report, *Preventing Crime: What Works, What Doesn't, What's Promising* was published. It had a methodological appendix in which criteria for the assessment of the quality of studies were described, currently known as the *Maryland Scientific Methods Scale*. Steadily this approach gained ground in social science research and evaluations.

BOX 5.1 THE MARYLAND SCIENTIFIC METHODS SCALE (MSMS) AS APPLIED IN CRIMINOLOGY

Level 1: Correlation between a prevention program and a measure of crime at one point in time (e.g. areas with CCTV [Closed Circuit TV] have lower crime rates than areas without CCTV)

Level 2: Measures of crime before and after the program implemented, with no comparable control conditions (e.g. crime decreased after CCTV was installed)

Level 3: Measures of crime before and after the program in experimental and control conditions (e.g. crime decreased after CCTV was installed in an experimental area, but there was no decrease in crime in a comparable area)

Level 4: Measures of crime before and after in (multiple) experimental and control units, controlling for the variables that influence crime (e.g. victimization of premises under CCTV surveillance decreased compared to victimization of control premises, after controlling for features of premises that influenced their victimization)

Level 5: Random assignment of program and control conditions to units (e.g. victimization of premises randomly assigned to have CCTV surveillance decreased compared to victimization of control premises)

Gough, Oliver and Thomas (2011) define the 'new'[3] approach to the former 'literature study' as 'a review of research literature using systematic and explicit, accountable methods'. When, after such a review, enough empirical studies remain eligible for further analysis, a statistical meta-analysis can be carried out (Gomm, 2008: 349).

Before going deeper into this world that Hansen and Rieper (2011) called *second-order knowledge production institutes* (see section 5.4 below), we first discuss the relationship between systematic research reviews and theories.

5.2 RELATIONSHIPS BETWEEN THEORIES AND RESEARCH REVIEWS

A first dimension of this relationship is that theories can be found (or stumbled upon) when doing a systematic research review. Suppose that you are involved in a review on dispute resolution and conflict behavior (in civil cases) and are not well trained in theories. The likelihood that, when doing the review, you will encounter several theories – like rational choice theory (giving an answer to the question why some persons invest time and money into a legal fight and others do not or refrain halfway) or Galantar's repeat player versus single shotter-theory – is high. Then one learns about 'theories' by doing the review.

Another link between theory and reviews has to do with the process of opening up the black box of assumptions about mechanisms that underlie the legal arrangement, device or policy under investigation. Often it is not a priori clear which mechanisms (are assumed to) play a role; they have to be articulated. In that situation a step-based, incremental and iterative process of finding and searching, including trial and error, of mechanisms takes place. Theories stimulate and help this process. On the one hand they produce insights about factors and variables relevant to take into account in a systematic search (as *key words*), while on the other hand factors that are already part of the search process can be enriched by linking them to theories with which the researcher might not have been familiar with. Sega et al (2012) show how this works in a paper with the fairly provocative title 'Theory! The Missing Link in Understanding the Performance of . . . '.

A third relationship between theory and review is when theories help explain the results.

5.3 THREE EXAMPLES: THE SCARED STRAIGHT AWARENESS INTERVENTION, MICROCREDIT AND ANNOUNCED/UNANNOUNCED INSPECTIONS

The first of these examples was published in the *Campbell Collaboration Series*, the second in the series of the *International Initiative for Impact Evaluation 3ie*[4] *and The Campbell Collaboration Series*, and the third in the academic journal *Health Policy*.

5.3.1 The Scared Straight Awareness Intervention

This study focuses on what is known about the impact on crime, respectively reoffending behavior of the *USA Scared Straight program* and a few other *Juvenile Awareness programs. Scared Straight* has often been evaluated. Petrosino et al (2003; 2013) summarized, analyzed and synthesized the results of dozens of these studies. The research question was what the 'effects are of programs comprising organized visits to prisons by juvenile delinquents (officially adjudicated or convicted by a juvenile court) or pre-delinquents (children in trouble but not officially adjudicated as delinquents), aimed at deterring them from criminal activity':

> The analyses show the intervention to be more harmful than doing nothing. . . . Given these results, we cannot recommend this program as a crime prevention strategy. Agencies that permit such programs, however, must rigorously evaluate them not only to ensure that they are doing what they purport to do (prevent crime) – but at the very least they do not cause more harm than good to the very citizens they pledge to protect' (Petrosino et al, 2012: 7)

In Box 5.2, more information on how this research review was done is summarized.

5.3.2 Microcredit/Microfinancing

The second example studied the impact of *microcredit/microfinancing* in the developing world. Over the past two decades, microcredit and microfinance activities have spread across the globe, reaching tens of millions of poor households with tailored financial services. Microfinance can best be described as a field of intervention rather than a particular instrument. Initially, microfinance usually meant microcredit for working capital and very small investments, but increasingly it has been broadened to include

BOX 5.2 A SYSTEMATIC REVIEW OF EVALUATIONS OF THE SCARED STRAIGHT AWARENESS INTERVENTION

The objectives of this review were 'to assess the effects of programs comprising organized visits to prisons of juvenile delinquents (officially adjudicated or convicted by a juvenile court) or pre-delinquents (children in trouble but not officially adjudicated as delinquents), aimed at deterring them from criminal activity'.

The criteria used to include or exclude studies in the review were strict: experimental and quasi-experimental studies were allowed, provided that they had a no-treatment control group (see Chapter 6 for information on research designs). Only studies involving juveniles, 17 years of age or younger or overlapping samples of juveniles and young adults (13–21 ages) were included. The types of interventions were also strict: only interventions that featured a visit by the program participants to a prison facility as its main component were included. The studies selected for review had to include at least one outcome of subsequent offending behavior, as measured by such indices as arrests, convictions, contacts with police, or self-reported offences.

Attention was also paid to the *intervention theory* underlying these programs. 'The underlying theory of programs like "Scared Straight" is deterrence. Program advocates and others believe that realistic depictions of life in prison and presentations by inmates will deter juvenile offenders (or children at risk for becoming delinquent) from further involvement with crime'.

The search strategy to identify the studies to be taken into account was the following. Several keywords like 'scared straight', 'prison awareness', 'prison aversion' or 'juvenile awareness' were used during the search actions. 'In order to minimize potential for publication bias (the possibility that journals are more likely to publish findings that reject the null hypothesis and find programs to be more effective than unpublished literature generally does), we conducted a search strategy designed to identify published and unpublished studies. We also conducted a comprehensive search strategy to minimize potential for discipline bias, for example evaluations reported in criminological journals or indexed in field-specific abstracting data bases might differ from those reported in psychological, sociological, social service, public health or educational sources.

First, randomized experiments were identified from a larger review of field trials in crime reduction conducted by the first author in the 1990s: more than 300 randomized experiments were collected. More recent studies were searched by using these and similar methods:

(1) broad searches of the Campbell Collaboration Social, Psychological, Educational & Criminological Trials Register (C2-SPECTR) and 14 other electronic databases like Criminal Justice Abstracts, Current Contents, Education Resource Information Clearinghouse and several social sciences databases;
(2) checks of citations from more recent systematic or traditional reviews to provide coverage of more recent studies and checking citation of documents relevant to 'Scared Straight' and similar programs;
(3) email contacts with researchers.

The *analysis of the studies* was done both in a quantitative and a qualitative ('narrative') way.

savings/deposits, (a limited range of) micro-insurance and payment services (including microleasing) as well as a somewhat broader range of credit products.

Vaessen et al (2014) carried out a systematic review of evaluations of the impact of microcredit/microfinancing on the empowerment of women over household spending:

> In line with three recent other reviews on microfinance (Stewart et al., 2010; Duvendack et al., 2011; Stewart et al. 2012) we found that the microcredit evidence base is extensive, yet most studies are weak methodologically. From those studies deemed comparable and of minimum acceptable quality, we concluded that overall there is no evidence for an effect of microcredit on women's control over household spending. Women's control over household resources constitutes an important intermediary dimension in processes of women's empowerment. Given the overall lack of evidence for an effect of microcredit on women's control over household resources it is therefore very unlikely that, overall, microcredit has a meaningful and substantial impact on empowerment processes in a broader sense. While impacts on empowerment may appear to have occurred in particular studies, the high risk of bias of studies providing positive assessments suggests that such findings are of limited validity. Our conclusions on the effects of microcredit on empowerment are also in line with previous systematic reviews by Duvendack et al. (2011) and Stewart et al. (2010) who report to a limited extent on empowerment effects. *Consequently, there appears to be a gap between the often optimistic societal belief in the capacity of microcredit to ameliorate the position of women in decision-making processes within the household on the one hand, and the empirical evidence base on the other hand.*

Box 5.3 presents more information.

5.3.3 Unannounced and Announced Inspections in Nursing Homes

Of a different 'weight' is the third example: what is known about the impact of *unannounced inspections* by the Inspectorate for Health (of the Netherlands government) in nursing homes? The background of this review is given by De Klerks et al (2013: 311):

> Politicians and regulators have high expectations of unannounced inspections. Unannounced inspections, unlike announced ones, would, they believe, lead to a clearer insight into the risks and a reduction of the regulatory burden. In order to verify these assumptions, a systematic review of the scientific literature and an exploratory study were conducted.

See Box 5.4. Although the third study did not report on a quantitative analysis, known as *meta-analysis*, because the number of studies was too small, the two others did. In a meta-analysis, data from individual studies

BOX 5.3 A SYSTEMATIC REVIEW OF EVALUATIONS OF THE IMPACT OF MICROCREDIT / MICROFINANCING ON WOMEN'S EMPOWERMENT (OVER HOUSEHOLD SPENDING)

The *objectives of this review* were 'to provide a systematic review of the evidence on the effects of microcredit on women's control over household spending in developing countries. More specifically, we aim to answer two related research questions: 1) what does the evaluative evidence say about the causal relationship between microcredit and specific dimensions of women's empowerment and 2) what are the mechanisms which mediate this relationship?'

Inclusion criteria: We only included studies that analyze the effects of microcredit schemes targeting poor women in low and middle income countries, as defined by the World Bank. Studies that did not include analysis on microcredit and the effect on one or more dimensions of women's control over household

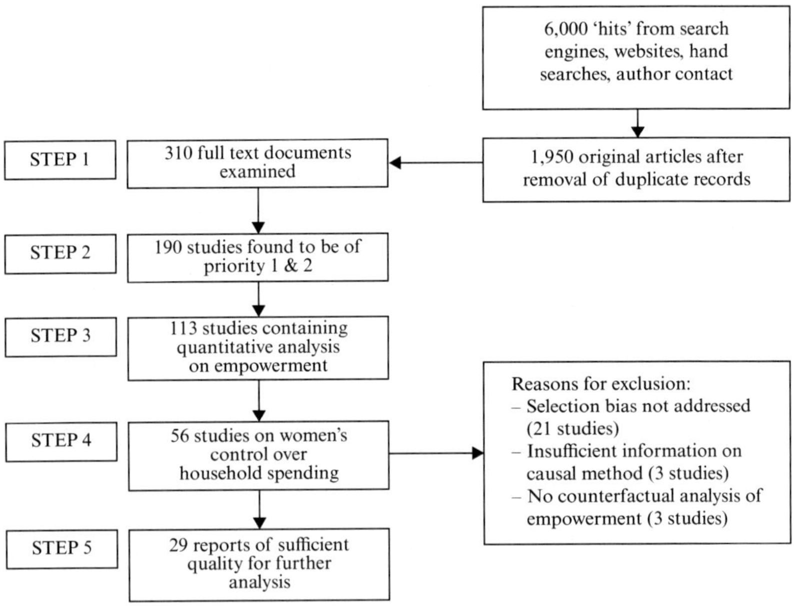

Note 1: For a description of steps see Figure 3.
Note 2: Duplicates were identified with the programme EndNote as well as manually through title screening. Annex 3 Table A3.1 provides the reasons for each study's exclusion at step 4.
Note 3: The 29 reports identified in Step 5 corresponded to 25 unique studies (see Section 3.3.1).

Figure 4 Search results

expenditures were excluded. Finally, remaining studies were screened for methodological design. Studies which gave evidence of addressing the attribution problem either through randomized design, quasi-experimental matching, or regression analysis, were included.

We included studies estimating the impact of micro-credit interventions on women's empowerment using the following measures relating to women's control over household spending: women's decision-making power, bargaining power, control over expenditures with respect to small purchases, large purchases, or expenditures regarding any type of consumption good, productive investment or acquiring of assets (e.g. clothing, education, health, food, house repairs, small livestock, large livestock, land).

Attention was also paid to the *intervention theory* underlying microcredit finance. This theory was reconstructed; the – earlier discussed – three types of mechanisms (institutional, action-formation and transformative, see Chapter 4) were part of this reconstruction.

The search strategy for identification of studies was done in English and several other languages, including Spanish. Some 15 keywords/search terms were used. Fifteen (web-based) search engines were searched including Web of Knowledge, Econpapers, IBSS (EBSCO), JSTOR, PsycINFO, SocINDEX and OECD. Also, six portals on MC, and websites of research organizations active in development aid/microcredit(s) were searched, while manually some 15 journals, some of which were not covered by the electronic databases mentioned earlier, were investigated.

Schematically, this operation looked as follows.

The *analysis of the studies* was done in a quantitative way (calculating effect sizes) and in a qualitative way (analyzing the mechanisms assumed to be at work when MC is used).

Note: Figure 4 was reproduced with kind permission of Vaessen et al, 'The Effect of Microcredit on Women's Control over Household Spending in Developing Countries: A Systematic Review' (Oslo: The Campbell Collaboration, 2014, p. 38 for further information on the notes).

are pooled quantitatively and re-analyzed using statistical methods. Just as individual studies summarize data collected from many participants in order to answer a specific research question (i.e. each participant is a separate data-point in the analysis), a meta-analysis summarizes data from individual studies that concern a specific research question (i.e. each study is a separate data-point in the analysis). An important aspect of this work is to be sure about the methodological quality of the studies included in the meta-analysis. As we will show in Chapter 6, the strength of the design, its internal validity and its relationship to the problem under investigation are *mucho importanto* when deciding which studies to include (and exclude). The work involved in checking the quality and applicability of the studies is called meta-evaluation. Apart from these

BOX 5.4 A SYSTEMATIC REVIEW OF EVALUATIONS OF ANNOUNCED AND UNANNOUNCED INSPECTIONS

The *objectives of this review* were 'to examine whether research exists on the difference between unannounced and announced inspections. The approach focused on quantitative and qualitative research on the difference between the two types of inspections'.

Inclusion criteria and search strategy: 'The data was collected until October 2011. We introduced the following three criteria for inclusion: (1) The article describes quantitative and/or qualitative research in which unannounced inspections were compared with announced inspections; (2) The article is published after the 1st of January 1995; (3) The article is written in English, German or Dutch.' The search strategy consisted of three parts. First, given that inspections take place in many different areas, the authors searched two medical databases (MEDLINE and CINAHL), a psychological database (PsycINFO), a sociological database (SocINDEX), an economic database (EconLit) and a database for educational research (ERIC). The second part consisted of a free search on Google Scholar according to the terms Unannounced, Announced, Inspection and Research, and published after 1 January 1995. Finally, the authors called for research on the difference between unannounced and announced inspections through a discussion group of Dutch regulators on Linked-In.

Table 1 Specification of the articles

Specification	Food safety	Primary education	Child care programs
Title	Beneficial effects of implementing an announced restaurant inspection program	Unannounced inspections in primary education, an inspection report	Unannounced vs. Announced Licensing Inspections in Monitoring Child Care Programs
Author(s)	Reske K, Jenkins T, Fernandez C, VanAmber D, Hedberg C	Dutch inspectorate of Education	Fiene R
Journal	Journal Of Environmental Health	–	National Association of Regulatory Administration
Year	2007	2007	1996
Country	US, Minnesota	The Netherlands	US, Pennsylvania
Peer reviewed	Yes	No	No
MSMS-level[a]	MSMS-2/3	MSMS-1/2	MSMS-2

a The Maryland Scientific Methods Scale (MSMS) for internal validity.

No attention was paid to the *intervention theory* underlying announced or unannounced inspections.

Findings: 'Only three relevant articles were found concerned with research into the difference between unannounced and announced inspections' (de Klerks et al, 2013: 311). 'Despite the strong political calls for unannounced inspections and the choice that several inspectorates make to inspect unannounced, very little research has been carried out into the difference between unannounced and announced inspections' (ibid., 313). See table 1 above.'

'None of the three studies were conducted in nursing homes. Knowledge is lacking on the difference, advantages and disadvantages, between announced and unannounced inspections' (de Klerks et al., 2013: 313). Therefore, the author's decided to launch a (new) empirical investigation focused on nursing home inspections.

BOX 5.5 GUIDELINES FOR SYSTEMATIC REVIEWS AND META-ANALYSIS

We refer to guidelines and other documents for more technical information about doing systematic reviews and meta-analysis: Field and Gillets (2010) [how to do a meta-analysis], http://www.campbellcollaboration.org/systematic_reviews/index.php, accessed 19 July 2015, and the 'gentle introduction' to systematic reviews and meta-analysis by Impellizzeri and Bizzini (2012).

selection activities, a meta-analysis consists of several other steps, one of them calculating the treatment effect with 95% confidence intervals (CI) for each individual study. A summary of statistics that is often used to measure treatment effects is the odds ratio (OR). This ratio is a measure of association between an exposure and an outcome. The OR represents the odds that an outcome will occur given a particular exposure, compared to the odds of the outcome occurring in the absence of that exposure.

What these three examples show is that systematic reviews use transparent procedures to find, evaluate and synthesize the results of relevant research. Procedures are explicitly defined in advance, in order to ensure that the exercise can be replicated. This practice is also designed to minimize publication bias. Studies included in a review are screened for quality, so that the findings of a large number of studies can be combined. Peer review is a key part of the process; qualified independent researchers control the author's methods and results.

The Evidence Library of the International Initiative for Impact Evaluation (3ie)[5] provides future producers of systematic reviews with guidelines, as do other organizations.[6]

5.4 OTHER APPROACHES

Despite the important role systematic reviews play, over the last 10 to 15 years other approaches have been developed. We discuss the most important ones.

5.4.1 The Rapid Review

Doing systematic research reviews often is a timely affair. Ganann et al (2010: 1) argue that 'policy makers and others often require synthesis of knowledge in an area within six months or less. Traditional systematic reviews typically take at least 12 months to conduct'. One of the more recent developments is the *rapid review*, which 'streamline traditional systematic review methods in order to synthesize evidence within a shortened timeframe' (ibid., p. 1). The 'rapid evidence assessment' (REA) – for example:

> is a tool in the systematic review methods family and is based on comprehensive electronic searches of appropriate databases, internet sources and follow-up of cited references. To complete REAs in a short timeframe, researchers make some concessions in comparison with a full systematic review. Exhaustive hand searching of journals and textbooks is not undertaken, and searching of 'grey' literature is necessarily curtailed. (Booth et al, 2012: 3)

Booth et al (2012) structured different approaches in terms of rigor, bias and results, while Khangura et al (2010) compared the systematic review and the rapid review (see Box 5.6).

5.4.2 The Realist Review and Synthesis Approach

Since the 1990s, *realist reviews and syntheses* are on the agenda. Realism is not a research method but an epistemological orientation; that is, a particular approach to developing and selecting research methods. It has its roots in philosophy (Bhaskar, 1978; Harré, 1979) and is intellectually linked to Popper's critical rationalism. The central theme of this approach is that (policy, including legal) interventions work by offering resources designed to influence their subject's reasoning and behavior (or take away resources). Whether that reasoning and action actually change also depends on the subject's characteristics and their circumstances:

> So, for example, in order to evaluate whether a training program reduces unemployment (O), a realist scholar would examine its underlying mechanisms M (e.g. have skills and motivation changed?) and its contexts C (e.g. are there local skill shortages and employment opportunities?). Realist research is thus all about hypothesizing and testing such *CMO configurations*. Putting this into

BOX 5.6 GENERAL COMPARISON OF RAPID REVIEWS VERSUS SYSTEMATIC REVIEWS APPROACHES

Table 1 General comparison of rapid review versus systematic review approaches[a]

	Rapid review	Systematic review
Timeframe[b]	≤ 5 weeks	6 months to 2 years
Question	Question specified *a priori* (may include broad PICOS)	Often a focused clinical question (focused PICOS)
Sources and searches	Sources may be limited but sources/ strategies made explicit	Comprehensive sources searched and explicit strategies
Selection	Criterion-based; uniformly applied	Criterion-based
Appraisal	Rigorous; critical appraisal (SRs only)	Rigorous; critical appraisal
Synthesis	Descriptive summary/categorization of the data	Qualitative summary +/− meta-analysis
Inferences	Limited/cautious interpretation of the findings	Evidence-based

[a] Specific to the KTA (Knowledge to Action) program – other groups have experimented with other approaches of rapid review and will therefore have other differences;

[b] Primary difference; other potentially important differences are noted in the cells. PICOS = population, interventions, comparators, outcomes and study designs; SR = systematic review.

> ordinary parlance we see, under realism, a change in emphasis in the basic question from 'what works?' to 'what is it about this intervention that works for whom in what circumstances?' (Pawson et al, 2004: 2)

The (Campbell Collaboration's):

> systematic reviews follow a highly specified and intentionally inflexible methodology, with the aim of assuring high reliability. A realist review, in contrast, follows a more heterogeneous and iterative process, which is less amenable to prescription. But that process should be equally rigorous, and it should be possible to 'look behind' the review and see how decisions were made, evidence sought, sifted and assessed, and findings accumulated and synthesized. (Pawson et al, 2004: 5–6)

Another distinct characteristic is that within realist studies the intervention theory is crucial, which is less so in the work of the Campbell Collaboration.

Four essential characteristics of the realist synthesis approach are highlighted by Pawson et al (2004: v, vi).

Pawson and others presented suggestions to help this process work and to increase its transparency, as there is a need for guidance and (evolving) standards. In 2010 the *RAMESES (Realist and Meta-narrative Evidence Syntheses: Evolving Standards)* project started which is in the process of producing methodological guidance, publication standards and training resources for those seeking to use the realist approach (Greenhalgh et al, 2011).

A flowchart of methodological steps and major review duties is presented by Molnaret et al (2015: 7) in a realist synthesis of the impact of unemployment insurance policies on poverty and health.

Realist synthesis is not primarily focused on producing statistical results but explanations and understanding (Pawson and Tilley, 1997; Pawson, 2006; 2013). By unraveling the CMO-configurations of policy programs, laws, regulations and other arrangements, the authors try to explain what makes them 'work'. Examples of realist syntheses are Pawson's work on grants and subsidies (Pawson, 2002a), his work on naming, shaming and blaming (Pawson, 2002b), Klein Haarhuis and Niemeijer's (2009) study on the impact of Dutch laws and Greenhalgh, Kristjansson and Robinson's (2007) school feeding programs study. Many other examples have been published over the last 10 to 15 years.

BOX 5.7 STAGES IN THE REALIST SYNTHESIS APPROACH

- The initial stage in which the scope of the review is defined involves a negotiation (with the commissioners or decision makers) intended to 'unpick' their reasons for needing the review and understand how it will be used. It also involves a careful dissection of the theoretical underpinnings of the intervention, using the literature in the first instance not to examine the empirical evidence but to map out in broad terms the conceptual and theoretical territory.
- The subsequent search for and appraisal of evidence is then undertaken to 'populate' this theoretical framework with empirical findings, using the theoretical framework as the construct for locating, integrating, comparing and contrasting empirical evidence. The search for evidence is a purposive one, and its progress is shaped by what is found. When theoretical saturation in one area is reached, and no significant new findings are emerging, searching can stop.
- The process is, within each stage and between stages, iterative. There is a constant to-ing and fro-ing as new evidence both changes the direction and focus of searching and opens up new areas of theory.
- The results of the review and synthesis combine both theoretical thinking and empirical evidence, and are focused on explaining how the intervention being studied works in ways that enable decision makers to use this understanding and apply it to their own particular contexts. The commissioners or decision makers are closely involved in shaping the conclusions and recommendations to be drawn from the review.

5.4.3 Combining the Campbell Collaboration Approach and the Realist Approach

Another development is to combine systematic research reviews and realist synthesis,[7] as each has something to offer to the other. To open up the black box of an intervention or arrangement is helpful for evaluators working according in line with the Campbell Collaboration's focus on experiments and quasi-experiments, as it enables them to better know *why* interventions do or do not work. As one of the problems for realist evaluators is to get relevant knowledge on board that is methodologically adequate, the realist approach could, vice versa, benefit from the (stricter) methodology suggested by the Campbell Collaboration.

An example of a combined approach was adopted in a review at the request of the Netherlands Ministry of Justice (Van der Knaap et al, 2008). The first goal was to provide the Ministry with an international overview of effective, or at least promising, measures to prevent violence in public and semi-public areas. And the second goal was to gain insights into the behavioral and social mechanisms that underlie effective or promising prevention measures and the circumstances in which these are found to be effective. The authors started with 454 titles of studies that seemed to be relevant. Titles and abstracts were checked to determine whether or not the study was an evaluation, whether it dealt with prevention of violence, and whether the study focused on violence in the (semi-) public domain. Of the 454 studies, 233 were selected for a second round of analysis. Sixty-four of these studies could not be retrieved or were not received in time to be included in our study. In total, 169 publications were included in the second round of literature selection. Criteria used to make the final selection were whether or not the dependent variable concerned violent behavior, whether there was information available about the contexts of the intervention and whether the evaluation focused on the behavioral effects of the intervention. A total of 48 studies into the effects of the prevention of violence in the public and semi-public domains were selected and included. In these studies 36 violence reduction programs were evaluated. The programs were categorized as effective, potentially effective, potentially not effective, and not effective, based on the findings of the studies and the methodological robustness of them. As will be clear, this approach so far was similar to what Campbell Collaboration standards suggest. The next step, however, was to address the question *what were the (behavioral) mechanisms, contexts and outcomes of the studies that were classified as 'living up to the Campbell Collaboration standards'*. The merging of Campbell standards and the realist approach took place *after* finishing the Campbell-style systematic review. This implied that only then attention was paid to the underlying mechanisms and contexts (described in studies of robust methodological quality).

The main conclusion of the *merging* of the two approaches was that there appeared to be (only) 'three overarching mechanisms to be at work when effective anti-violence programs have been implemented. The first is of a cognitive nature, focusing on learning, teaching and training. The second concerns the way that the social environment is rewarding or punishing behavior (through bonding, community development and the targeting of police activities). And the third is risk reduction'.

5.4.4 The Browsing for Evidence – Approach

This approach reviews and synthesizes a batch of studies on a specific topic within a specific period of time. Kleemans et al (2007) describe this approach. They reviewed and synthesized 31 evaluation studies, covering one policy field (law enforcement) in one period (January 2002 to May 2004) in one country (the Netherlands). The 31 studies related to a broad spectrum of policy interventions, they used different methods and designs, and their results ranged from information about mechanisms and implementation issues to evidence about output. The central goal was *how to produce a reliable and useful synthesis of research results for policy makers, given the diversity and abundance of evaluation studies*.

The authors first mapped the different law enforcement interventions used in the Netherlands over that period. The cross-section diverged widely from the typical interventions evaluated under the auspices of the Campbell Collaboration. The authors showed that most interventions were not directly aimed at individuals or clients, who may be treated in different ways, but at institutional actors, organizations or the law enforcement chain. Second, the authors took a closer look at the studies evaluating these interventions and strategies. They screened all studies and appraised their methodological quality in line with four criteria. The first was *internal validity* of the evaluations: does a study unambiguously demonstrate that an intervention produced a certain outcome? This criterion implies that the research design should exclude confounding factors as much as possible. For the evaluation of internal validity, they employed the Maryland Scientific Methods Scale (MSMS) (see above). According to the MSMS, all 31 evaluations were level 1 or level 2 studies, meaning that internal validity was limited.

The second criterion was the *descriptive validity* of the studies: the overall adequacy of reporting information. Two main elements were discerned: how well the research design was described and accounted for (including the selection of methods); and whether multiple information sources had been used to measure the dependent and independent variables. The descriptive validity of the studies turned out to be generally adequate. Designs, sample sizes and measurements of variables are relatively well described and accounted for. Most of the studies used data from multiple information sources.

The third criterion assessed whether the evaluations determined *the degree to which an intervention has in fact been implemented.* Research has shown that program integrity, i.e. the implementation of a program or intervention in accordance with the plan, is often inadequate[8] (Nas, van Ooyen-Houben and Wieman, 2011). It was found that all evaluations provide evidence on the extent to which the (policy) interventions have been implemented. They provided insight into the 'program integrity' and thus met one important, though basic, precondition for a relationship between policy interventions and outcomes.

The fourth and final criterion assessed whether or not evaluators did pay *attention to the assumptions underlying law enforcement policy interventions (intervention theories)* and whether or not they were confronted with reality. It was found that more than a third of the 31 evaluations provided a clear description of intervention theories.

5.4.5 The (Systematic) 'Review of (systematic) Reviews (aka Meta-reviews)'

Another relevant approach is the (systematic) review of (systematic) reviews, sometimes called meta-reviews. In a meta-review, only reviews and meta-analyses are included and the results of those studies are summarized. One of the reasons to do a systematic review of reviews is to make sure that in the reviews under review, most, if not all, of the relevant and available primary studies are covered. Reviews of reviews are also likely to be helpful when a review question is very broad, when several reviews have already been published and when there is a debate about the differences in findings and conclusions from these reviews (covering the same topic). However, the different inclusion criteria adopted by the various reviews can also make synthesis and interpretations problematic (Centre for Reviews and Dissemination (CRD), 2008). Nagtegaal's (2012) meta-review of systematic reviews looking into self-reported problems following child sexual abuse is an example of a meta-review.

5.4.6 Syntheses of Qualitative Studies[9]

Snilstveit et al (2012: 414ff) are of the opinion that 'unlike quantitative synthesis that converts information into a common metric and synthesizes these data to test a theory using statistical meta-analysis, qualitative synthesis aims to synthesize qualitative data, which is commonly text-based. Such reviews adopt a narrative, as opposed to statistical, approach and seek to generate new insights and recommendations by going beyond the summary of findings from different studies as in traditional narrative reviews'. Snilstveit et al discuss weaknesses in this approach (like the lack of transparency and the lack of clarity on methods and formal guidance on how to conduct these syntheses), but they also offer guidance on different approaches to qualitative synthesis. As will be discussed later in Chapter 8, software has become available which allows qualitative researchers to do content analysis in a more transparent (and 'quantitative' way).

Greenhalgh et al (2005) developed the meta-narrative review. A meta-narrative is the unfolding 'storyline' of research in a particular scientific tradition, defined as a coherent body of theoretical knowledge and a linked set of primary studies in which successive studies are influenced by the findings of previous studies. The authors distinguish several phases when doing a meta-narrative. They applied this approach to the question of what the determinants are of the diffusion of innovations in health service organizations (Greenhalgh et al, 2004).

Noblit and Hare (1988) discuss a 'meta-ethnography approach'. Three types of analyses are characteristic for such a study. One involves the 'translation' of concepts from individual studies into one another, thereby evolving overarching concepts or metaphors. Noblit and Hare called this process *reciprocal translational analysis (RTA)*. *Refutational synthesis* involves exploring and explaining contradictions between individual studies. And *Lines-of-argument (LOA) synthesis* involves building up a picture of the whole (i.e. culture, organization) from studies of its parts'.[10]

5.5 SOME GUIDANCE

- Use *second-order knowledge production institutes* that publish reviews and synthesis; sometimes they are called *clearing houses*. An example is the Evidence for Policy and Practice Information and Coordinating Centre (EPPI Centre).[11] An example focusing on crime and justice is CrimeSolutions.gov of the US Office of Justice Programs and the US National Institute of Justice (NIJ). Its portal uses research to inform practitioners and policy makers about what works in criminal justice, juvenile justice and crime victim services. A third example is the What Works Clearinghouse of the Institute of Education and Sciences in the USA,[12] while in the UK the Evidence Network provides impact assessments for innovation.[13] It is organized by the University of York together with the UK National Institute for Health Research.[14] Other examples are the Impact Evaluation Repository (an index of impact evaluations of development interventions) of 3ie, the Coalition for evidence-based policy and the Best Evidence Encyclopedia (empowering educators with evidence on proven programs).[15]

- The Cochrane Collaboration, the Campbell Collaboration and several other organizations have handbooks for systematic reviews of interventions (and evaluations), protocols and other 'help desk'-type documents. EPPI has made *software* available 'for all types of literature review', including systematic reviews, meta-analyses, 'narrative' reviews and meta-ethnographies.
- *EPPI-Reviewer 4* was launched in autumn 2010. It has been used by hundreds of reviewers across hundreds of projects covering a large range of diverse topics and review sizes, some containing over 1 million items.[16]
- *A word of caution*. Sometimes it can be heard that this painstakingly precise review work is not necessary, because a high speed visit to Google Scholar also works and leads to basically the same results. Boeker et al (2013: 1) showed that Google Scholar, used alone, cannot replace the other search engines:

  > Currently, Google Scholar does not provide necessary elements for systematic scientific literature retrieval such as tools for incremental query optimization, export of a large number of references, a visual search builder or a history function. Google Scholar is not ready as a professional searching tool for tasks where structured retrieval methodology is necessary.

- The likelihood that your research problem will be completely answered by using results from research reviews and syntheses is small. One reason is that reviews publish contradictory results, or have not taken into account differences between (legal) contexts which may lead to comparing apples, oranges and motorbikes. There may also be a simple lack of robust studies.

Then, *new empirical research is needed. So, get ready to think and decide about the research design.*

ENDNOTES

1. See Logan (1972) for criminology and MacDonald et al (1992) for social work.
2. For more information on the recent history, see Leeuw (2009b).

3. It should be stressed that for legal researchers this may be new, for medical and health researchers it is not and the same is true for research in the social, behavioral and economic sciences. One indicator of the importance of this 'new approach' is that for health, there has been a specialized journal, *Systematic Reviews*, which discusses design, conduct and reporting of systematic reviews.
4. 3ie, the International Initiative for Impact Evaluation, funds impact evaluations and systematic reviews that generate evidence on what works in development programs and why (http://www.3ieimpact.org/, accessed 25 November 2015). The Campbell Collaboration is an international research network that produces systematic reviews of the effects of social interventions. It is based on voluntary cooperation among researchers of a variety of backgrounds (see http://www.campbellcollaboration.org/artman2/uploads/1/Petrosino_2013_EC_Reflections_Genesis_of_the_Campbell_Collaboration.pdf, accessed 25 November 2015).
5. http://www.3ieimpact.org/media/filer/2012/05/07/quality_appraisal_checklist_srdatabase.pdf, accessed 25 November 2015.
6. An example is: http://www.prisma-statement.org/, accessed 25 November 2015. PRISMA stands for Preferred Reporting Items for Systematic Reviews and Meta-Analyses. The aim of the PRISMA Statement is to help authors improve the reporting of systematic reviews and meta-analyses. The focus is on randomized trials, but PRISMA can also be used as a basis for reporting systematic reviews of evaluations of interventions. The PRISMA Statement consists of a 27-item checklist and a four-phase flow diagram.
7. See also Caracelli and Cooksy (2013) who incorporate qualitative evidence in systematic reviews.
8. See the journal *Implementation Science* (http://www.implementationscience.com/, accessed 25 November 2015).
9. Barnett-Page and Thomas (2009: 4–5) published an ESRC National Centre for Research Methods Working Paper (Series Number 01/09). It was their aim to 'identify every distinct approach to the synthesis of qualitative research. Papers which used or discussed methods of qualitative synthesis were identified . . . Relevant papers were also retrieved using the "pearl-growing" technique, i.e. further references were identified using the bibliographies of relevant papers the authors were already aware of, the bibliographies of which were – in turn – checked, until saturation point was reached. In addition, the contents pages of the following journals were hand-searched: Qualitative Health Research, International Journal of Social Research Methodology, Qualitative Research, International Journal of Qualitative Methods, The Qualitative Report, Forum: Qualitative Social Research, Evidence and Policy and BMC Medical Research Methodology . . . Two-hundred and three papers were found. Amongst the many syntheses of qualitative research, nine distinct methods of synthesis were identified'.
10. See also: http://eppi.ioe.ac.uk/cms/Default.aspx?tabid=188, accessed 25 November 2015. Repositories like the Cochrane Library or the Campbell Collaboration of specialized, qualitative meta-studies do not, as we know, exist yet.
11. http://eppi.ioe.ac.uk/cms, accessed 25 November 2015.
12. http://ies.ed.gov/ncee/wwc/, accessed 25 November 2015.
13. http://www.theevidencenetwork.com/, accessed 25 November 2015.
14. http://www.crd.york.ac.uk/prospero/, accessed 25 November 2015.
15. http://www.3ieimpact.org/en/evidence/impact-evaluations/impact-evaluation-repository/; http://coalition4evidence.org/and http://www.bestevidence.org, accessed 25 November 2015.
16. http://eppi.ioe.ac.uk/cms/Default.aspx?alias=eppi.ioe.ac.uk/cms/er4, accessed 25 November 2015.

6. Research designs: raisons d'être, examples and criteria

6.1 WHAT ARE RESEARCH DESIGNS?

De Vaus (2001: 8) clarifies this concept by using the following analogy:

> When constructing a building there is no point ordering materials for completion of project stages until we know what *sort of building* is being constructed. The first decision is whether we need a high-rise office building, a factory for manufacturing machinery, a school, a residential home or an apartment block. Until this is done we cannot sketch a plan, obtain permits, work out a work schedule or order materials. *Similarly, research needs a design or a structure before data collection or analysis can commence. . . .* The function of a research design is to ensure that the evidence obtained enables us to answer the initial question as unambiguously as possible. Obtaining relevant evidence entails specifying the type of evidence needed to answer the research question, to test a theory, to evaluate a program or to accurately describe some phenomenon. In other words, when designing research we need to ask: *given this research question. . . . what type of evidence is needed to answer the question in a convincing way?*

What does this analogy mean when empirical legal research is involved? An example may help. Suppose you are asked to investigate *what the impact is of a new law on preventing and reducing domestic violence in country X?* The law was implemented in 2015 for the northern part of the country and in 2016 for the rest of the country. The law focuses on intensifying law enforcement activities and reducing domestic violence.

Researching the impact of this law first makes it necessary to study the prevalence and incidence of domestic violence (over a number of years).[1] It may turn out that *after* the law was implemented, there was a *change* in numbers (let's assume a lower prevalence and incidence). Can this change be attributed to the implementation of the law? No, because there may be other, '*rival*' *factors* that are the *engines* behind the change and explain the drop in numbers. For rival factors, think of public information campaigns on domestic violence that were implemented in the same period and that (could) have had an impact on behavior. Or think about newly established civic society organizations to alert society and offenders to the domestic violence problem. That also can have contributed to the drop in numbers. To assess the impact of the *new law* (in a valid and reliable way), it is necessary to work with a *research design* capable of addressing the (causal) *attribution issue*: *can the drop in numbers of domestic violence in country X (or a part thereof) be attributed to the new law*? Which designs will (*not*) be applicable?

A *simple post-test (only) design* – in which a representative sample of inhabitants of the country one or two years after the implementation of the law is asked whether the new law has made them change their behavior – will *not* do. Such a design (sometimes incorrectly labelled as 'experimental') does not address the attribution problem.[2] Neither will a *(one group) pre-test/post-test design* produce valid information on the impact of the new law, because it (and also the simple post-test-only design) does not allow for comparing what people *would have done* had there been *no new law on domestic violence*. In methodological terms: information on the *counterfactual* is missing, because a *control group (or condition)*[3] is missing. Another problem (which relates to data collection) is that what people say is not always equal to what they do (or did).

Now it must be acknowledged that finding the counterfactual when an impact evaluation of a law is at stake is difficult, if not impossible: laws are often implemented for everybody in society at the same time. Only when a law and/or its implementation is spread over time and/or over regions, it is possible to work with a design that addresses – to some extent – the counterfactual problem: see section 6.3 below.[4] In the (hypothetical) example we used, the law was implemented in the northern regions in 2015, and a year later in the rest of the country. Then a *pipeline comparison research design* could be used; the communities/inhabitants of that part of the country where the (legal) arrangement is not yet implemented, can (*under certain conditions!*) be used as comparison groups for the communities/inhabitants of the *other part* of the country.[5]

6.2 TYPES AND EXAMPLES OF DESIGNS FROM EMPIRICAL LEGAL RESEARCH

In this section, main types (and subtypes) of designs are discussed. We follow De Vaus' (2001) distinction between *experimental, quasi-experimental, cross sectional, longitudinal* and *case study designs*, but we add *the comparative design* (as it is often referred to in legal studies).[6] Flick (2009), who writes from the perspective of *qualitative research*, refers to the same types of design, but does not include the (quasi-) experiment. There are also other distinctions suggested, like between descriptive designs (e.g. a 'case study'), correlational designs (e.g. a 'cross-sectional study'), causal designs ('experimental and quasi-experimental designs') and meta-analytical designs (the statistical part of the systematic review and synthesis work, referred to in Chapter 5). However, these categories are overlapping and non-excludable.[7] Another distinction is between fixed and flexible and quantitative and qualitative designs; these categorizations easily create misunderstanding about what these words mean. Sometimes, methods of data collection ('survey', 'questionnaire') are confused with research designs.

Some readers may wonder when research approaches like the '*theory-driven approach*', '*the Delphi method*', '*secondary analysis*' and '*action research*' will be discussed. These approaches, however, are *mistakenly* seen as research designs. The theory-driven approach is not a design but a method of how to detect underlying intervention theories (see Chapter 4). The Delphi method is a data collection method, which we will discuss in Chapter 7, which is also the case for 'secondary analysis' (using and analyzing existing (administrative, 'stored') data) (see Chapters 7 and 8). 'Action research' we do not discuss at all.[8]

6.2.1 Experimental Research Designs

The central characteristic of this design is the random assignment of subjects (persons, courts, prisons, lawyers, offenders) to treatment and control groups.[9] A treatment group is the group confronted with the intervention (a behavioral modification program to reduce antisocial behavior, a new organizational regime in a prison, a regulation and inspection program, a

BOX 6.1 RESEARCH DESIGNS AND VALIDITY THREATS

Wortman (1983: 225, 6), based on earlier work by Campbell, Stanley and Cook, was among the first to discuss these threats and included 'testing, history, instrumentation, selection, maturation, experimental mortality, statistical regression, and selection-maturation and other interactions'. He used the mnemonic *THIS MESS* (the first letters of Testing, History etc.). Later the list was expanded with more threats. See below for more information.

Bijleveld (2013: 110ff) listed assumptions of an ontological nature that are important for designs addressing causality (and for statistical analysis in general). For instance, the units of analysis (people, prisoners, patients, classes) are assumed to behave in ways independent of what others are doing; if there is full imitation or persuasion of the units of analysis, implying that they all would look and act in a similar way, this assumption would not hold. Another assumption is that the units of analysis are representative for 'a population' (and are 'more than their own unicity' (p. 111)).

BOX 6.2 RANDOMIZED EXPERIMENTS EXAMPLE 1: DO INFORMATION AND AN E-COACH HELP PERSONAL INJURY VICTIMS?

A first example is a randomized controlled trial by Elbers et al (2013: 1–2): 'Participants were individuals aged over 18 at the time of enrollment, who had been injured in a traffic crash less than two years ago and were claiming compensation for financial losses. Furthermore, they were required to speak Dutch and to have access to the internet. . . . [They] were recruited by three Dutch claims settlement offices. . . . The study design was a randomized controlled trial. An intervention website was developed with (1) information about the compensation process, and (2) an evidence-based, therapist-assisted problem-solving course. The control website contained a few links to already existing websites. Outcome measures were empowerment (of victims), self-efficacy, health status (including depression, anxiety, and somatic symptoms), perceived fairness, ability to work, claims knowledge and extent of burden. The outcomes were self-reported through online questionnaires and were measured four times: at baseline, and at 3, 6 and 12 months.'

soft law or a website for victims). The control group is the group that does not 'get' the intervention. Pre-test and post-test measurement is part of the design. The usual name for it is RCT: randomized controlled trial. Most methodologists consider this design as the most robust choice to address causal questions ('attribution'), including questions on the impact of interventions. Randomization of subjects makes the only difference between treatment and control situations the intervention itself (see the Maryland Scientific Methods Scale, mentioned in Chapter 5). This design, when implemented in an adequate way, is capable of detecting causality. It is a strong 'antibiotic' to validity threats.

Rossi, Lipsey and Freeman (2003) stress the point that random does not mean haphazard or capricious. On the contrary, randomly allocating targets to experimental and control groups requires taking extreme care to ensure that every unit (person, organization, etc.) in a target population has the same chance as any other to be selected for either group. White's blog on 'ten things that can go wrong with randomized controlled trials (experiments)' is interesting reading material (White, 2014).

Trochim and Donelly (2007),[10] Campbell and Stanley (1963), Shadish, Cook and Campbell (2002) and Kirk (2009) describe a number of subtypes of the experimental design, including the *one-group double-pretest posttest design*, *the randomized block design* and the *Solomon four group design*.

The *stepped wedge design* measures the intervention that is rolled-out sequentially to the experiment's participants (either as individuals or

BOX 6.3 RANDOMIZED EXPERIMENTS EXAMPLE 2: ARE SUPPLEMENTARY INCOME PAYMENTS BY THE US GOVERNMENT, UNDER THE NEW JERSEY-PENNSYLVANIA INCOME MAINTENANCE PROJECT, WORK DISINCENTIVES?

The experiment was launched by the Office of Economic Opportunity (the executive agency of US President Lyndon B Johnson's War on Poverty/Great Society program). The experiment started in 1968 and was carried on for three years. The experimental study was aimed at a target population of intact (i.e. not broken) families whose income was below 150% of the (then) poverty level and whose male heads were aged between 18 and 58. There were eight treatments that consisted of various combinations of guarantees, pegged to what was then the poverty level and the rates at which payments were taxed (adjusted to earnings received by the families). Other treatments consisted of working with different tax rates. A control group consisted of families who did not receive any payments.

The experiment was conducted in four communities in New Jersey and one in Pennsylvania (USA). A household survey was undertaken to identify eligible families. Identified families were invited to participate; after agreement was achieved, families were randomly allocated to one of the experimental groups or to the control group. Although about 1300 families were initially recruited, by the end of the experimental study 22% had discontinued their cooperation. Others had missed one or more interviews or had dropped out of the experiment for varying reasons. Fewer than 700 remained for analysis (Rossi and Freeman, 1993: 274ff).

BOX 6.4 BLOCKING

Blocking is a procedure for isolating variation attributable to a nuisance variable. Nuisance variables are undesired sources of variation that can affect the dependent variable. These are factors that have some effect on the response, but are of no interest to the experimenter; however, the variability it transmits to the response needs to be minimized or explained. Typical nuisance factors include different *operators of experiments*, the *pieces* of test equipment, when studying a process, and *time* (shifts, days, etc.), where the time of the day or the shift can be a factor that influences the response. Failure to block is a common flaw in designing an experiment (Kirk, 2009: 24).

clusters of individuals) over a number of periods. The order in which the different individuals or clusters receive the intervention is determined at random. By the end of the random allocation, all individuals or groups will have received the intervention. Stepped wedge designs incorporate data collection at each point where a new group (member) (*step*) receives the intervention (Brown and Lilford, 2006: 2).[11] A *double blind experiment*

BOX 6.5 EXPERIMENTS AND ONLINE CROWDSOURCING

Azzam and Jacobson (2013) have explored the viability of a new approach to create comparison groups in experimental studies: *online crowdsourcing*. Their study compares survey results from a randomized control group to survey results from a matched-comparison group created from Amazon.com's M(echanical) Turk crowdsourcing service to determine their comparability. Study findings indicate that online crowdsourcing is a potentially viable resource for research designs where access to comparison groups, large budgets and/or time is limited.

is a design wherein both researcher and subjects are unaware of which is the treatment group and which is the control group. This design is used to prevent research outcomes from being 'influenced' by the placebo effect or observer bias (the argument goes that it can be relatively easy for a researcher to influence experimental observations).

6.2.2 Quasi-experimental Research Designs

Quasi-experimental designs (QEDs) are designs that aim to study interventions like legal arrangements in an experimental way, but without randomization. Similar to randomized trials, quasi-experiments aim to demonstrate causality between the intervention/arrangement and the outcome. These studies use both pre-intervention and post-intervention measurements as well as non-randomly selected control groups. QEDs seek to match (instead of randomize) the characteristics of the treatment and control groups as closely as possible to eliminate selection bias as far as possible (Bamberger et al, 2012). Statistical matching means that with regard to crucial variables like demographics, socio-economic status and others known to be relevant for the specific research project, both groups (regions, persons, schools, hospitals, police districts, etc.) are 'made' – as much as possible – similar.[12]

A special type of design are *natural experiments*. Unlike randomized controlled trials or quasi-experimental designs, researchers do not have the ability to assign participants to treatment and control groups. Rather, divergences in law, policy or practice can offer the opportunity to analyze populations *as if* they had been part of an experiment. In essence, one population has received an intervention, while the other has not. The validity of these studies largely depend on the premise that the assignment of subjects to the 'treatment' and 'control' groups is random or 'as if' random.[13]

There are several sub-types of QEDs. We discuss a few.[14] Three have we mentioned: *the pipeline comparison group design*, *the propensity score*

BOX 6.6 QED EXAMPLE 1: DOES HOT SPOTS POLICING REDUCE VIOLENT CRIME RATES?

Braga et al (2012) investigated the Boston Police Department's Safe Street Team (SST) hot spots program. Using computerized mapping and database software, a micro-level place database of violent index crimes at all street segments and intersections in Boston was created. The SST hot spot areas were comprised of street segments and intersections. These 'micro places' were used to develop equivalent comparison units for the evaluation study (propensity score matching[1]). Data were collected (such as the yearly counts of violent index crimes between 2000 and 2009) and related to the treatment (SST hot spots) and comparison street segments and intersections.

[1] Bijleveld (2013: 123) describes the conceptual part of this (sub)design as follows. The problem she starts with is to find out the effects of an offender treatment program on juvenile sexual delinquents: Propensity score matching assumes that some offenders have a larger probability to receive a treatment than others. Juvenile abusers of very young children, as an example, will have a larger probability to get treated by a behavioral intervention program than juvenile abusers of juveniles. Some sexual delinquents of children will have had treatment in earlier years, although that is not evident. And some others will have been more active in their delinquent behavior than others. When propensity score matching is applied, the following groups can be compared: offenders of which it could be expected that they had had earlier treatment, but in fact didn't get such a treatment versus offenders of which it could also be expected that they were part of a treatment procedure and indeed were treated. These persons resemble each other in terms of the probability to be treated and their risk profiles are almost equal, but the one group did get the treatment and the other did not. An important assumption is that 'enough' data are available on the matching variables. When a study compares groups in this way, the logic of propensity score matching is followed. Remler and van Ryzyn (2011: 446) give another example. 'We might have administrative data on college students, including their exact age, gender, major, year in college, grade point average and so on and use these data to estimate a statistical equation that predicts volunteering for a stress reduction program (at the university). The resulting equation produces a predicted probability ("propensity") of being a volunteer (for that program). Those with high propensity scores but who did not volunteer for the stress program are used to create the comparison group'. Tollenaar, van der Laan and van der Heyden (2012) give a third example. They estimated 'the incapacitation effect and the impact on post-release recidivism of a measure combining prolonged incarceration and rehabilitation, the so called ISD measure for high frequency offenders (HFOs) (implemented in the Netherlands), compared to the standard practice of short-term imprisonment. The authors applied a quasi-experimental design. The intervention group consisted of all HFOs released from ISD in the period 2004–2008. Two control groups were derived from the remaining population of HFOs who were released from a standard prison term. To form groups of controls, a combination of multiple imputation (MI) and propensity score matching (PSM) was used. It was found that the ISD measure seems to be effective in reducing recidivism and crime. The estimated incapacitation effect showed that a serious portion of criminal cases and offences was prevented'.

matching design and *the natural experiment*. Another subtype is the *regression discontinuity (RD) design*. In this design, participants are assigned to the experimental or control groups solely on the basis of a cutoff score on a pre-program/intervention measure. This cutoff criterion is appropriate when the goal is to target a program or treatment to those who most need or deserve it. As Bamberger et al (2012: 577) make clear:

BOX 6.7 A NATURAL EXPERIMENT: WHAT IS THE IMPACT OF AN EXOGENOUS BOOST OF FAMILY INCOMES (DUE TO THE ESTABLISHMENT OF A CASINO) ON POVERTY REDUCTION AND CHILDREN'S PSYCHIATRIC DISORDERS?

Remler and van Ryzin (2011: 428) gave an example, known as the Cherokee casino study (Costello et al, 2003). A representative population sample of some 1500 rural children in the USA (Great Smokey Mountains) were given annual psychiatric assessments over a period of eight years (1993–2000). One quarter of the sample were American Indian, the remaining, predominantly white. Halfway through the study, a casino (opening in the Indian reservation) gave every American-Indian an income supplement that increased every year. This increase moved 14% of the study families out of poverty, while 53% remained poor (the others were never considered poor). The incomes of non-Indian families were not affected. The decision to establish a casino gave a boost to family incomes independent of whatever habits, motivations, dispositions or other factors being capable of influencing the mental health of the children. 'In other words, the families on the reservation did not *self-select* into behavior (such as getting a college degree) that resulted from their higher income – the boost in income just happened, like winning the lottery' (Remler and van Ryzyn, 2011: 428). Costello et al (2003: 2023) found that the 'Casino intervention' that moved families out of poverty for reasons that cannot be ascribed to family characteristics, 'had a major effect on some types of children's psychiatric disorders, but not on others'.

An important aspect of natural experiments is 'the ability to make comparisons – either over time or to a group that did not get the treatment. In the Casino study, the researchers began collecting data before the casino opened. Therefore, they had a *before* measure (or *pre-test*) of mental health to compare with mental health measures *after* the casino opened (*post-test*). This pre-test measure provided an estimate of the *counterfactual*: What would have been the mental health status of the children *had the casino not opened*? By comparing the change, the researchers were able to infer the causal effect of income on mental health' (ibid.). The researchers gathered data on families not living on the Cherokee reservation and thus not eligible for the sudden additional income from the casino. This unexposed *comparison group* also provides an estimate of the counterfactual' (Remler and van Ryzin, 2011: 428–9).

this design requires the definition of a target population (e.g., prisoners being released from jail) while an assignment variable must be identified. Normally this will be related either to need or to likelihood of success [like reduction of recidivism in this example]. The scale must be ordinal or interval with precise and measurable positions and it must be possible to rate everyone on the scale. A precise and measurable eligibility cutoff must also be defined, and it must be clear who falls about or below the cutoff. A strict selection procedure must be applied, so that everyone above the cutoff point is accepted and everyone below the cutoff is rejected. Once selection has been completed and the program implemented, the evaluation involves comparing subjects just above cutoff

> point with those just below it. . . . If the project had an effect, there will be a discontinuity ('jump') in the regression line at the cutoff point.

Berk and Rauma (1983) give an example when they estimated the effects of a program providing eligibility for unemployment insurance payments to released prisoners in California.

The *difference-in-difference design (DID)* recognizes that in the absence of random assignment, treatment and control groups are likely to differ for many reasons. Sometimes, however, treatment and control outcomes move in parallel in the absence of treatment. When they do, the divergence of a post-treatment path from the trend established by a comparison group may signal a treatment effect (Angrist and Pischke, 2014: 178). In its simplest set up, it is one where outcomes are observed for two groups for two time periods. One of the groups is exposed to a treatment in the second period but not in the first period. The second group is not exposed to the treatment during either period. In the case where the same units within a group are observed in each time period, the average gain in the second (control) group is subtracted from the average gain in the first (treatment) group. This removes biases in second period comparisons between the treatment and control group that could be the result of permanent differences between those groups, as well as biases from comparisons over time in the treatment group that could be the result of trends.

6.2.3 Longitudinal Research Design

A longitudinal study is an observational research study that collects information on the same sample (like individuals or households) at repeated intervals over an extended period of time. It means that researchers record information about their subjects without manipulating the study environment. Decisions that researchers usually have to make which determine the precise type of design are the following (De Vaus, 2001: 113ff): will the same 'cases' (persons, organizations, countries, courts) be followed over time? And: will data be collected at different points of time, as is the case in the prospective longitudinal design where groups (i.e. including members of organizations) are chosen that will be studied, tracked and re-studied at one or more moments in the future?

Longitudinal studies can also be retrospective or bidirectional. A retrospective study looks back and investigates 'history', for example by doing interviews and analyzing documents. Monahan and Swanson (2009) used such a design when they addressed the question how careers of a (University of) Virginia lawyers class have developed over the years. They used (stored) data to characterize the start of the careers and a survey to collect information on later moments in life. A bi-directional design combines both approaches.

Sometimes the expression 'cohort studies' is used. Such a study is usually based on a group of people who share the same (significant) event (birth cohort, marriage cohort, etc.) and are followed. Rather than sampling on the basis of a (significant) life event, panel surveys sample a cross-section of the population, and then follow them up at regular intervals (like household panel studies or product testing panels). Several sub-designs exist.[15]

6.2.4 Cross-sectional Research Design[16]

A cross-sectional design is also observational in nature. The defining feature of such a study is that it looks into *different population groups* at *a single point in* time (where populations can also be organizations or institutions). Think of it in terms of taking a snapshot. In the standard cross-sectional design, data are collected at one point in time. The cross-sectional design has three distinctive features: no time dimension, reliance on existing differences rather than change (due to a policy or another 'outside' intervention) and groups based on existing differences rather than random allocation (De Vaus, 2001: 170).

BOX 6.8 LONGITUDINAL DESIGN EXAMPLE 1: HOW DO BOYS FROM LONDON DEVELOP IN RELATION TO CRIME AND NON-CRIME OVER A PERIOD OF 50 YEARS? THE CAMBRIDGE STUDY IN DELINQUENT DEVELOPMENT

An example of a prospective longitudinal design is the Cambridge Study in Delinquent Development. The study was initiated by Donald West in 1961. David Farrrington joined him in 1969 and became sole director of the project in 1981 (http://www.icpsr.umich.edu/icpsrweb/NACJD/studies/08488, accessed 27 November 2015). Data collection began in 1961–62 when most of the boys were aged between eight and nine. It is a 50-year follow-up of 400 London males. Recently, their adult children were interviewed to make this a three-generation study. Using a mixture of self-reports, in-depth interviews and psychological testing, the researchers collected both qualitative and quantitative data to explain and understand the intricacies and influences of anti-social and pro-social tendencies in both criminal and non-criminal young men. See also http://www.integrated-sociopsychology.net/cambridge_study_delinquent.html, accessed 5 July 2015.

BOX 6.9 LONGITUDINAL DESIGN EXAMPLE 2: WHAT CAN BE SAID ABOUT THE IMPORTANCE OF BIOLOGICAL AND GENETIC FACTORS IN EXPLAINING PERSISTENT ANTISOCIAL BEHAVIOR?

The Dunedin Multidisciplinary Health and Development Research Study (http://dunedinstudy.otago.ac.nz/, accessed December 13, 2015) ('the Dunedin Study') has been ongoing since 1972–73. It is a longitudinal study of the health, development and well-being of a general sample of New Zealanders. They were studied at birth (1972–73), followed up and assessed at the age of three when the longitudinal study was started. Since then they have been assessed every two years until the age of 15, then at ages 18 (1990–91), 21 (1993–94), 26 (1998–99), 32 (2003–2005) and 38 (2010–2012). The study, with an original focus on the effects of environmental factors on human development, has since evolved and grown to include genetic and genomic data, to explore how genes and environments interact, and to inform policy decisions. In the early 1990s Moffit and Caspi (http://www.moffittcaspi.com/AntiBehav-empirical, accessed 27 November 2015) started to analyze data about crime, antisocial behavior, genetics and variables from neurosciences and neuropsychology.

BOX 6.10 LONGITUDINAL DESIGN EXAMPLE 3: DOES A COUNTRY'S LEGAL ORIGIN AFFECT THE CONTENT OF ITS SUBSTANTIVE LAW IN THE AREA OF SHAREHOLDER PROTECTION?

Armour et al (2009) used a panel data set covering a range of developed and developing countries and showed that common law systems were more protective of shareholder interests than civil law systems in the period 1995–2005. However, civil law systems were catching up, suggesting that legal origin was not much of an obstacle to formal convergence in shareholder protection law. This study is a (longitudinal) test of the Legal Origines hypotheses (La Porta et al, 2008). Four data sets were produced. Three of them are five-country data sets for the period 1970–2005, covering the fields of shareholder protection, creditor protection and labor regulation. A fourth dataset was used which covers shareholder protection, but does so for a wider range of countries over a shorter period of time (20 countries over the period 1995–2005 including developed systems like Canada, France and Germany, developing countries (India, Malaysia, South Africa) and transition systems (China, Latvia). The period was chosen because this was a time in which almost all systems worldwide were undergoing a general move to liberalize their economies, as part of which legal reforms aimed at strengthening shareholder protection were on the policy agenda.

BOX 6.11 CROSS-SECTIONAL DESIGN EXAMPLE 1: WHAT ARE THE PATHS TO JUSTICE OF THE DUTCH POPULATION?

An example of a cross-sectional study is the WODC Paths to Justice study that provides a quantitative overview of the 'landscape of disputes', as seen from the perspective of Dutch citizens (Van Velthoven and Klein Haarhuis, 2010). Who – in the Netherlands – are having what (legally relevant) problems, who solves them and through which ways, who is 'entering the legal arena' and what are the results? These studies are repeated every so many years, with different samples. They are part of a larger research program looking into the same problem in several other countries by making use of a similar approach.

BOX 6.12 CROSS-SECTIONAL DESIGN EXAMPLE 2: WHICH OFFENCES, SUCH AS ASSAULT, BURGLARY, ROBBERY, SEXUAL OFFENCES OR PERSONAL THEFTS, WERE EXPERIENCED OVER THE LAST 12 MONTHS? THE INTERNATIONAL CRIME VICTIMS SURVEY (ICVS)

The ICVS was designed to produce data that allows valid cross-country comparisons and covers over 30 countries. The survey goes back for several decades. The results show substantial differences between countries. The ICVS also tracks the percentage of crimes reported to the police by victims. Several countries not only participate in the international victims study, but also have a victimization survey for their own country (like the USA and the Netherlands). http://www.unicri.it/services/library_documentation/publications/icvs/, accessed 2 July 2015.

6.2.5 Case Studies Design

According to Yin (2003: 2) 'the distinctive need for case studies arises out of the desire to understand complex social phenomena'. Yin describes a case study as an empirical study that investigates a phenomenon within its real-life context. Case studies aim at providing as complete an understanding of an event or situation as possible. They focus on (social) phenomena 'in one or a few of its manifestations, in its natural surroundings, during a certain period, focusing on detailed descriptions,[17] interpretations and explanations that several categories of participants in the system attach to the (social) processes' (in a courtroom, prison, boot camp, lawyer's office). Yin considers that they are best used to answer 'how and why' questions through in-depth analysis of one situation, event or location.

BOX 6.13 CASE STUDY DESIGN EXAMPLE 1: WHAT IS THE IMPACT OF REGULATORY DISCLOSURE OF NAMES OF OFFENDING COMPANIES ON THE BEHAVIOR OF COMPANIES IN THE NETHERLANDS?

An example of a study using this design was given by Van Erp (2010) on regulatory disclosure of names of offending companies. This type of public sanction is increasingly popular as an alternative to traditional command and control regulation in Western countries. The study aimed to contribute to a better understanding of the underlying working mechanisms of regulatory disclosure of offenders' names through a case study of the Dutch Authority for Financial Markets' (AFM) policy: 'First, a document analysis was performed of legal and parliamentary documents, jurisprudence, Internet sources, annual reports, and the press releases of the AFM. This analysis included the public warnings and public sanctions issued in 2007 and 2008. Second, some 30 interviews were held with regulators and supervisors, experts and compliance officers. Third, telephone interviews were conducted with sanctioned companies on effects of publication on their reputation. Last, an analysis of the media coverage of public warnings and sanctions in national and regional newspapers was performed through LexisNexis' (ibid., p. 415).

BOX 6.14 CASE STUDY DESIGN EXAMPLE 2: DO ASSUMPTIONS ABOUT SOLICITOR ADVERSARIALISM IN DIVORCE MATTERS IN THE UK HAVE ANY EMPIRICAL VALIDITY?

Webley (2010: 944ff) summarized this study done by Eekelaar et al (2000) as a case study of lawyer-client interactions in a divorce context. The study examined the work of a small sample of individual solicitors. Eekelaar et al used a three-fold methodology. First they *observed* ten partner-level solicitors at work for a day (14 days observation), recording what the solicitors did in descriptive terms. The second mode of data collection was to *conduct interviews* with 40 solicitors who were asked to talk about pre-selected cases from the beginning of the case to the present position. These solicitors were from four regions in England and Wales. Once all the data had been collected, the interview transcripts were analyzed using *content analysis*, while illustrative quotes were included in the write-up of their findings as evidence of what they had observed and heard.

One distinguishes between single and multiple case studies. The N=1 trial (with one person) which has its origin in medicine and is also used in forensic research is an example of a single case study, also known as a 'single-subject design'. A multiple case study enables the researcher to

BOX 6.15 CASE STUDY DESIGN EXAMPLE 3: WHAT ARE THE KEY FEATURES OF RELIABLE SELF-REGULATING PRIVATE THIRD-PARTY CERTIFICATION, AND WHAT ARE THEIR COMPARATIVE INSTITUTIONAL ADVANTAGES OVER ADMINISTRATIVE REGULATION BY GOVERNMENT AGENCIES?

Private certification as a means of risk regulation and quality assurance can offer advantages over government regulation, including superior technical expertise, better inspection and monitoring of regulated entities, increased responsiveness to consumers, and greater efficiency. In this study, two cases of reliable private certification in regulatory arenas are reported: fire safety and kosher food (Lytton, 2014). The author illustrates how brand competition, professionalism, bureaucratic controls, a shared sense of mission and social networks support reliable private certification. These factors are mechanisms related to different theories like Aviram's theory on network regulation (Aviram, 2003) and social capital theory.

explore differences within and between cases. Because comparisons will be drawn, it is imperative that the cases are chosen carefully so that the researcher can predict similar results across cases, or predict contrasting results based on a theory (Yin, 2003).

Case studies are also undertaken on a macro level (for example in the field of the position of countries on rule of law indicators and human rights indicators) (Evans and Price, 2008). In the evaluation world, the Qualitative Comparative Analysis (QCA) (sub)design (Ragin, 2008) is becoming popular. It claims to combine traditional, 'qualitative' case studies with a quantitative approach: 'QCA can be usefully applied to research designs involving small and intermediate-size N's (e.g., 5–50). In this range, there are often too many cases for researchers to keep all the case knowledge "in their heads", but too few cases for most conventional statistical techniques' (ibid., p. 4).[18]

6.2.6 The Comparative 'Design' (aka Comparative Law Research)

Compared to the other designs we discussed so far, it is less clear what this 'design' entails. In fact there is serious doubt that there is such a thing as *the (or 'a')* comparative design. Sometimes it is seen as a name for a variety of methods of looking at law, sometimes it is a variety of 'perspectives' (Legrand, 1996; Oderkerk, 2014) and sometimes the focus is on the 'functional method of comparative law' (Michaels, 2006: 340ff), which 'has become both the *mantra* and the *bête noire* of comparative law. For its proponents it is the most, perhaps the only, fruitful method; to its opponents it represents everything bad about mainstream comparative law'.[19] Palmer (2004: 1–2) is of the opinion that 'all lawyers are comparatists in a natural sense, as when they make distinctions, draw deductions or look for a case in point'.

Husa's (2007: 8–9) answer to the question 'how does the (comparative) method work in practice, i.e. what steps to take?' is this: 'the process of comparative law is, roughly, as follows: 1) Pose a functional question (how is – loosely understood – socio-legal problem X solved?), 2) present the systems and their way of solving problem X, 3) list similarities and differences in ways of solving problem X, 4) adopt a new point of view from which to consider explanations of differences and similarities, and 5) critically evaluate discoveries (and sometimes judge which of the solutions is "best")'. Husa (2007: 17) suggests to work with 'a flexible methodology' when making comparisons; however, what 'flexibility' and 'methodology' is, remains unclear, and the same is true for several of the other steps.

In his progress report on comparative law over the last 50 years, Reimann (2002: 685) contended that '[w]hile comparative law has been a considerable success in terms of producing a wealth of knowledge, it has been a resounding failure with regard to its more general development as a field of inquiry'. Ten years later, Orücü (2012: 573) concluded that 'we cannot talk of a "comparative law methodology" nor of a "methodology of comparative law", but must speak of methods employed in comparative law research, since there is no single method or single perspective [or design] exclusive to comparative law'. Oderkerk (2014) is at least as critical.

To help articulate what the basic principles of 'the' comparative research design are, we turn to Lijphart (1971). He showed that it resembles the experimental design, but only in a 'very imperfect way' (ibid., p. 685).[20] Two 'principal problems facing the comparative method are causing this: many variables, small number of cases'. Lijphart points at the 'method of difference' and the 'method of concomitant variations' (coined by John Stuart Mill):

> The method of difference consists of comparing instances in which (a) phenomenon does occur, with instances in other respects similar in which it does not . . . the method of concomitant variations is a more sophisticated version: instead of observing merely the presence or absence of operative variables, it observes and measures the quantitative variations of the operative variables and relates these to each other. (Lijphart, 1971: 687–8)

Eberle (2009: 452) articulated four steps in comparative legal research:

> The first part (Step 1) is acquiring the skills of a comparativist in order to evaluate law clearly, objectively, and neutrally. The second part (Step 2) is the

BOX 6.16 COMPARATIVE (LEGAL RESEARCH) DESIGN EXAMPLE 1: WHAT IS THE COMMON CORE CONTRACT LAW? THE CORNELL PROJECT AND THE TRENTO PROJECT

The Cornell project was sponsored by the Ford Foundation and guided by Schlesinger (1968); it focused on realizing a better 'understanding of the formation of contracts (and their common core) and to develop knowledge and teaching materials for the teaching of law courses in the future. It is thought that in the future the average practitioner will have to have a familiarity not just with the common law of the United States but with a common core of law of the world' (Shadoan, 1968: 263). The Trento project broadened the scope of the Cornell project beyond contract law and has put emphasis on contract, property and tort, with a number of sub topics such as commercial trusts, mistake and fraud in contract law. The project relies on what in the world of legal comparativists is known as the 'factual approach', that is, fact-based, in-depth research methodology, presenting a number of cases, 15 to 30, to national reporters and asking for solutions offered by their legal systems (Orücü, 2012: 567).

BOX 6.17 COMPARATIVE (LEGAL RESEARCH) DESIGN EXAMPLE 2: HOW ARE STATE-FINANCED LEGAL AID SYSTEMS ORGANIZED IN COUNTRIES A. . . .N? WHICH MINIMUM REQUIREMENTS FOR STATE-FINANCED LEGAL AID CAN BE DEDUCED FROM THE EUROPEAN CONVENTION OF HUMAN RIGHTS AND FROM CASE LAW OF THE EUROPEAN COURT OF HUMAN RIGHTS?

In this study the authors 'have compared legal aid systems of nine countries and assessed how they perform within the framework of the fundamental right to access to justice protected by Article 6 European Convention on Human Rights (ECHR). Besides describing the systems, the goal is to identify trends, in relation to the costs of services, alternative ways of delivering legal assistance and the effectiveness of services provided. The research focuses on a number of subquestions, like: what are the eligibility criteria, financial thresholds, own contributions, merits criteria, excluded and exempted groups and types of problems? What are the budgets of state-financed legal aid and, if available, the different contributions per contributor? What are the scopes of the legal aid services, and what are limitations and exclusions? Which (preliminary, mandatory) services are available? What are the effects of legal aid systems on the quality of access to justice and the effects on people with limited means, and on conflict resolution?

Data collection was done through a questionnaire. Reports available on the internet were used from all countries in native languages. Interviews were conducted with national experts from legal aid boards or from academia. These specialists also verified information collected through desk research. For France, Scotland, and England & Wales, recent reports and public sources provided sufficient information' (Barendrecht et al, 2014: 5; 27ff).

BOX 6.18 COMPARATIVE (LEGAL RESEARCH) DESIGN EXAMPLE 3 OF THE COMPARATIVE DESIGN: HOW DOES THE EUROPEAN COMMISSION FOR THE EFFICIENCY OF JUSTICE (CEPEJ) APPROACH WORK IN PRACTICE WHEN MEASURING COURTS AND JUDICIAL SYSTEMS AND WHILE FOCUSING ON THE REDUCTION OF DELAYS IN COURT PROCEEDINGS?

The European Commission for the Efficiency of Justice (CEPEJ) is one of the intergovernmental activities of the Council of Europe. When the CEPEJ was created in 2002, one of its first tasks was to develop a methodology for comparatively evaluating the composition and functioning of European judicial systems. The original questionnaire was composed of 123 questions designed to provide an overview of the judicial structure and operation in the individual countries. The questionnaire sought both general information and specific details regarding the country's court system:

- access to justice and to courts;
- the functioning of the nation's court system and its relative efficiency;
- use of information technology in the court system;
- whether the judicial system provides litigants with a fair trial;
- information regarding judges, public prosecutors, and lawyers;
- information regarding the system's enforcement agents and the execution of court decisions.

To facilitate the process of data collection, the experts decided that each country should nominate a 'national correspondent' (Albers, 2008). More recent CEPEJ studies work with a somewhat changed methodology.

> evaluation of the law as it is expressed concretely, in words, action; we can refer to this as the external law. Once we get an understanding of the law as actually stated, we can move on to the third part (Step 3) of the methodology: evaluating how the law actually operates within a culture. We might refer to this as law in action or the internal law. . . . After we have evaluated the law as stated and the law in action, we can assemble our data (Step 4) and conclude with comparative observations that can shed light on both a foreign legal culture and our own.[21]

Örücü (2012: 565) makes the point that 'the possibility of comparison is dependent upon the existence and availability of data. Data can best be obtained by employing social science methodology'.[22]

Researchers *of course* combine designs. In fact this often is commendable. The following are a few examples.

- Using a *cross-sectional design* to take a snapshot and find potential areas of interest and next use a *longitudinal design* to find trends (and their explanations).

  Take the example of the Paths to Justice studies. The group of civilians having the largest number of socio-legal problems and are most unsatisfied with solutions to these problems offered by the justice system, could be followed longitudinally to find explanations, but also to see if there is progress made in the 'treatment' of this population group by the justice system.

- Using *longitudinal design* but where the time line is interrupted by a certain intervention, for example new legislation (linked to natural experiments).

  The *interrupted time-series design* works with multiple pre-test and post-test observations spaced at certain intervals of time. Such a design is one in which a string of consecutive observations equally spaced in time is interrupted by the imposition of a treatment or intervention. A classic example in empirical legal research is Campbell and Ross's (1968) evaluation of the impact of the Connecticut Crackdown on speeding on the number of traffic fatalities. Another example is Muller's (2004) study of the repeal of Florida's motorcycle helmet law by tracking monthly motorcycle fatalities for several years before and after the law's repeal. This sub-design is called 'interrupted', because the time series is confronted with (and interrupted by) the implementation of a treatment/policy/law.[23]

- Combining a *longitudinal (cohort) study* with an *experimental design*.

  Here the Montreal Longitudinal and Experimental Study (MILES) of boys with low socioeconomic status is an example. It was initiated in 1984 and included a randomized prevention program delivered over a 2-year period when boys were aged 7–9 years. The program targeted disruptive behavior and included two main components: social skills training for the boys at school and training for parents during family visits. This prevention program has been shown, on the basis of an (experimental) evaluation, to have short- and long-term effects on disruptive, antisocial and delinquent behavior, identified as the study's primary outcomes, as well as academic performance and drop out from school. (Castellanos-Ryan et al, 2013: 188)

- Using a *single case study approach and a quasi-experimental design*). Here the focus usually is on one person (e.g. a (serial) killer, patient, police officer, judge).

  One such study evaluated the effectiveness of a behavioral treatment for panic disorder in a 10-year-old boy (Barlow et al, 2009). In this study, the boy, Michael, had frequent and repeated panic attacks, which were unsuccessfully treated in a previous play therapy. Michael was next treated using a modified version of the Panic Control Treatment, a manualized treatment developed and evaluated for adults. The treatment was carefully administered. In addition to using semi-structured clinical interviews at pre- and post-treatment to evaluate symptoms of panic disorder, Michael and his mother both completed and turned in daily logs of the number of panic attacks experienced as well as his overall level of global anxiety each day.

- Using a *cross-sectional survey* in which Dutch pictograms *Kijkwijzer* and *PEGI (Pan European Game Information)* were studied with *mystery guests* (visiting and calling producers and sellers of audiovisual products for children to find out if they used the pictograms), where content-analysis was applied to TV programs to find out if movies were correctly pictogrammed and where a *quasi-experimental design* was implemented to find out to what extent these pictograms were attractive and informative for consumers.

  The pictograms were placed on covers, packing materials, posters, and other advertising materials and were also shown at the start of a movie or television program. The pictograms primarily meant to inform parents and teachers about the harmfulness of audiovisual products for children below certain ages. In addition, *Kijkwijzer* helps the audiovisual business to comply with the Dutch Media Law and the Criminal Law, which state that children under the age of sixteen must be protected against harmful media. (Gosselt et al, 2008: 175–200)

BOX 6.19 FURTHER (TECHNICAL) INFORMATION OF RESEARCH DESIGNS

Angrist and Pishke (2014); Bamberger et al (2012); Stern et al (2012); Sherman (2010); Leeuw and Vaessen, (2009); Gomm (2008); and classics like Campbell and Stanley (1963); and Cook and Campbell (1979).

6.3 CRITERIA ASSESSING THE ADEQUACY OF RESEARCH DESIGNS

Although the list presented below is not exhaustive, these criteria are crucial in judging the applicability, appropriateness and quality of a design: *internal validity, external validity, descriptive validity, problem relevance (of designs), relationship with theories and ethical and legal aspects of designs.* There are several criteria for judging the quality and adequacy of empirical legal research that deal with sampling, representativeness, selection of units, operationalization of concepts and variables, data collection, data-analysis and reporting. These will be discussed in the next two chapters.

Earlier, we referred to *threats to validity* diagnosed over the years when studying, in particular, causal relationships. More than 30 threats have been formulated. We refer to Cook and Campbell (1979) and to lists available on the internet.[24]

6.3.1 Criterion 1: Statistical Validity

Quintessentially this means talking about the statistical significance of the quantitative relationship between variables. To check its significance, use is made of statistical tests.

6.3.2 Criterion 2: Internal Validity

Gomm (2008: 12–13) describes validity by saying that 'it means something like truth. Most researchers accept that we can never know the truth for sure, so in research what is valid is that which hasn't as yet been invalidated, despite attempts to do so'. He relates this position to Popper's falsificationist epistemology. Internal validity is the extent to which the structure of a research design enables researchers to draw unambiguous conclusions. The way in which the study is set up (e.g. tracking changes over time, making comparisons) can eliminate alternative explanations for the findings. 'The more the design of a study eliminates these alternative interpretations, the stronger the internal validity of that study' (de Vaus, 2001). In a paper assessing internal validity of business administration studies, Berg et al (2004) put it like this: 'Studies with high internal validity provide results that are not subject to flaws whereas designs with low internal validity produce results that are subject to third-variable effects and confounds' (Campbell and Stanley, 1963; Cook and Campbell, 1979).[25]

Internal validity is largely only relevant in studies that try to establish or test a *causal relationship*. If studies do not use words like 'explanation', 'cause' or 'causal relationship', but de facto address these topics, internal validity is also crucial. An example of such a situation is when an evaluator is claiming to investigate the impact (consequences) of new legislation on companies, but does not use words like 'causation' or 'causal explanation'.

Internal validity is also a relevant criterion when pilots (of projects, regulation, etc.) are designed and tested and when researchers look into the relationship between implementation fidelity and impact of an intervention.

6.3.3 Criterion 3: External Validity

External validity is defined as the extent to which a specific result of a study can be generalized to a wider population (Perry et al, 2010). Recall that validity in general refers to the approximate truth of propositions, inferences or conclusions. That means that external validity refers to the approximate truth of conclusions that involve generalizations. External validity usually distinguishes between population validity (the extent to which the results of a study can be generalized from the specific sample that was studied to a larger group of subjects) and ecological validity (the extent to which the results of an experiment can be generalized from the set of environmental conditions created by the researcher to other environmental conditions (settings and conditions)).

6.3.4 Criterion 4: Descriptive Validity

In its simplest form, this criterion addresses the overall quality of the reporting of a study, as we saw in Chapter 5. Farrington (2003) developed a 14-item checklist which includes a range of different elements (e.g. design of the study, hypotheses to be tested, and effect sizes). Recently, the *Consort Statement* was developed comprising a 25-item checklist.[26] The list focuses on reporting how the randomized control trial (the focus of this Statement) is designed, analyzed and interpreted. Attention is paid to the title and abstract, introduction and background, methods (including information on participants, interventions, objectives, outcomes, sample size, randomization, blinding and statistical methods), results (including information on participant flow, recruitment, baseline data, numbers analyzed, outcomes and estimation, ancillary analyses and adverse events), interpretation, generalizability and overall evidence of the randomized control trial (RCT). It has been used to increase the standard of reporting RCTs in medicine and has been endorsed internationally by journal editors and professional bodies.

Perry et al (2010) used the Consort Statement in a study that had as 'the overall aim to assess the descriptive validity in a representative sample of crime and justice trials. The sample comprised of 83 RCT's that had been previously identified by Farrington and Welsh (2005)'. Unfortunately, the conclusions were not very positive: 'Overall, the findings suggest that crime and justice studies have low descriptive validity. Reporting was poor on methods of randomization, outcome measures, statistical analyses, and study findings, though much better in regard to reporting of background and participant details'.

While the CONSORT Statement has randomized controlled studies as its focus, for *observational designs* the *STROBE Statement* (also a list of items) gives methodological guidance which is related to the CONSORT list.[27]

Next to these three types of validity, there is validity (and reliability) of data collection instruments and construct validity (the adequacy of the operational definition and measurement of the theoretical constructs that underlie the intervention and the outcome): we refer to Chapters 7 and 8 for more information.

6.3.5 Criterion 5: Problem Relevance of Research Designs and the Danger of Success Bias

Choosing the design of a study is related to the type of problem under investigation, as the (hypothetical) example from section 6.2 showed. *To assume that designs always 'fit' problems and that every design 'will do', is a mistake.* Although some (types of) research problems are not very selective in their design choice,[28] other research problems are highly selective. The reason is that *the choice of an adequate, commendable, i.e. 'fitting' research design is a conditio sine qua non for the production of valid and reliable evidence.* This has to do with the *strength of the design*. Strength is largely dependent upon the criteria discussed above, and in particular internal validity. Designs vary in the extent to which they can control various forms of error, and hence some designs provide more reliable evidence than others.

In the literature several scales have been suggested describing the relative strengths of designs. Sometimes they are called 'evidence or design hierarchies'. An example used in criminology is the Maryland Scientific Methods Scale (Sherman et al, 1997) (see Chapter 5). Usually, the experiment (RCT) is at 'the top' of the scale, while correlational studies with only one measurement moment are at 'the bottom'. The criteria the Campbell Collaboration uses when decisions are taken as to which research designs to include and which to exclude from systematic reviews are more or less the same. In the medical and health research world, the Cochrane Library also follows such a typology, although other approaches are accepted. The next two boxes summarize two other 'hierarchies' (Nutley, Powell and Davies, 2012) but also refer to well-known critique on the hierarchy concept.

In the methodological literature, the negative consequences of working with designs not fitting the research problems have been addressed. For evaluations of policy programs, Rossi (1987) coined the '*Stainless Steel Law of Evaluation*': the weaker the design of an impact evaluation is (i.e. quasi-experimental design is weaker than the experimental; cross-sectional

BOX 6.20 TWO EXAMPLES OF HIERARCHIES OF EVIDENCE, BASED ON THE RESEARCH DESIGN

- Level I: Well conducted, suitably powered randomized control trial (RCT)
- Level II: Well conducted, but small and underpowered RCT
- Level III: Non-randomized observational studies
- Level IV: Non-randomized study with historical controls
- Level V: Case series without controls

Source: Bagshaw and Bellomo, 2008: 2.

1. Systematic reviews and meta-analyses
2. RCTs with definitive results
3. RCTs with non-definitive results
4. Cohort studies
5. Case control studies
6. Cross sectional surveys
7. Case reports

Source: Petticrew and Roberts, 2006: 527.

BOX 6.21 POINTS OF CRITIQUE ON HIERARCHIES OF EVIDENCE

- Schwartz and Mayne (2005) discuss other standards of quality that are not necessarily related to these scales/designs. Burrows and Walker (2013) suggest ways for assessing expert (opinions).
- Pawson and Tilley (1997) and Pawson (2006; 2013) do not focus on hierarchies but on the contribution of research (designs) to theory development and explanations.
- Hierarchies do not take into account how different designs are used in the world of practice. Studies describing how (randomized) experiments – as an example – are carried out point to major deficiencies. See Farrington (2003) and Greenberg and Barnow (2014) (in their analysis of 'eight, somewhat overlapping, types of flaws that have occurred in evaluating (through RCT's) the effects or impacts of social programs'.
- Designs lower down the ranking are not always superfluous. For example, the link between smoking and lung cancer was discovered via cohort studies carried out in the 1950s.

is weaker than longitudinal; single case studies are weaker than multiple case studies), the larger the likelihood that positive findings are found compared to the situation when stronger designs are used. Gomm (2008: 96–9) refers to this problem as 'the bias towards success verdicts in effectiveness studies'. For criminology, Logan (1972) found that when there were no

Table 6.1 Experimental control and experimental results: research on programmes to reduce crime and delinquency (after Logan, 1972 and Gomm, 2008: Table 1)

Experimental control and experimental results: research on programmes to reduce crime and delinquency

	Number judged successful (%)	Number judged unsuccessful (%)
19 studies with randomized control groups	7 (37)	12 (63)
23 studies with non-randomized control groups	16 (70)	7 (30)
58 studies with no control groups	50 (86)	8 (14)

How to read this table
Logan reviewed 100 studies of programmes designed to reduce criminal behaviour; 58 of these had designs with no control groups – that is, they featured only people receiving the programme, and not anyone receiving any alternative treatment or no treatment at all. The remainder had control groups, 23 with non-randomized control groups and 19 with randomized control groups (see Chapter 3, Section 3.3). The table shows that where there were no control groups the researchers were very likely to judge the programme as a success, and that where there were randomized control groups they were much more likely to judge the programme as a failure.

Source: After Logan (1972: Table 1).

control groups used in the design, the findings were much more positive than when randomized control groups were used. He looked into 100 criminological studies; Table 6.1 presents the evidence (see Logan, 1972; Gomm, 2008: 97).

The differences indicate that when an experimental design is used, impact evaluations are more precise (and – in this case – critical) in their outcomes than when less robust designs are used.

Since Logan (1972), other studies with similar findings have been produced in social work (MacDonald et al, 1992), in medicine (Moher et al, 2001) and in criminology (Lipsey, 1995; Weisburd et al, 2001 and Welsh et al, 2011). Welsh et al (2011) partially replicated the Weisburd et al (2001) study (does the robustness of the research designs have an influence on study outcomes?) and found similar results that 'the overall correlation between research design and study outcomes is moderate but negative and significant (Tau-b= −.175, p=.029). This suggests that stronger research designs are less likely to report desirable effects or, conversely, weaker research designs may be biased upward' (Welsh et al, 2011).

Gomm (2008: 96) summarized the evidence on this complicated issue:

> Studies of effectiveness without any control groups at all are very poorly equipped to provide evidence to determine whether some intervention was the cause of any outcomes recorded. . . . It also seems to be true that where randomization is used to create control groups (i.e. 'real experiments'), findings of effectiveness are less likely than when control groups are created in other ways.

He adds a list of some 15 'recipes for bias' (ibid., p. 98).

6.3.6 Criterion 6: Relationship with Theories

As indicated before, theories with a small 't' or a capital 'T' are important in ELR. It is therefore not commendable to see the selection and construction of a research design as a purely technical exercise. Such an attitude creates the risk that singular hypotheses are studied without connecting them to more general (explanatory or intervention) theories. If hypotheses are deduced from existing theories, testing them is more efficient in realizing accumulation of knowledge than working with stand-alone hypotheses.

6.3.7 Criterion 7: Ethical Aspects of Design Choices, in Particular Randomization

One of, if not the most often discussed questions in design choices is if, and to what extent, *randomization of persons/other actors* to either the experimental group or the control group is ethically correct. The argument against a positive answer is that some people, who could benefit from the intervention, and are in dire need of improving their (social, legal or medical) situation, may become part of the control group and are 'left behind'. The argument in favor of matched or random assignment is first that it is not known whether the intervention will work (to find that out is exactly the goal of the study) and secondly that it is unethical, if society faces unintended and negative side effects of the intervention, simply because it was not evaluated in a proper and valid way. With regard to court experiments Lind (1985) described RCTs (or 'close approximations to them': p. 73) that examined innovations in civil procedures. He refers to a committee which not only saw no general conditions to prohibit working with random designs, but also agreed with the adage that disparity in treatment is harmful. The point was that the harm can be overcome by the benefits that can result from randomized research (Lind, 1985: 79–80).

More recently, Weisburd (2003: 336) argued that:

> in fact there is a moral imperative for the conduct of randomized experiments in crime and justice. That imperative develops from our professional obligation to provide valid answers to questions about the effectiveness of treatments, practices, and programs. It is supported by a statistical argument that makes randomized experiments the preferred method for ruling out alternative causes of the outcomes observed.

However, and as was mentioned in Box 6.21 above, the way in which experiments are carried out in real life, including the deficiencies and flaws related to them, makes the idea of a 'moral imperative' for conducting RCTs an overclaim.

Other aspects of designs that are part of the discussion on ethics include the way in which data are collected and analyzed. Codes of conduct are concerned with the issue of informed consent, privacy and confidentiality. In general the starting point is that researchers should do everything to uphold professional integrity. More recently, replicability, associated with scientific fraud and plagiarism, is also on the ethical agenda.

6.4 SOME GUIDANCE

- Moving from the (type of) research problem to the (type of) design is not a 'free choice'. Given the 'specs' of the research problem and the role of theories, methodological criteria help indicate which design(s) can and should be used and which should not be used (or are at least less desirable). Put differently, there are methodological restrictions imposed on the process of selecting a research design: it is neither a 'one size fits all', nor 'every size will do'. Some guidance is appropriate. Guidance means giving advice and formulating suggestions, based on earlier studies and (methodological) handbooks and textbooks; it does *not* mean *instructing* researchers *how* to handle things and what exactly to do.
- Do not forget to organize enough time and advice when designing and/or selecting the design of the empirical projects. Never jump from the research problem to collecting data, thinking that choosing the people to be interviewed, the documents to be analyzed or the data to be scrutinized is equal to the development of the design of the study.
- How to take care of practical restrictions? The answer is threefold:
  - First, try as hard as possible to go for the best (i.e. commendable) design.

- Second, if there continues to be practical (i.e. financial, administrative, time) restrictions, as will sometimes be the case,[29] opt for lowering the ambition of the study. When the original ambition was to sort out the *causal effects* of new procedures in civil law on efficiency and satisfaction levels of parties involved, which puts '*attribution*' right into the heart of the study, opt for replacing 'attribution' by '*contribution*' (Mayne, 2012). As attribution analysis implies robust designs, contribution analysis can work with less robust designs, while partly compensating the 'loss' of 'validity' by using strong, i.e. corroborated theories and research evidence from repositories as sources of information to back up empirical findings and to follow the *general elimination method* (GEM), in which the hypothesis that the intervention can explain the outcomes, is 'bashed', i.e. seriously criticized, while doing the same to rival explanations.[30]
- Third, if these options are practically impossible, refrain from doing the study.

ENDNOTES

1. Prevalence is a measure of how commonly a 'condition' occurs in a population. Incidence measures the rate of occurrence of new cases of a 'condition'.
2. Campbell and Stanley (1963: 6) call such a design 'pre-experimental'.
3. Usually one refers to a 'control group' when using an experimental design (as randomization ensures that there is no systematic difference in the distribution of subject characteristics between the two groups) and a 'comparison group', when working with a quasi-experimental design (Bamberger et al, 2012: 217).
4. For differences between experiments and quasi-experiments, see section 6.2 below.
5. An example is the evaluation of the change in the soft drugs policy of the Netherlands government by van Ooyen-Houben et al (2014). Implementation of several elements of the new policy started in the southern provinces of the Netherlands in 2012 (stage 1 of the evaluation). It was planned that in 2013 implementation would take place in the central and northern parts of the country (stage 2). During 2014 several other aspects of the policy change would finally be implemented. However, in the course of 2013 the policy (and implementation) changed (drastically) due to political developments (Ooyen-Houben et al, 2013), making this pipeline design no longer applicable.
6. Sometimes authors refer to what they call 'design approaches' (Stern et al, 2012). One of the consequences of using this word is that 'theory-driven studies', 'systematic research reviews' and 'participatory studies' are brought under this label. However, experiments, quasi-experiments, case studies and the other designs all can 'use' a theory-driven approach, as well as a systematic research review. Then the term 'research design' no longer has a distinctive value.
7. The multiple case study and the meta-analysis are – as an example – capable of detecting correlation and suggestions for causal relationships.
8. One way to describe what 'action research' entails is this. The essentials follow a characteristic cycle whereby initially an exploratory stance is adopted, where an understanding

of a problem is developed and plans are made for some form of interventional strategy. Then the intervention is carried out (the 'action') during which time, pertinent observations are collected in various forms. The new interventional strategies are carried out, and this cyclic process repeats, continuing until a sufficient understanding of (or a valid implementation solution for) the problem is achieved. We refer for more information to Kemmis and McTaggart (2000) and Reason and Bradbury (2001).

9. It is generally agreed that the 'seminal ideas for experimental designs can be traced to Sir Ronald Fisher. The publication of Fisher's Statistical methods for research workers in 1925 and The design of experiments in 1935 gradually led to the acceptance of what today is considered the cornerstone of good experimental design: randomization. Prior to Fisher's work, most researchers used systematic schemes rather than randomization to assign participants to the levels of a treatment' (Kirk, 2009: 24).
10. http://www.socialresearchmethods.net/kb/index.php, accessed 27 November 2015.
11. Cook and Campbell were possibly the first to consider the potential for experimentally staged introduction in a situation when an innovation cannot be delivered concurrently to all units (Brown and Lilford, 2006).
12. This is the younger brother of the QED: variables that are not yet known or are still without data cannot be matched.
13. http://www.gov.scot/resource/doc/175356/0091395.pdf, accessed 27 November 2015.
14. See Bamberger et al (2012: 216ff) and Remler and van Ryzin (2011) who refer to subtypes like the truncated pre-test, post-test and comparison group design. The core of the instrumental variable (IV) approach can be illustrated as follows. Suppose prisoners with a certain cognitive-behavioral problem are treated in prison center 1 always with intervention A and in prison center 2 always with B. If it is by mere chance (i.e. random) who is to stay in which center, then both groups of prisoners are comparable. And if the treatment in these centers – apart from the choice between intervention A or B – is the same, then the comparison between center 1 and center 2 implies a comparison between the effectiveness of intervention A and intervention B. If there is a difference in results between the centers, then this difference can be attributed to the difference in treatment. In technical terms, 'center' is the *instrumental variable*. Amodio (2015) gives an interesting example in the field of crime prevention, studying the relationship between levels of crime, crime protection technology and potential crime victims' knowledge about experiences with criminality of friends and family that do not live in the same region or community as the persons interviewed. Angrist and Pishke (2013) present examples in the field of education.
15. An example is the case-control design, often used by epidemiologists, which compares a group of persons with a particular outcome to an otherwise similar group of people without the outcome (the controls).
16. See also Mann (2003).
17. Also known as 'thick descriptions'. The term was used by Clifford Geertz in his 'The Interpretation of Cultures' (1973: 5, 6, 9, 10).
18. However, Thiem (2014) detected several pitfalls in the 20 evaluation studies that applied this design. They regard the number of cases, the role of 'necessity relations', model ambiguities and several other problems.
19. Zweigert and Kötz (1998) are seen as the founding fathers of the functionality 'school' in comparative legal research. Orücü (2012: 561) defines this school of thought as an approach that 'answers the question: which institution in System B performs an equivalent function to the one under survey in System A or that solve the same problem, that is, similarity of solutions'. This 'method' in law strongly resembles the sociological school of thought, called functionalism, which studied 'functional prerequisites of societies' and was made well-known by Robert K. Merton.
20. He also compares the case study design with the comparative.
21. Those who would have thought that Eberle is positive about the methodology (or the 'design') of comparative legal studies will be disappointed: 'it is clear that comparative law is in need of an overhaul if it is to take its rightful place as an important legal

science. . . . First, we need to focus on developing and applying a sound methodology, as employed in law and economics' (Eberle, 2009: 486).

22. Orücü (2012: 570) sketches the relevance of 'evaluation' as one of the steps of a comparative law study. 'For instance, the comparativist could be looking for the most 'efficient' rule and therefore using the 'law and economics' approach as the touchstone or she could be looking for other values such as 'cheapness of procedure', 'speed of procedure', 'better protection of the victim', 'user-friendliness' and so on'.
23. This design could also be presented as an example of the longitudinal design (see section 6.2.3 above).
24. http://www.psyconsult.de/lehre/ws02_03/Materialien/Cook_Campbell_Threats%20to%20Validity.pdf.
25. Although internal validity is very often used in quantitative studies, there are alternative concepts that are mainly used in qualitative studies: credibility and authenticity. See Chapter 8.
26. See http://www.psyconsult.de/lehre/ws02_03/Materialien/Cook_Campbell_Threats%20to%20Validity, accessed 27 November 2015.
27. STROBE stands for an international, collaborative initiative of epidemiologists, methodologists, statisticians, researchers and journal editors involved in the conduct and dissemination of observational studies, with the common aim of Strenghening The Reporting of OBservational studies in Epidemiology (http://www.strobe-statement.org) (http://www.strobe-statement.org/fileadmin/Strobe/uploads/checklists/STROBE_checklist_v4_combined.pdf, accessed 27 November 2015).
28. Also ethical and practical (like financial) aspects have to be taken into account but are not discussed here.
29. This is the reason why Bamberger et al (2012) referred to 'real world evaluations'. See also Nelen (2008) who makes the point that (quasi-)experiments are not always possible in the world of crime and justice, because of problems of coverage, ethics and bureaucratic complexity.
30. Scriven (1976; 2008) introduced this 'method' in the 1970s, which is intellectually related to Popper's falsificationist approach. A crucial element of GEM is to try to eliminate the explanation that the intervention or program under review has 'caused' the outcomes.

7. Data collection methods

7.1 UNITS OF ANALYSIS, OPERATIONALIZATION AND CODING

Thinking about the '*units of analysis*' is an important task in empirical research; units of analysis include individuals, groups, families, officials, organizations, municipalities, courts, prisons, but also contracts, wills, guidelines, protocols and verdicts. Once the units of analysis have been selected, the next question is: who (or what) is *in* the unit? Are all courts within a country selected or just a sample? Is it a sample of victims under 25 or over 65, or is it the complete demographic spectrum? Are all the documents found in registers and dossiers on procurement fraud the units of analysis, or a sample from those that are less than three years old? When a population is sufficiently large, one can work with *samples*. If the sample is selected randomly and high-quality data collection methods are used (see below; and Chapter 8), statistical techniques to infer information about the broader population (inferential statistics) can be used. Sampling may look simple, but 'is perhaps the messiest part of inferential empirical work'.[1] As sampling is strongly related to the statistical analysis of data, in Chapter 8 we will discuss more in depth (statistical) aspects of sampling.

Often complicated, and also dangerously messy, is *the operationalization of central concepts of the study into variables that can be measured*. Concepts (also known as constructs) are generalizable properties or characteristics associated with objects, events or people (Whetten, 1989; Bhattacherjee, 2012: 26–8). They may have different levels of abstraction and are (sometimes) part of the theory(ies) involved in the research project. Some concepts, such as a person's age are precise and easy to operationalize, while other concepts, such as a person's personality, are more abstract and difficult to operationalize. The former instance (age) is a one-dimensional construct, while the latter is a multi-dimensional construct (i.e. it consists of multiple underlying dimensions). In the theories outlined in Chapter 5, concepts like 'innovation diffusion', 'repeat player versus single shotter', 'deterrence' and 'cognitive dissonance' are multi-dimensional. The same is true for legal constructs like gap-filling (in contracting), public private partnerships, human rights, procedural justice and rule-jungling.

A variable is a measurable representation of a concept. For instance, a person's intelligence is often measured as his or her IQ score, which is an index generated from tests. In this case, intelligence is the concept, and IQ score the variable, measured by using an IQ test. Variables that explain other variables are called independent variables, those that are explained are called dependent variables (Bhattacherjee, 2012). The link with theories will be evident. Operationalization is the process of 'transforming' concepts into variables that can be measured. In Box 7.1 examples of how to operationalize are presented.

After operationalization, decisions on how to collect data and how to code them is the next step. We start with the coding process:

> Coding data . . . is [the] task in empirical scholarship that is universal, no matter whether the data are quantitative or qualitative, from where the hypothesis and data come. . . . Coding is the process of translating properties or attributes of the world (variables) into a form that is susceptible to systematic analysis. The process itself entails, first, developing a precise scheme to account for the values of each variable and, second, methodically and physically assigning all units a value for each variable. (Epstein and Martin, 2014: 95)

Codes can be based on theories but also on themes, topics, concepts, terms or keywords found in the data. Having codes is not enough; a coding list ('a detailing of each variable of interest along with the values of each variable, such as the variable "prosecutor's gender" with the values: male and female') is necessary but, again, not enough. The reason is simple: ELR will hardly ever deal with only one or two variables. To allow for data analysis, the researchers have to assign all units of study a value for each variable. That implies making a codebook to 'house the scheme and other relevant information and to determine how they will ultimately enter their data into a statistical software package so that they can analyze them' (Epstein and Martin, 2014: 106).[2]

Let us move to the three types of data ELR usually works with: stored data, primary data and Big Data.[3]

7.2 TYPE I DATA: STORED DATA, INCLUDING REGISTER AND ADMINISTRATIVE DATA

Data are stored in data warehouses of national science foundations, universities, research organizations and (national) statistical offices and other organizations, and are – sometimes – available for analysis by the scientific community. Given the attention paid to the Open Data policy in Europe and the USA, availability will probably be increasing. *Stored data*

BOX 7.1 FROM SIMPLE TO MORE COMPLEX OPERATIONALIZATIONS

Example 1

The *research problem* is: what causes growth problems of children in country X, region Q? The *hypothesis* is: children in that region don't eat enough vegetables (and children who do grow more quickly). To study this hypothesis, concepts need to be operationalized. What is meant by children? What age are they? How is growth defined? Is it weight, height, mental growth or strength? What is enough? What does the expression 'more quickly' mean? What timescale will be used to measure this? What are vegetables? There are dozens of (types of) vegetables, each containing different levels of vitamins and minerals. Are the children fed raw vegetables, or are they cooked?

Source: http://www.experiment-resources.com/operationalization.html#ixzz23gWk2x8K, accessed 6 July 2015.

Example 2

The *research problem* is: will more European funds to SMMEs (small, medium and micro enterprises) and more government-sponsored 'business-links brokerage' organizations stimulate the establishment of SMME's and contribute to economic growth and job creation in countries X,Y and Z?

The *theory* is that government funding through subsidies will work as prompts for entrepreneurs stimulating them to get their business going and/or brought to a higher gear, while business-links brokerage organizations will help inform them about rules, regulations, market chances, partners, networks, etc., which will also give a boost to economic growth and job creation.

Operationalization:

What are SMMEs: are demarcations clear and can they be applied to organizations (when is an organization small, medium?).

When is something a government fund?: subsidies, credits, loans? Will all types of subsidies (cash, in kind) and all kinds of credits be included?

When is something a business-links brokerage: are demarcations between general consulting firms and focused brokerage organizations '*klip und klar*'? Can sole traders act as a business-links brokerage? Is there a registration of criteria and characteristics of these brokerages?

What is economic growth?

What is job creation?

Source: Carmichael (2009).

Example 3

The *research problem* is: 'previous studies on contractual complexity employ objective measures such as the number of pages, the number of kilobytes, or the number of provisions to measure this complexity. . . . We argue that the degree to which a contract imposes a cognitive load on contract parties should be taken as another important dimension of contractual complexity' (Hagedoorn and Hesen, 2009). The research problem is to what extent quantitative objective measures of complexity (e.g. length), objective elements of cognitive load (e.g. time on-task) and subjective elements of cognitive load (e.g. mental effort) do measure different aspects of contractual complexity.

The *theory*: Hagedoorn and Hesen (2009) developed 'a conceptual model of the complexity of contracts using a multidimensional perspective where both objective and subjective dimensions are taken into account. Our empirical analysis combines a sample of nearly 400 R&D alliance contracts in the biopharmaceutical industry with a measurement of the cognitive load of these contracts.

Operationalization:
First, the well-known measures of contractual complexity were used (kilobytes, number of words and number of pages). The authors also developed a questionnaire for the pilot study with five questions based on validated and widely used items found in the cognitive load literature. Cognitive load comprises mental load, mental effort and performance. For example: as an indirect subjective measure, the participants (of the pilot study) were asked to report the invested mental effort necessary to understand the materials, adopted from an already existing scale. The measurement of experienced stress levels was adopted from the Subjective Workload Assessment Technique (SWAT) and the National Aeronautics and Space Administration – Task Load Index (NASA-TLX). In cognitive load research, seven-point Likert scales are frequently used to measure the invested mental effort and the difficulty of the materials.[1]

[1] We have picked a few items from this study that analyzed hundreds of contracts in a pilot stage and during the actual study.

Source: Hagedoorn and Hesen (2009).

have already been collected, coded and cleaned. Researchers use these data not only for answering substantive research questions, but also for replications of studies, to find out if the findings and conclusions hold when different conditions, different populations or different time periods are part of the study. Sometimes researchers are engaged in replications to review the quality of the data (analysis).

For empirical legal research, several organizations store relevant register data and data from other sources (like surveys). One is the *(national) statistical office*. Statistics Netherlands for example is responsible for statistics to be used in practice, by policy makers and for scientific research. The information this organization publishes incorporates a multitude of societal aspects, from macro-economic indicators such as economic growth and consumer prices to judiciary decisions (verdicts, number of victims, number of crimes), health and cultural participation. Of particular importance is its Social Statistical Database (SSB), which consists

BOX 7.2 OPEN GOVERNMENT DATA (OGD)

Relatively new are *Open Government Data (OGD)*. This concept refers to data that governments actively publish on the internet for public reuse and which can be assessed without restrictions and used without payment (Grimmelikhuijsen and Meijer, 2014). The European Union uses the term 'Public Sector Information' to refer to OGD. More governments are starting the development and implementation of OGD infrastructures (Conradie and Choenni, 2014).

of a number of interconnected registers, where demographic and socio-economic micro-data are included. In addition, there are SSB satellites that describe a particular topic in detail based on combinations of registers including information on variables and stemming from governmental and other organizations. Examples of satellites are crime and justice, economic development, labour force and unemployment and health. Because the information is coupled for a number of years on the level of individual (anonymized) persons, people can be followed over time. Ministries, municipalities, courts and other (legal) actors usually also collect and store data, though it is often less readily available.

International organizations like the World Bank, the IMF, the OECD and *Eurostat* also collect large amounts of data on topics relevant for ELR (e.g. public private partnerships).

Data-archives of social science research organizations store survey data (like opinion surveys, victim's surveys, housing and health surveys) and data from behavioral studies. An example is *DANS*: Data Archiving and Networked Services Netherlands, which promotes sustained access to digital research data. *DANS* encourages researchers to archive and reuse data in a sustained manner, e.g. through online archiving systems.

Another type of *data archive is the one that deals with typically legal topics like wills, contracts, guidelines, verdicts and rulings etc*. The Stanford Law Faculty has several (Gordon, 1998). One is the Intellectual Property Litigation Clearinghouse. This free online tool provides real-time data on intellectual property litigation. A private-venture outgrowth of that clearinghouse, *LexMachina* (LM), is a web-based software and data analysis service that creates structured or tagged data sets of judges, lawyers, parties and patents gleaned from case dockets and documents obtained from the Public Access to Court Electronic Records system, the US International Trade Commission's Electronic Documents Information System and the US Patent and Trademark Office. All sources are processed by a natural-language processing engine, which cleans up data (e.g. makes consistent case and party names), codes or classifies it, and then tags it for searching and analysis via LM's web application. It is getting close to Legal Big Data (see section 7.4 below).

An example from the Netherlands is the *WODC database of neurolaw cases.* In order to answer the question, to what extent neuroscience plays a role in Dutch civil law cases, out of a pre-selection of 1500 cases, approximately 300 cases, in which neuro-scientific information plays a role, have been selected for further investigation. This data base of neuro-law cases is expanded annually (Kogel and Westgeest, 2015).

Finally, there are *databases (of research organizations) in which administrative data from governmental organizations (active in the field of law, regulation, crime and justice) are stored.* Examples are data from (penal) law cases or other judiciary processes. In the Netherlands the WODC of the Dutch Ministry of Security and Justice has a *data warehouse on the criminal law chain.* It consists of data from various organizations, each of which operate relatively autonomously and independently. This means that each organization registers data in its own way and in its own operational systems. Important databases of these organizations are the national database(s) of the Dutch police (containing information about crime reports and suspects), of the Public Prosecutor Service, which contains information about judicial cases, the Prison Agency, the Child Care and Protection Board, Probation Officers, and the Central Fine Collection Agency. These organizations all contain data about individuals and their actions. However, the systems are not built from the same perspective, and they differ in many other aspects (see Figure 7.1).

Making combinations, following persons and/or cases through the penal law chain, analyzing caseloads and elapsed time, checking for 'missing cases (and persons)' and many other topics could not have been studied, had there been no data warehouse – the central repository of data collected from these different sources. These data are stored and structured in such a way that

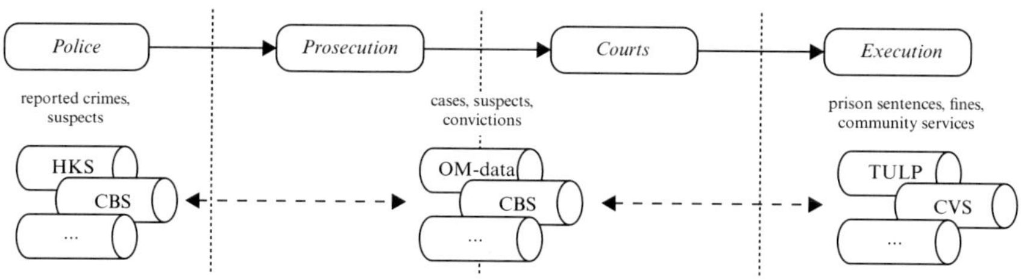

Figure 7.1 Examples of databases in the Dutch criminal law chain

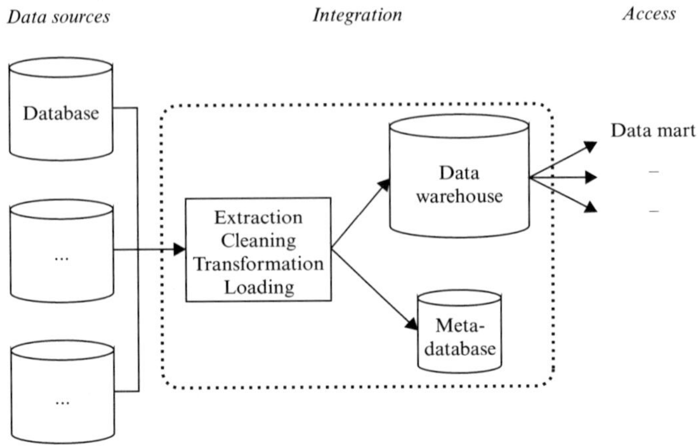

Figure 7.2 An overview of the data warehouse approach

querying and reporting are facilitated. It provides a uniform data model for all data regardless of their source (van den Braak et al, 2013) (see Figure 7.2).

Box 7.3 gives an example of a study made possible through this data warehouse.

BOX 7.3 ON THE DEVIANT AGE-CRIME CURVE OF AFRO-CARIBBEAN POPULATIONS. THE CASE OF ANTILLEANS LIVING IN THE NETHERLANDS (JENNISSEN, 2014)

Jennissen investigated the extent to which the 'conventional' age-crime curve (characterized by quickly rising crime figures during puberty, which peak in the late adolescence and early adulthood but then go down to a comparatively very low level for people in their middle-ages) also applied for Antilleans, Moroccans, Turks, Surinamese and people of Dutch native heritage. For this study, the author used the national database of the Dutch police to construct the age-crime curves. These data were coupled on a person-to-person basis with the SSB (Social Statistical Database, Statistics Netherlands; anonymized). To a large part a cohort study design was applied (see Chapter 5).

The study found that the crime figures among Antilleans (people from islands in the Caribbean Sea) residing in the European country of the Netherlands remain high for offenders in their twenties and thirties, unlike other major ethnic groups residing in the Netherlands. The research comprises a quantitative analysis of data regarding people who are registered as offenders in the Netherlands. This study has found indications that the high level of broken families might be related to comparatively high rates of offenders among adult Antillean men aged up to approximately 45 years.

The UK Ministry of Justice's Justice Data Lab (JDL) (Lyon et al, 2015) is to some extent an equivalent of the WODC's data warehouse. JDL works with large sets of government administrative data. JDL has 'as of September 2014 provided 117 analyses to charities, social enterprises, public and private sector organizations in England and Wales' (ibid., p. 233).[4]

All these examples mostly deal with *public records*. There are also *personal documents* (NSF, 2002). These:

> first-person accounts of events and experiences are 'documents of life' and include diaries, portfolios, photographs, artwork, schedules, scrapbooks, poetry, letters to the paper, etc. Unlike other sources of qualitative data, collecting data from documents is relatively invisible to, and requires minimal cooperation from, persons within the setting being studied. Information from documents also can be used to generate interview questions or identify events to be observed.

7.3 TYPE II DATA: PRIMARY ('NEW') DATA AND METHODS

Data collection methods can be *quantitative or qualitative*, *obtrusive or unobtrusive* and *multi-method* and *multi-source*.

In *qualitative studies* data are usually collected through four main methods, used individually or in combination: observation, interviews, document analyses and the analysis of movies, pictures, audio and (other) (internet) sources. As Webley (2010: 928) makes clear, 'the data can take a number of forms. It may include notes made by the researcher that provide a detailed description of what, where and how people did what they did, their interactions, processes or a description of the researcher's observation to text-based sources, sounds, video or images, transcripts of meetings, etc.'. Focus groups are part of the toolkit. *Quantitative methods* involve the use of numerical measurement: quantitative data is data in number form.

Obtrusive data collection is data collection where the researcher makes his presence clear to participants; participants know they are part of a study; they know that they will be asked questions, react to vignettes, mail back an envelope (in postal surveys) or answer a computer-assisted questionnaire online. The researcher asks questions on attitudes about a new penal sanction, another wants to know what you think about the existing refugee law, or is asking what your current income is (or when you plan to finish your PhD). As people lie and cheat (for whatever reason) and forget (as they are sometimes sloppy 'time managers'), there is no a priori certainty about the truth level of their statements, i.e. to what extent they reveal what the people 'really' think, believe, plan and do.

Unobtrusive data collection is more or less the opposite; the respondents or 'units of analysis' do not know (or see or experience) that they or their behavior, or the consequences of their behavior, is/are measured. Unobtrusive measures are measures that do not require the researcher to intrude in the research context (of 'respondents'). They are hidden, and are often low-key. Instead of asking what people drink during a party, an unobtrusive approach would collect empty cans and bottles from the relevant garbage dump (or garden), count their numbers (and the number of party goers) and analyze brands and labels. There are other examples: to ascertain popularity of journals in waiting rooms in hospitals, one can observe their wear and tear. Entry counters in a supermarket provide evidence from which side the customers come in. Hidden cameras can show consumer behavior in the store.

While a few decades ago in the social sciences, paradigm wars were fought between adherents of the qualitative or quantitative 'schools', these 'wars' nowadays have more or less disappeared. One, if not the most important, reason is that researchers 'from both sides' have reached the conclusion that *multi-method and multi-source research* is often more appropriate than single method studies. Later we will come back to this, including a short discussion on what is meant by the buzz word 'triangulation' (see also Chapter 8).

We start with methods that are *typically obtrusive*, then discuss *typically unobtrusive* methods, and we end with methods that, depending on the way they are operated, can be *obtrusive or unobtrusive*.

BOX 7.4 OBTRUSIVE METHODS OF DATA COLLECTION

The survey (using questionnaires)

Surveys are a popular form of data collection, especially when gathering information from larger groups, where standardization is important. Surveys can be constructed in many ways, but they always consist of two components: questions and responses. Standardization is realized by working with structured interviews.[1] An example is the international crime victim survey (ICVS) (see http://english.wodc.nl/onderzoeksdatabase/icvs-2005-survey.aspx?cp=45&cs=6798, accessed 27 November 2015).

There are different kinds of surveys: *face-to-face, telephone, paper, pencil and online surveys*. Surveys usually focus on *actual situations* but *hypothetical question surveys* are also used. Then, respondents are confronted with information on policy measures, legal arrangements or products/devices that do not (already) exist. Sometimes respondents' decision-making processes are followed and registered by asking if and to what extent their behavior *would change, would have been changed or would not change, if* (legal) intervention Y had been implemented (or legal arrangement P made available). An example is Thompson and Appelbaum's (1974) study of the social acceptance of population policy in the USA. Related to the hypothetical question-surveys are *'stated preference surveys'*, *'willingness to pay (and to accept)' surveys* and *'vignette surveys'*. Short descriptions of situations or persons (vignettes) are shown to respondents in order to elicit their opinions/judgments or (behavioral) intentions.

The (in-depth) interview

In a study by Wijkhuis et al (2011) the 'pardon regulation', which took effect in the Netherlands in 2007, and meant that residence permits would be officially granted to a delimited group of asylum seekers, was evaluated in terms of its social acceptance and impact. In-depth interviews were conducted with 59 respondents. In another evaluation (of the Dutch naturalization ceremony) some 45 in-depth interviews were carried out (Wubs et al, 2010).

Sometimes in-depth interviews are conducted with (only) key informants (NSF, 2002).

The focus group method[2]

Focus groups are a form of group interview that capitalizes on communication between research participants in order to generate data. Although group interviews are often used as a quick and convenient way to collect data from several people simultaneously, focus groups explicitly use group interaction as part of the method. This means that instead of the researcher asking each person to respond to a question in turn, people are encouraged to talk to one another: asking questions, exchanging anecdotes and commenting on each other's experiences and points of view.
Kromhout and van San (2003) studied the issue of whether ethnic groups in the Netherlands, other than the 'big four' (Surinamese, Antillean/Arubans, Turks and Moroccans), accounted for the relatively large share of juvenile crime, with the goal of finding out whether there is a need for preventive measures. The study concerned juveniles aged 12 to 17 years and young adults aged 18 to 24 years and was limited to first-generation members of ethnic minorities (Western and non-Western). Next to quantitative data, 10 focus group meetings were organized involving 77 professionals whose day-to-day work brought them into contact with juveniles from diverse ethnic groups.

The Delphi method

This method was originally developed as an interactive forecasting method which relied on a panel of experts.[3] The experts answered questionnaires in two or more rounds. After each round, a facilitator provided an anonymous summary of the experts' forecasts from the previous round as well as the reasons they provided for their judgments. Experts were encouraged to revise their earlier answers in light of the replies of other members. It is believed that during this process the range of the answers will decrease and the group will converge towards the 'correct' answer. Finally, the process ended after a pre-defined stop criterion (e.g. number of rounds, achievement of consensus, stability of results). Over the years this method has been applied for more than just forecasting and is also used in evaluation studies and in surveys in general (Hsu and Sandford, 2007).

Measurement scales
Guttman, Thurston and Likert scales measure attitudes, opinions, behavioral intentions and reported behavior. The research project 'Judged by the general population: A study of sentencing preferences in the Netherlands' by Ruiter et al (2011) used several scales. This project studied how the Dutch public, given the opportunity, would sentence perpetrators of different types of crime. One of the scales used was the 'Algemene Bezorgdheid Criminaliteit (ABC)' scale (a scale on the general concern about crime).

[1] Usually there are three modes of doing the survey: *capi*, *cati*, *cawi*. Capi stands for computer-assisted personal interviews, cati for computer-assisted telephone interview and cawi for web interviewing.
[2] Robert K. Merton (Merton et al, 1956) was the first social scientist to develop and use this method in communication studies to explore the effects of films and television programs.
[3] The Delphi technique was mainly developed by Dalkey and Helmer (1963) at the Rand Corporation.

BOX 7.5 DEVICES AND SOFTWARE TO HELP RECORD, SYSTEMATIZE AND CONTENT–ANALYSE

Several technical/digital devices are available (often with low costs) to be used while doing interviews. An example is the *ethnocorder* (http://ethnocorder.com/features/index.php) which has over 20 types of multimedia elements that can be used in either questions or responses including iPhone's built-in microphone, camera and video recorder.

Software programs categorize and analyze data coming from (qualitative) interviews (i.e. content analysis):
Dragon NaturallySpeaking
http://www.nuance.com/for-individuals/by-product/dragon-for-pc/home-version/index.htm
http:// atlasti.com
N6 http://www.qsrinternational.com/
NVivo http://www.qsrinternational.com/
Maxqda http://www.maxqda
http://www.qsrinternational.com/products_nvivo.aspx

All websites accessed 27 November 2015. See also Chapter 8 for more information on qualitative data analysis.

A disadvantage of *interview or questionnaire-oriented methods* is that the interviewee or participants (in a focus group) may distort information through recall error, selective perceptions, desire to please the interviewer or simply because they feel 'the need' to give answers, but do not know right from wrong. Self-report studies may lead to biased reporting. The selection process as to who participates in focus groups and/or surveys is crucial, as are group dynamics, as they can distort the validity of the findings.

With regard to the use of measurement scales, NSF (2002) sees providing objective information on what the test taker knows and can do as advantageous; they (usually) can be scored in a straightforward manner and most of them are accepted by the public as credible indicators. Disadvantages are that the test may be oversimplified and superficial; they may also be time-consuming and may be biased against some groups of test takers.

Box 7.5 mentions devices and software programs that help to record and systematize data collected in (in-depth) interviews and focus groups.

Of a different nature are *institutionalized forms of data collection* like *public hearings*, *truth commissions* and *parliamentary inquiries*. A *public hearing* is often a formal meeting to receive testimony on a proposed (government) action, like legislation. Testimony is usually recorded for public record, and a report summarizing the key points is generated. Sometimes hearings take place before a court. A public hearing may also be less formal. Rowe and Frewer (2000) give an overview of approaches and their restrictions and opportunities.

Frequently, public hearings are applied in conjunction with other types of data collection, like expert panels and systematic research reviews. An interesting example of involving the public is the way in which the US National Academies work with their 'Committee Meetings'.[5] They:

> gather information through – amongst others – meetings that are announced in advance through the National Academies Web site. . . . In accordance with federal law and with few exceptions, [these] meetings of the committee are open to the public, and any written materials provided to the committee by individuals who are not officials, agents, or employees of the National Academies are maintained in a public access file that is available for examination.

Truth commissions have become common components of post-conflict policy throughout the world. Gonzalez et al (2014:10) present data of some 30 truth commissions installed over a period of less than 30 years, while Sirleaf (2014: 2265), looking at a longer historical period, found almost 70. He defines a truth commission as:

> an officially sanctioned non-judicial body organized for a limited time. They are usually set up at a time of transition for the specific purpose of examining serious human rights violations. They aim to achieve restorative-justice goals by combining elements of public truth seeking, victim-offender confrontation, public apology, and historical accounting.

BOX 7.6 UNOBTRUSIVE METHODS OF DATA COLLECTION

Reading lenses

Reading lenses are used when documents are analyzed. One example is the analysis of the impact of neurosciences on US Supreme Court decisions about adolescents' culpability by applying content analyses of the decisions (Steinberg, 2013). For the Netherlands Kogel and Westgeest (2015) undertook something related: 'To assess how neuroscientific and behavioral genetic information are used in criminal justice practice in the Netherlands, we systematically collect Dutch criminal cases in which neuroscientific or behavioral genetic information is introduced. . . . Although cases are diverse, several themes appear, such as pre-frontal brain damage in relation to criminal responsibility and recidivism risk, and divergent views of the implications of neurobiological knowledge about addiction for judging criminal responsibility' (p. 1). Another example is Klein Haarhuis and Niemeijer's (2009) meta-evaluation and synthesis of 59 evaluations of (the impact of) Dutch laws. They applied reading lenses to categorize and analyze the content of the legislative evaluations. One of their tasks was to categorize types of policy interventions, their underlying mechanisms and the results of the evaluations.

Mystery guests

There is a long history of the use of mystery guests in (applied) research, evaluation studies, marketing and auditing. Perhaps one of the oldest studies in which a kind of mystery guest was used and described in a systematic way, was LaPiere (1934). He traveled through the USA together with a 'young Chinese student and his wife. Both were personable, charming, quick to win the admiration and respect of those with whom they had the opportunity to become intimate' (ibid., p. 231). They approached 67 hotels, auto camps and tourist homes for accommodation and ate at 184 restaurants and cafes. LaPiere kept detailed records of the responses of hotel clerks, bell boys, elevator operators and waitresses to the presence of the Chinese couple. So that reactions would not be unduly altered because of his presence, LaPiere often let the Chinese couple secure the room or other accommodations while he took care of the luggage, and whenever possible he allowed them to enter restaurants before him. Next, LaPiere mailed questionnaires to all of the establishments they had visited. He allowed six months to pass between the actual visit and the mailing of the questionnaire, in order to reduce the effect of the Chinese couple's visit. The question of primary interest on the questionnaire was, 'Will you accept members of the Chinese race as guests in your establishment?' These questionnaires were returned by 81 of the restaurants and cafes and 47 of the lodging establishments. This was a response rate of 51%. To ensure that the questionnaire responses were not directly influenced by the Chinese couple's visit, LaPiere also obtained responses to the same questionnaire from 32 hotels and 96 restaurants located in the same regions of the country, but not visited by the travelers. After nearly three years, LaPiere had the data necessary to make a comparison of social attitudes with social behavior. The conclusion was that 'nearly all (over 90%) of the hotels, campgrounds, tourist homes, restaurants, and cafes visited by LaPiere and the Chinese couple replied that they would *not* serve Chinese individuals. In addition, the distribution of responses from the establishments not visited were virtually the same, indicating that the findings were not somehow caused by the travelers' recent visit'. Conclusion: between behavior, attitudes (and behavioral intentions) a *serious discrepancy existed.*

Over the years, the mystery guest method (*simulated patients, pseudo patrons and surrogate shoppers*) has become popular. An important advantage of mystery shopping is that mystery guests are well trained in observations, know the processes of the organization or situation and have only one activity to do: to behave (in a certain way).

Methods measuring products of human behavior that can be found in places and situations where the 'producer' did not know that data would be collected
Ort et al (2014: 1338ff) present an example: *measuring the size of illicit drug use in certain geographic areas by wastewater analysis (WWA)*. 'Illicit drug use is a covert and hidden activity that presents methodological challenges for drug surveillance systems. Questionnaire-based survey methods have traditionally been an important component of the approaches employed to monitor drug use, but it is recognized that these methods are not sufficient to monitor trends in drug use adequately and quickly, and require complementary data from other sources. The analysis of the excretion products of illicit drugs in wastewater [WWA] has been explored since 2008 as an additional approach for estimating illicit drug use within specified regions, i.e. the catchment areas of wastewater treatment plants. While the approach cannot provide information on the behavior of single users and on their demographics, there are a number of ways in which WWA can complement other survey methods and provide additional information to understand the illicit drug situation more clearly. Wastewater data can be obtained within short timeframes, are not prone to response biases and can help in identifying the spectrum of illicit drugs being used by a population. . . . Wastewater studies in different countries have also detected regional variations in illicit drug use. The influence of urbanization on the use of illicit drugs was evaluated in Oregon (USA) and South Australia and Queensland (Australia), concluding that the use of illicit drugs was higher in urban regions compared to more rural areas. Wastewater analysis has also been applied to detect transnational differences in illicit drug use. The consumption of five substances was evaluated by analyzing wastewater from 19 European cities for a 1-week period in 2011.'

Often interviews are an important type of data collection but register data are also used. Sirleaf (2014: 2340ff) reports on problems with the credibility of truth commissions, including the ways in which statements were recorded.

In a study of 88 parliaments worldwide, Yamamoto (2007) presents examples of the tools used by different parliaments to oversee their governments. One of them is the *parliamentary inquiry*. These are established 'to examine the positive and negative aspects of particular policies and to pursue the responsibility of the officials in charge'. Seventy-six of the 88 parliaments surveyed by Yamamoto (2007: 39) have procedures for these committees of inquiry. Hearings under oath are one of the characteristics of (some of) these committees, but other methods are also applied (like administering surveys of opinions and experiences, expert panels and literature reviews).

Unobtrusive measures[6] are measures that do not require the researcher to intrude in the research context.

There are also data collection methods that *can be either used in an unobtrusive or an obtrusive way*.

BOX 7.7 DATA COLLECTION METHODS TO BE USED IN AN OBTRUSIVE OR UNOBTRUSIVE WAY

Observational methods

Observation guides, checklists and recording sheets are examples. Eekelaar, Maclean and Beinart (2000) studied 'the work of solicitors in divorce cases in England and Wales. They observed 10 partner-level solicitors at work for a day (14 days' observation in total as 2 researchers observed some of the solicitors), recording what the solicitors did in descriptive terms)' (Webley, 2010: 946).

The *FaceReader*™ is a software tool for analysis of the six basic facial expressions: happy, sad, scared, disgusted, surprised and angry. In addition, the software tracks the head orientation, enabling tracking of 3D orientation of the head, classifies mouth open-closed, eyes open-shut, and eyebrows raised-neutral-lowered (http://www.noldus.com/content/facereader-4-automatic-facial-expression-analysis-and-emotion-detection, accessed 27 November 2015).

Neurobiological methods: imaging techniques, neuropsychological and physiological instruments

Bio-data are collected in studies looking into biological, neurological and psychological aspects of aggression and persistent antisocial behavior and in studies on neurolaw. They make use of basic neurobiological measurements (including neuropsychological assessments (like the Trail Making Test, the D2 Cancellation task, verbal fluency tests, Iowa Gambling Task, Stroop-Color-Word test and Stop-it task) and resting heart rate assessments) and more complex neurobiological measurements (including physiological measurements of hormones like cortisol or oxytocine and brain imaging techniques ((f)MRIs) and pet-scans (Gao et al, 2012; Wilson and Scarpa, 2012; Cornet, 2015).

Sensor-based data, remote monitoring and webometrics

Due to the digitization of life many more possibilities for unobtrusive and obtrusive data collection have come available. Miller (2012) published the '*Smartphone Psychology Manifesto*' and one of his points is this: 'By 2025 more than 5 billion people on our planet will be using ultra-broadband, sensor-rich smartphones far beyond the abilities of today's iPhones, Androids, and Blackberries. Although smartphones were not designed for psychological research, they can collect vast amounts of ecologically valid data, easily and quickly, from large global samples. If participants download the right "psych apps," smartphones can record where they are, what they are doing and what they can see and hear, and can run interactive surveys, tests, and experiments through touch screens and wireless connections to nearby screens, headsets, biosensors, and other peripherals'. This type of data collection has and will have direct consequences for data collection in many fields of study, including ELR (de Haan et al, 2011: Chapter 23).

Bail (2015: 1, 3) introduced *social media survey apps (SMSAs)* that 'adjoin computational social science methods with conventional survey techniques in order to enable more comprehensive analysis of collective behavior online. Although most apps are designed to improve the convenience of computing technology – often via mobile technology – I argue that app technology also provides a powerful new platform for social science research. SMSAs (1) enable researchers to request permission to access public and nonpublic data from an organization's social media page, (2) survey these organizations in order to capture additional data of interest to a researcher, and (3) return the results of a scholarly analysis back to the organization as incentive for them to share their data and participate in social science research'. Although social media websites such as Facebook and Twitter provide an unprecedented amount of qualitative data about organizations and collective behavior, these new data sources lack critical information about the broader social context of collective behavior – or protect it behind strict privacy barriers. Working with SMSAs is designed to solve both problems.

The rapid decline in the cost of audio and video recording devices, the ability to transmit the information over the internet, and the availability of free or low-cost tools such as Google Earth enable organizations to get much more raw data about what is actually happening on the ground (for example in developing countries) and to make sense of that data by using annotation and sharing features in tools. An example of this type of *remote monitoring* is a tool called FORMA (Forestry Monitoring for Action), developed by the Center for Global Development and the Danish government. It uses satellite imagery to produce monthly maps of deforestation down to a very small scale (Hammer et al, 2009; http://datalab.wri.org/blog/forma-a-near-real-time-alert-system-for-tropical-forest-loss, accessed 27 November 2015).

The research field of *webometrics* (including web care) encompasses various forms of web-based link and text analyses. Webometric studies have included large-scale analyses of social network sites and social websites like Flickr, Twitter and YouTube, as well as areas of the traditional web, such as university websites.[1] The international operating Dutch data sciences firm Coosto has data available from 2009 onwards.

[1] See Mike Thelwall's keynote talk from the OII Symposium 'Social Science and Digital Research: Interdisciplinary Insights', March 2012, http://podcasts.ox.ac.uk/webometrics-evolution-digital-social-science-research-field, accessed 27 November 2015.

7.4 TYPE III DATA: BIG DATA

Strongly related to sensor data and webometrics are *Big Data*. Two messages from a sociologist and a lawyer introduce what Big Data are (Box 7.8).

BOX 7.8 TWO MESSAGES ON BIG DATA

Message 1

Bail (2014: 465) published a paper on the relevance of Big Data for researching organizational cultures and started as follows: 'More data were accumulated in 2002 than all previous years of human history combined. By 2011, the amount of data collected prior to 2002 was being collected every two days. This dramatic growth in data spans nearly every part of our lives from gene sequencing to consumer behavior. While much of these data are binary or quantitative, text-based data is also being accumulated on an unprecedented scale. Yet social scientists – and cultural sociologists in particular – have largely ignored the promise of so-called Big Data'. Bail also reported that 'the rise of the Internet, social media, and digitized historical archives has produced a colossal amount of text-based data in recent years. While computer scientists have produced powerful new tools for automated analyses of such Big Data, they lack the theoretical direction necessary to extract meaning from them'.

Message 2

Zahorsky (2015) mailed the following message to colleagues: 'Lawyers be warned: Big data analytics, such as programs that predict settlement outcomes by a few percentage points, computers that universally interpret and comprehend state and international laws, and competitors who deliver legal services more quickly, cheaply and successfully than traditional bricks-and-mortar law offices are permanently shifting the legal landscape'.

Big Data consist of (call) logs, mobile-banking transactions, online user-generated content such as blog posts, social media, sensor apps and online searches and satellite images, including data held in emails, weblogs, intranets, extranets, etc. As 'older' (paper) documents like wills, contracts, treaties and other legal case material, as well as books, newspapers and TV programs, are digitized, the larger this '(legal) Big Data' become. Usually Big Data are not collected by researchers but generated by machines, networks and human interaction on systems like social media. They are 'born digital'. However, Big Data can also be 'produced' by *digitization* of existing material like legal documents, videos, audio tapes, pictures, archives, company administrations and health reports.[7]

Bail (2014) described the background of this development. The central topic is that huge amounts of text-based information about behavior, attitudes, rules, institutions, decisions and emotions are now available that were unthinkable 20 years ago:

> Between 1995 and 2008 the number of websites expanded by a factor of more than 66 million, recently surpassing 1 trillion. Although sociologists were concerned about digital divides in years past, these inequalities appear to be

> steadily decreasing. According to a 2012 survey, roughly half of all Americans visit a social media site such as Facebook or Twitter each day, producing billions of lines of text in so doing. These trends are markedly higher among younger people, suggesting these trends may only continue to grow over time. Most of the text from social media sites is readily accessible via simple computer programs. Yet the outgrowth in text-based data on the Internet is not limited to social media sites. Screen-scraping technologies can be used to extract information from any number of Internet sites within time frames that are only limited by digital storage capacity. And the potential to collect such data is not only tied to the future, but also the past. Since 1996, the Internet Archive has been storing all text from nearly every website on the Internet. The outgrowth of text-based data is also not confined to the Internet. Thanks to new digital technologies from fields as diverse as library science and communications, an unprecedented amount of qualitative data is being archived. Google alone has already created digital copies of nearly every single book ever written in collaboration with more than 19 million libraries worldwide. Academic data warehouses such as LEXIS-NEXIS or ProQuest now contain digital copies of most of the world's journals, newspapers, and magazines. The Vanderbilt Television News Archive contains copies of most major newscasts produced since 1998. An unprecedented amount of text-based data that describe legislative debates, government reports, and other state discourse is also now available on websites such as the National Archives of the United States and Great Britain.

Data on OECD countries are available and show for many countries similar trends. For the developing world, the UN Global Pulse organization's White Paper 'Big Data for Development: Challenges & Opportunities' describes the spectacular increase in the use of mobile phones/smart phones that produces massive datasets:

> The spread of mobile-phone technology to the hands of billions of individuals over the past decade might be the single most significant change that has affected developing countries since the decolonization movement and the Green Revolution. Worldwide, there were over five billion mobile phones in use in 2010, and of those, over 80% in developing countries. . . . Across the developing world, mobile phones are routinely used not only for personal communications, but also to transfer money, to search for work, to buy and sell goods, or transfer data such as grades, test results, stock levels and prices of various commodities, medical information, etc. (UN Global Pulse, 2012: 9)[8]

Although '*born digital*' Big Data are relevant for empirical legal research, the same is true for information *not* 'born digital' but 'transformed' into Big Data. As the legal profession has been active for centuries in registering decisions, motivations, contracts, litigation and much more, there is a plethora of digitazible material. Stevenson and Wagoner (2014) describe an example of the relevance and the 'transformation' of legal material 'into' Big Data. The authors focus on litigation in the USA:

BOX 7.9 EXAMPLES OF THE PERVASIVENESS OF SENSORS, DIGITAL SERVICE DELIVERY AND LEGAL BIG DATA

Smart roofs to help NYC cops fight crime and collect data

New York Police Commissioner Bill Bratton announced in June 2014 the use of urban infrastructure as a new form of surveillance. The murder rate in New York City is lower than ever, but in public housing projects, shootings are up 32%. In addition to flooding those areas with additional police officers, New York Police Department commissioner is launching a two-year, $1.5 million pilot program to install microphone-based rooftop sensors in select locations. ShotSpotter, which makes the sensors, aims to help police work more effectively by providing data on gunfire incidents, many of which go unreported. The sensors use triangulation to pinpoint the location of a gunshot in real-time. Analysts can then separate noise like firework explosions from the recorded data, and ultimately – hopefully – make police deployment more effective over time.[1]

Digital delivery of legal services

Many jurisdictions see the benefit of a website which offers itself as a resource on the law, sources of legal assistance and venues of determination of dispute for those on low incomes. The precise form of provision, already available or planned, reflects particular local circumstances. Roger Smith (http://www.thelegaleducationfoundation.org/digital-report, accessed 27 November 2015) addressed the question whether the internet could transform legal services for people on low incomes. He discussed several examples of portals where digital delivery is up and running, covering examples from Canada, the UK, the Netherlands and the USA: Advice Portals; Interactive information; Parental support – developing skills; Online communities; Developing avatars; Remembering basics; and Challenges for government. These portals are services but at the same time data 'collecting' machines.

'Should we graph the entire justice system?' Puig and Garcia Torrent's (Stanford University) work on a project 'Big data and the law: should we graph the entire justice system' states: 'Justice Systems can be represented as a graph: a network of nodes linked by different kinds of relationships. This approach allows for the discovery of emerging patterns and features otherwise unnoticed within the massive amounts of disjointed data generated by courts and tribunals – therefore shedding new, much needed light on the interactions of all players and constituent elements involved in law. . . . The goal is to create a semantic web covering entire jurisdictions, enabling a much deeper analysis of every player and constituent part, as well as a better understanding of the Justice system as a whole' (https://experiment.com/projects/can-we-improve-international-justice-using-analytics, accessed 27 November 2015).

[1] See http://www.citylightcap.com/news/2014/ShotSpotter/2014-06-16-smart-roofs-to-help-nyc-cops-fight-crime.php, accessed 27 November 2015).

> Litigation data means (1) the basic information about a given case, such as the names of the parties, attorneys, nature of suit, and other characteristics about the case (otherwise referred to as 'case meta-data'); (2) information reflected on the electronic docket sheet for a given case; and (3) the electronic court records associated with a given case. . . . When aggregated on a large scale and then filtered using software, patterns and trends begin to surface that shed light on how parties, attorneys, and judges typically behave during the litigation process. (ibid., p. 16)

The active final active category of litigation data that the authors discuss are court records:

> Court records tell the story of a given case. To initiate a lawsuit in district court, a plaintiff must file a complaint that sets forth a valid legal basis for relief and factual allegations that would, if true, justify such relief. A defendant will then respond to the complaint by filing an answer, motion to dismiss, or any number of other legal instruments. After reaching a final decision in a given case, a judge may issue an order, ruling, or judgment accompanied by a written opinion in which the judge will articulate his or her findings of fact and conclusions of law in support of their decision. (ibid., p. 28)

Information on these processes and outcomes nowadays are digitally trackable and researchable through PACER,[9] also part of the (Legal) Big Data World.

Van Rijmenam (2015) gives a few examples from the world of US legal firms. One refers to Lexis Advance MedMal Navigator that offers predictions on potential medical-malpractice cases. LexMachina offers for patent lawyers what MedMal Navigator does for malpractice. This web-based service crawls the internet for data from all known, reliable sources of patent law information and auto-loads it into a master database (Dysart, 2013). Ravellaw.com (a legal search engine) is a third example.

BOX 7.10 RAVEL LAW AS AN EXAMPLE OF VISUALIZED LEGAL BIG DATA

Ravel Law[1] shows what working with and visualizing legal Big Data looks like: 'If you sign on to Ravel Law, you will find a simple search field with no instructions. Plug in a term – let's say: climate change. While working with *Westlaw* and *Lexis* you will receive a list of cases, in Ravel Law you receive something very different. Ravel Law gives you the list of cases, to be sure, but it also displays an interactive graphic representation of the citation network of all cases using the search term. The visual representation allows the user effortlessly and instantly to identify cases citing cases, the strength of each case as a citation source for others, and the timeline of cases in the network. So, if a practitioner wants to identify the "big case" in a topic, or to quickly trace the growth of the topic in case law, Ravel Law finds it for you in seconds, whereas piecing that together through traditional searches would take hours and a lot of mental gymnastics'.

[1] https://www.ravellaw.com/, accessed 27 November 2015. This is based on J. B. Ruhl's 'Law 2050' post on http://law2050.com/tag/ravel-law/, accessed 27 November 2015.

Is a (research) world with Big Data a world *without (methodological or statistical) difficulties?* That would be a gross misunderstanding. Harford (2014: 17) mentions two:

> Because found (Big) Data sets are so messy, it can be hard to figure out what biases lurk inside them – and because they are so large, some analysts seem to have decided the sampling problem isn't worth worrying about. . . . An example is Twitter. It is in principle possible to record and analyze every message on Twitter and use it to draw conclusions about the public mood. (In practice, most researchers use a subset of that vast 'fire hose' of data.) But while we can look at all the tweets, Twitter users are not representative of the population as a whole. (According to the Pew Research Internet Project, in 2013, US-based Twitter users were disproportionately young, urban or suburban, and black. . . . 'N = All' is often a seductive illusion. (ibid., p. 18)

The second difficulty of Big Data is that they 'do not solve the problem that has obsessed statisticians and scientists for centuries: the problem of insight, of inferring what is going on, and figuring out how we might intervene to change a system for the better' (ibid., p. 19). In Chapter 8, section 8.7, examples of how to work with Big Data are presented.

7.5 MIXED METHODS RESEARCH AND TRIANGULATION

Nielsen (2010: 953) describes mixed or multi-method research (MMR) as:

> any research that uses more than one research technique to study one or several closely related phenomena. Research that employs multiple 'tactics' for observing and understanding is more reliable than a single study, if the studies are of comparable quality. The term 'triangulation' is often used to describe deployment of multiple methods.

The methodological assumption is that combining two (or more) methods pays off in improved instrumentation for all data collection approaches and in sharpening the researcher's understanding of

BOX 7.11 EXAMPLES OF MIXED METHODS IN EMPIRICAL LEGAL RESEARCH

The *Civil Litigation Research Project (CLRP)* (Nielsen, 2010: 957) studied civil litigation in the USA by making use of a survey in five federal judicial districts in the USA, to study the claiming behavior of individuals involved in disputes that might have become lawsuits, quantitative data on the 'litigation explosion', and observations of lawyers and non-lawyers in a variety of advocacy settings.

Youth delinquency trends in the Netherlands have been studied by Van der Laan and Blom (2011). The research problem was as follows: *Which developments occurred in the proportion, nature, and settlement of juvenile delinquency in the period of 1996–2010?* The authors combined methods on the basis of self-reported delinquency on the one hand, and police and judicial statistics on the other hand. By means of self-reporting, they obtained insight into the number of young people who stated that they had been guilty of committing an offence in a specific period, the 'self-reported offenders'. Police statistics provided them insight into the number of arrested suspects of an offence. The judicial data provided insight into the number of prosecuted offenders in respect of whom the Public Prosecution Service considered it advisable to initiate criminal proceedings and whose offence had been settled in court.

findings. A typical study might start out with a qualitative segment such as a focus group discussion alerting the researcher to issues that should be explored in a survey of program participants, followed by the survey, which in turn is followed by in-depth interviews to clarify some of the survey findings.

We referred to using (self-report) surveys and register data (police, public prosecutor) with regard to criminal offenses. To what extent one source is more reliable than the other (and to what extent there is over- or under-reporting of criminal offenses) has been an issue for quite some time. In a special issue of *Criminal Behaviour and Mental Health*, Farrington and Ttofi (2014) studied differences and similarities between (self-report) surveys and official records of arrests/convictions:

> These two methods have different advantages and problems. For example, official records include only the 'tip of the iceberg' of offending, but the offences are recorded quite accurately and completely for very large samples. Self-reports, on the other hand, reveal more of the 'dark figure' of offending but they have problems of exaggeration and concealment and also problems of missing data in interviewed samples compared with target samples. The most delinquent people are often the most difficult to interview. . . . One of the main aims of this special issue [of the journal] is to compare information about criminal careers from official records with information from self-reports. (ibid., pp. 225ff)

Some conclusions from seven longitudinal studies done in four countries are as follows:

- Self-reports of offending show that many more (over 20 times as many) crimes are committed compared with offences that lead to convictions.
- The vast majority of males have committed an offence that, in theory, could have led to a conviction.
- Generally, the most frequent offenders according to self-reports are the most likely to be convicted.
- Self-reports of offending predict future convictions.
- Criminal careers last longer according to self-reports than according to official records of convictions.
- The age of onset of offending is a few years earlier in self-reports than in convictions, providing an opportunity for early intervention to prevent persistence and escalation in offending. (ibid., p. 228)

Although these findings only go back to the criminological problem of how to measure (re)offending, for other fields covered by ELR, these insights are relevant too (conflicts mentioned in surveys versus those addressed by mediators and courts; digital piracy, etc.).

Recently, Blok and Pedersen (2014) published a paper with the challenging sub-title 'Quali-quantitative experiments in a Big Data world'. The authors add to the menu, *mixing Big Data with traditional data-collection methods*. They describe how in their project this remixing mixed methods takes place (ibid., p. 2):

> The Copenhagen Social Networks Study is a large-scale cross-disciplinary research program . . . to make continuous recordings of social interactions at all communication channels among an entire freshman class (N>1000) of the Danish Technical University students, using smart phones distributed to students as measurement devices ('socio-meters'). This allows us to digitally map out the 'complete' social network of an entire freshman class, including face-to-face encounters via Bluetooth, geo-location proximities via GPS, social network data via apps, and telecommunication data via call logs. . . . Also, by way of 'embedding' an anthropologist, 'thick' ethnographic fieldwork data on friendship and other social relations amongst the same group of students [is done]. Simultaneously, researchers track different components of the social fabric via the application of established survey methods.

7.6 QUALITY CRITERIA

Gomm (2008) for empirical research in general, and Epstein and Martin (2014) for ELR in particular have suggested several criteria.

7.6.1 Criteria 1 and 2: Validity and Reliability

Validity and reliability of measurement instruments are – together with objectivity[10] – 'the traditional criteria by which scientific research is judged. This is accepted by most quantitative researchers and by many qualitative researchers. *Validity*, for an instrument, is about whether it gives accurate measures of what it purports to be measuring. *Reliability* is whether the instrument does this consistently; whether it gives the same results in the same circumstances' (Gomm, 2008: 33ff). There are subtypes of these criteria (ibid., pp. 34–9). With regard to qualitative (empirical legal) research, Webley (2010: 935) adds the criterion of 'dependability' (or 'integrity' or 'trustworthiness'), indicating to which extent researchers and their findings are free from bias. Epstein and Martin (2014: 50ff) discuss 'face validity', 'unbiasedness' and 'efficiency', while mentioning the caveat 'that meeting all of them isn't always necessary, and together they are not always sufficient even though collectively they are often helpful in understanding when a measure is more or less valid'. *Face validity* is when 'a measure is consistent with prior evidence of all sorts: including all quantitative, qualitative and even impressionistic reports or anecdotes'. They warn the reader that going for face validity is not a casual armchair judgment, but instead a careful comparison of the new measure and extant evidence (ibid., p. 51). Data collection is *unbiased* when the measures 'are right on average across repeated applications'. *Efficiency* means that when there are several unbiased measures to choose from, those with lesser registered errors are to be preferred over others.

Demand characteristics and other *bias-inducing characteristics of data-collection instruments* should also be mentioned. 'Demand characteristics' is a term to denote the situation wherein the results of an empirical study are biased because the researchers' expectancies regarding the performance of the participants (people interviewed for example) on a particular task, create an implicit demand for the participants to perform (or answer) as expected. They are 'the biases that result from the adoption of a specific role by the subject who believes that he or she has discerned the objective of the study, or provoked by a reaction to the decoding of an (experimental) manipulation'.[11] MacCoun (1998) and Kirk (2009) give an overview of these biases (in psychological research and related to designs and data collection methods) and several ways to combat them.

Validity and reliability are related to the *measurement theory* that guides

> **BOX 7.12 EXAMPLES OF DEMAND CHARACTERISTICS, PARTICIPANT-PREDISPOSITION EFFECTS AND EXPERIMENTER-EXPECTANCY EFFECTS**
>
> *Social desirability* means if study participants consistently give the answer that the investigator wants to hear, then information bias would occur.
>
> *Recall decay* means the decline in the ability to retrieve information from memory as the event to be remembered recedes in time.
>
> *Forward telescoping* means the misperception that an event occurred more recently than it really did.
>
> *The halo effect* is a cognitive bias in which our judgments of a person's character can be influenced by our overall impression of him/her. It can be found in a range of situations – from the courtroom to the classroom and in everyday interactions. It will also happen when the wording of questions and the order in which they are asked are formulated in one direction (i.e. a positive one).

the work of researchers when collecting data. Why certain scales are used, why a telephone survey is preferred over an online survey, why register data on fiscal items are believed to 'speak the truth' and interviews are not or are less likely to do so, and to what extent expressing a person's response to an item in a test is associated with the underlying 'latent variable', which is meant to be known through using this test, are questions addressed by measurement theory. The underlying latent variable in – for example – forensic psychological investigations could be a feeling of a depression: to what extent can a researcher be certain that scores on a depression-scale, and in particular the items X to Z, are corresponding with reality?

In Chapter 8 we pay attention to reliability (and validity) when statistical indicators are used to judge – among others – scales.

7.6.2 Criterion 3: Ethics

Collecting data on attitudes and behavior in general, but perhaps even more so when it concerns attitudes and behavior regarding legal issues, requires careful procedures that are ethically (and legally) sound. Miles and Huberman (1994) list several issues that researchers should consider when analyzing data. They caution researchers to be aware of these and other issues before, during and after the research has been conducted. Some of the issues involve the following:

- Informed consent (Do participants have full knowledge of what is involved?)

- Harm and risk (Can the study hurt participants?)
- Honesty and trust (Is the researcher being truthful in presenting data?)
- Privacy, confidentiality, and anonymity (Will the study intrude too much into group and/or individual behavior?)
- Intervention and advocacy (What should researchers do if participants display harmful or illegal behavior?)

Three of these we discuss more in depth. The first is *consent*. There are instances in which consent is inferred, such as when the researcher is observing participants in public, or when consent to participate was previously gained by another researcher or agency. When data are collected directly from participants (e.g. via surveys or interviews) for the first time, the researcher must assess the participants' willingness and ability to voluntarily consent to participation. Researchers need to explain how they will assess and record voluntary participation. Often, researchers create scripts and/or forms to aid in gaining and recording voluntary consent.

The other issue is to take care of *privacy*. This also related to the risk of disclosure when data are collected or come from administrative sources. As Kalidien et al (2010) show with regard to criminal justice data, due to the general societal trend to make organizations transparent, there is a growing demand from users to make crime statistics accessible online for several reasons: with online statistics, combining and analyzing data will become easier and may give a better insight into certain phenomena. However, applying data mining or Web 2.0 technology, such as mash ups on crime data online, can lead to undesirable consequences like violation of privacy laws, and disclosure of the identity of groups of people. Choenni, van Dijk and Leeuw (2010) have described ways to avoid these problems.

A third ethical issue is *fraud in scientific research*. Fabrication, falsification and plagiarism, summarized as FFP, are distinct forms of fraud in science. Fabrication is the creation of data as if they were real. Falsification is the manipulation of data ('counterfeiting') and other results of research, including the selective omission of certain information (misrepresentation).[12] Plagiarism, according to Freeland Judson (2004: 185), is misappropriation. Self-control, working with protocols and guidelines, transparency in procedures about data-collection, peer reviews and similar approaches are there to prevent fraud in any way. That includes software capable of detecting plagiarism. Schuyt (2014) recently presented a socio-criminological theory to explain why these perversities appear within the scientific world.

With regard to Big Data, ethical issues are also at stake. One is the privacy and civil liberties consequences of being swept up in Big Data's net. Lerman

(2013: 57, 59) however takes a different approach, focusing on the risks of exclusion: the threats that Big Data pose to those whom it overlooks:

> the non-random, systemic omission of people who live on big data's margins, whether due to poverty, geography, or lifestyle, and whose lives are less 'datafied' than the general population's. In key sectors, their marginalization risks distorting datasets and, consequently, skewing the analysis on which private and public actors increasingly depend. They are big data's exclusions. The consequences of exclusion could be profound:
>
> - those left out of the big data revolution may suffer tangible economic harms. Businesses may ignore or undervalue the preferences and behaviors of consumers who do not shop in ways that big data tools can easily capture, aggregate, and analyze. Stores may not open in their neighborhoods, denying them not just shopping options, but also employment opportunities;
> - politicians and governments may come to rely on big data to such a degree that exclusion from data flows leads to exclusion from civic and political life – a barrier to full citizenship.

7.7 SOME GUIDANCE

- Data can be almost everything: stored, born digital, made digital, obtrusive, unobtrusive, numerical or qualitative. Often they have to be collected, increasingly they are stored in registers, data warehouses or archives, or they are 'collected' automatically (Big Data).
- Think before you leap to well-known, often used types of data collection: interviewing victims, litigators, magistrates, prison personnel and others can easily lead to suboptimal information if existing data in administrative systems or in data archives are omitted (or considered dull or 'a waste of time', because of the 'not-invented-here' syndrome some researchers have).
- Think outside the box. Wastewater analysis to measure illicit drug use is an example, as is working with Big Data.
- Keep in mind the relevance (and complexity) of measurement theory.
- Big Data are an important new development for ELR, though not without (some) problems. However, traditional 'data' (collection methods) are *also* confronted with problems and, moreover, are not geared to measuring *real time* developments in the digital world.
- Be transparent and log your actions when working with data, first, to make replications possible and second, to prevent integrity problems.

ENDNOTES

1. This statement and several others come from http://library.law.yale.edu/news/writing-empirical-legal-study-design-primer, accessed 27 November 2015.
2. We refer to Chapter 5 of Epstein and Martin (2014) for more information, including a practical exposé on how to deal with missing data and how to work with data entry programs like Microsoft Access or Filemaker. Not long ago 'the easiest way to enter the data into a computer [was] to just type the data in directly. However, that process created mistakes and in order to assure the highest level data accuracy, it was suggested to use a procedure called double entry. In this procedure one person enters the data once. Then, a special program makes it possible to enter the data a second time and check each second entry against the first. If there is a discrepancy, the program notifies the user and allows the user to determine the correct entry. This double entry procedure significantly reduces entry errors. Data preparation also implies documenting all steps that have been taken to be able for data-auditors to come and evaluate all actions and decisions' (ibid., p. 106).
3. Van den Braak, Choenni and Bamberger (2016) distinguish between user-generated data (e.g. from social media or websites, surveys, interviews), machine-generated data (e.g. tracking data, sensor data or application logs) and registry data (e.g. data that governmental organizations need for their operational tasks). These data are often stored in database systems that are essentially organized collections of the data which model reality to a certain extent.
4. Information about the Justice Data Lab works can be found at https://www.gov.uk/government/publications/justice-data-lab, accessed 27 November 2015.
5. http://www.nationalacademies.org/studyprocess/index.html#st2, accessed 27 November 2015.
6. http://hafeezrm.hubpages.com/hub/Data-Collection-Methods, accessed 27 November 2015.
7. We do not discuss differences and similarities between 'coding' in the world of Big Data and when working with other types of data.
8. See also http://www.unglobalpulse.org/monitoring-evaluation-toolkit, accessed 27 November 2015.
9. PACER is an online repository for court records, docket sheets and case metadata maintained by the Administrative Office of the United States Courts. It should be noted that there is critique on this repository and its usability because of (outdated) technology.
10. Usually this means free of biases of any kind, like political, ideological, personal, cognitive and those related to stakes a researcher may have.
11. In the psychological literature on demand characteristics and experiments a distinction is made between several 'roles' respondents can play. In the 'good-participant role' the participant attempts to discern the experimenter's hypotheses to confirm them. In the negative-participant role he/she attempts to discern the experimenter's hypotheses, but only in order to destroy the credibility of the study. The faithful-participant role implies a participant following the instructions given by the experimenter to the letter. And in the apprehensive-participant role the participant is so concerned about how the experimenter might evaluate the responses that the participant behaves in a socially desirable way. This point is part of the literature on measurement theory (see below).
12. This 'type' of falsification is completely different from the epistemological concept that was introduced by Popper.

8. Analyzing and visualizing quantitative and qualitative data

Data analysis is a body of methods that helps to describe facts, detect patterns, develop explanations and test theories. *Quantitative data analysis* describes, explains and evaluates phenomena by using mathematically based methods (in particular statistics) (Aliaga and Gunderson, 2005). *Qualitative data analysis* is the process and procedure whereby researchers move from qualitative data into (some form of) exploration, explanation, understanding or interpretation of people, situations, arrangements and 'products'. More and more qualitative data are 'digitized' and become accessible to quantitative methods. For a long time 'paradigm wars' existed between both 'branches' but, partly due to innovations in the field of computer-assisted methods and Big Data (including sensor data), these 'wars' are disappearing.

Sections 8.2 to 8.4 below deal with *quantitative data analysis*, while section 8.5 focuses on Big Data analysis, and section 8.6 on *qualitative data analysis*. Section 8.7 discusses *combining qualitative and quantitative analysis*, while section 8.8 presents information on *data visualization*. Section 8.9 discusses *criteria to assess the (methodological) quality* of *data analyses* while section 8.10 gives some *guidance*.

8.1 QUANTITATIVE DATA ANALYSIS AND ELECTIONS: A PREVIEW

Empirical (legal) research can make use of a wide variety of research designs and methods (see Chapters 6 and 7). Most of these designs are based on a defined population: e.g. the inhabitants of a specific country, a municipality, the labour market population, judges within courts, detainees in prisons, students at universities, or employees of a company. Usually only a selection of units within the specified population are studied. Where this selection is based on a strategy, these selected units may constitute a *sample*. A well-known example of the connection of the two concepts – sample and population – can be found in the survey. A survey collects data on a number of units based on a (random) sample from a defined population. In the Netherlands, for example, a random sample of 4000 units could be taken from a population of 10,245,782 eligible voters.

In the next two sections the sample method, the data-collection methodology, the response, the reasons for not-participating (= non-response) and methods to reduce the bias originating from a non-response are described. The statistical methods to analyse the data will be outlined – from simple descriptive statistics, such as the mean value of a given distribution, to inferential statistics used for drawing general conclusions on the defined population based on the sample.

Although up to this point various *examples* of *theories, research designs and data collection methods* have been presented, with regard to quantitative data analysis this chapter takes *another route*. All methodological and statistical issues and examples focus on *one field of research: elections*. When the goal is to inform readers on the *breadth and width of methods and approaches* of ELR, a *smorgasbord* menu is enlightening and attractive. However, when *doing quantitative data analysis and statistics*, it is crucial that the reader *experiences* what it means to *dig* into data (topics) as concretely as possible.

We have selected four election studies to help unravel what empirical legal researchers are doing when they work with quantitative data. The first is the *Dutch Parliamentary Election Study*. The second example is retrieved from the *European Social Survey*: a cross-national survey conducted in some 30 countries, covering social and political attitudes. The third example is a *study on OSCE (Organisation for Security and Cooperation in Europe) Election Observation Missions* in which polling stations are observed. And the fourth study deals with an *experiment* on how to enhance response rates through incentives. Three of the studies belong to the family of observational designs, while one is an experiment. The studies differ in the *units of analysis: eligible voters* in the first study, *citizens* in the second, *polling stations* in the third, and *households* in the fourth. *Voters*, *citizens* and *households* are (natural) people; *polling stations* are organizational units that are part of the voting process and have characteristics of their own. Polling stations as such cannot be 'asked questions' but officials responsible for these organizations can.

Although these units of analysis are rather divergent, we will demonstrate how relevant and applicable a range of statistical methods and techniques is, both when sampling and collecting data and when analysing the results. We start with the backbone of the surveys: the registers from which samples are drawn. Subsequently, the data-collection methods will be discussed. We will touch upon the quality of a survey by detailing the response and non-response bias (for an overview of the Total Survey Error, see Groves et al, 2009; Groves and Lyberg, 2010; Biemer, 2010). This will be followed by a brief introduction of statistical methods when analysing data. In boxes, information on measurement levels of variables and validity and reliability when working with statistical data is presented.

BOX 8.1 ON ELECTIONS AND REGULATION

Elections are at the heart of democracies. The fundamental freedoms and political rights necessary for democratic elections were established by the Universal Declaration of Human Rights (UDHR) adopted by the UN General Assembly in 1948 and the International Convention on Civil and Political Rights (ICCPR) in 1996. The UDHR has been accepted by all members of the UN and represents the international standard. The ICCPR is legally binding upon all ratifying countries. In Article 25 the right to participate in public affairs and voting rights is outlined. There exist a number of regional declarations and commitments, often based on the UDHR and ICCPR. Examples include the African Union Declaration on Principles Governing Democratic Elections in 2007, the Arab Charter on Human Rights in 1994, the American Declaration of the Rights and Duties of Man in 1948 and the Code of Good Practice on Electoral Matters (2002) adopted by the European Commission for Democracy through Law ('the Venice Commission').

Elections are a part of national constitutional law as well as the various International Commitments based on the member states of international organisations, including the Organisation for Security and Cooperation in Europe (OSCE). Based on the 1990 Copenhagen Commitments, the OSCE Office for Democratic Institutions and Human Rights (OSCE/ODIHR) in Warsaw observes the elections of its almost 60 member states, which includes countries in Europe and Eurasia, the USA and Canada. For this purpose Election Observation Missions (EOMs) are conducted, to assess the various phases of an election: before, during and after Election Day. This is a common practice for the assessment of elections for countries in transition or new democracies.

With regard to elections at the European Union,[1] the European Parliamentary Research Service[2] issues infographics describing major characteristics of the system for voting at the European Parliament: compulsory voting (or not), the voting system, the number of MPs, the minimum age of candidates and whether or not there is an electoral threshold for parties.[3]

[1] Regarding elections in the Netherlands the Electoral Council is a central electoral committee, an advisory body and an information center in the field of franchise and elections. Its mandate is enshrined in the Elections Act, also called the Act of 28 September 1989 containing new provisions governing the franchise and elections. The Netherlands has had an Elections Act since 1850. For a long time, the right to vote was reserved for the male elite. It was not until 1919 that the right to vote was given to men and women. Equality of the vote is today found in the Dutch constitution (since 1983; Elzinga, 1997: 25). Before the recent changes, the constitutional character of elections could only be deduced from international law documents and treaties. An important difference with other constitutional ('founding') rights is that elections are a right for Dutch citizens only, while other founding rights in the Netherlands protect all persons living in the Netherlands.

[2] http://www.europarl.europa.eu/aboutparliament/en/000f81b2e3/European-Parliamentary-Research-Service.html, accessed 27 November 2015.

[3] http://www.europarl.europa.eu/eplibrary/InfoGraphic-2014-European-elections-national-rules.pdf, accessed 27 November 2015.

8.2 POPULATION CENSUS, SAMPLING, RESPONSE AND WEIGHTING

8.2.1 Population Census

We start with the *Dutch Parliamentary Election Studies (DPES)*. For many reasons knowledge of a population and its units is vital. First, knowing the population of eligible voters requires a database with records of the population, including characteristics such as age and citizenship. To produce such a database, a population census is needed in which basic characteristics from all individuals are collected for a specific point in time. On average, countries connected to the United Nations Economic Commission for Europe (UNECE) conduct a census every ten years. To this end, most UNECE countries conduct face-to-face interviews using paper questionnaires. Other modes of collecting information include the telephone, internet and self-completed questionnaires. Some countries – Denmark, Finland, Norway, Sweden, the Netherlands, Austria and Slovenia – compile their censuses from existing registers ('stored data'), sometimes in combination with large-scale surveys, and do not collect additional data (Schulte Nordholt, 2014). The register-based approach is used because of financial considerations (interviewing people is much more expensive than using stored data), and because populations are becoming less willing to participate in surveys. A third aspect is that when using register data, social desirable answers to interviewers – e.g. on the consumption of (hard) drugs, cigarettes, alcohol – given during interviews are not possible.

In surveys only a narrow selection of units in the defined population is usually approached. If the selection is based on a random sample, i.e. the chance to be selected is equal for all units, we can draw general conclusions based on the specific population. Clearly, there are many ways to draw a sample, and there exists a long tradition of study in this field to that end. In 1906 Sir Arthur Bowley pioneered the use of sampling techniques in (social) surveys, and demonstrated that, using 'selection at random from the population', a measure for accuracy of estimates could be obtained. In 1934 Neyman showed that a stratified sample method has many merits compared to a non-stratified sample (Neyman, 1934). In a stratified sample the population is divided in a number of subpopulations, often linked to the groups in whom the researcher is interested, e.g. men and women, youngsters and the elderly, natives and ethnic minorities, people living in rural and urban areas, etc. The samples are drawn from the subpopulations, optimizing the comparison of these groups.

Ten years later Hansen and Hurwitz (1943) introduced the multi-stage stratified sample. In a first stage the primary units are selected with probabilities proportional to their size; and in a second stage, within the selected primary units, a fixed number of secondary units are selected. This method is still a common practice sampling strategy in social surveys. For example, in the first stage a random selection of the municipalities in a country is made, ensuring that the probability to be included is higher as more inhabitants live in the municipalities. In the second stage a random selection of a fixed number of people will be made within the selected municipalities. A typical example is the selection of 200 out of 430 municipalities in the Netherlands, followed by a selection of 20 people from each municipality, resulting in a sample of 4000 people.

We will now elaborate on the stratified sampling technique applied to the *Dutch Parliamentary Election Study 2006* (DPES 2006). The initial gross sample included 4000 Dutch people, aged 18 or older. The sample was drawn from the Municipal Basic Register, which includes the whole population living in the Netherlands. This register contains detailed regional information (as addresses are available), gender, age, country of origin, marital status and citizenship. For the DPES only citizens with Dutch nationality and aged 18 or older on election day should be included in the sample. Note that the DPES does not cover eligible voters living abroad, nor does it cover eligible voters living on the small islands in the northern part of the Netherlands. Also excluded are people who do not live in private households, but instead, for example, reside in hospitals and care-centres. This deliberate exclusion of a part of the target population is called 'non-coverage'.[1]

In Chapter 7 we discussed ways in which data can be collected. Nowadays, the *mixed mode approach*[2] is becoming increasingly popular

BOX 8.2 MIXED MODE RESEARCH AND STATISTICS NETHERLANDS

At Statistics Netherlands a mixed internet/telephone/face-to-face modus is generally used. The main reason for starting with data collection through the internet is cost reduction: it is by far the cheapest method. If the selected person does not respond, two reminders will be sent. If that is not successful either, and a telephone number is available, the next mode in this sequential design is the telephone interview. If the selected person cannot be reached by telephone, the face-to-face mode is used as a last resort to get the selected person to respond. Per selected person, a maximum of nine contact attempts will be conducted spread across three days and three daily shifts within the data collection period which varies between two and four weeks. After this period, the selected person is denoted a non-response due to non-contact (Luiten, 2013).

in large-scale fieldwork. This approach is mixed because it uses interviews by an interviewer, either face to face or by telephone, and/or without the interference of an interviewer, e.g. by mail or internet (De Leeuw, 2005).

A mixed-mode data-collection strategy brings with it certain problems and challenges. The questions in the questionnaires have to fit nicely into the various data collection modes. This, however, is not always easy to realize. For example, how is it possible to create for respondents the 'do not know' option to suit the different environments of an internet version of a questionnaire and that of a face-to face interview? Oftentimes, if a 'do not know' option is clearly provided for a respondent on the internet, it will be used more frequently than in a face-to-face or telephone interview where the 'do not know' option is not immediately available. Many experiments have revealed that *interview data-collection mode effects* exist (Kappelhof, 2015), precisely as we alluded to in the previous chapter. Researchers have to cope with the problems of trend breaches due to changes from uni-mode to mixed-mode designs.[3]

8.2.2 Response, Non-response Bias and Weighting

Response rates are often considered to be a quality indicator in surveys. If all selected people in a sample were to participate, the response rate would be 100%. Error due to non-response would not exist, and we would only have to cope with other errors in the design, collection, processing and analysis of the survey data. Ultimately, however, most or all surveys suffer from non-responsiveness, which is an important part of the Total Survey Error. One part of the non-response factor is caused by failure to establish contact with selected persons in the sample. In surveys conducted by Statistics Netherlands, some 4% of samples are made up of non-contacts (Luiten, 2013). Yet, the main reason for not participating in a survey is a person's refusal to do so. Some 20 to 25% of respondents are not willing to cooperate. This means that most surveys have an average response rate of some 60 to 65%, and consequently a 35 to 40% non-response rate.

Let us look more specifically at the DPES 2006. The DPES was conducted from six weeks to shortly before election day (first interview) and shortly after election day (second interview) among the same selected people in the sample. This implies that the DPES was a two-wave panel-study. During the first wave, the response rate of the DPES 2006 was 66.9%. Non-responsiveness was usually the result of respondent refusals to participate (21%) and unavailability of participants during the fieldwork period (6%). Other reasons were failure to make contact (3%), complications associated with people moving to other municipalities (2%) and language barriers (1%).

BOX 8.3 RESPONSE IN THE DUTCH PARLIAMENTARY ELECTION STUDY (DPES) 1972–2012

In the DPES, the response in the second wave has been below 50% since 1972, reaching an all-time low of 27% in 2002. These low response rates were partly caused by panel attrition as the DPES is a two-wave study, conducted shortly before and after elections. For the DPES in 2006, a substantial improvement in the response – to 55% in the first wave and 45% in the second wave – was the main target. This target was easily achieved with 72% and 64% responses to the two waves. In 2010 the response rates were lower: 67% in the first wave and 57% in the second. Due to cost constraints, in 2012 only one interview after election day was conducted without a re-approach to the non-response. This resulted in a response rate of 62%. Taking the response as an indicator, the quality of the DPES in 2006 was significantly better than the DPESs in 2010 and 2012.

In the DPES the method of refusal conversion was applied. Refusal conversions are the procedures used by survey researchers to gain cooperation from a sampled respondent who has refused an initial survey request. In the DPES, refusing people were re-approached via another data-collection mode: telephone or mail. To this end, a shortened questionnaire was used. Re-approaching non-contacts and refusals resulted in additional responses of 3.3% by telephone and 1.4% by mail. Because of panel attrition,[4] approximately 7% were lost in the second wave. Consequently, the second wave face-to-face response was 60.2%. Again, refusal conversion and additional contact attempts added a further 4.1%, resulting in a final second-wave response rate of 64.3%.

As previously stated, samples can be drawn from the Netherlands Municipal Basic Register which includes basic information for all those resident in the Netherlands. This register also serves as a tool for the production and dissemination of various demographic statistics. The Municipal Basic Register is linked with other registers such as tax authorities' registers on income, and (large-scale) surveys, such as Housing Demand Surveys, Crime Victimization Surveys and Labor Force Surveys. All these data are included in the Social Statistical Database (SSB, see Chapter 7), which enables Statistics Netherlands to produce social statistics and to draw samples based on the whole Dutch population and (very specific) subpopulations. Such a subpopulation could for example include all non-Western immigrant females, aged 18 to 24, living in rural areas. All such information is already found in the database (so-called background variables), and consequently there is no need to collect this information from additional surveys.

Above we discussed the quality of a survey, and demonstrated that the DPES in 2006 had a higher quality than those in 2010 and 2012. However, all three DPES studies still suffer from selection bias, because non-voters are clearly underrepresented compared to official turnout figures. For the DPES in 2006 and 2010 only one in three non-voters participated in the survey, while in 2012 the DPES was slightly more representative as one in two of the non-voters was willing to answer the questions. The reason for this is the change of the survey design, from a two-wave panel study to a one-wave study after the election. This change meant that the DPES 2012 did not need to account for panel attrition.

But, even more importantly, participation in a survey can also change attitudes and behaviour. There is some evidence that potential non-voters who do participate in election surveys in fact change their behaviour and go to the poll on election day, reducing the proportion of non-voters in a sample even further. This finding is based on a quasi-experiment conducted in 2006 in which the questions on voting behaviour were asked in November of that year (Schmeets, 2010). The questions on voting behaviour were also addressed to a fresh sample of some 10,000 people aged 18 or older in the Labour Force Survey (LFS) and some 800 in the Permanent Life Situation Study (POLS). In the DPES the turnout was 93%, and in the LFS and POLS 88% while the official turnout figure was 80%. This implies that the turnout bias was substantially higher (13%) in the DPES than in the LFS and POLS (8%). The 5% difference between the two figures – 13% minus 8% – is attributed to the stimulus-effect. The other 8% bias in all three studies can be attributed to a combination of (a) selection bias: a higher share of voters participate in social surveys than non-voters (Brehm, 1993) and (b) social desirability: respondents do not want to admit that they did not vote. Based on other studies (Traugott and Katosh, 1979; Swaddle and Health, 1989; Van der Kolk and Aarts, 2001; Voogt, 2004), we can assume that the 8% bias is caused by 2% social desirability and 6% selection biases. In the DPES 2012, the design changed to a one-wave study, conducted after the elections on 12 September. The official turnout was 74.6%, but the DPES indicated that 86% said that they had cast their vote that year (Schmeets and Van den Brakel, 2015), while more than half (14.0/25.4 = 0.55) of non-voters actually participated in the DPES. This result compares to the LFS and POLS findings in 2006, which also found that slightly more than half of non-voters participated.

We have shown that the Social Statistical Database has many merits: it is cost-effective, lowers the respondents' burden, and serves as a tool for the production of many social statistics. But there is another advantage: as key characteristics of the Dutch population are available for both respondents and non-respondents, we can explore the over- and underrepresentation of some groups in the sample. This information is particularly useful for correcting for bias in the findings, simply by increasing the provided answers from the underrepresented group and likewise reducing the answers from the overrepresented group. To put it differently: the answers are *reweighted* to ensure that the unequal distribution in the sample is adjusted in line with the distributions in the population. Take a population, for example, where the gender distribution in the population is 50% male and 50% female, whereas in the sample the distribution is 60 versus 40. Weighting enables us to make sure that the higher share of male answers and the lower share of female answers will be adjusted accordingly by using a higher weight for the answers provided by women and lower weights for men. In sum, information from respondents and non-respondents enables us to assign higher weights to the underrepresented groups, and likewise to lower weights of the overrepresented groups. The application of such tailored weighting procedures may improve the representation of the sample and consequently the quality of the statistical estimates.

8.3 QUANTITATIVE DATA ANALYSIS AND STATISTICS

8.3.1 Descriptive Statistics

We now turn to the analysis of quantitative data. First, we need to explore the data in a descriptive manner. This means looking at how we use statistics as a tool for providing an overview of the main characteristics of the individual (micro) data, e.g. the answers provided by the respondents and stored in a database, where the rows represent the respondents and the columns represent the variables. Let us first look at individual variables. By producing a frequency table, the numbers and percentages of the answer categories are listed. The most commonly used measure to indicate the center of a distribution is the *mean*: all observations are summed and divided by the total number of observations (e.g. six respondents: $(3 + 4 + 8 + 8 + 6 + 7)/6 = 6$). We might also look at the category with the highest frequency: the *mode*. In the above example the mode is 8 as two respondents have provided this answer. Another measure is the *median*: the point at which half of the total number of observations is reached. It is a measure of central tendency and divides the distribution in half, so that 50% of the scores are above the median and 50% below. Therefore, we need to rank the answers – 3, 4, 6, 8, 8, 7 – and find that the median is 6. Another measure is the *range*, which indicates the difference between the maximum and minimum score in a distribution (in the example: $8 - 3 = 5$).

Given the measures above, it is possible to calculate measures for the variation in the scores: the *variance* and the *standard deviation. Variance* measures the squared distances to the mean, while the *standard deviation* is the average distance of all scores from the mean. Again, we use six respondents and the already calculated mean value 6. The sum of all distances (−3; −2; 0; 2; 2; 1) is always 0. For the variance we calculate the squared distances: $(3^2 + 2^2 + 0^2 + 2^2 + 2^2 + 1^2)$ divided by 6 = 22/6 or 3.67. The *standard deviation is* the squared root (√) of the variance (σ): √3.67 = 1.91. Note that these calculations are based on the assumption that the six respondents are a population, and not a sample. If they made up a sample distribution, the squared distances would need to be divided by the number of cases minus 1. In the formula for sample variance, this is represented by $n - 1$. For this sample, therefore, the variance would equal 22/5 or 4.40, and the standard deviation would equal 2.10. Clearly, the lower the standard deviation and variance compared to a given mean, the more we can be sure that the mean of this specific variable is a good predictor for all values provided by the respondents in the sample.

The mean and the standard deviation are linked to an important feature in statistics: the *normal distribution. Normal distributions* are symmetric and have bell-shaped density curves with a single peak. For a normal distribution, almost all values (97.5%) lie within three standard deviations of the mean. If the distribution is not normal, for example in cases where the distribution is heavily skewed to the right or to the left, there is a risk that statistics showing whether or not a correlation is statistically significant are wrong. In such cases the statistical significance should be based on a binominal distribution.[5]

Now let us move from the descriptive statistics of one single variable, called *univariate* statistics, to *bivariate* statistics. *Bivariate* statistics examine the statistical relationship between two variables. Two variables are positively related when low and high values on one variable coincide with low and high values on the other variable. Likewise, when low values on one variable go together with high values on the other variable, the relationship is negative. Because numerical descriptions of bivariate relationships are often generalized to a population, we need to know how sure we can be *that the descriptive relationship based on the sample will also be found in the population.* Put differently: *is the relationship statistically significant or not*? To assess this statistical significance we need to explore *inferential statistics.* Box 8.4 gives basic information on variables and their measurement levels, which is important to understand which statistical operations are possible (and allowed).

BOX 8.4 VARIABLES AND MEASUREMENT LEVELS

In statistics, variables can be categorized into one of following levels of measurement: Nominal; Ordinal; Interval; Ratio.

Nominal variables represent the lowest measurement level. The categories of these variables are only distinguished by their names. The numerical codes representing the categories therefore can be chosen arbitrarily as long as they are uniquely associated with one category. An example of a nominal variable is *Party choice*. This variable's categories are not logically ordered (e.g. Labor, Christian Democrats, Liberals).

Ordinal variables cannot be coded arbitrarily because the categories are rank ordered. For example, the variable *Education Level* is ordinal as it is assumed that levels can be ordered according to the amount of knowledge that has been attained by the respondent. Generally, the lowest knowledge level has been attained when people complete (1) only primary school education. Higher levels are obtained by those with (2) lower vocational education, (3) secondary education, (4) middle vocational and (5) higher vocational or university degree education. To express this ranking, the codes of an ordinal variable must be in ascending or descending order, from (1) to (5).

In contrast to ordinal variables, *interval variables* have exact known differences (or intervals) between subsequent categories. An example of an interval variable is 'year of birth'. The categories of this variable are rank ordered and the intervals between subsequent categories (e.g. one year) are equally distanced from one another. *Ratio variables* have an additional absolute 'zero-point', for example income (200 euro is twice 100 euro) or age (10 years is twice 5 years). A typical example of an interval variable, but not a ratio variable, is degrees Celsius (20 degrees is not twice as hot as 10 degrees).

Dichotomous variables are a special category of variables. They always have exactly two categories, like *Gender*.[1] These variables allow the researcher to rank observations in terms of presence/absence (or yes/no). For the variable *Gender*, respondents are female or they are not (male). In addition to this, it becomes irrelevant whether or not there are equal intervals between all categories because there is only one interval. Therefore, mathematically, a dichotomous variable has the same characteristics as an interval variable.

[1] Note that there are some exceptions, e.g. transgender.

8.3.2 Inferential Statistics

In inferential statistics, the sample size is important as the calculations are based on the fact that more respondents increase the likelihood that the calculations will be representative of the greater population. Additionally, the standard deviation is also important. The lower the standard deviation, the more we can be sure that the mean value in the sample is a good estimate of the value in the greater unstudied population. As previously mentioned, the standard deviation reflects the average distance to the mean value found in the sample. The smaller this distance is, the better the estimate of the mean value drawn from respondents in the sample population. The two aspects – sample size (n) and standard deviation – comprised the *standard error* ($\sigma\bar{x}$) measure found by dividing the standard deviation by the square root of the sample size: $\sigma/\sqrt{n}$. Suppose we have a sample of 100 respondents, and that the standard deviation is exactly the same in the example based on the six respondents: 1.66. For this case the standard error is 0.17 (calculation: $1.66/\sqrt{100}$). The standard error is an important feature as it enables us to calculate the *confidence intervals* around the estimates. It tells us in which range we might expect that, for example, 95% of all possible sample means would be located within this range. A rough calculation of this interval is by multiplying two standard errors and by subtracting/adding this value to/from the mean value. In our example, $6 \pm 2 * .17 = 5.66$ and 6.34.

Many National Statistical Institutes and other research organizations also provide the Confidence Intervals (CI) in addition to the estimates (the mean values) in order to understand how reliable an estimator is. Very large CIs would indicate that the estimator does not say much about the defined (sub)population. The CI are also useful for testing research hypotheses. In the above example, a hypothesis expecting the mean value to be less than 5.50 would have been rejected. However, in statistical analysis, another strategy is to use the *level of significance* (notation: α). Common levels of significance are 10%, 5% and 1%. When a sample result falls beyond these intervals, it falls into a *rejection area* and the null hypothesis is similarly rejected as a result (see also Chapter 4). The exact probability (also known as 'p-value' or just 'p') can be calculated with any statistical software package. This p-value can either be one-tailed or two-tailed, depending on whether there is a notion of whether the expected value of one group is higher or lower than that for the other group (one-tailed), or whether there is no idea (at all) (two-tailed).

The Statistical Package for Social Sciences (SPSS) includes tests to assess whether or not relationships between two or more variables are statistically significant, and what the strength of the associations are. One test to compare (the differences between) mean values of two groups is the *t-test*. A comparison of more than two groups is possible using the *analysis of variance (ANOVA)* (comparing between the group means). If the variance between the group means (between group variance) is small, we often will not find a great statistical difference between two groups. Likewise, if the variance around the group means (within group variance) is large, the mean is not a good estimator (i.e. large CI), and consequently we will not find that the mean values of the groups will differ statistically. The combination of low between group variance and high within group variance will hardly result in the finding that the groups differ. This combination is reflected in the divide between group variance/within group variance, and is expressed in the *F-value*. A large F-value is associated with relatively large between variance compared to the within variance, and conversely a low F-value is associated with a low between variance and high within variance. In an experimental design the hypothesis tests whether the treatment effects the average of the experimental groups. Often a variance-analyses is applied, depending on the exact setup of the experiment. If the means of the groups differ, it is important to verify which treatments are causing the changes. A common approach is to make use of the t-test. Montgomery (2005) details various experimental designs and the appropriate analyses of variance. In the following section on the analyses of data, the basics of this method are further elaborated upon.

Now let us continue with the analysis of tables. *Contingency tables* are commonly used to describe the association or relationship between variables with low numbers of categories (preferably < 10), and are often used only for nominal and ordinal variables. These tables consist of two or more columns and rows, depending on the number of categories. The inner cells contain the observations for each combination of columns and rows. The outer cells are called the marginals, in which the total number of observations for each column and each row are presented. The total sum of all marginals is the total number of observations and is shown in the lower right of the contingency table. One measure of association applicable to all tables is the chi-square (χ^2). The height of this chi-square indicates the difference between the observed and the expected counts in the inner cells of a contingency table. The expected numbers are calculated from the hypothetical situation where there is no statistical relationship between the variables. The exact chi-square is calculated by taking the difference between the observed and the expected counts of each cell. These differences are squared, divided by the associated expected count, and finally summed. Thus the chi-square indicates the level of discrepancy between the observed table and the table without any statistical relationship. High chi-square values indicate a high level of relationship and vice versa. Based on the chi-square, the association measurement *Cramér's V* has been developed for tables in which at least one variable is ordinal. The merit of Cramér's V is that its values are *always* between 0 (no relationship) and 1 (perfect relationship). A value lower than 0.25 demonstrates a low relationship, and a value of 0.35 and higher a strong relationship. For only ordinal variables the association measurement *Kendalls Tau B* (number of categories are equal) and *Kendalls Tau C* (unequal number of categories) are often used. The values vary between −1.00 (perfect negative association), and 1.00 (perfect positive association), where 0.00 represents no relationship.

Another measurement of association based on ordinal variables is the *Spearman's Rho* rank order correlation. The benefit of Spearman's rank correlation is that it is quite similar to *Pearson's correlation coefficient*, which is an important measure of association for interval-/ratio variables. The Pearson's correlation (r), however, requires an approximately linear relationship, which is not required for Spearman's correlation. The linear association may be perfectly negative ($r = -1.00$, if every unit increase of x results in a one unit *decrease* of y) or perfectly positive ($r = 1.00$). The relationship between two variables can also be demonstrated by values on a dependent (y) variable predicted by scores on an independent (x) variable. This technique is called *regression analysis*. In such an analysis a line is drawn that minimizes the distances between the dots of the two variables in the scatter plot. The increase of one unit of the independent variable is associated with a concomitant increase of x units in the other, dependent, variable: this is the *b-coefficient*. The *intercept* or constant (a) is also an important parameter in addition to the b-coefficient (b) as every straight line can be mathematically ascribed to a formula $y = a + bx$. The intercept (a) is the value of y where the line crosses the y-axis. It can be found by extending the regression line to the y-axis. If all scores of y are located exactly on the regression line, the linear relationship is perfect, and the explained variance is 1.00 (100%). In such a (theoretical) regression model, all values of variable y can be precisely predicted based on the values of variable x. In usual practice, the explained variance is much lower. The explained variance can be increased by adding more x variables (x2; x3; . . . xN) to the model. The inclusion of more independent variables refers to *multiple regression analysis*.[6]

A specific, often-used type of regression analysis is *logistic regression analysis*. This is used if the dependent (y) variable is dichotomous, where it consists of only two categories (see Box 8.5). The independent variables are included either as interval variables or as categories in which one category will serve as the reference category. The values of all other categories reflect the distance from this reference category, expressed b-values and odds ratios (OR). An OR of 1.00 indicates that there is no change compared to the reference category; if the OR is significantly lower or higher than 1.00, the OR expresses the likelihood that this category has lower, respectively higher scores on the dependent variable in comparison to the reference category.

In all the examples above the variables are linked to each other in such a way that the scores on independent variables predict – to some extent – the scores on a dependent variable in a *regression model*. *Structural Equation Models* (SEMs) allow the inclusion of many regression models simultaneously. In many cases, two or more dependent variables are included. SEMs also permit the inclusion of *measurement models* in which various variables

BOX 8.5 A SUMMARY OF STATISTICAL MEASURES/LEVELS OF VARIABLES

Dependent variable (y)	Independent variable(s) (x1; x2; x3 . . . xN)		
	Nominal	**Ordinal**	**Interval or Ratio**
Nominal	Chi square Cramér's V	Chi square Cramér's V	Chi square Cramér's V
Dichotomous	Chi square Cramér's V Logistic regression	Chi square Cramérs' V Logistic regression	Chi square Cramér's V Logistic regression
Ordinal	Chi square Cramér's V Ordinal regression	Kendalls tau-b and tau-c Spearman's Rho Ordinal regression	Kendalls tau-b and tau-c Spearman's Rho Ordinal regression
Interval or Ratio	Pearson's R T-test and F-test (multiple) Linear regression	Pearson' R T-test and F-test (multiple) Linear regression	Pearson's R T-test and F-test (multiple) Linear regression

are linked to a 'latent' concept, in fact (assumed to) represent the different factors (see Box 8.6). There are various 'goodness of fit' measures presenting to what extent the model reflects the empirical data (the correlations) well.

In an ideal world all models would be based on (explanatory) theories. These theories would specify the variables and, in particular, the mechanisms assumed to be capable of influencing other (i.e. dependent) variables. Although explanatory theories are available (see Chapter 4), not all models can be based on them. One reason is that these theories are not true or valid a priori (for all situations). Another reason is that in research new situations are analyzed that have not yet been the object of a theoretical analysis. When the social media revolution first infiltrated society and the question was asked what the impact of Facebook and Twitter on voting behavior would be, a *new* set of variables entered the equation about which no explanatory theories had been developed, let alone been tested.

The absence of applicable and tested theories also extends to simple models in which one dependent and one independent variable are included,

BOX 8.6 CALCULATING VALIDITY AND RELIABILITY, SCALES AND MEASUREMENT MODELS

Validity refers to whether a measurement actually measures what it intends to measure. Questions can measure something quite differently to what is intended.

Reliability relates to the (lack of) random error of the measurement: under similar circumstances a repeated measurement should (roughly) result in a similar outcome. For example, the possibility that a measurement is unreliable increases when questions are used that can be interpreted in multiple ways. If a researcher is interested in measuring a concept with more than one indicator, answers can simply be summed to create a *Likert scale*. This scale's reliability will be higher than that of each separate question. This of course does not mean that reliable measurements are also valid.

It is also possible to calculate the *reliability of a concept (measured) that consists of a number of variables*. In SPSS various measures are available, of which *Cronbach's alpha* is the most often used. It is based on the number of variables (also indicated as items), and the correlation between all variables. The more items and the higher the inter-item correlation, the higher the alpha measure. An alpha lower than 0.60 demonstrates that the reliability is low and the concept is not reliable (measured). Where the alpha measure falls between 0.60 and 0.70 the reliability is moderate, and above 0.80 it is considered high. If the reliability is not satisfactory, a solution is to include more items in the Likert scale. If an item shows a weak correlation with other items, a solution is to delete such item in the scale. SPSS calculates the alpha if an item is deleted.

Apart from the Likert scale, there are other possibilities for creating a scale based on multiple variables. In *measurement models*, scales are calculated based on the correlations between the included variables. A number of variables are reduced to one or a few new variables: the factors representing (a selection of) those variables. Such analysis are 'factor'-analysis, of which the *Principal Component Analysis (PCA)* and the *Principal Factor Analysis (PFA)* are mostly used. The judgment of whether the provided factor solution is appropriate depends on the theoretical assumptions and the statistical figures, such as the explained variance of the factor(s), and the loadings of the single variables on the selected factors.

as well as to complex models, such as SEMs with many independent and dependent variables. When using theories, it is necessary to ascertain whether or not the relationship between the examined variables is spurious, in other words, whether any correlations may be due to *other variables unaccounted for* in the original analysis.

An example will help. Dutch statistics show that non-Western immigrants in the Netherlands are more healthy than the native population. However, a 'third' variable could explain the spurious nature of this seemingly odd finding. In this case, for example, one unexamined factor could be the age discrepancy between the native population and non-Western

BOX 8.7 SUBSUMATION

What can help is to deduce from *existing theories on interpersonal communication and behavior in the digital world*, insights into how Facebook and Twitter may interact with voting behavior. These theories point to cognitive and behavioral mechanisms that play a role in different communication settings. By subsuming Facebook and Twitter's interpersonal communication under these more general mechanisms, relevant variables may be found. Leeuw (2012) gives examples.

immigrants. Non-Western immigrants in the Netherlands are on average much younger, and younger people are usually healthier than older people. If we account for age in the model, the fact that non-immigrants are actually less healthy than natives is revealed.

Needless to say, many more variables could be included in such a model, including education level (higher educated people are healthier than less educated). In (regression) models, we should be aware that the results show the effects of the *unique contributions of the included independent* variables *controlled for* other independent variables. The independent variables should be selected on the basis of theories and earlier (robust) research evidence. In this example, theories from demography and epidemiology help to find these variables (and to explain the findings), but this is not always the case. As a rule of thumb, the more variables that are included, the more difficult the interpretation of them will become. Taking the example of the country of origin and health, for all included variables we rule out the differences (e.g. in age, education, and so on) between the non-Western immigrants and the native population. However, such differences still do exist, revealed in the bivariate statistics. By comparing the *bivariate associations* with the results based on *more complex models*, we are forced to provide a proper explanation, which is often more difficult than expected at first glance. In fact researchers have to deal with two dilemmas:

- *simple (bi-variate) associations between variables found through descriptive statistics are describing the actual factual statistics, but can also be misleading as other variables might play a crucial role, while*
- *the findings based on complex models are often not comprehensible because ever more variables get included in the statistical analysis, often (or at least sometimes) without being related to small or capital t (T) theories.*

For clarity's sake, then, we recommend building complex models in steps, starting from a simple model, and then enlarging the model by including a few more variables for each subsequent step. We try to do that in such a way that explanatory or intervention theories can play their role.

8.4 FOUR EXAMPLES

Until now we have been describing different methods of working with quantitative data, both at a descriptive level and at an inferential level. We now present examples that describe how the results of this kind of analysis look when dealing with specific, and practical, questions. The first example concerns the level of satisfaction of Dutch people with Dutch democracy, with data from the DPES. The second example uses the *European Social Survey* as a source. The third example looks into empirical research on the *quality of election's in OCSE countries*. Finally, the fourth example details an *experiment on the impact of incentives* in advance letters on the *response behaviour* in surveys.

8.4.1 Example 1: The Dutch Parliamentary Election Study (DPES) on the Satisfaction Levels of Dutch Society with Dutch Democracy

In Table 8.1 the satisfaction of Dutch citizens with democracy is presented and compared based on differences in gender and education levels. Let us first look at the column below with the total percentages. It reveals that, based on the 1633 respondents in the DPES 2012, 13% are very satisfied with Dutch democracy, a further 66% are fairly satisfied, 18% are not very satisfied and 2% are not at all satisfied. These four percentages add up to 100% and cover the answers of all 1633 respondents. In the third and fourth column the gender distribution is given showing that 16% of the male respondents and 11% of the female respondents are very satisfied. The table evidently shows that the highest educated voters, in particular, are more satisfied than the less educated voters.

Another way of presenting the findings is by using a bar chart (Figure 8.1). Looking at the black colour, it becomes obvious that a greater share of highly educated respondents are 'very satisfied with democracy' than is true of the less educated. On the other hand, looking at the grey and light grey colour, we see that the 'not very' and 'not at all' answers are more prevalent among the less educated than the higher educated.

Furthermore, if we were to consider this satisfaction indicator as an interval variable, ranging from (1) very (223 cases), (2) fairly (1092 cases), (3) not very (308 cases), to (4) not at all (39 cases), the mean (average) value would be 2.1, which is very close to the 'fairly satisfied' position. The median and mode value would be 2.0, and the range 3.0. The standard

Table 8.1 Satisfaction with Dutch democracy by gender and education, 2012 (n = 1633)

	Total	Gender		Education				
		Men	Women	Elementary	Lower vocational	Secondary	Middle vocational	Higher vocational / University
					%			
Very satisfied	13	16	11	7	5	11	12	24
Fairly satisfied	66	63	68	64	64	71	67	66
Not very satisfied	18	18	19	23	27	15	19	10
Not at all satisfied	2	3	2	5	4	4	2	1

Source: DPES/CBS.

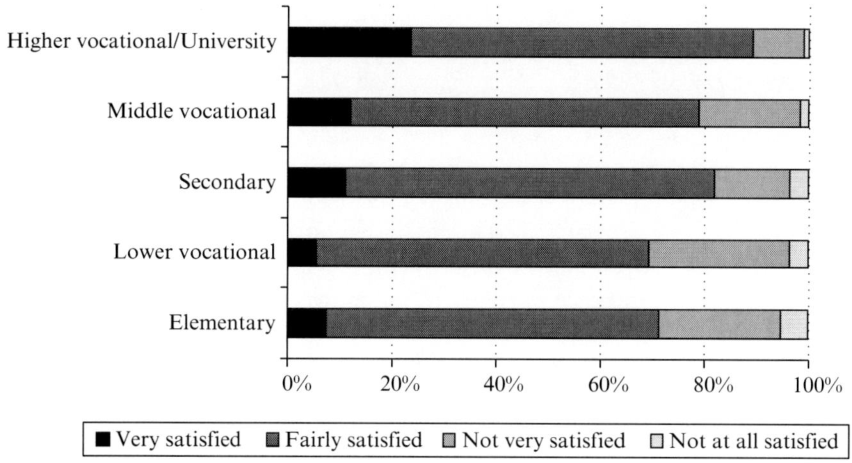

Source: DPES/CBS.

Figure 8.1 Satisfaction with Dutch democracy by education (n = 1633)

deviation is calculated by the average of all absolute differences between all the 1662 cases that provided the answers, ranging from 1 to 4 (223 + 1092 + 308 + 39) and the mean value. This standard deviation (figure of 0.64) is usually calculated using computer software programs, such as SPSS. The variance is 0.41 (0.64 * 0.64).

Inferential statistics show that the standard error is 0.016. Just to remind you, we calculate standard error by dividing the standard deviation by the square root of the sample size (0.64/40.3 = 0.016). By multiplying the standard error by 1.96, we get 0.03. If we add and subtract this figure (0.03) from the mean value of 2.1, the confidence intervals emerge: 2.08 and 2.13.

Inferential statistics can be used to calculate the association measures between the characteristics. We have revealed that there is an association between education and satisfaction with democracy: Cramérs V = 0.14; $p < 0.001$. There is also a relationship with gender: Cramérs V = 0.08; $p = 0.014$. Note that this relation is less clear as the association measure is lower (0.08), and the p-value is higher, but still clearly below the 0.05 threshold.

8.4.2 Example 2: The European Social Survey (ESS) and the Level of Trust in Institutions

The European Social Survey (ESS) is a cross-national survey which aims to describe and explain the interaction between Europe's changing institutions and the social and political beliefs and behavior of European citizens. The population used by the ESS is all people aged 15 and over in each participating country. The data have been collected by face-to-face interviews bi-annually since 2002. Research leaders of the ESS have gone to great efforts to improve survey accuracy. In all countries, systematic random samples were drawn and agreement was reached among the research teams as to the exact composition of the sampling frames. Several measures were taken to increase response rates, such as incentives for participants and specific training for interviewers. Response rates have exceeded 60% in most cases. Non-response error has been closely monitored to ensure representativeness. Additionally, efforts have been made to decrease measurement error by paying close attention to the translation of survey questions.

The ESS covers many topics, including trust in other people and in institutions like the judiciary, the police, parliament and political parties. One of the questions in the survey asks: 'Please tell me on a score of 0–10 how much you personally trust each of the institutions I read out. Zero (0) means you do not trust an institution at all, and 10 means you have complete trust.' The cross-country comparison reveals that the Netherlands is a high trust country (Linssen and Schmeets, 2010). Together with other social-democratic welfare states – including Norway, Finland, Denmark and Sweden – the Netherlands has a high ranking. A vast majority, 64%, of the Dutch population trust other people. This contrasts sharply with trust levels in many Eastern and Southern European countries. In Turkey, Bulgaria and Portugal social trust is less than 20%. Another finding was that many (72%) Dutch citizens trust the police (score 6–10). Only in some Nordic countries, in particular Denmark and Finland, do more people trust the police. Some 63% of the Dutch population has trust in the judicial system. Only in four other countries – Switzerland, Norway, Denmark and Finland – is trust in the judicial system higher. In Belgium, trust is substantially lower at 44%, a figure comparable to those in France and the UK. Lower trust levels are found in Ukraine, Bulgaria and Croatia. The majority of the Dutch also have trust in political institutions: in parliament, in politicians and in political parties. These trust levels are higher than in most other countries and are similar to those found in Norway, Finland, Denmark and Sweden. Especially low trust levels are found in Eastern European countries, such as Poland, Bulgaria, Ukraine and Hungary. In some of the Mediterranean countries, such as Greece and Portugal, trust in political institutions is low in comparison to other European countries. In addition, turnout rates in parliamentary elections are high in the Netherlands: only in Denmark, Sweden and Norway do more people go to the polls. This is also true for Belgium and Cyprus, where compulsory attendance has been introduced. However, when it comes to other political activities, such as demonstrating, contacting politicians, signing petitions and boycotting products, the Netherlands takes a middle position in the European ranking (see Table 8.2).

In Table 8.3 the correlations between the various trust indicators and the voter turnout are displayed. Using rank order correlations (Spearman's Rho), a strong correlation between the two is revealed. Most correlations measure 0.80 or higher. These high correlations imply that if the countries' position on one trust indicator is available, we can make a fairly good prediction what the countries' position in the rank will be for the other trust indicator. The highest correlation found trust in political parties and trust in politicians (0.99). However, not all trust indicators are strongly correlated. This is particularly true for the correlation between trust in the European parliament (EP) and voter turnout (0.36). Note that this is also the only insignificant correlation ($p > 0.05$). An inspection of the figures in the table shows why this correlation is low: a high turnout does not often go together with great trust in the EP, and that also applies to the combination of low turnout and low levels of trust in the EP.

The Spearman's rank order correlation value usually comes very close to Pearson's R value, and this is also true for correlations between the above eight indicators. The R-square (R^2) is the explained variance and tells us the share of the variance of the dependent variable (y) explained by the values on the independent variable (x). Another term for the R^2 is the fit of the model (in this case the regression between variables x and y).

Let us now look at an example by explaining the variance of trust in police versus trust in the judicial system. The scatter gram (Figure 8.2) shows that R^2 equals 0.82. Note that this corresponds with the Pearson's R value of 0.90 (the correlation) by taking the square root of 0.82. Note also that this correlation R value of 0.90 corresponds to exactly the same value as expressed in the Spearman's Rho correlation in Table 8.3. In addition, the regression equation is displayed. The mean values demonstrate that trust in the police is on average higher (57%) compared to trust in the judicial system (44%). The intercept of the regression line is 20.56, which equals the position of trust in the police and the 0% trust in the judicial system. The slope (the b-value) is 0.88, which indicates that on top of the 20.6% trust, a 0.88% trust has to be added for each 1% trust in the judicial system. For example, if trust in the judicial system is 70%, the prediction for trust in police is: 20.56% + (0.88 * 70%) = 82.16%. Note that this effectively mirrors the position of Switzerland (70% and 82% respectively).

Table 8.2 Trust in other people and (political) institutions, turnout in 28 countries (%)

	Year of Survey	Other people	Judicial System	Police	Politicians	Parliament	Political parties	European Parlement	Turn-out
Belgium	2012	46	44	66	31	44	30	47	89
Bulgaria	2012	18	10	23	4	7	4	32	52
Cyprus	2012	21	40	44	9	18	9	32	79
Denmark	2012	78	86	90	47	63	48	45	88
Germany	2012	41	60	77	20	39	18	32	72
Estonia	2012	48	42	58	16	26	14	36	64
Finland	2012	74	79	93	41	61	41	44	67
France	2010	27	40	54	13	24	10	28	55
Greece	2010	26	28	39	3	7	3	12	62
Hungary	2010	31	36	44	15	29	14	37	62
Ireland	2012	48	46	73	15	21	13	33	70
Iceland	2012	59	60	90	23	31	18	33	81
Kosovo	2012	22	19	49	11	19	12	48	43
Croatia	2010	35	17	32	4	8	4	15	54
Netherlands	2012	65	67	77	50	52	48	45	75
Norway	2012	75	82	83	44	66	43	35	78
Ukraine	2010	29	6	10	4	6	5	25	57

Austria	2006	44	60	66	16	40	17	28	75
Poland	2012	26	20	46	6	13	6	29	49
Portugal	2012	20	19	51	4	9	3	16	58
Russia	2012	32	21	20	13	18	14	23	60
Slovenia	2012	35	18	49	7	15	7	23	66
Slowakia	2012	24	15	27	10	15	10	22	59
Spain	2012	44	25	59	7	21	7	26	69
CzechRepublic	2012	33	30	42	14	19	14	28	59
United Kingdom	2012	48	52	73	21	31	19	18	66
Sweden	2012	63	66	74	38	60	38	36	83
Switzerland	2012	54	70	82	45	63	41	35	49

Source: ESS.

Table 8.3 Trust in other people and (political) institutions, turnout in 28 countries: Spearman's Rho

	Other people	Judicial System	Police	Politicians	Parliament	Political parties	European Parlement	Turn-out
Trust: other people	1.00							
Trust: judicial system	0.84**	1.00						
Trust: police	0.83**	0.90**	1.00					
Trust: politicians	0.85**	0.91**	0.83**	1.00				
Trust: parliament	0.84**	0.93**	0.88**	0.96**	1.00			
Trust: political parties	0.84**	0.88**	0.78**	0.99**	0.95**	1.00		
Trust: European parliament	0.48*	0.57**	0.56**	0.69**	0.67**	0.67**	1.00	
Turnout Parliamentary elections	0.63**	0.66**	0.60**	0.59**	0.60**	0.58**	0.36	1.00

Notes:
* $p < 0.05$ (two-tailed).
** $p < 0.01$ (two-tailed).

Source: ESS.

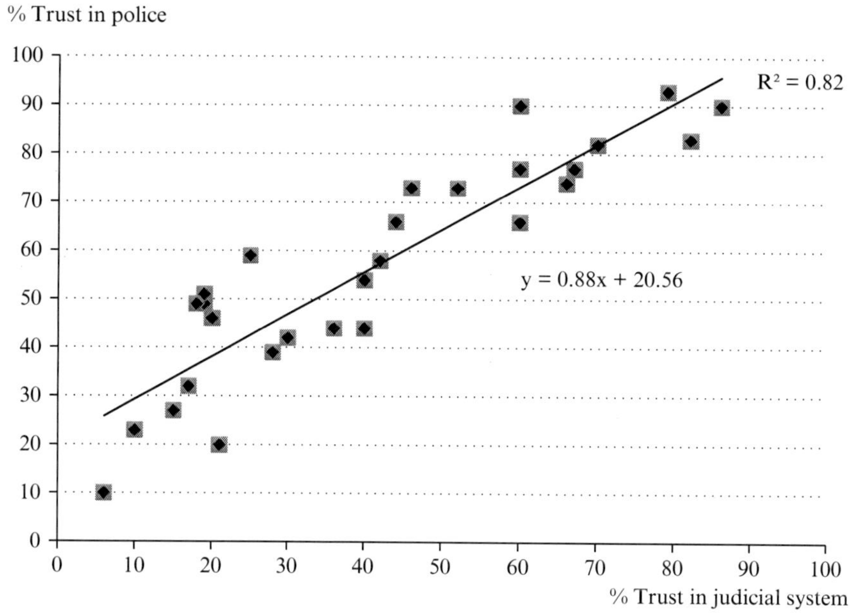

Figure 8.2 Trust in police and trust in judicial system: scatterplot (n = 28 countries)

8.4.3 Example 3: Election Observation Missions: The Quality of OSCE Polling Stations Measured

Of a different nature is the third example: *empirical research on the quality of elections in the OSCE region*. The OSCE is the Organization for Security and Co-operation in Europe (OSCE); it addresses a wide range of security-related concerns, including arms control, human rights, national minorities, democratization, policing strategies, counter-terrorism and economic and environmental activities. All 57 participating states enjoy equal status, and decisions are made by consensus on a politically, but not legally binding basis.[7]

Polling stations are an essential element of the electoral process. They are the sites where voting takes place and where votes are counted by the election administration. Election Observation Missions (EOMs) play an important role in evaluating the quality of elections. The OCSE has developed handbooks, including a handbook on *Media Monitoring for Election Observation Missions* and a brochure describing the main methodology of this work.[8] The methodology of an EOM is based on the participation of international election observers. To this end, all OSCE member states are requested to send international observers: long-term observers (LTOs) to cover the whole election period of two to three months, and short-term observers (STOs) who stay for a week around election day. The Office for Democratic Institutions and Human Rights (ODIHR) provides the methodology and coordination for EOMs. Core teams of 10 to 20 international election experts, along with local staff, are put into place on the ground. The OSCE/ODIHR deploys hundreds of STOs. On average some 330 STOs are on the ground per election, with this number increasing from slightly more than 200 in 1996 to 400 in 2010 (Schmeets, 2011). STOs are paired in teams of two, and together with a driver and interpreter they visit some 10 to 12 polling stations and report their observations at each station by answering over 50 questions on a 'Observer Report Form'. Soon after, usually in the afternoon on the day after election day (within 24 hours after the closing of the polling stations), the OSCE/ODIHR releases a preliminary statement about the elections and publishes a final election report with recommendations within approximately six to 10 weeks after the completion of the electoral process.

The 'quality of an election', including the assessment based on the observations inside the polling stations, is analysed on the basis of several criteria focusing on the question of whether the elections are in line with the specific paragraphs in the 1990 Copenhagen commitments, which require elections to be equal, fair, secret, free, universal, transparent and accountable.[9] Apart from full-scale EOMs, another approach for observing elections is a limited election mission, without STOs, which is called an *Election Assessment Mission (EAM)*. EAMs have become more popular in recent years as a tool for covering the elections in other member states, including 'old' democracies like the Netherlands, the USA and the UK.

With regard to methodology and statistics, a first point to mention is that EOMs do not need to struggle with the issue of non-response. Essentially all the approached polling stations have to co-operate: the chairperson of a polling station, as stated in the election law and observers' code of conduct, cannot refuse the presence of (accredited) international observers. However, in some states parts of the country cannot be covered. In the Russian Federation, observers are on the ground only in the west and the south of the country. Recently, in the 2014 presidential and legislative elections in the Ukraine, no observers were sent to the Luhansk and Donetsk regions due to safety risks. This problem is basically a population issue: the sample is based on a part of the population and all conclusions are not related to the country as a whole, but a defined part of it.

In a typical EOM, the OSCE/ODIHR requests a number of international observers, often between 300 and 600. In a deployment plan the regions are selected in which LTOs operate. A number of international observers are allocated to the LTO regions. For example in the recent 2014 Presidential Election in Ukraine, a total of 40 LTO teams were deployed. Within the LTO region a number of districts are selected where specifically assigned observer teams should observe on polling day. Although there is no selection bias due to non-response (for various reasons), more polling stations are observed in urban than in rural areas (Bader and Schmeets, 2014). The main reason is that remote polling stations are more difficult to access, and polling stations located close to the observers' accommodation are more often in urban than in rural areas. How severe this selection bias is depends on the correlation between urban/rural and observers' assessments. If the findings of observers in rural areas do not differ from those in urban areas, signifying no correlation, the estimates will not be affected by selection bias. However, if a correlation does exist, e.g. the situation in urban areas is more positive than in rural areas, the result will be too positive. A panacea would then be to reweigh the data: urban located polling stations would receive a lower weight, and rural stations a higher one.

Observers cover the opening of the polling stations, the voting process, the vote count and the tabulation of the results. For all four phases, observers fill in their observations in a special observer report form. On election day and night up to 8000 report forms, based on these observations, are handed over or faxed to the EOM headquarters. Recently, these forms have been sent and processed automatically using software in the pens of the observers when filling in the observer report forms. Severe irregularities, such as ballot box stuffing, intimidation of voters and observers, are checked for. The answers to one question in the four observer report forms, in particular, comes under close scrutiny: 'The conduct of the [opening; voting; counting; tabulation] process is very bad/bad/good/very good'. This overall indicator is a very important tool in the assessment of the elections based on the findings of the short-term observers. The importance of this question in the observer report forms is highlighted in the observers' briefings and de-briefings. It also serves as the key figure in the statements as well as in the negotiations with various delegations involved in the joint statements, made in a typical EOM by the Parliamentary Assemblies of the OSCE and Council of Europe, and the EU Parliamentary Delegation.

Apart from the overall indicator, some 50 other specific questions relating to problems and irregularities are included in the observer report forms. Observers are also requested to give further written comments and details. These comments provided by observers in special forms are processed in order to produce an overview in a database of problems and to identify significant violations.

Clearly, the methodology in an EOM is based on a mixture of quantitative and qualitative approaches. The comments provide further insights of what was seen and heard during the observations, and accompany the more statistical nature of the quantitative information. If clear quantitative violations (e.g. ballot box stuffing) are not expanded upon by comments, this will be investigated and the data – if needed – will be cleaned accordingly.

The estimates as well as the correlations are compared with the findings of other EOMs. For example, if intimidation is observed in 5% of the polling stations in an election, and intimidation is observed only in 2% of all elections, this signals that there is a serious problem in that particular election. On the other hand, a 5% 'family or group voting' figure is low and might even be considered as a positive indication of the greater observance of the principle of 'secrecy' in that election. Clear violations of the various principles should go together with a (very) negative judgement overall. Some problems and irregularities are more strongly correlated with the overall indicator, and consequently have a stronger impact on observers' decisions whether the assessment is either (very) bad or (very) good, than others.

Observers' findings are studied from a comparative perspective. In Schmeets (2011), based on 96 EOMs in the 1996–2010 period, a *benchmark* was introduced in order to evaluate observers' findings based on the overall indicators. The best quartile of the voting process overall assessments consists of a group of elections with up to 3% negative reports. The next quartile includes between 3 and 6.5% negative reports, followed by the group ranging between 6.5 and 10%, and the worst quartile consists of more than 10% negative reports. Similarly, the four election groups are selected based on the overall assessments of vote count observations: the best group consists of elections in which less than 9% of the reports are negative, the next group falls in the range from 9 to 16.9%, the third group from 17.0 to 27.4%, and the worst group comprises elections whose vote count observations were over 27.5% negative. This benchmark shows that the voting process in Tajikistan and the Southern Caucasus – Azerbaijan, Georgia and Armenia – fall in the worst category (more than 10% negative reports) and consequently are labeled 'very bad' elections. Elections in Albania, Belarus, Kazakhstan and Macedonia are found in the third quartile ('bad'). Other countries are characterized as either 'good' or 'very good'. The picture changes for the vote count. Tajikistan (55%) and Belarus (52%) exceed the 27.5 threshold and fall in the worst quartile with more than half of the observer reports negative. This also holds true for Azerbaijan (38%) and Kazakhstan (32%). Another way of presenting the figures is in a graph in which the assessment of the voting process is the x-variable, and the assessment of the counting process is the y-variable (see Figure 8.3). A total of 81 EOMs are included and for some EOMs the labels are also included. Let us look at one of the two EOMs in Croatia in

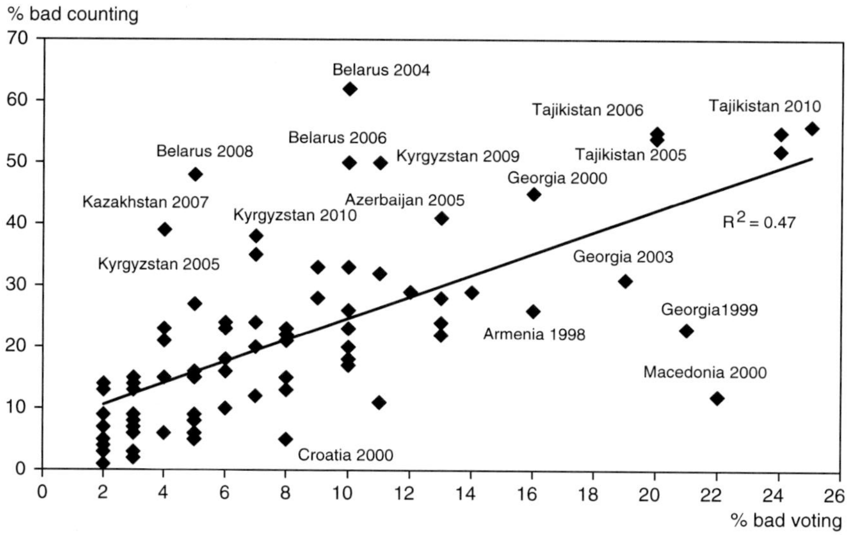

Figure 8.3 *Bad to very bad assessed voting and counting stations in 81 elections, 1996–2010*

2000: observers assessed 8% of the stations in the voting process and 5% of the stations in the counting process negatively. In Kazakhstan in 2007 4% of voting stations were assessed as either bad or very bad, as were 39% of the counting stations. Note that both assessments, the voting and counting process, are linked to each other. The regression line shows that a negative overall assessment of the voting process is associated with a negative overall judgment of the vote count in an EOM ($R^2 = 0.47$). In other words, if the observer teams concluded that only in a very limited number of polling stations the process was bad or even very bad, they were also mild in their overall assessment of the counting process.[10]

This overview clearly shows that the cross-country variation is substantial. Moreover, the overall assessment of the voting process is evidently more positive in comparison to the counting process. An explanation for this finding is that observer teams stay for approximately 30 minutes in a polling station observing the voting process, whereas they stay from the beginning until the end to observe the counting procedures. They may notice more problems and irregularities during their stay of at least two to three hours observing the counting procedures than during their observation of the voting process. A further explanation is that it might be easier to manipulate the counting process than the voting process, and consequently more violations will be noticed during the vote count.

8.4.4 Example 4: An Experiment to Enhance Response Rates by Incentives in the Dutch Labour Force Study 2005

An appropriate design to test the impact of a treatment is a randomized controlled experiment. The exact design of an experiment is important in that it allows us to draw general conclusions. Randomization and blocking are two crucial principles (see Chapter 6 for more information). When national statistical institutes change their data-collection methodology, this often has an impact on the statistical estimates, for example residents' assessment of their neighbourhood as safe or unsafe. In order to measure the impact of such a change in the methodology, i.e. the trend breach, the sample is divided into two blocks, with one block benefiting from the traditional data-collection method, and the other from a new data-collection method. The interpretation of the difference between the findings based on the two samples is the change in data-collection methodology. The estimates are surrounded by margins, and consequently it is crucial to ascertain the accuracy of the findings beforehand, which involves careful selection of the sample size of the experimental and control groups.

An example of such an experiment is a *revision of the advance letter* in order to assess the impact on response rates. That type of research has a long history in which a wide range of measures have been discussed and tested as ways of enhancing response rates (Stoop, 2005). Groves and Couper (1998) distinguish factors under researchers' control such as the survey design, the topic and length of the questionnaire, the selection and motivation of interviewers, and the number of contact efforts. However, the sociodemographic, behavioural and attitudinal characteristics of the people to be interviewed are also important. Other factors are related to the interaction between the interviewers and the selected persons. Dillman et al (2009) refer to 'respect for the respondent' as a crucial element for facilitating cooperation. The advance letter is an important element for getting respect (and participation). An advance letter should aim to establish a rapport between researcher and respondent by demonstrating why the survey has to be conducted and why the cooperation of the respondent is important.

Feskens (2009), Stoop (2014) and Kappelhof (2015) elaborate on tailored strategies for hard-to-survey groups, such as ethnic minorities. And, among others, Dillman (1991) refers to the use of unconditional incentives. There is a large body of literature showing that unconditional incentives, even in small amounts, enhance the cooperation of persons in surveys. Interestingly, the literature does not claim the same for rewards for participation in a survey (Groves and Couper, 1998; Singer, 2001; Dillman et al, 2009). The effect of prepaid incentives on the response rate is often explained with reference to *social exchange theory*. The potential respondents receive an incentive from the research institution without having to give something back. According to this theory, an incentive is seen as an act of kindness and a token of trust and this kindness evokes the norm of reciprocity. In accepting the gift, the potential respondent feels more or less obliged by social norms to respond in kind.

In the Netherlands, a large-scale experiment (n = 10,995), based on the Dutch Labour Force Survey (LFS), was conducted in November–December 2005 by Statistics Netherlands. The experiment found that the response rate increased from 66% to 73% if 10 postage stamps (value: €4) were included in the advance letter (Wetzels et al, 2008). The LFS is designed as a rotating panel with five waves. Each month a sample of about 7500 addresses are drawn by stratified two-stage sampling. The monthly samples of November and December 2005 were randomized over four treatment groups with no stamps, 5 stamps, 10 stamps and 20 stamps. In total, 6960 addresses were approached in November and 6029 in December. The addresses were allocated over the four treatment groups as: (1) No incentive, 6195 addresses; (2) Incentive valued €2 (5 stamps), 3146 addresses; (3) Incentive valued €4 (10 stamps), 3148 addresses; (4) Incentive valued €8 (20 stamps), 500 addresses.

The purpose of this experiment was to investigate the following research questions: (1) What is the effect of €2, €4, and €8 incentives on the response rates? (2) Do incentives improve the selectivity, i.e. decrease the variation in response rates between different subpopulations?

A response account of the fieldwork under the four treatment groups of the experiment is given in Table 8.4. The response increases substantially when stamps were included in the advance letter. Compared to the group without incentives, the jumps in the response rate equal 5.3, 7.8 and 7.4% for the groups with 5, 10 and 20 stamps respectively. Note that this is caused by lower refusal percentages of 5.1, 7.1 and 10.1% respectively.

Table 8.4 Response and non-response in households by variant incentives

	0 stamps		5 stamps		10 stamps		20 stamps	
		%		%		%		%
Refusal	1211	23.2	476	18.1	432	16.1	57	13.1
No opportunity	240	4.6	125	4.8	123	4.6	26	6.0
Language problem	78	1.5	37	1.4	51	1.9	5	1.2
No contact	262	5.0	127	4.8	106	4.0	29	6.7
Response	3419	65.6	1865	70.9	1964	73.4	317	73.0
Total	5210	100.0	2630	100.0	2676	100.0	434	100.0

Source: CBS.

The second research question deals with the selectivity in the response, i.e. whether incentives decrease or increase the variation in response rates between different subpopulations. The response distributions of the explanatory variables for the four treatments show only minor effects of the incentives on the selectivity for most variables. There are, however, effects on the response distributions over regions and country of origin. The influence on response distributions is particularly strong for the three largest cities in the Netherlands – Amsterdam, Rotterdam and The Hague – which have the highest non-response rates. A 10-stamp incentive results in a response rate increase from 53 to 65%, whereas outside of those three cities there was a moderate increase, from 70 to 76%. On the other hand, the incentives did not increase the response among non-Western ethnic minorities. Some 60% of the group that did not receive an incentive participated in the survey. Of the non-Western minorities which received an advanced letter in which 10 stamps were included, 58% participated. This contradicts the findings found among the native population (an increase from 69 to 77%) as well as among Western foreigners (from 64 to 73%). Consequently, the gap in response rate between the non-Western ethnic minorities and the native population increased. This is also true for the gap between the non-Western and Western ethnic minorities. The effect of incentives on response behavior is also tested with a logistic regression analysis. Interaction effects between the incentives and the other social-demographic variables on response rates indicate an increase or decrease of selectivity. Therefore response behavior (1 = response; 0 = other response categories) is given in a logistic regression model using the following explanatory variables: (1) Treatment (no incentive, 5 stamps and 10 stamps); (2) Age (15–34/35–44/45–54/55–64/65 and older); (3) Gender (male/female); (4) Household size (1/2/3/4/5 or more members); (5) Household income (standardized); Region (three largest cities/other areas); (6) Country of origin (native Dutch population/Western foreigners/non-Western foreigners). Apart from the main effects of the included independent variables on the dependent variable (the response – yes/no), Statistics Netherlands included so-called *second order interactions* with incentives in the regression model. Two significant interactions were found: (a) incentive × region and (b) incentive × country of origin. The results affirmed the findings in the bivariate associations that the difference in response rates between non-Western migrants and both Western migrants and the native Dutch population increased *due to the incentive*. The discrepancy in response rates between the three largest cities and the other areas shrank. In other words, if we focus on the region, there is less selectivity if we use a 10-stamp incentive. However, looking at the country of origin indicates an increase in selectivity.

This example shows how to analyze the impact of a treatment in an experiment. Starting with cross-tables, the subsequent regression model (in this case a logistic regression as the dependent variable is dichotomous) provides the information on the main-effects and the interactions between the treatment and the other independent variables.

We leave the stage of these types and examples of quantitative data analysis regarding elections and we move to something different: Big Data analysis.

8.5 BIG DATA ANALYSIS

Big Data usually include data sets with sizes beyond the ability of commonly used software tools to capture, curate, manage and process the data within a tolerably elapsed time. A number of open source processing and analyzing frameworks have become entrenched in the Big Data arena, for instance Apache Hadoop (http://hadoop.apache.org/). This section describes two examples of how Big Data can be analyzed: one from computational legal linguistics (Katz and Bommarito, 2013) and one from working with Google search data (Willemsen and Leeuw, in press).

8.5.1 Example 1: Computational Legal Studies

Katz and Bommarito (2013: 3–4) studied how complex legal rules are (in the USA):

> This question is particularly challenging, as law must operate in both a static and dynamic context, both in the moment and across time. While current circumstances typically dictate how legal rules are crafted, innovation in social interaction, economic exchange, and political behavior yield an increasingly complex world whose conduct the law is subsequently called upon to regulate. Thus, as a society or economy becomes more complex, legal rules arguably must adapt to match this complexity. While this idea is clear in theory, when one observes a society and its complex body of legal rules, it is difficult to objectively assess the necessity of this complexity. Observed legal complexity may be driven by a genuine effort to keep pace with ongoing developments in society. Alternatively, it may only be the by-product of politicians' efforts to deliver particularized benefits to specific individuals or interest groups. Politicians may seek to maximize their own reelection function by modifying legal rules in a manner consistent with the preferences of their core constituency.

To help sort this out, Katz and Bommarito developed a method to measure complexity as objectively as possible. Their focus was the *United States Code* featuring a total of some 50 Titles. In published form, it contains hundreds of thousands of provisions and tens of millions of words. Their theory centered upon a hypothetical individual engaging in a knowledge acquisition process (ibid., p. 1):

> Knowledge acquisition, a field at the intersection of psychology and computer science, studies the protocols individuals use to acquire, store, and analyze information. Using ideas developed in this field, we develop and apply an acquisition protocol for the *Code* . . . and conceptualize complexity as the cost of carrying out the acquisition protocol. Our protocol indicates that the three primary qualitative features of the *Code* that contribute to its complexity are structure, language, and interdependence. . . . This conceptual justification allows us to move discussion of legal complexity past assessments akin to the adage 'I know it when I see it'. Having identified these three aspects of complexity, we *empirically measured* them by applying computational techniques that scale to the scope of this large body of information.

In this research project an XML representation of the 49 active Titles of the US Code in 2010 was used. Information on the data set was provided by the Cornell Legal Information Institute and can be accessed at http://hula.law.cornell.edu/uscode_xml_dist/usc-xml-2010-10-28/ (accessed 17 July 2015).

8.5.2 Example 2: Google Search Terms, Google Correlate and Predicting the Number of Bankruptcies in the Netherlands

Willemsen and Leeuw (in press) studied the development of bankruptcies in the Netherlands by using Google's online, automated method for query selection: *Google Correlate*.[11] This method determines which queries best mimic the data; these *search queries* can serve to build an estimate of the *true value* of the phenomenon. Google Correlate searches millions of candidate queries in order to find the best matches for a targeted time series.[12] An early example was Google Flu Trends (GFT). GFT was created in 2008 and worked with search algorithms to track flu activity based on individuals' searches for flu-related terms.[13] Although the results were spectacular, GFT also encountered serious criticism.[14] Therefore we set ourselves the challenge of finding out how well this approach could work, when taking on board a problem well-known in (empirical) legal research: bankruptcies in the Netherlands.

When a company, institution or natural person is no longer in a position to meet their financial obligations, in the Netherlands, they – or one or more of their creditors – may file for bankruptcy at a District Court level. The number of bankruptcies pronounced per month partly depends on the number of days the District Courts are in session during that month, and may fluctuate strongly from month to month. See Figure 8.4 for the administrative legal data downloaded from Statistics Netherlands.

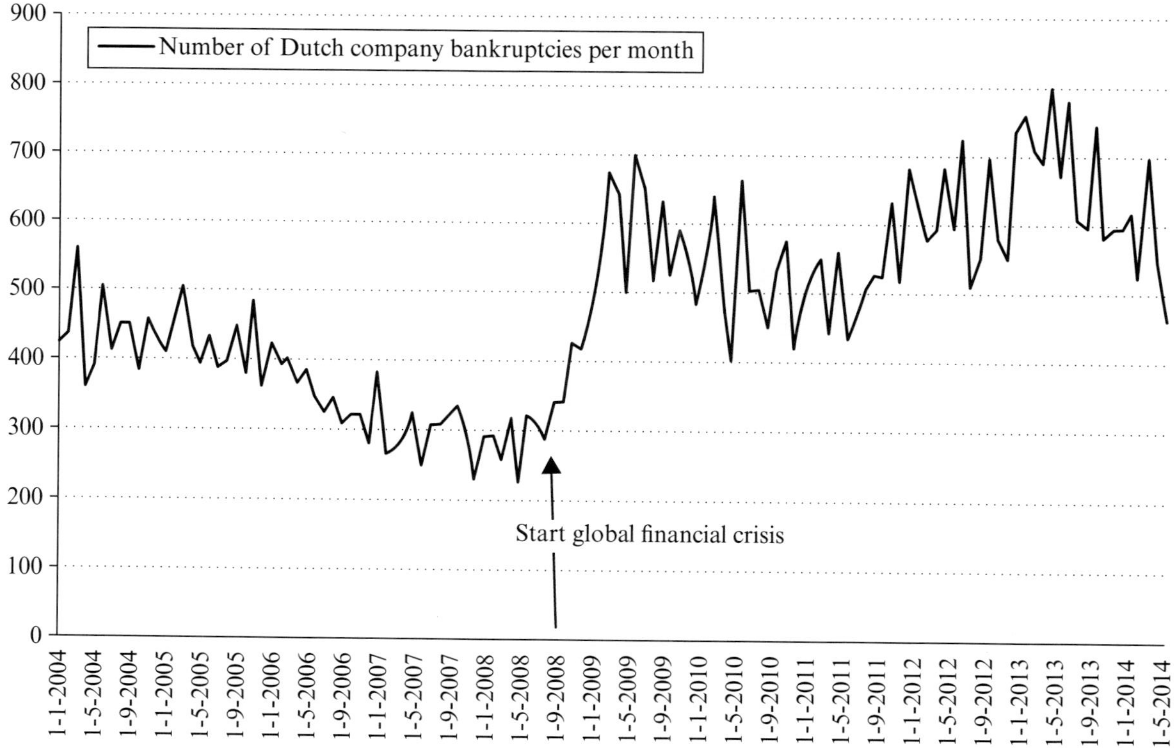

Figure 8.4 *Business bankruptcy per month in the Netherlands (2004–2014)*

Figure 8.4 shows that the start of the global financial crisis had a very serious impact on the number of bankruptcies in the Netherlands. Beginning with the bankruptcy of Lehman Brothers on 14 September 2008, the financial crisis entered a critical phase marked by failures of prominent banks and efforts by the American and European governments to rescue financial institutions. This reduced the possibilities for companies to obtain new loans to continue their businesses.

Willemsen and Leeuw (in press) uploaded the bankruptcy time series into the Google Correlate spreadsheet. Only two variables were uploaded – a date (month and year) and the number of bankruptcies for every month – while no labels or relevant file names were attached. Next, correlation coefficients (r) were calculated between the (Statistics Netherlands) time series and the frequency time series for every query in the Google database. Google Correlate employs an approximate nearest neighbor (ANN) algorithm over millions of candidate queries in an online search tree to produce results in seconds. The queries that Google Correlate shows are the ones with the highest correlation coefficient (see Table 8.5).

The Dutch queries in Table 8.5 are most highly correlated with the uploaded target pattern (bankruptcy). Variation in the queries could predict the number of bankruptcies in the near future, for which clues are also found in Figure 8.5. It shows that the query with the highest correlation (='WW-uitkering' [unemployment benefits]) has the same shape as our uploaded time series from Statistics Netherlands (representing the administrative and 'real' numbers of bankruptcies). The fact that the query also acted very well in times of very serious changes is remarkable (i.e. the sudden start of the global financial crisis in September 2008).

We next turned to the question of what the role of a *small-t theory*

Table 8.5 Top queries for bankruptcy time series in Google Correlate

Correlation (r)	Query (in Dutch)	Translation
0.900	WW Uitkering	Unemployment benefits
0.872	WW	Abbreviation for Dutch unemployment legislation
0.857	Berekenen WW	Calculate unemployment benefits
0.856	To excel	To excel
0.848	Doorstart	Relaunch (of a business)
0.847	Credios	Dutch debt collection agency
0.847	Uitkering	Unemployment benefits
0.844	Faillissement	Bankruptcy
0.842	Hoogte WW	The amount of the benefit

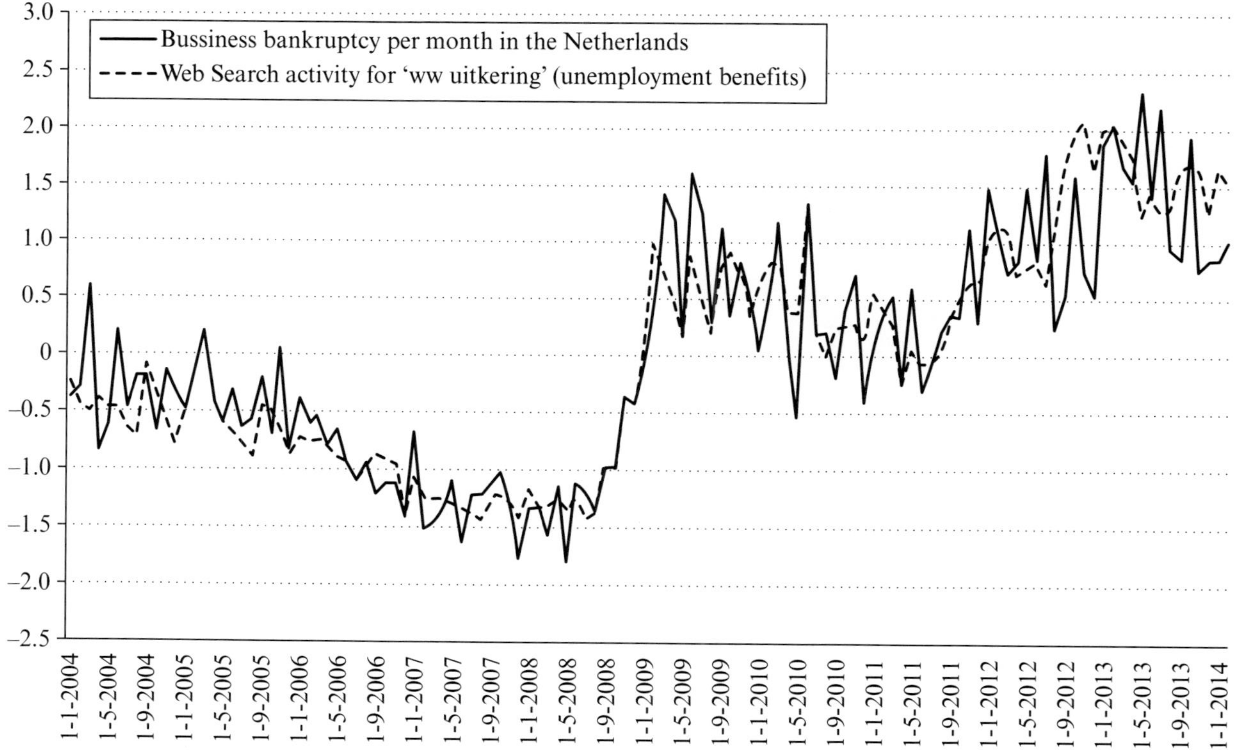

Figure 8.5 *User-uploaded activity for Business bankruptcy per month in the Netherlands. Web Search activity for 'wwuitkering' (unemployment benefits) (r = 0.900)*

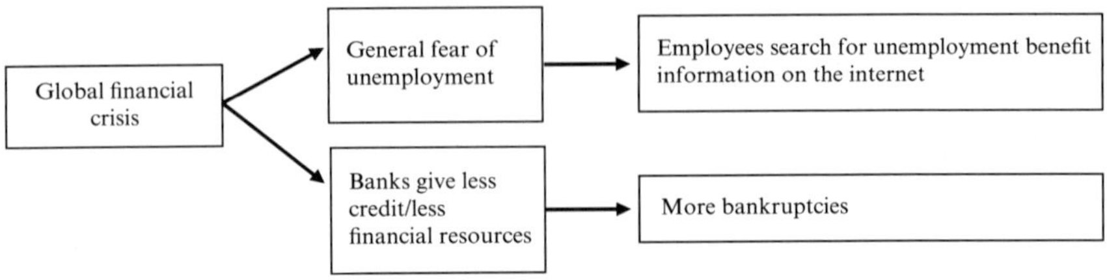

Figure 8.6 Small-t theory on mechanisms regarding the relationship between the global financial crisis and bankruptcies

may be in understanding this finding. Our *small-t theory*, that is to say, expectations about how the world works and what is needed to understand phenomena of interest (Lempert, 2010: 887) (see Chapter 4) argues that employees of companies with severe financial problems are using these search terms to find relevant information, *even before bankruptcies are pronounced at a District Court*. The *small-t theory* also suggests that the global financial crisis causes two other mechanisms: *fear of becoming unemployed* and a *lack of financial resources*. The first mechanism causes more queries for 'unemployment benefits' and lookalike terms, the latter more for bankruptcy (related terms). By linking these behavioral mechanisms (from our small-t theory) with the global financial crisis makes the Google findings understandable (see Figure 8.6).

Having found correlated queries that can be related to this theory, the next step was to export the normalized scores of these queries and use them to build *new predicting models* in SPSS. To judge the predictive power of these models, we have to make sure that models that contain query data predict *better* than simple autoregressive models.[15] To find this out, we used the stationary bankruptcies trend from 1 January 2004 to 1 October 2008. We then tried to predict the next four months (when the numbers of bankruptcies in reality exploded) with a regular ARIMA[16] model (Figure 8.7a) and a similar time series model to which *we added normalized query data* from Google Correlate (Figure 8.7b). The figures show that the forecast (behind the dotted line) of the second model is much better than the forecast using the regular ARIMA model.

We summarize a few characteristics of working with Big Data:

- The correlation coefficients [r] are extremely high (around .90).
- Working with a small-t theory is important because it addresses the why question and it helps the forecasters to understand which mechanisms may be involved.[17]
- The cost of data collection and analysis is, when compared to other,

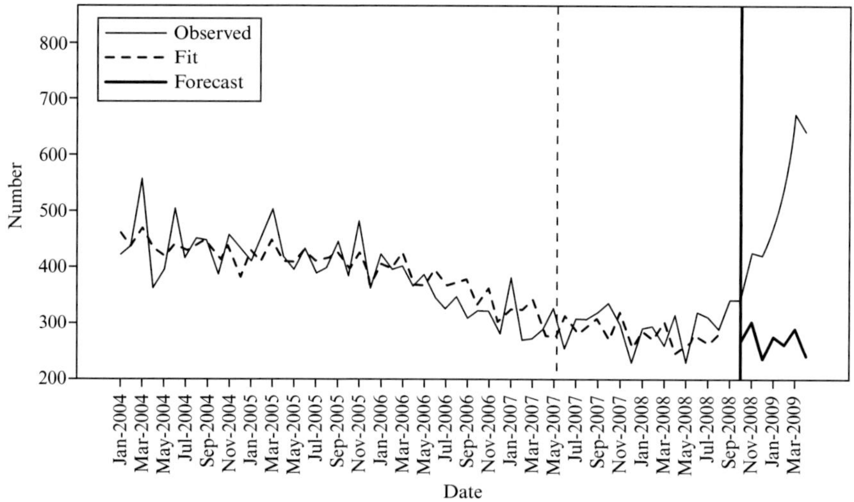

Figure 8.7a Regular ARIMA model (historical bankruptcies data only)

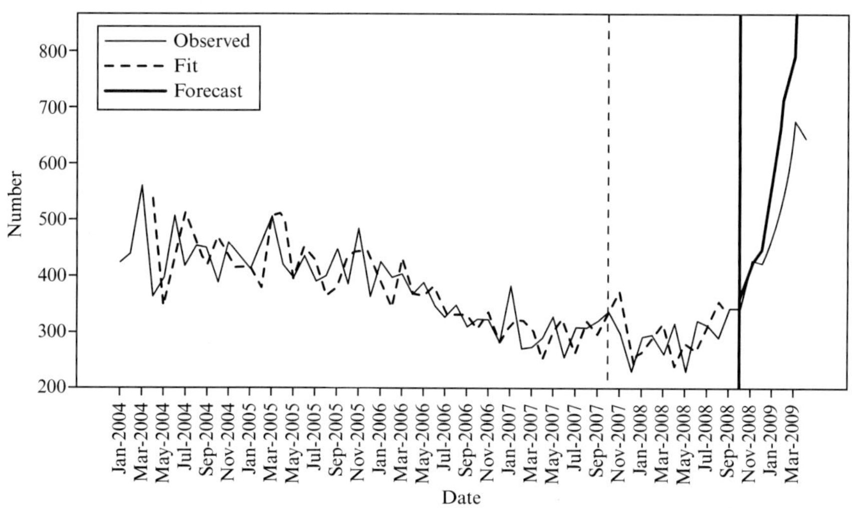

Figure 8.7b ARIMA model plus normalized query data as an independent variable

more classic approaches, extremely low. The reason is simple: data are not 'collected' but to some extent 'presented' to the researchers; software is free and the time it takes to do the (many) queries is very limited.

8.6 QUALITATIVE DATA ANALYSIS

Though the 'paradigm wars' between qualitative and quantitative analysis are disappearing, there still are important differences. Sources of qualitative data include interviews, observations and documents, but also audio and video recordings, graphics, artwork, pictures and photos, available both offline and online. In qualitative studies the focus usually is:

- more on meanings, including 'thick descriptions', than on measurement of specific variables and quantifiable phenomena;
- more on depth and detail and sensitivity to context rather than finding generalizations; and
- more on the impact of the researcher's and others' values on the course of the analysis rather than presuming the possibility of value-free inquiry.

In this book we restrict ourselves largely to *texts and documents ('narrative data')*. These can be in paper and/or digital form, structured but also unstructured, and 'official' (like wills, claims, verdicts or policy statements) but also 'informal' and personal.

Why this restriction? First, because in the legal world this type of data is (still) predominant. Second, because software programs for content analysis of narratives, are capable of analyzing other types of sources, like video or audio (see Box 8.8 for references to programs). What can be learned from content analysis of texts and documents, is also relevant for these other types of content analysis.

Text or narrative data come in many forms and from a variety of sources. Taylor-Powell and Renner (2003) and Dholakia and Zhang (2004) have inventoried a number of them:

- open-ended questions and written comments on questionnaires may generate single words, brief phrases or full paragraphs of text;
- websites;
- testimonials, either in person or in written correspondence;
- individual interviews in the form of notes, a summary of the interview or word-for-word transcripts;

BOX 8.8 SOFTWARE FOR QUALITATIVE DATA ANALYSIS INCLUDING CONTENT ANALYSES[1]

In 2006 Hall and Wright made a plea for applying content analysis from the social sciences to understanding case law: 'Content analysis is more than a better way to read cases. . . . We are not proselytizers of this method. It has certain advantages, along with substantial limitations, compared to conventional legal analysis. What we claim is that, when one reads cases this way, one engages in a uniquely legal empirical method – a way of generating objective, falsifiable, and reproducible knowledge about what courts do and how and why they do it. Content analysis aims for a scientific understanding of the law itself as found in judicial opinions and other legal texts. We maintain that content analysis makes legal scholarship more consistent with the basic epistemological underpinnings of other social science research'.
Ten years later, software programs are widely available for doing this work. They organize, evaluate, code, annotate and interpret all kinds of data, create easy-to-read reports and visualizations, and connect and share with other researchers. They usually come with YouTube instruction and demo videos but there are also textbooks available (like Krippendorf, 2013 and Barzelay and Jackson, 2013).

NVivo 10:
http://download.qsrinternational.com/Resource/NVivo10/NVivo-10-Overview.pdf.
https://www.youtube.com/watch?v=7bLZ7fqSEEc

Atlas.ti:
http://atlasti.com/qualitative-data-analysis-software/

Maxqda:
http://www.maxqda.com/

QDA Miner Lite:
http://provalisresearch.com/products/qualitative-data-analysis-software/freeware/

Coding Analysis Toolkit (CAT):
http://cat.ucsur.pitt.edu/

Transana (for qualitative researchers who want to analyze video, auditory and still image data):
http://www.transana.org/
All websites accessed 26 November 2015.

How to analyze photos, films, TV, videos, YouTube, graffiti and similar data sources
To perform a comparative analysis of drawings/photographs/videos, each image or frame is examined and coded, codes are chunked and chunks are clustered and labeled as themes until data saturation, informational redundancy and/or theoretical saturation is reached. Programs like CAQDAS (e.g. QDA Miner 4.0) facilitate the coding of drawing, photographs, paintings and other types of visual documents. Other programs (e.g. Transana, Atlas.ti) facilitate the coding of audio and video data.

Another way of using visual data is to *videotape specific aspects of behavior*. Videotaping has become a familiar everyday technique to document experiences, like holidays or festivities. It is also present in public places, underground stations and the like, which are subject to video camera surveillance. *Analyzing YouTube movies* is also a source of information. The same is true for *ready available multimedia data (soaps, news, advertisements, online materials), and private visual data (family movies – documentation analysis) and CCTV recordings*.

References
Heath et al (2010); Jewitt (2012).
Ball and Snizek (2007) analyzed *desk top graffiti* within universities to measure student culture and campus climate.

[1] Chambliss and Schutt (2015: 350) have a box describing three of the most popular programs to illustrate how they work: HyperRESEARCH, QSR NVivo and ATLAS.ti. (A free trial version of HyperRESEARCH and tutorials can be downloaded from the ResearchWare site, at http://www.researchware.com.)

- discussion group or focus group interviews can involve full transcripts and notes from a moderator or observer;
- blogs, journals and diaries;
- observations might be recorded in field notes or descriptive accounts as a result of watching and listening;
- stories may provide data from personal accounts of experiences and results of policy programs in people's own words;
- documents, reports, verdicts, narrative field logs, email exchanges and news articles or any written/digitized material also present large volumes of qualitative data, including the following:
  - Bulletin Board Systems (a medium that displays all messages that have been posted on it and their respective replies);
  - online communities;
  - chat rooms/Whatsapp;
  - Twitter accounts and other social media data, including search behavior (for example on Google).

Chambliss and Schutt (2015: 325) describe activities:

> that are shared by most approaches to qualitative data analysis.[18] They include the documentation of the data and the process of data collection (incl. data management), the organization/categorization of the data into concepts, connections between the data, the 'corroboration/legitimization', by evaluating alternative explanations, disconfirming evidence, and searching for negative cases and the reporting of the findings.[19]

8.6.1 Sampling, Documentation and Data Management

Sampling is, as is the case in quantitative research, a crucial step in the empirical cycle. Often, qualitative researchers aim at comparing groups, persons, organizations, documents or events. Flick (2009: Chapter 11) distinguishes between theoretical sampling and purposive sample and refers to some 10 subtypes of samples. Onwuegbuzie and Leech (2007) identify 22 sampling schemes. Regardless of which sampling typology is used, disclosing information on sampling decisions is crucial, including the type of sample and its rationale.

Data for a qualitative study can easily produce serious 'volumes' of information. A one-hour interview can generate 20 to 25 pages of single-spaced text (Kvale 1996:169). Miles (1979) remarked that qualitative data are usually voluminous, messy, unwieldy and discursive – 'an attractive nuisance'. This may take the form of extensive fieldnotes, hundreds of pages of transcripts from interviews or focus groups, documents, photographs or videos, and the researcher must find a way of getting a handle on the data. Working with blogs or (legal) documents can also easily fill many DVDs and USB sticks. Again: how should one handle this? Consequently, *data management and reduction* is an important task in qualitative analysis.

8.6.2 Conceptualization, Reduction, Coding and Categorizing

Identifying and refining concepts is a key part of the iterative process of qualitative data analysis. 'Read, read, read', is the adage. Sometimes, conceptualizing begins with a simple observation that is interpreted directly, 'pulled apart' and then put back together more meaningfully. A well-designed chart, or matrix, can facilitate the coding and categorization process. Taylor-Powell and Renner (2003: 3) add the following:

> Some people refer to categorizing information as coding the data or indexing the data. However, categorizing does not [automatically] involve assigning numerical codes as you do in quantitative analysis where you label exclusive variables with preset codes[20] or values. To bring meaning to the words before, you: a) identify themes or patterns – ideas, concepts, behaviors, interactions, incidents, terminology or phrases used; and b) organize them into coherent categories that summarize and bring meaning to the text. This can be fairly labor-intensive, depending on the amount of data. But this is the crux of qualitative analysis. It involves reading and re-reading the text and identifying coherent categories.

One of the more popular approaches when doing qualitative data analysis (QDA) is to work with sensitizing concepts. The term originated with Blumer (1954: 7) who contrasted definitive concepts with sensitizing concepts:

> A definitive concept refers precisely to what is common to a class of objects, by the aid of a clear definition in terms of attributes or fixed bench marks. . . . A sensitizing concept lacks such specification of attributes or bench marks and consequently it does not enable the user to move directly to the instance and its relevant content. Instead, it gives the user a general sense of reference and guidance in approaching empirical instances. . . . Sensitizing concepts merely suggest directions along which to look.

As Bowen (2006: 2) argued, (social) researchers tend to view sensitizing concepts as interpretive devices. Although Blumer (1954) suggested that these concepts can be tested, there is a serious risk that they turn out to produce immunization practices as guidance on when data must be labelled disruptive or confirmative to the sensitizing concept, often is not available.[21]

Miles, Huberman and Saldana (2014: 12) refer to these activities as *data condensation*: 'the process of selecting, focusing, simplifying, abstracting and/or transforming the data that appear in the full corpus of written-up field notes, interview transcripts, documents and other empirical materials . . . Data condensation occurs continuously throughout the life of any qualitatively oriented project'.

One can start with a list of themes or categories in advance, based on the theory that has been selected during earlier stages of the empirical cycle; from this theory concepts have been deduced that can be compared with the (documentary) evidence. It is crucial to understand what one is looking for. One approach is to search – in the data – for confirmation or verification of the insights deduced from the theory. This is not recommended because verifying a theory is only relevant if attempts to refute the conjecture also take place.[22]

Another approach is, instead of working with (largely only) preconceived themes or categories, you read through the text and find the themes or issues that recur (and emerge) in the data. These then become (new) themes or categories. They may be ideas or concepts that you had not thought about (Taylor-Power and Renner, 2003).

Coding is a crucial activity for qualitative data analysts. Miles, Huberman and Saldana (2014: 74ff) distinguish between different types: descriptive coding, process coding, emotion coding, values coding, dramaturgical coding and others. Spencer, Ritchie and O'Connor (2003: 202) suggest two ways of working:

> cross-sectional 'code and retrieve' methods, and in situ, non-cross-sectional analysis. . . . In cross-sectional code and retrieve methods, the researcher devises a common system of categories which is applied – manually or with a computer – across the whole data set and is used as a means of searching for and retrieving chunks of labelled data. This approach is felt to offer a systematic overview of the scope of the data; to aid finding themes or examples which do

> not appear in an orderly way in the data; to aid locating conceptual, analytical categories in the data; and to help getting a handle on the data for making comparisons or connections.
>
> Non-cross-sectional data organization involves looking at particular parts of the data separately, each of which may require a different conceptualization of categories. This approach is seen by some to offer better opportunities than cross-sectional analysis to gain a sense of the distinctiveness of particular sections of the material; to understand complex narratives or processes; to organize the data around themes which do not appear in all parts of the data; and to identify overall structures within each case or interview. Also included within non-cross-sectional approaches are cross-referencing systems which do not segment text but enable the analyst to browse and create pathways through the data, mainly through the use of computer software packages.

Reading need not only be done by natural persons. Over the years a number of useful software programs for *content analysis* have been developed and tested. We refer to Box 8.8 for more information. These do not fall prey to the problem of 'research(ers) fatigue', with selectivity and biases as negative consequences. The work of machines is fully replicable and auditable.

8.6.3 Examining Relationships and Displaying Data Including Verification/Falsification

Examining relationships is the centerpiece of the analytic process because it urges the researcher to move from description of the people and settings to explorations and explanations of why things happened as they did. Usually the goal is to find recurring themes in the documents, patterns, time sequences, or whether or not there exist certain clusters of participants, respondents or actors and their activities, statements or attitudes.

The process of examining relationships can be captured in a matrix that shows how different concepts are connected. Chambliss and Schutt (2015: 330) give an example. It starts with this matrix (Figure 8.8).

The figure:

> displays a matrix used to capture the relationship between the extent to which stakeholders in a new program had something important at stake in the program and the researcher's estimate of their favorability toward the program. Each cell of the matrix was to be filled in with a summary of an illustrative case study. In other matrix analyses, quotes might be included in the cells to represent the opinions of these different stakeholders, or the number of cases of each type might appear in the cells. . . . Keeping this approach in mind will generate ideas for structuring a qualitative data analysis. The simple relationships that are identified with a matrix like that shown in [this] exhibit can next be examined and extended to create a more complex *causal model*.

Exhibit 10.5 **Coding Form for Relationships: Stakeholders' Stakes**

	Favorable	Neutral or Unknown	Antagonistic
High			
Moderate			
Low			

Source: Chambliss and Schutt, 2015: 330.

Figure 8.8 Coding Form for Relationships: Stakeholders' Stakes

Such a causal model resembles a *theory* with a small t (see Chapter 4).

Miles, Huberman and Saldana (2014: 115–19; 277, 283) describe several ways to analyze matrix data. Some of them are as follows:[23]

- Start with a 'quick scan' . . . 'eyeballing' down columns and across rows.
- Pay attention to finding patterns, themes, making contrasts, comparisons and clusters, and then . . . count.
- Data displays never speak for themselves . . . Always make your interpretations and explanations explicit.
- Make contrasts/comparisons.
- Subsume particulars into the general.
- First insights have to be checked against the primary data. Look at the raw data to guard against the situation that these insights do not ring true at the 'ground level'.
- Be sure the descriptive understanding is clear at the individual or within-case level first before you try to understand cross-case patterns.

It is crucial during this step in the process of qualitative data analysis that relationships between processes, people and situations detected in the data are not interpreted without critical reflection. When explanatory theories are used, from which concepts are deduced and confronted with data, searching *only* for confirmation or verification in the data is not advisable. As is the case when working with quantitative data, it is crucial to reflect on the relationships in the empirical material and try to refute the theories used. Part of this process is to find out which *alternative explanations* are capable of explaining the relationship.

When *no* explanatory theories are used, the likelihood of *confirmation bias* may seem smaller, but can be bigger (as researchers might work with 'implicit theories' that are in dire need of 'being verified'). The same is true for qualitative data analysis that is done in line with 'Grounded Theory' and 'sensitizing concepts' (see below).

8.6.4 Representing the Findings

Finally, the results of the data analysis are presented. See section 8.8 for information on data visualization.

8.6.5 Some Examples

In line with Webley (2010) we restrict ourselves to three approaches: discourse analysis, the grounded theory approach and netnography.

Discourse analysis, according to Webley (2010), is not a single mode of data analysis but a *genre* including conversation analysis (focusing on the use of language, syntax, pauses and repetitions in the discourses being studied). Gill (2000: 174) sees four main themes in this genre: 'a concern with the discourse itself, a view of language as constructive and constructed, an emphasis upon discourse as a form of action and a conviction in the rhetorical organization of discourse'. Chambliss and Schutt (2015: 337) discuss one of the well-known members of the genre family – conversation analysis. This:

> is a specific qualitative method for analyzing the sequential organization and details of conversation. . . . It focuses on how reality is constructed, rather than on what it is. From this perspective, detailed analysis of conversational interaction is important because conversation is 'sociological bedrock': . . . a form of social organization through which the work . . . institutions such as the economy, the polity, the family, socialization, etc. is accomplished.

The grounded theory approach is the second example. This approach sees 'theory' develop *as the research process proceeds*. In Chapter 4 we discussed theories with a capital 'T' and a small 't', which are put to test *through empirical research*. The grounded theory approach is come-and-go, wherein – while researching – concepts pop up, confronted with evidence, discussed, sometimes 'stay' and get enriched, and sometimes 'go'. It is called 'grounded theory' because it is grounded in, or based on, the observations 'in reality'. The grounded theorist first summarizes observations into conceptual categories, and 'tests' the coherence of these categories directly in the research setting with more observations. Over time, as the researcher refines and links the conceptual categories, a 'theory' might evolve (Chambliss and Schutt, 2015: 341). Although this approach is often used, criticisms have been leveled against it (see Webley, 2010: 944–5).

Netnography, also termed cyberethnography and virtual ethnography, is the third example; it uses ethnographic methods to study online communities. While ethnography looks into communities in (common) physical locations, netnography looks into relationships that develop online. A netnographer keeps both observational and reflective field notes, but unlike a traditional ethnographer, can return to review the original data – the posted test – long after it was produced. The data can

BOX 8.9 NETNOGRAPHY ON SEXTING

This study (Ringrose et al, 2012) looked at 'sexting'. 'Sexting has been conventionally defined as 'exchange of sexual messages or images' and 'creating, sharing and forwarding of sexually suggestive nude or nearly nude images' (Lenhart, 2009) through mobile phones and/or the internet. The legal interest has been in under-aged sexually explicit images which are a form of child pornography. Quantitative research on sexting has found rates as wide as 15% to 40% among young people, depending on age, and the way what is understood as sexting is measured. The purpose of the qualitative research referred to in this box, was to respond to and enhance our understandings of the complex nature of sexting and the role of mobile technologies within peer teen networks. Ringrose et al. (2012) conducted focus group interviews with 35 young people aged 8 and 10 in two inner-city London schools: 'At the focus groups we asked participants to friend us on Facebook, with a research Facebook profile. The majority of our participants accepted (31); two participants did not accept our request and two did not have a Facebook account. We created a research based Facebook page, with settings so that the list of our "friends" could not see each other's posts or the list of participants. We then were able to follow public profile updates from each Facebook friend. On the basis of both focus group discussions and the online content of Facebook we selected a smaller sample of case study participants (22), with whom we followed up issues around sexual communication and representation on Facebook in individual interviews. We also interviewed key teachers and staff at the schools'. Context analysis of text messages took place where different 'sexting scenarios' were described as well as several other activities and factors active in the digital and 'classic' reality.

then be coded, annotated with the researcher's interpretations, checked against new data to evaluate the persistence of social patterns, and used to develop a theory that is grounded in the data (Chabliss and Schutt, 2015: 335).

8.7 COMBINING QUALITATIVE AND QUANTITATIVE ANALYSIS

In 1993, Caracelli and Greene published a paper in which they discussed the transformation of qualitative data into quantitative data, and quantitative data into qualitative data. Others suggested that such a combination could assist in practical solutions to overcome limitations of mono-method research. And, indeed, it can be seen from the work of Tashakkori and Teddlie (2003) and Onwuegbuzie and Leech (2007) that there now is broad agreement on the use of multiple methods with complementary strengths and different weaknesses. Part of that agreement is that the conversion of qualitative data into quantitative data ('quantitizing') and the conversion of quantitative data into qualitative ('qualitizing') is seen as an important development. Sandelowski (2000: 253) describes these processes. Quantitizing implies 'a process by which qualitative data are treated with quantitative techniques to transform them into quantitative data. The researcher must first reduce verbal or visual data (e.g., from interviews, observations, artifacts, or documents) into items, constructs, or variables that are intended to mean only one thing and that can, therefore, be represented numerically'. The author gives several examples. The opposite, qualitizing, 'refers to a process by which quantitative data are transformed into qualitative data. As in quantitizing, qualitizing can be used to extract more information from quantitative data. An example of this process is the use of scores on instruments to profile participants – to create verbal portraits or typologies of them – around target phenomena'. Tashakkori and Teddlie (1998: 130–133) described five kinds of narrative or qualitative profiling: modal, average, comparative, normative and holistic.

The *first example* is the *Dutch Organized Crime Monitor* study (Kleemans, 2014; Kruisbergen et al, 2015). In the late 1990s the Research and Documentation Centre (WODC) of the Netherlands Ministry of Justice formed a group of researchers from several organizations. Together, they conducted a systematic analysis of closed police investigations of criminal groups. Reports to Parliament were published in 1998, 2002, 2007 and 2012:

The main sources for the Monitor are the closed police files of criminal groups, often spanning a period of several years. During the period 1996–2012, 150 large-scale investigations (case-studies) were systematically content-analyzed. Each case study started with structured interviews with police officers and/or public prosecutors. Subsequently the police files are analyzed and a case report is written, using an extensive checklist.

BOX 8.10 THE CHECKLIST USED IN THE NETHERLANDS' ORGANIZED CRIME MONITOR TO ANALYSE THE 150 + CASES

1. Case Data
2. *Summary of the police/law enforcement investigation (see below)*
3. The way(s) in which criminals operated (top-down/network/hub etc.)
4. Activities, method (modus operandi) and damage done
5. Contacts with the environment
6. Extent of, distribution of and use of illegally obtained assets (criminal earnings)
7. Criminal prosecution
8. Evaluation of the case and possibilities for learning/prevention

Zooming in on point 2: Summary of the police/law enforcement investigation

- what was the reason for the investigation?
- what made the police decide to do the investigation (traces, earlier information, other reports etc.)?
- the offenses and suspects under investigation: who are they?
- any significant issues and changes that have occurred in the course of the investigation
- all deployed detection/police methods used. [Make a note of each deployed method in terms of what it produced (evidence etc.)]. Which of the methods has yielded reliable information?
- is there any special software used to search large data files, categorize or analyze? If so, what software was this? And what was the result of the use of the software?
- which people were detained and interrogated and which were not; who were heard by the police?
- what is the reason that some people have not been arrested or answered questions?
- have suspects made statements? To what extent did they confess? Were suspects granted access to the police and other law enforcement agencies' computers etc. by issuing passwords and the like (e.g. to contribute to decrypt files)?
- how much information has been collected with regard to the case (such as money laundering, exports, imports, developing malware)?
- have there been international contacts (by suspects and police/law enforcement) officials? Are there any requests for legal assistance? If so, what was the purpose of the applications, what is the result and what is the time span?

The police files contain the results of all police activities that were deployed in a case, such as wiretapping, observation techniques, undercover policing, gathering intelligence, interrogations of suspects, victims and witnesses, the confiscation of goods, and financial investigation. The strength of this data set was found in its combination of breadth of scope and depth of content. Yet it should not be understood as a representative sample, as using intrusive policing techniques to shed light on a hidden phenomenon, such as organized crime, means that a complete or random sample is rarely conceivable. Furthermore, all samples are, in some way, selective and influenced by police priorities (as well as the failures of criminal groups to escape police attention and shield their activities effectively). Therefore, the Dutch Organized Crime Monitor employs a strategic selection of cases from a total population of all closed criminal investigations of national and regional investigation teams (including the fiscal police). This strategically selective sample focuses not only on traditional drug trafficking cases (cocaine, heroin and cannabis) (37 cases), but also on other – less frequently prioritized – phenomena such as synthetic drugs (production and export) (15 cases), mixed cases (including traditional drugs and synthetic drugs) (21 cases), human smuggling (16 cases), sex trafficking (18 cases), fraud and money laundering (32 cases) and other criminal activities (11 cases).

Using the data from the 150 cases of this *Organized Crime Monitor* Kruisbergen et al (2015) investigated how (Dutch) organized crime offenders invest their money in the legal economy (real estate objects, companies, bonds and options, leaving aside investments in criminal activity as well as any form of consumption, such as spending money on nightlife, clothing, cars, boats and jewelry). The empirical data consisted of a dataset of 1196 individual assets of (suspected) participants in organized crime. It covered various crimes and also included information on foreign assets. Every case report (N = 150) was content-analyzed for available information on the offenders' assets. These 1196 assets as well as the 'surrounding' qualitative and quantitative information was analyzed through SPSS to allow for quantitative analysis (see Kruisbergen et al, 2015 for results).

Another example with a different subject matter is a study by Nielsen (2010: 175–6). The study analyzed:

> the *outcomes of employment discrimination lawsuits filed in US federal Court* from 1988 to 2003. Our analysis is informed by four theoretical models: formal legal, rational action/economic, legal mobilization, and critical realist, while three datasets were used. . . . The first is an expanded replication of Donohue and Siegelman's earlier research on employment discrimination case filings. We collected a random sample of employment civil rights cases filed in federal courts between 1988 and 2003 in seven regionally diverse federal districts. A

> second data set consists of more than 100 in-depth interviews with plaintiffs, defendants, and their lawyers. We randomly drew a subsample of cases from our filings sample in two districts. Where possible, we interviewed opposing parties and lawyers in the same case. The interviews were taped, transcribed, and coded. A third set of data is the confidential charge data file obtained from the EEOC[24] for the years 1991–2002, which contains the universe of complaints submitted to the EEOC or state fair employment agencies. . . . Rather than analyze litigation outcomes in binary terms (did the plaintiff win or lose?), we analyze case outcomes as a sequential variable. This approach better captures the dynamic character of the litigation process and the dilemmas that parties and courts face in adjudicating claims. By including distinct categories of outcomes that are largely unmeasured and therefore invisible in other research, our analysis more clearly reveals the social organization of discrimination litigation.

A *third example* studied *governance and safeguarding institutions* in Aruba and regarded the quality of governance in this microstate (Klein Haarhuis et al, 2015). According to the literature, realizing counterweights to public administration is a challenge in small-scale settings: human capital is limited and people regularly encounter each other in various social roles. Therefore, the question was asked (by the Dutch government and Aruba) to what extent safeguarding institutions in Aruba succeeded in performing their monitoring and checks and balancing tasks.

Between 2009 to 2011, Klein Haarhuis et al studied the state of governance and the enforcement of law and order in Aruba. The rationale behind the study was to describe and analyze the then current situation, including its problems with regard to good governance and to find out how much room for improvement there was. The problems pertained to alleged corruption or conflicts of interest; a poor functioning of the 'Staten' and thus of democracy; and the failure to keep to a number of the agreements set down in earlier agreed-upon protocols. Next to articulating several theories on microstates and governance issues, Klein Haarhuis et al studied written material related to aspects of good governance on Aruba. It included studies and evaluations by fact-finding or advisory committees of international organizations such as the International Monetary Fund (IMF) (on government finances) and studies by individuals. The authors also studied sources from both checks and balances and enforcement institutions, such as annual reports, or reports that dug deeper, such as studies by the General Accounting Office and the Central Auditor's Service, or the Advisory Council. The authors also obtained material from the Criminal Investigation Bureau and the Public Prosecution Service. These documents were content-analyzed and were also used for the preparation and the validation of (findings from)

86 semi-structured, anonymous interviews. Among the interviewees were representatives from safeguarding institutions, politicians – including members of the 'Staten' and the government –, officials, representatives from enforcing institutions, immigration services, the business world and civil society, and several former functionaries.

8.8 DATA VISUALIZATION

Data visualization is 'a process that (a) is based on qualitative or quantitative data and (b) results in an image that is representative of the raw data, which is (c) readable by viewers and supports exploration, examination and communication of the data' (Azzam et al, 2013). Data visualizations may look like a new 'kid on the block' but have a long history. The 'invention' by John Tukey in 1965 of the histogram to present information on the frequency of phenomena and the even older development of the 'Cholera Death Map' (John Snow) are examples from the past. The introduction of the PC around 1984 and Apple software was also a landmark. Rosling's (2007) TED talk, using bubble charts to depict life expectancy trends over time and across the globe, was a game changer (see Azzam et al, 2013: 10–13 for more historical examples). As an *amuse guelle*, see the following video: https://public.tableau.com/s/ for an amazing tool; and see https://public.tableau.com/s/authors for information, accessed 26 November 2015. The underlying idea of data visualization is that it will help potential readers and users to better receive, read and work with the evidence, more than when evidence is presented in 'old-fashioned' tables or statistics (for quantitative ELR) or in 'thick-descriptive' 'narratives' (in qualitative research).

What are important examples of data visualization?

We start with quantitative data. Lysy (2013) mentions *bubble charts*, where traditional scatter plots, based on large amounts of data points, are visually presented in such a way that the reader is much more able to see the forest instead of a thousand trees. *Pie charts*, a circular statistical graphic, which is divided into slices to illustrate numerical proportion and *infographics* (composed of graphs, diagrams and/or illustrations often related to a single topic), are other examples. *Mashups* integrate heterogeneous digital data and applications from multiple sources. *Dashboards* (sometimes used for benchmarking goals) often implies working with mashups.

These visualizations are usually non-interactive. Lysy (2013: 42) discusses interactive data presentations that 'can be manipulated directly and simply by the user in a free-flowing manner, including such actions

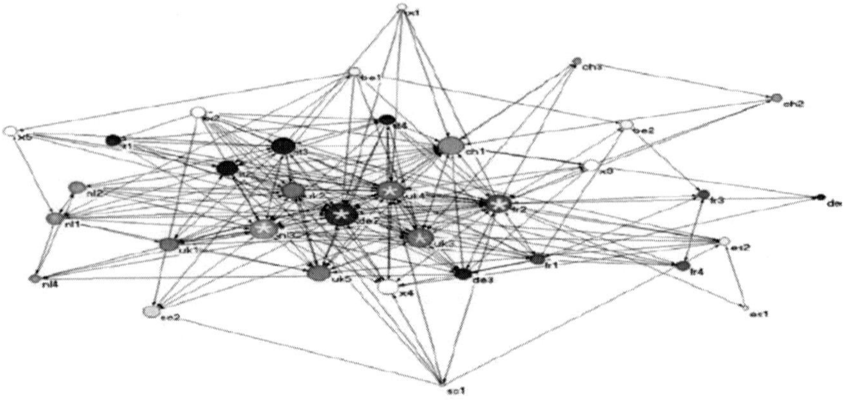

Figure 8.9 Visualization of the personal discussion network among European IP judges belonging to the Venice Forum

as filtering the data and drilling down into details'. *Interactive maps* of – for example – crime developments in communities, cities or countries are well-known examples. Part of interactive visualizations are animations, of which Rosling's *Gapminder* is a prime example (http://www.gapminder.org/, accessed 26 November 2015). *SocialNetworks* form an important focus of ELR. Lazega (2012) gives an example in his study on the mapping of judicial dialogues across national borders addressing the question if and how European intellectual property judges learn from lobbying. He used social network analysis to map a social network of judges (belonging to the *Venice Forum*), including High Court judges, that describes the ways in which they look at the work of other judges across borders and learn from each other.

Visualization (see Figure 8.9) of *qualitative data* is also becoming popular (and important) (Henderson and Segal, 2013). We have already discussed *software for content analysis* and working with *matrices*. Given the importance that documents play in empirical legal research (think of jurisprudence, political speeches and historical records), using Wordle (http://www.wordle.net) or TagCrowd (http://www.tagcrowd.com) makes *word clouds* (visual displays of word counts from one or more texts). Related visualization software does not deal with words but with sentences, while 'phrase nets highlight the connections of word pairs rather than whole sentences'. Of a different nature is the process of *argument diagramming* to aid the process of reconstructing underlying assumptions by using ICT-driven approaches, often called computer-supported argumentation or computer-supported argument visualization. Since creating argument diagrams by

BOX 8.11 TOOLOGRAPHY (KISTLER, EVERGREEN AND AZZAM, 2013)

The authors offer descriptions of a selection of the *tools* used in the field of social science research, evaluation and policy studies. It provides readers with a general estimate of their ease of use, whether they are available for free and their strengths and weaknesses, along with guidance on how to access further information and alternatives to the tool. The authors expect that the number of tools available will grow rapidly. They also look at data visualization suites, mapping tools, qualitative tools, world cloud generators and social network analysis tools.

hand, using pen and paper, is laborious, researchers have turned to the development of software tools that support this process (van den Braak, Choenni and Bamberger, 2015). Examples are Belvedere, Compendium and Cohere. These are user-friendly and allow for an ease of use of the interface.

8.9 CRITERIA FOR ASSESSING DATA ANALYSIS

8.9.1 Criteria for Assessing Quantitative (Statistical) Data Analysis

Statistics Canada (2002) mentions '*fitness for use*' of statistical information as a quality criterion and operationalized it in terms of six dimensions: *relevance, accuracy, timeliness, accessibility, interpretability, and coherence of statistical data (analysis)*:

> The relevance of statistical information reflects the degree to which it meets the real needs of clients. It is concerned with whether the available information sheds light on the issues that are important to users. The accuracy of statistical information is the degree to which the information correctly describes the phenomena it was designed to measure. It is usually characterized in terms of error in statistical estimates and is traditionally decomposed into bias (systematic error) and variance (random error) components. It may also be described in terms of the major sources of error that potentially cause inaccuracy (e.g., coverage, sampling, nonresponse, response). The timeliness of statistical information refers to the delay between the reference point (or the end of the reference period) to which the information pertains, and the date on which the information becomes available. The accessibility of statistical information refers to the ease with which it can be obtained. The interpretability of statistical information reflects the availability of the supplementary information and metadata necessary to interpret and utilize it appropriately. The coherence of statistical information reflects the degree to which it can be successfully brought together with other statistical information within a broad analytic framework and over time.

Although these dimensions are overlapping and interrelated, as Statistics Canada (2002: 3) alluded to, 'every dimension has to be adequately managed if information is to be fit for use; failure in any one dimension will impair or destroy the usefulness of the information'.

One of the ways to address criteria like accuracy and coherency is to do a *data review*: look for problems or anomalies regarding the sample, coding, data collection (missing values, deviations from standard operating procedures) and the assumptions underlying the data quality, including the sampling and analysis plan, the selection of statistical tools and the objectives of the researchers when doing the analysis (EPA, 2006). Data review is a part of what is known as *data governance*.

8.9.2 Criteria for Assessing Qualitative Data Analysis

Flick (2009: 384) started a discussion on quality criteria in qualitative research as follows:

> The problem of how to assess qualitative research has not yet been solved. . . . Should qualitative research be assessed with the same criteria and concepts as quantitative research or are there any specific ways of how to assess qualitative research? Are there any generally accepted criteria or strategies for assessing qualitative research and its results? Can research be 'valid' and 'reliable' without being subject to the traditional ways of assessing validity and reliability? Such questions have dominated the discussions about the value.

He presents criteria that can be applied when doing quality assessments and which follow from possible *deficiencies* of qualitative research and data analysis.

One deficiency is '*selective plausibility*': interpretations in and results of qualitative research are made transparent and comprehensible for the reader, only by the interweaving of 'illustrative' quotations from interviews or observation protocols. Especially where researchers use this as 'the only instrument for documenting their statements', the credibility passed on is not sufficient (Bühler-Niederberger, 1985: 475). Another deficiency is the lack of *authenticity checks*, in particular when (in-depth) interviews are carried out (Flick, 2009: 388–9). Earlier we referred to a third deficiency: *confirmation/verification bias*.

Flick (2009) and Miles, Huberman and Saldana (2014: 310ff) specify eight criteria for assessing the soundness of qualitative (data) analysis: confirmability (sometimes referred to as 'objectivity'), reliability/dependability/auditability and internal validity/credibility/authenticity.[25] Golafshani (2003) compares how validity and reliability are assessed in quantitative and qualitative research.

Confirmability

This criterion refers to the degree to which the results of studies can be confirmed or corroborated by others and not only by the qualitative researcher him/herself. Confirmability is *not* the same as searching for confirmation of the results. There are a number of strategies for enhancing confirmability. The researcher can document the procedures for checking and rechecking the data throughout the study. Another researcher can take a 'devil's advocate' role with respect to the results, and this process can be documented. After the study, a data audit can be conducted to examine the data collection and analysis procedures, including the likelihood of bias or distortion.[26]

Reliability/dependability/auditability

Reliability focuses on the question whether or not the 'process of the study (and analysis) is consistent, reasonably stable over time and across researchers and methods' (Miles, Huberman and Saldana, 2014: 312). A study scores positive on auditability if an audit trail can be carried out, looking into field notes and other records kept of what the inquirer does, sees, hears, etc. Dependability emphasizes the need to account for the changing context within which the research occurs.

Validity/credibility/authenticity

Flick (2009: 387) keeps it simple: 'the question of validity can be summarized as a question of whether the researchers see what they think they see'. This criterion is also called the 'truth value': are the data collected and analyzed genuine and of unquestionable origin? Questions to be asked are 'how credible was the informant? Were statements made by someone with whom the researcher had a relationship of trust or by someone the researcher had just met? Did the informant have reason to lie? Were statements made in response to the researcher's questions, or were they spontaneous?'

As is the case with quantitative data analysis, *ethics* are also part of the research toolkit. Chablis and Schutt (2015: 353) outline their perspective:

> The qualitative data analyst is never far from ethical issues and dilemmas. Data collection should not begin unless the researcher has a plan that others see as likely to produce useful knowledge. Relations developed with research participants and other stakeholders to facilitate data collection should also be used to keep these groups informed about research progress and findings.

Privacy, anonymity and confidentiality are the first topics they discuss. Given the often smaller distance between the researcher and the researcher's subject (persons, groups) in qualitative rather than in quantitative studies, the issue 'what to do when I see harmful, illegal, or wrongful behavior on the part of others during a study? Should I speak for anyone's interests besides my own? If so, whose interests do I advocate?' cannot be neglected. Miles, Huberman and Saldana (2014: Chapter 3) discuss the worthiness of a research project, informed consent, benefits, costs and reciprocity, harm and risk, honesty and trust and use and misuse of the results.

8.10 SOME GUIDANCE

- Although data analysis may seem to be a standalone activity, this is a misconception. Data analysis should take place in alignment with the research problem, the design of the study and the theory/ies used and not as a 'technical' action alone.
- The techniques and tools of quantitative data analysis are built on hundreds of years of scientific heritage (in mathematics, statistics, epidemiology, etc.). For many people, including legal researchers, this world may sometimes resemble a dangerous jungle. Now that computer-assisted statistical packages, including YouTube movies on 'how to do it', have become widely available, this jungle is more under control but there is also a new danger: that quantitative analyses are carried out by persons without a basic understanding of relevant parts of their statistical and mathematical background. Therefore, when engaging in this kind of work without training in basic 'stats and math', it is commendable to have somebody on board who does have such an understanding.
- Compared to quantitative analysis, the techniques and tools of qualitative analysis have a much shorter and less advanced scientific heritage. Quality control from within this research orientation is less regulated by epistemological 'rules' than is the case with quantitative methods and statistics.
- It is commendable to present data and conclusions in a reader- and user-friendly way and on time. Data-visualization, including modes of transfer and communication, in person as well as in virtual reality are important factors for successful reception of research results by audiences outside the research profession. Chapter 9 is dedicated to that issue (and to one other).
- To help the reader finds his/her way into literature on quantitative data analysis, these few references will help.
    - M. Te Grotenhuis and T. Van de Weegen, *Statistical Tools. An overview of Common Applications in Social Sciences* (Assen:

Van Gorcum, 2011). There are also YouTube instruction videos available.

- W. G. Cochran, *Sampling Techniques* (New York: John Wiley and Sons, 1977).
- *Research Methods in Education and Social Sciences* (Routledge, Taylor & Francis Group Publishers or Sage) (various publications).
- L. Epstein and A. Martin, *An Introduction to Empirical Legal Research* (Oxford: Oxford University Press, 2014).
- D.A. Dillman, *Mail and internet surveys: The tailored design method* (Hoboken, New Jersey: John Wiley and Sons, 2007).
- J. Bethlehem, F. Cobben and B. Schouten, *Handbook of nonresponse in household surveys* (Wiley Handbooks in Survey Methodology) (Hoboken, New Jersey: John Wiley and Sons, 2011).

ENDNOTES

1. The DPES sample is drawn up around two months before the fieldwork starts. Problematically, information in the register is sometimes not updated. This means that the units in the sample do not necessarily correspond to the actual situation. Of the 4000 selected eligible voters it was revealed that in 80 cases for various reasons the respondent could not be approached (e.g. he/she had died, moved abroad, etc.) and so these units are considered sample frame errors.
2. Also known as the 'mixed method' approach. Sometimes the sequential mixed method/mode approach is referred to in order to highlight the steps taken during the data collection process.
3. One example is retrieved from the Dutch Survey on Social Cohesion and Well-being. According to this survey, Dutch citizens are quite happy people: 89% report to be happy or very happy over the 1997–2010 time span, showing a very stable trend. In 2010 the sample was split into a uni-mode Face-to-Face survey and a mixed-mode Internet/Telephone/Face-to-Face survey. Again 89% of the uni-mode respondents said that they were happy. For the mixed-mode respondents, the happiness level dropped to 84%. In 2012 and 2013 the mixed-mode variant was applied. The results in these years equalled the 2010-findings with a 84% share of the adult Dutch population reporting that they were happy to very happy.
4. Attrition is the process of dropout from a panel study.
5. See also: http://www.youtube.com/watch?v=sQkB-AlJgPI, accessed 26 November 2015.
6. In many books the inclusion of more than one independent variable is labeled as multivariate (regression) analysis, which is however not correct as multivariate stands for more than one dependent variable.
7. http://www.osce.org/who, accessed 26 November 2015.
8. http://www.osce.org/odihr/elections/92057?download=true; http://www.osce.org/odihr/elections/17165?download=true, accessed 26 November 2015.
9. Six out of these seven principles are covered by *observation on polling day*. Voters should have equal access to the polling stations; safeguards should be implemented to guarantee that the principle of 'one person, one vote' is not violated, such as no proxy voting, and that the voter has to cast his/her vote in person. Secrecy can only be guaranteed if the

voter casts his/her vote alone; only a single person should be allowed in a polling booth. Fairness refers to voters' exposure to basic information about all contestants in the election and the fundamental issues they represent. On polling day it is forbidden to have campaign material in the vicinity or inside the polling station. Voters should mark their ballots in a free manner, without any intimidation or pressure. Furthermore, universal suffrage refers to the fact that no (groups of) eligible voters should be refused their vote. This also implies that voters' lists are updated and accurate. Transparency is crucial in an election as international observers, NGOs and party or candidate representatives should have a clear view inside the polling stations. Accountability refers to the period after the election and verifies whether elected people take office. The will of the electorate needs to be guaranteed and the elected must take their seats in parliament or other institutions.

10. However, there are some outliers in this pattern. The three elections in Belarus are characterised by a very negative count – which was mainly caused by a lack of transparency; observers were kept at a distance and had no clear view on the procedures – whereas the assessment of the voting procedures was not that negative (e.g., for the 2010 elections see OSCE/ODIHR, 2011).
11. http://www.google.com/trends/correlate, accessed 26 November 2015.
12. For more information about the algorithms which power Google Correlate, see D. Vanderkam et al, 'Nearest Neighbor Search in Google Correlate', n.d. (http://www.google.com/trends/correlate/nnsearch.pdf, accessed 25 November 2015). See also http://research.google.com/pubs/pub41694.html, accessed 26 November 2015.
13. https://www.google.org/flutrends/intl/en_us/about/faq.html, accessed 26 November 2015.
14. Lazer et al (2014: 1204–1205) present critical remarks on algorithms and statistics (not using a theory to understand the findings) but also make the points that '[Big Data] are the most exciting frontiers in studying human behavior' and that the 'large errors in flu prediction [by Google] were largely avoidable, which offers lessons for the use of Big Data'.
15. An 'example' of such a model can be found when predicting the weather in Las Vegas. In that city the sun shines more than 320 days a year. The model that uses 'today's weather' is almost always an adequate forecast for tomorrow.
16. In statistics, and in particular in time series analysis, an autoregressive integrated moving average (ARIMA) model is a generalization of an autoregressive moving average (ARMA) model. These models are fitted to time series data either to better understand the data or to predict future points in the series (forecasting). They are applied in some cases where data show evidence of non-stationarity, where an initial differencing step (corresponding to the 'integrated' part of the model) can be applied to remove the non-stationarity.
17. As we discussed in Willemsen and Leeuw (in press), it is our assertion that by working along these lines, this will help to protect Big Data analysts from making the same mistake that was made with Google Flu Trends.
18. Elsberg and Heise (2005), based on Miles and Huberman (1994), use different words but the activities are the same: data reading (also known as data immersion) and coding, data reduction, data display and conclusion drawing. See also http://www.slideshare.net/tilahunigatu/qualitative-data-analysis-11895136, accessed 26 November 2015.
19. The authors also refer to the 'representation of the account', a topic we will discuss below when criteria are mentioned to assess the quality of qualitative data analysis.
20. Miles, Huberman and Saldana (2014: 71) define codes as 'labels that assign symbolic meaning to the descriptive or inferential information compiled during a study'. Codes are usually attached to data 'chunks'.
21. The so-called 'theoretical saturation' process (that is, when additional data failed to uncover any new ideas about the sensitizing concepts) and the 'grounded' theory approach both increase the likelihood that immunization strategies will occur, making statements untestable and killing informative content as a criterion.
22. Ellsberg and Heise (2005: 214) make a point when suggesting the qualitative researcher

to do 'negative case analysis': seeking cases actively that appear to be exceptions to the general pattern, as a way of testing and refining hypothesis. The method relies on the analysis of 'outliers' to improve the credibility of the findings'.

23. See Miles, Huberman and Saldana (2014: 161–273) for more information on how to describe, order, explain and predict from qualitative data.
24. The US Equal Employment Opportunity Commission.
25. They see 'utilization/applications (of the research)' as the fourth standard but we disagree, as the utilization of (qualitative) research in principle does not say anything about its methodological robustness of QDA.
26. http://www.socialresearchmethods.net/kb/qualval.php, accessed 26 November 2015.

9. Transferring research results to legal professionals, utilization and the fact-value dichotomy

9.1 KNOWLEDGE TRANSFER, DEFINITIONS, EXAMPLES AND MECHANISMS

The times that publishing a report of 232 pages with statistics, references and a summary finalized a project, have gone. Not only is data visualization indispensable, but after the report is finished, factsheets ('two pagers'), seminars, webinars, YouTube movies and TED (like) communication activities are needed to stimulate the *transfer, dissemination and utilization* of findings and conclusions. To ensure that lawyers, legislators and policy officials *get to know* the findings, *take notice* of them and *decide to use* them, more actions are needed, as Box 9.1 shows.

This section looks into the transfer and utilization process and summarizes insights from (review and synthesis) studies dealing with topics like 'evidence-based policy making' and 'knowledge utilization'.

However, the transfer and utilization of results from ELR into legal scholarship and practice is more than just communication and persuasion. It also implies an *epistemological issue*, as the dominant legal tradition is *doctrinal*, while the type of knowledge produced by ELR is *descriptive, exploratory or explanatory*. Doctrinal legal research is 'to a large extent, a discipline which *takes normative propositions and makes choices among values and interests*' (van Hoecke, 2011: 10, emphasis added). In section 9.2 we will discuss this issue.

9.1.1 Definitions

Knowledge (or: research) transfer is the process by which relevant research information is made available and accessible for practice, planning, policy making, law-making and other activities. It is a process of moving research into practice and going beyond traditional methods of publishing research results. It is a two-way process that supports the production of research and the dissemination and use of research results by others.

BOX 9.1 TRANSFER/UTILIZATION OF RESEARCH IN THE LEGAL FIELD IS NOT AN EASY PIECE OF CAKE

Police/law enforcement

Lum et al (2012):

'In policing, concern over the gap between research and practice . . . seems to be a recurring lament: research may not have made as significant, or at least as coherent, an impression on policing as scholars like to think. . . . Nor has research led to widespread operational changes even when it has been accepted as true.'

Lum (2009) noted the lack of research in daily policing, suggesting that better translation of research was needed in order for evidence-based policing to be realized.

Private law/civilology

Pape (2011: 420) studied research from cognitive psychology and ergonomics regarding warnings and product liability to examine whether the presumptions of lawyers about behavior and products and warnings in European product liability law (e.g. do warnings really prevent damage?) are correct. After reviewing and synthesizing research (results), Pape suggested a toolkit with a number of principles on how to best design warnings etc. Courts, in her perception, 'can use these to facilitate the evaluation of the adequacy of a warning' (ibid., p. 441). Although this approach is an interesting example of empirical legal research in the field of private law, Pape does not address the problem that courts may not or only partly *use* the toolkit. Nor does she address the problem of various evidence levels that can be distinguished, including conflicting evidence.

Judges and juries

Two Dutch PhDs published around 2008 found that 'the way judges come to an "acceptable judgment" mainly comes down to intuition' (van Rossum, 2010). In one study, five lawsuits were reconstructed on the basis of documents and interviews with parties, lawyers, judges and others, while the other PhD researcher also interviewed judges to find out how they come to their verdicts (van Rossum, 2010: 2467). Of a different nature is the transfer and utilization problem in neurolaw and neurosciences: not 'under-utilization' of findings and methods, but the '*seductive allure*' neuro-imaging may have for (mock) juries (Weisberg et al, 2008). Due to this 'allure', results from neuro-imaging may create a bias in the judges' and jurors' decision-making. Some studies in the USA examined the persuasiveness of neuro-imaging on mock jurors' willingness to find a criminal defendant *not guilty by reason of insanity* (NGRI). When mock jurors were presented with evidence that included expert testimony based on structural neuro-imaging plus an expert's testimony, they were 1.3 times more likely to render a verdict of NGRI than the same expert testimony that lacked neuroscience-based evidence. However, Baker et al (2013) did not find such an effect.

Bullis (2014: 2) (though not based on systematic investigations) discussed the distance between social scientists and lawyers from a practitioner's perspective: 'Miscommunications yield miscues, misunderstandings and missed opportunities. Expectations can be unmet when either attorneys or social scientists do not "hear" what the other party is saying. The different assumptions and frames of reference between a lawyer's world and the social science world are largely the culprit. Legal research and social science research have different methods and ends in mind. The communication problem becomes acute when the two professions need to collaborate.'

BOX 9.2 SAUNDERS (2012) TYPES OF KNOWLEDGE UTILIZATION

1. *Instrumental*: when decision-makers in private or public organizations use the research findings to modify their policies/programs/interventions (including legislation and other legal arrangements).
2. *Conceptual*: when the findings help policy makers and other decision-makers understand the policy/interventions (including legislation and other legal arrangements).
3. *Enlightenment*: when the research findings add knowledge to the field which may be used by anyone, not just those involved with the program/interventions/legislation.
4. *Process use*: cognitive, behavioral, program and organizational changes resulting from engagement in the research process and learning to think in line with the research (findings).
5. *Symbolic use*: when a researcher is hired to study a program/intervention in order to legitimize a decision that has already been made prior to the research work.

Knowledge (or: research) utilization is a step further: the evidence produced by empiricists has not only been received, but is acknowledged and used. Saunders (2012: 425) distinguished several types of *knowledge utilization* (see Box 9.2).

Over almost a hundred years researchers and practitioners have studied transfer, dissemination and utilization processes in society. The first wave started in the 1920s in the USA, with studies on the diffusion of agricultural innovations to farmers and new teaching ideas to school personnel (Backer, 1991: 228–30). Rogers (1983) sees the hybrid seed corn study by Ryan and Gross (1943) as a frontrunner. The focus was on individuals.[1] A second wave started around the 1960s, as (in particular) US organizations made funding available for research on methods of utilization and for providing technical assistance to researchers and to potential adopters to increase the application of federally sponsored research. The Center for Research on the Utilization of Scientific Knowledge (CRUSK) at the University of Michigan was one of the first think tanks in and of this field that soon followed suit in – among others – the Netherlands.[2]

In the 1970s an important development in medicine occurred, when Archie Cochrane published his book *Effectiveness and Efficiency* (1972). Cochrane's criticism was that medicine had not organized its (collective) knowledge in any systematic, reliable and cumulative way; the result was chaotic, individualistic, and sometimes harmful. He encouraged health practitioners to practice *evidence based medicine*. Later the work Cochrane started transformed into the Cochrane Collaboration with a library (a collection of databases that contain different types of high-quality, independent evidence to inform healthcare decision-making), including Cochrane reviews. In the latter part of the 1990s a sister organization, the Campbell Collaboration, was established which looked into the effectiveness of *social interventions* (see Chapter 5). The organization was named in honor of Dr Donald T. Campbell (1916–1996) who advocated the (Popperian) idea that (governmental) interventions can be seen as societal experiments to which scientific rules of evidence can be applied.

Evaluators and policy researchers also study the transfer and utilization problem. Leviton and Hughes (1981: 525) identified 13 factors affecting utilization and clustered them into five categories of variables: (1) relevance of evaluation to the needs of potential users; (2) extent of communication between potential users and producers of evaluations; (3) translation of evaluations into their implications for policy and programs; (4) credibility or trust placed in evaluations; and (5) commitment or advocacy by individual users. Fifteen years later Shulha and Cousins (1997: 195) undertook a review and synthesis of the literature published since 1986, while Johnson et al (2009) did the same and covered a period spanning 1986 to 2005. The attention became so large that Patton 'created' a special paradigm, utilization-focused evaluations.

The third wave started around the mid-1990s. Crucial elements were the uptake of evidence-based policy, policing, social work and education, distinguishing between levels of evidence (based on methodological criteria; see Chapter 5) and – from the launch of the internet – new forms of data visualization and transfer activities (search engines, Wiki's, blogs, digital watchdogs and digital fact-checkers).

9.1.2 Mechanisms

What are important *mechanisms* driving this process? Following Crona and Parker (2011), the '*engineering model*' suggests that research will be used by policy makers and others if it is methodologically sound and of high scientific quality. This model has been criticized for failing to recognize the importance of *social contexts and social relations* in knowledge transactions. In contrast, *socio-organizational explanations* suggest that knowledge utilization is determined primarily by the character of social relations between researchers and those addressed.

In the literature a range of other factors is mentioned:[3]

- the *setting or context* in which the transfer of research to practitioners takes place (such as the political climate, competing information from other studies, including Google and other search engines, contractual obligations and financial aspects);
- the *communication and information processes* (two-way formal or (more) informal); the channels used for communication (no-media, mass-media, social media), presentation styles, the social interactions between researchers and recipients ('social capital'; trust);
- the 'absorptive *capacity*' of the potential user: the ability to recognize the value of research evidence for one's own practice;
- the *credibility of the research* (robustness of its methodology; informative content);
- the *difficulty* in finding relevant research evidence (fragmentation of disciplines and the heterogeneity of terminology);
- the *'stickiness' of knowledge* (knowledge adheres to particular people and is hard to move to another 'location' without a great deal of effort);
- the *relevance and timeliness of the research*; and
- the *user involvement* (advocacy or enlightenment).

An interesting model on how transfer and utilization of knowledge takes place has been developed by Henry and Mark (2003). They focused on (social, behavioral and cognitive) *mechanisms* stimulating or hampering these activities and conceptualized utilization as 'influence'. Next, they distinguished between multiple levels of mechanisms: individual, interpersonal and collective:

> These three levels correspond to different kinds of change processes that have been studied in the social and behavioral sciences. The first level, individual, refers to those cases when evaluation processes or findings directly cause some change in the thoughts or actions of one or more individuals . . .The second level, that is, the interpersonal, refers to a change brought about in interactions between individuals, or more precisely, to a process or outcome that predominantly takes place within interactions among individuals. And the third level, the collective, refers to the direct or indirect influence of evaluation on the decisions and practices of organizations, whether public or private. More precisely, the collective level of analysis is involved when a change process or outcome operates predominantly within some aggregate social organizational body. (Henry and Mark, 2003: 297–8)

Examples of individual mechanisms are the valence of an attitude (policy makers, politicians, lawyers may hold positive or negative beliefs about the intervention or one or more of its underlying assumptions) and salience (the importance of an issue as judged by an individual).

Examples of interpersonal mechanisms are justification (research findings support previously held positions) and persuasion (communication of results through credible organizations persuades decision-makers that programs or interventions should be supported). Examples of collective mechanisms are diffusion (evidence of a policy's success in another jurisdiction influences the adoption of similar policy elsewhere) and policy-oriented (organizational) learning (relative enduring alterations of thought or behavioral intentions resulting from experience and/or new information and that can present itself in several ways, for example single loop learning or double loop learning).[4]

9.2 THE FACT-VALUE GAP[5]

Where are we? Let us suppose that we are in a situation in which empirical findings and conclusions are *noticed* by potential users from the legal (and policy) world, while they have a *positive attitude* towards *using* them, when drafting legislation or developing other legal devices and arrangements. However, decision-making in the legal world often is *normative, while ELR produces facts, correlations, causes and information on impact*. Smits (2014: 81) states:

> The legal discipline reflects what it is that individuals, firms, states, and other organizations ought to do, or ought to refrain from doing. Typical legal questions are thus: whether disinheriting one's children should be permitted, whether the death penalty should be imposed for criminal offences, under which circumstances it is justified to go to war, when constitutional review should be allowed, and whether ship-wrecked sailors may eat their weakest companion if they are likely to die of starvation.

This is true not only for legal scholarship but even more so for legal practice. This means that there is a serious *gap* between *empirical evidence* on – for example – the deterrent effect of the death penalty or the consequences for the well-being of children, when they are disinherited, on the one hand, and the *legal-normative argumentation* to be in favor or against the death penalty or disinheritance, on the other.

The topic *how to relate results from empirical (descriptive/causal) research to normative legal questions* is by no means a novel one. David Hume (1711–76) may be one of the first to have addressed it. Max Weber, in his study 'Die Objektivität sozialwissenschaftlicher und sozialpolitischer Erkenntnis' (1904)[6] also discussed this problem and made the point that 'eine empirische Wissenschaft vermag niemanden zu lehren, was er soll, sondern nur, was er kann und – unter Umständen – was er will' [an empirical (social) science should nobody ever tell what he should (do), but only what he can and – under circumstances – what he wants]. According to Weber, the social and cultural sciences including economics are never capable 'bindende Normen und Ideale . . . [zu] ermitteln, um daraus für die Praxis Rezepte ableiten zu können' [to identify binding norms and ideals in order to derive from them 'prescriptions for practice']. Lepsius (2005) concluded that even a thorough way of establishing facts will not do away with the *Bewertungsproblem*, 'the problem of adding normative value to facts (*as no legal obligation follows from empirical facts*)'.[7]

The following issues are at stake.

- *Is it necessary that legal decision-makers and researchers know about this fact-value dichotomy and approaches to deal with it?*

The answer is yes. Not being aware of it will lead to refraining from using empirical evidence, to compare apples and oranges without knowing the differences, or to pick and choose research results but deny others (as they seem not to fit or 'verify' the normative statements already formulated).

- *Is it necessary to try to bridge the gap?*

Our answer is yes and a great many authors agree (Robbenolt, 2002; Lepsius, 2005; Vranken, 2014; Mertz, 2008, 2011; and Giesen, 2015). One argument goes back to Nathan Roscoe Pound and Oliver Holmes (see Chapter 1): *law in the books and blackletter law* is important, but definitely not enough to understand how 'law' *develops, what it does and does not to society, how it can be made (more) effective and – sometimes – less harmful.* A second argument is that when lawyers decide on normative issues, formulate verdicts, and introduce rules and legislation, with often far-reaching consequences, and they do not know right from wrong regarding behavioral mechanisms, effects and side-effects, this will create legal arrangements without a 'reality check' (Van Boom, 2013).

9.2.1 Approaches to Analyze and Handle the Fact-value Gap

Giesen's due process approach

Giesen (2015: 11) scanned several approaches to this problem and concluded that 'the available methodological literature does not really get us much further. We do know that the issue is real and serious enough; we do know that we need to work on it. But how?'. He took the challenge to develop a (new) approach, called 'Due Process', and started by saying that one needs to be:

> cautious when using insights from elsewhere in a legal discussion leading to legal consequences; law is not only about psychology, or sociology or economics, it is also (and perhaps mainly) about value judgments being made at a given point in time at a given place. This cautious approach would then have it that a judge, practitioner or legal scholar is only 'allowed' – in the scientific sense of the word – to leap from extralegal insights to legal solutions if certain (formal, procedural) criteria have been satisfied: if due process is attended to. The following non-exhaustive set of criteria that ultimately deal with rather common methodological problems (such as construct validity, internal validity and external validity biases) might be listed here as relevant criteria that the judge or scholar should consider and weigh, taken together, before using empirical insights in his legal reasoning:
>
> - whether the empirical work is in fact relevant for the question of law that arises,
> - whether the work is up to the current state of the art in the field methodologically, as well as regards its research design, etc., and its implications,
> - whether (more generally) the research is valid and reliable,
> - whether there is conflicting empirical work on the same issue,
> - whether the study has been replicated and confirmed or not,
> - whether the study is but one building block of a larger set of studies needed for policy implications,
> - whether the researcher is objective, independent and an expert, and so on.
>
> With regard to these factors, and others that might be added, the reasoned justification provided by the user of the extralegal information (the judge deciding the case) would be crucial. That justification would, for instance, need to deal with the issue, raised above, that aggregated data are used in individual cases. But if and when these criteria have been duly considered, weighed against one another, and justified, the extralegal materials can be considered reliable (enough) and may thus be used in the decision-making process (again, there would be no obligation to do so). The legal or public policy outcome may then be inspired by the empirical insights found. To put it differently: *the Sein can then be used to answer the Sollen, basically because all possible safeguards have been put in place*. . . . An important consequence of the Due Process approach advocated here is of course that it asks of judges, practitioners and scholars to be or at least become 'somewhat' familiar with the methodology of the social science at stake. (Giesen, 2015: 16)[8]

Although Giesen's approach to the gap problem is interesting, one crucial difficulty is not addressed: *how to leap from valid (and relevant) empirical evidence (compliant with due process criteria) to normative statements?* An example clarifies this point. It concerns microcredit/microfinance programs, well-known in the developing world as a policy instrument based on (soft) laws and regulation. Recently, four systematic research reviews[9] were published. A systematic review (see Chapter 5) summarizes the results of empirical studies evaluating the impact of microcredit programs. The (primary) studies have been reviewed and scrutinized on the basis of a protocol which includes Giesen's methodological due process criteria and others (but is more sophisticated).[10] The review process is to distinguish the wheat from the chaff; only those studies that pass the methodological criteria are used for the analysis and synthesis. The four systematic reviews raise serious doubts about what the impact of microcredit on women and society is. They challenge received wisdom. One of the conclusions Vaessen et al (2014: 8, 10) present is that:

> there appears to be a gap between the often optimistic societal belief in the capacity of microcredit to ameliorate the position of women in decision-making processes within the household on the one hand, and the empirical evidence base on the other hand. We conclude that there is no consistent evidence for an effect of microcredit on women's control over household spending. Given the overall lack of evidence for an effect of microcredit on women's control over household resources it is therefore very unlikely that, overall, microcredit has a meaningful and substantial impact on empowerment processes in a broader sense.

Although the evidence from this and other reviews and is strong and convincing, the question remains: *how do legal counselors, legal scholars and policy advisors in the field of microcredit and development aid, operate when they are confronted with these results?* How do they 'move' from the sophisticated and crystal clear findings about the absence or near-absence of the impact on women's empowerment of microcredits to answering the question *whether or not to continue, to abandon or to modify microcredit programs*. How can the empirical results help or guide the people that have to advise on or decide about such an issue?

A simple answer would be: 'abandon this intervention, as robust research has found that . . . '. This is too simple, as there can be other factors – normative (including ideological) and political – at stake, that value microcredits so high that instead of abandoning the intervention, the robust research evidence is 'abandoned', i.e. not used. Normative beliefs may and sometimes do outweigh the evidence, precisely as Giesen (2015: 18) indicated: 'but the novel insight [in this case: robust results from several systematic reviews] itself is not enough; there might be one or more good reasons not to follow up on that insight, given the other arguments presented to the decision maker'. Even when following a due process approach, the gap problem *continues to exist*.

Given this situation, we decided to look ourselves for approaches capable of trimming down the gap problem (Leeuw, 2015). The first characterizes law as an *argumentative discipline*, the second has as its background *evaluation studies* and the third is *empirically informed ethics*.[11]

The law as an argumentative discipline

Smits (2014: 82) defines legal science as an argumentative discipline:

> The core of legal science is the behavior of the homo juridicus (what it is that people should do as a matter of law) . . . If one's research question is not what the law says, but what it should say, empirical material can be used to test whether some idea or argument was already used elsewhere and how it was received in that other jurisdiction. In my view, the most important research method to evaluate arguments is therefore the comparative one. . . . Other jurisdictions should in this respect be seen as 'experimenting laboratories'.

He adds that 'the aim of legal studies is not to put an end to normative uncertainty but to take this uncertainty as a starting point. . . . This leads to a characterization of legal studies as the discipline of conflicting arguments'. A crucial question Smits (2009b: 53, 54) asks is:

> how we should establish what is the better argument? For some part the answer must be found in the normative presuppositions underlying the acceptance of an argument . . . I agree that each argument can only be assessed within a certain normative framework. But in doing so, we should not forget that in many jurisdictions there is already such a framework available in the form of a doctrinal system. Each jurisdiction has its own 'internal morality' as a reflection of the prevailing normative views within that jurisdiction. . . . This view of legal methodology implies that each normative scholarly exercise consists of two steps.
>
> - The first is to identify the relevant arguments in favor of and against a certain solution. Several methods can be used to do this, including empirical approaches, but in the end the comparative method is the most promising one.
> - The second step is to see whether these arguments fit into an already existing normative setting.

What, then, are the criteria to compare and weigh normative statements like values? Smits did not answer that question, but Ball (1995) and Lint (2014) did. The first is *completeness*. To what extent does the argument address all key aspects that are at stake and to what extent are important ones left out? This requires that one is aware of all important values, by, for example, studying the history of the policy or regulation and by examining public opinion. The second criterion is that of *relevance*. The question is, to what extent are the embodied values appropriate and checkable in a similar vein as for completeness? In Ball's words, do the 'reasons offered in support of the value goals of a policy argument appertain to those goals'? The third criterion is the matter of *consonance*: 'To what degree do the claimed values contradict each other?' The idea is that while complete consonance is difficult to attain, inconsistencies in the set of values would undermine the argument's power. Insights from the world of decision-support systems may help to address this weighting problem (Comes et al, 2011). In principle *multi-attribute decision-making* (MADM), *multi-actor multi-criteria analysis* (MAMCA) and *decision-maps* can make this process transparent, especially now that digital tools are available to engage professionals in such a process simultaneously (Macaris et al, 2012; Palenberg, 2011: 56–61).

Unravelling and unpacking arguments and speech-acts (Astbury and Leeuw, 2010; Searle, 1964)

This approach is related to intervention theories and how to find them, as discussed in Chapter 4. It starts with unravelling arguments that are said to be normative (or ideological) into parts that can be empirically tested and parts that cannot (as they are *sui generis* normative[12]). Let us take an example of voting by ethnic minorities in a Western industrialized country. Suppose that the voting rate of ethnic minorities in this country is considered 'too low' compared to the voting rate of the rest of the population. It is seen as desirable ('good') to have the rate increased by at least 30%. Suppose also that a law is implemented to help realize this goal. The law specifies two actions. One is to have all documents on voting/programs of political parties translated in every language spoken by ethnic minorities in the country. The second is to have three or more times the number of ballot boxes operating in geographic areas populated by a certain percentage of ethnic minorities.

The research problem is to investigate whether this law (and its two interventions) leads to an increase of at least 30% in voting by ethnic minorities. The first question is: can this law be empirically tested? That seems doubtful, as one of the law's underlying central assumptions (*it is good, desirable or commendable to stimulate voting by ethnic minorities with at least 30%*) is normative in nature. What is good for believers can be 'bad' for non-believers. Framed in this way, it may be concluded that an empirical evaluation of the law is *not possible, given its normative character*. However, by using Searle's theory on speech acts, a different conclusion can be reached (Hage 2013: 57). Searle distinguished between several types of speech acts.[13] The first are *assertives*: they commit the speaker (i.e. policy maker or lawyer) to something's being the case: for instance, the statement that less than X% of the eligible ethnic minorities in country A vote. Assertives have the word-to-world direction of fit; they are successful if they are true. That means that they can be put to an empirical test, which applies to our case.

Directives, a second category of speech-acts, are the attempts of someone to get another to do something. This is a statement that 'I, as policy maker or legislator, will do something about the underrepresentation in voting of minorities'. Directives (commands, requests, entreaties) have a world-to-word direction of fit, and are successful if they are effective (i.e. a policy maker is indeed doing something about this situation). Again, the success of the law can be measured in an empirical sense.

Commissives (the third category) commit a person to some future course of action. They also have, according to Searle, the world-to-word direction of fit. For instance, the sentence 'I promise to realize that I will help minorities in making voting easier, so that under-representation will disappear' is such a commissive of a policy maker. And again, this type of statement can be empirically researched as it stays in the domain of facts and not of oughts.

The evaluation can also look into the two practical interventions and their consequences. First, by reconstructing (and testing) the *underlying intervention theory*: why is it believed that adding ballot boxes and translating voting documents will contribute to a higher voting rate by ethnic minorities (up to 30%)? This can be done by searching for empirical evidence on these and lookalike approaches in research repositories (in the field of law and politics for example) and by collecting new data through experimental or other designs measuring the impact of interventions.

Contrary to the original answer ('this law cannot be evaluated because it is inherently normative in nature'), there is now another situation: by unravelling the assumptions and speech-acts, it appears that almost every item of this 'normative' law can be empirically tested. The only issue that cannot be handled in this way is the normative adjective that it is '*good*' to stimulate voting, as the number of voting minorities is believed to be '*too low*'. That belongs to the core of the (sui generis) normative part of the law.[14] Decision-makers therefore still have to *weigh* empirical findings and *this* normative statement. This *Bewertungsproblem* has not been solved, but strongly trimmed.

Empirically informed ethics

In the last 25 years, ethicists have combined empirical (usually social science) research with normative-ethical analysis and reflection (De Vries and Gordijn, 2009). Christian and Alfano (2014) distinguish three ways. The first is to empirically describe the *framing of a normative problem*: what are the concepts and variables related to – for example – the discussion whether or not it is legally and normatively acceptable to do research on stem cells and what are the societal discourses about this question? Finding *empirical data as an indicator of the feasibility of ethical thought* is a second potential aspect. One of the examples of Christian and Alfano is this:

> Data emerging from patients with focal lesions in the prefrontal cortex that play a significant role in arguments for the significance of emotions as a 'foundation' of moral intuitions and for practical decision making are remarkably imprecise with respect to what kind of emotions are affected. Such findings are also highly prone to misinterpretations driven by prejudices about what the data should demonstrate.

Related to this approach is to study how lawyers (and others) in practice handle ethical and normative issues by asking them and learning from the empirical results. Perry et al's (2009: 462) study on the 'Ethical Health Lawyer' is an example. The primary research question was how health lawyers respond when they encounter ethical or moral dilemmas in their practice for which the law fails to offer a bright-line solution. The authors developed:

> a survey instrument aimed at capturing empirical data about how health lawyers deliberate and act when they encounter an ethical or moral dilemma in their practice. . . . We drafted hypothetical scenarios and questions designed to highlight the tension between what the law and rules of professional conduct might allow and what might more broadly be understood as the right or just course of action. Most questions (in these scenarios) used the term 'ethical dilemmas' and several measurement scales used by the researchers applied the options 'Definitely ethical' or 'Definitely unethical'.

The third way of relating empirical research to ethical and normative topics is that *data can be seen as foundations of normative theories, in particular when performing thought experiments.* Experiments are set up in such a way as to elicit assent to or even certitude in certain (normative) judgments (Christian and Alfano, 2014: 14–17). Neuroscientists are engaged in this work as they are interested in what is happening inside the brain, when individuals who have available relevant empirical evidence are confronted with moral dilemmas. The Trolley Problem is an example of such an approach. It originated with Foot's 1967 article, 'The Problem of Abortion and the Doctrine of Double Effect'. It consists of two scenarios. Here we focus on the first (the Switch case). A runaway trolley is about to kill five workers on the track. A bystander notices that he can throw a switch, thereby turning the trolley onto a spur where there is only one worker who would be killed (the empirical evidence). What to do? (the normative/ethical problem). Neuro- and cognitive scientists have designed experiments that look into the workings of 'moral grammars' that people use to guide their normative opinions and behavior (Lanteri et al, 2008). The idea is that encountering such a conflict evokes both a strong emotional response as well as a reasoned cognitive response that tend to oppose each other. In neuro-scientific studies, Greene et al (2001) asked research subjects to contemplate both the Switch case and the other (i.e. the Footbridge case, where 'you and a man are standing on a footbridge over the tracks. His body is large enough to stop the trolley if you push him onto the tracks. He will die but the five others will be spared. Many people believe that it would be morally wrong for you to push the big man onto the tracks').

The core of this approach is to address the fact-value gap by studying what is happening inside the brain, when people have to deal with normative/ethical problems, while evidence on the consequences of choices is available. Instead of producing normative statements on what people should do to leap from empirics to values (when confronted with the trolley or lookalike problems[15]), cognitive and neuroscientists open the black box of decision-making mechanisms that guide a person's perspectives and behavior. Knowing which mechanisms are 'at stake' and how they work when linking 'IST' and 'SOLL' can help find the pathways that judges, prosecutors, regulators and legal scholars follow when they are confronted with the option to cross the bridge between facts, values (and emotions).

These three approaches do not solve the fact-value problem, nor did Giesen (2015). It may very well be that there is no solution to this problem. The purpose of presenting several approaches is primarily to empower both empiricists and normativists with some (*argumentative*) '*tools*' to handle the gap problem in a transparent way.

9.3 SOME GUIDANCE

- Understanding what the social and behavioral mechanisms are that may hamper the transfer and dissemination process is important, as are ways that help understand this process and reduce these restrictions.
- For reasons of efficiency, effectiveness, economy and ethics, it is highly commendable that the evidence produced by empirical legal

research is transferred (in a smart way) to the legal profession, including doctrinal legal research.

- To know that there is a gap problem between facts and values, respectively between ELR and legal-normative scholarship and practice is crucial, as is knowing where this problem comes from. One of its origins is the empirical legal researcher who produces evidence that contradicts certain legal arrangements, practices, positions or expectations. ELR then basically functions as a 'reality check' (though is not always a welcome guest). A second origin is that, due to limited experience with data (collection and analysis), legal scholars' interpretations of evidence can be methodologically incorrect. A third possibility is that the evidence is (too) complex, making it difficult for lawyers and legislators to understand what has been found, which may result in putting aside (certain) facts and figures.
- Several approaches have been highlighted to help understand this process:
  - recognize the importance of (Giesen, 2015) the due process approach but also its limitations;
  - pay attention to the translation of legal concepts in empirical ones and vice versa;
  - work with explicit criteria to compare and weigh normative statements like values;
  - unravel and unpack arguments and speech-acts to prevent all arguments being lumped together;
  - work with and learn from insights from empirically informed ethics.

ENDNOTES

1. Apart from these traditions, there is C. P. Snow's famous 'Two Cultures' essay, in which he criticized the cultural divide that separates two areas of human intellectual activity, 'science' and 'the arts'. Snow argued that practitioners in both areas should build bridges to further the progress of human knowledge and to benefit society (Snow, 1959).
2. Mark van de Vall (a sociology professor at the University of Buffalo and Leyden University) established in the late 1970s LISPOR (Leyden Institute for Social Policy Research) in which CRUSK-type work was done.
3. See Cousins (2003) and Leonardi and Meyer (2014). Some of these references come from Mimi Crijns, who works on a PhD on evaluation utilization at the Netherlands Open University.
4. Single-loop learning describes the type of learning that takes place when the objective is to fix problems within the present context, so that the system (policy, intervention, regulation) will function better, and does not attempt to alter the structure of the system. Double-loop learning is concerned with understanding the basis for the tasks being

completed, rather than a more efficient process for completing. Chris Argyris was one (if not the) inventor of these concepts.

5. This section is partly based on Leeuw (2015) and Giesen (2015).
6. See: M. Weber (1985; 1904): 'Die "Objektivität" sozialwissenschaftlicher und sozial politischer Erkenntnis, in Max Weber (Hrsg.), *Gesammelte Aufsätze zur Wissenschaftslehre*, [The "objectivity" of social science and social political knowledge, in Max Weber (ed.), Collected Essays on epistemology], Tübingen: J. C. B. Mohr, pp. 146–214.
7. See Giesen, 2015: 5. Another way to describe this problem is to ask the question: can (and how) normative value be added to facts as no legal obligation follows from empirical facts?
8. To some extent his approach is related to the Daubert Standard, which Giesen (2015) mentions on pp. 4, 8 and 20. It is the standard used by trial judges in the USA to make a preliminary assessment of whether an expert's scientific testimony is based on reasoning or methodology that is scientifically valid and can properly be applied to the facts at issue. Under this standard, the factors that may be considered in determining whether the methodology is valid are: (1) whether the theory or technique in question can be and has been tested; (2) whether it has been subjected to peer review and publication; (3) its known or potential error rate; (4) the existence and maintenance of standards controlling its operation; and (5) whether it has attracted widespread acceptance within a relevant scientific community. Faigman (2002: 339–40) is of the opinion that 'although it has taken more than 200 years, [Daubert] initiated a scientific revolution in the law'.
9. Stewart et al (2010); Stewart et al (2012); Duvendack et al (2011) and Vaessen et al (2014).
10. See Gough et al (2012).
11. This selection does not claim completeness. Although we have used some insights from philosophy, a great many others we have not even mentioned (like 'Cornell Realism', which claims, 'among other things, that moral knowledge can be acquired in the same basic way that scientific knowledge can' (Long, 2014: 174–83). See also the *Journal of Value Inquiry* for interesting papers.
12. See McNaughton and Rawling (2003) for a discussion on the concept of sui generis normative statements and properties.
13. Searle (1964: 44) referred to two more speech-acts: declarations and expressions. See also Hage (2013: 45).
14. This resembles the well-known example from literature: 'Few debate that one ought to run quickly if one's goal is to win a race. A tougher question may be whether one "morally ought" to want to win a race in the first place'.
15. The trolley problem belongs to the world of moral dilemmas. There is a certain kind of conflict between the rightness or wrongness of the actions one thinks about and – finally – carries out, and the goodness or badness of the consequences of the actions taking place.

10. Empirical legal research: booming business and growth of knowledge?

10.1 AN EMPIRICAL REVOLUTION IN LAW?

'Traditional legal scholarship is under pressure. Debates are taking place on the aims and methods of the academic study of law'. These are some of the introductory words by Smits (2012) in his book on the state of the legal sciences. Debates address a wide range of topics, ranging from the methodology of legal research, the curriculum and the future of the profession to the 'disruptive' influence that digitization, machine learning and Big Data may have. At the same time the message can be heard that there is an (empirical) *revolution* going on in the legal sciences. Ho and Kramer (2013) advocate this thesis. They counted the proportion of *Stanford Law Review* articles mentioning the word 'empirical' over a period of almost 60 years, which made them call the development a revolution. A *word count* is a thin indicator of the 'empirical engagement' of legal researchers, as using this word does not necessarily imply that empirical research has been done. Diamond and Mueller (2010: 587) searched deeper and analyzed the *content* of 60 law review volumes published between 1998 and 2008: 'Our content analysis revealed that by 2008 nearly half of law review articles included some empirical content. Production of original research is less common'.[1] They also reported that 'evaluating the place of empirical scholarship in law reviews, has attracted a flurry of attention and a variety of approaches' (ibid, pp. 12–14). Klick (2011) studied the content of eight journals publishing in the field of law and economics (like the *Review of Law and Economics* and the *Journal of Law, Economics and Organization*) and analyzed the empirical market share of these journals. Data were collected from the journals' first issue on. He found that the share of empirical articles declined for only one journal while for the others it increased, though not in a dramatic or revolutionary way. Engel (2012) studied the coverage of *behavioral law and economics* within one journal (*Journal of Empirical Legal Studies*) devoted to empirical contributions. He found 77 articles since the journal's inception (in 2004) that focus on this topic, 32 addressing behavioral papers on private law, 27 covering an issue from criminal law and five dealing with public law. In the field of *international*

law, Chilton and Tingley (2013) interpreted the development as an 'empirical turn in the study of international law' that took place in the first decade of the twenty-first century. Simmons and Breidenbach (2011: 220) also mention the 'empirical turn in legal scholarship [that] generally has been pretty well-documented. Indeed, there is even a law school ranking [in the USA] based on institutional strength in empirical legal studies. In the specific area of *international economic law*, the trend is less noted, but is on the rise'.[2]

Although the impression may arise that the empirical turn in legal studies is something that happened in the last two decades, reality is different, as we have made clear in Chapter 2. Although it is an exaggeration to call the more recent developments a *revolution*, empirical legal research indeed is *blossoming*, or, as Van Dijck (2011: 1105) suggests, *booming*. What are underlying causes of this phenomenon? We list six of them:

- *Reason 1: Transparency and accountability have hit the shores of the world of law, regulation and other legal arrangements. Finding out how transparent, accountable and effective the legal world and its institutions is cannot be done without empirical research.*

The growing importance attached by governments, parliaments and society to know and understand what the diverse legal arrangements, devices and institutions accomplish (and cost) is almost everywhere (in the Western world). That drive is directly related to the transparency and accountability debate, which has been going on for several decades (in public, semi-public and private organizations). In the latter part of the 1990s, Power (1999) launched the concepts of the 'audit explosion' and the 'audit society', describing the growth and pervasiveness of auditing activities focused on transparency, legality and accountability of organizations and their policies and programs. A little later, these arrangements themselves no longer were taken 'for granted' in terms of their relevance and effectiveness. 'Arrangements-in-the-book' can differ from 'arrangements-in-action', as we know, and the same is true for legal devices.

- *Reason 2: The growth in numbers of laws and regulations puts pressure on the need to know about transparency, accountability and effectiveness.*

The number of regulations increased strongly in many (Western) countries after World War II. In the Netherlands the growth has been serious, despite continuous governmental pleas for de-regulation since the early 1980s (De Jong and Herweijer, 2004). On 1 January 2007, 1785 laws existed, 2489 cabinet regulations and Royal Decrees and 6402 ministerial regulations. The total number of laws has increased since 1980 by approximately 700.

In *Belgium* Parmentier and van Houtte (2003: 21–2) show that:

> in recent decades, the amount of law in Belgium has increased spectacularly. Already in the 1980s, some commentators spoke in an ornate language about the 'inflation of legislation' and 'hyperlexis', about 'legal pollution' and 'legal elephantiasis'. . . . In the 1990s it was no better. In 1999 the Belgian Bulletin of Acts and Decrees (*Moniteur Belge*) contained over 50,000 pages, 50,560. . . . The production of law is not restricted to the legislative work of the Parliament, on the contrary there is a noticeable shift in the production of rules towards the executive power. If one compares for the period 1985–1995 just the number of laws and Royal Decrees, the ratio is 8,5% to 91,5%. This 'pseudo-legislation' leads, together with the 'normal legislation' to a significant rule density in modern society.

According to the EUABC.com in 2015 'there are now more than 40,000 legal acts in the EU. There are also 15,000 Court verdicts and 62,000 international standards, all of which must be respected and obeyed by citizens and companies in the EU'. Some acts are legally binding, such as regulations, directives, decisions and international agreements. Some are not, such as white papers, green papers and communications.[3]

In the *USA* Dawson (2007: 16–18) measured the amount of federal regulation by counting the number of pages in the Code of Federal Regulations (CFR) from 1949 to 1999. The CFR is the US Government publication that prints all federal regulations in existence during a given year:

> Regulation grows almost all the time, but its growth rate varies a great deal. Periods of negative growth are infrequent, and, when negative, the magnitude of the growth rate always is small. High growth rates occur in the 1970s, even though that period saw important deregulation in transportation, telecommunications, and energy.

Given these demographics of rules and regulations,[4] it is evident that society wants to know facts and figures about their functioning, including effects and side-effects, for example on economic productivity.[5]

- *Reason 3: The growth in numbers and activities of organizations enforcing laws and regulations (inspectorates, oversight authorities, public prosecutors, magistrates) are also drivers behind the need to know what is happening in reality through ELR.*

More or less parallel to the increase in numbers of regulations, there has also been an increase in (legal) institutions enforcing rules and regulations: inspectorates, oversight organization and authorities, public prosecutors, organizations studying and fighting fraud and corruption, and many more. Jordana and Levi-Faur's (2004) study of regulatory agencies in *49 countries* is a first source. It looks into the years between 1920 and 2002 and 'found that the number of regulatory agencies rose sharply in the 1990s. Indeed, the rate of establishment increased dramatically: from fewer than five new autonomous agencies per year from the 1960s to the 1980s, to more than 20 per year from the 1990s to 2002' (Braithwaite, 2008: vii).

For *the Netherlands*, data are available on inspectorates for almost 25 years (from 1989 onwards) in terms of their number of employees (full-time equivalents (ftes)) and spending (Willemsen, Leeuw and Leeuw, 2008; Morawski, Leeuw and Otto, 2013). In 1989 inspectorates were spending a little less than €300 million annually, while the costs more than tripled in 2007 (€1.1 billion). However, between 2007 and 2013 the number of full time equivalents in these organizations was reduced by 8% (implying a reduction in costs of personnel) but the costs of the operations were 13% higher (Morawski, Leeuw and Otto, 2013).

For the *United Kingdom* Hood et al (1998: 62) have data on the numbers of staff in regulators' organizations over two decades:

> We identified no fewer than 134 separate bodies regulating the UK public sector at national government level in 1995. They directly employed almost 14,000 staff, and cost £766M to run – just over 30 pence in every £100 spent by UK government (if we take out the biggest transfer payments in the forms of debt interest and cyclical social security [HM Treasury, 1996]).

Hood et al's estimate of 'the overall staff increase in regulatory bodies inside UK government is 90% between 1976 and 1995, and that is a conservative figure. This dramatic staff growth contrasts sharply with what happened to staffing in the public sector as a whole, with a fall of more than 30% in total civil servants and over 20% in local authority staff' (Hood et al, 2010: 64).

Finally, data on the development in *numbers of public prosecutors* per 100,000 inhabitants in 30-plus European countries can be presented. The data show that a steady increase in numbers took place between 1995 and 2011.[6] The mean annual growth for 1995–2000 was 2.15%, for the years 2003–2007 it was 2.48% and for the most recent years (2007–2011) 1.56%. The range in numbers is interesting; while Bulgaria in 2007 had 24 public prosecutors per 100,000 inhabitants, the Netherlands had 4.19, Germany 6.18 and Belgium 8.5.

- *Reason 4: The juridification of societies also triggers a greater interest in ELR.*

Juridification has to do with the role laws, regulation and judges play in a society. Hirschl (2008: 119) uses the concept of judicialization to describe the reliance on courts and judicial means for addressing core moral predicaments, public policy questions and political controversies. In descriptive terms some see this development as 'the proliferation of law' or as 'the tendency towards an increase in formal (or positive, written) law';[7] others see it as 'the monopolization of the legal field by legal professionals', the 'construction of judicial power' or the 'expansion of judicial power'. Here we refer to the first two interpretations (proliferation and tendency towards an increase of formal law). The 'actors' involved, broadly speaking, are governments, legislatures, administrations, the judiciary, legal experts and (other) non-state actors including individuals as well as institutional and corporate actors.

One of the factors behind juridification is the development and implementation of the welfare state. Maus (1986) puts it as follows: 'the welfare paradigm (of law) deploys a particular form of law; substantive, purposive, goal oriented, and implemented through regulations, standards, and rules. This materialized law aims at achieving specific goals in concrete situations'. Teubner (1987:18–19) made the point that juridification 'does not merely mean proliferation of law', but 'signifies a process in which the interventionist social state produces a new type of law, regulatory law . . . characterized by material rationality as opposed to formal rationality'.[8] Law indeed is applied in 'new' areas: family, labor, environment, intimacy and so on. The spread of law and legislation in this manner means that 'relationships hitherto governed by other values and expectations come to be subjected to legal values and rules'. Tugendhat and Croft (2013: 16) used the expression '*legal mission creep*' to characterize this phenomenon.[9] These developments stimulate the need for empirical knowledge, not only showing what is 'going on' in reality, but also with what (expected and unintended) consequences.

- *Reason 5: Contractualization of society also stimulates the interest in ELR.*

Contractual arrangements between central governments and local governments and between governments and NGOs and other organizations have gained importance since New Public Management was introduced in the 1980s in many (Western) countries. O'Flynn (2007: 355) refers to the 'emergence of a new contractualism, while for others contracts and competition became the basis for changing the fundamental nature of the public sector; . . . contracting has been established as a standard form of policy delivery – indeed as an instrument with few limits, preferable in most circumstances to traditional public bureaucracy' (2001: 76). The development of Public Private Partnerships can be linked to the increased importance attached to contracts. However, there is also a third development. Chassagnard-Pinet and Delalieux (2010: 1–2) sketch it thus:

> The decline of the Welfare state in developed countries, along with the globalization of trade with emerging countries, have promoted a major change in the role of governments as producers of norms and as a result a proliferation of norms issued by private bodies. . . . The Sovereign states, whose legal action is mostly limited within their national borders, are struggling in their attempt to rule transnational economic activities . . . The weakening of the State is favoring the emergence of various stakeholders, who nonetheless take part in the development of norms but also implement them (agencies of regulation, private bodies, NGO . . .)

To organize these relationships use is made of contracts and soft laws, for example in the field of corporate social responsibility. Smits (2010: 8–10) links this development with private global norm-production. With this term, he refers to codes of conduct for corporate social or environmental responsibility, to rules of standardization (such as the 'codex alimentarius') and to other types of self-regulation including, in contract law, the age-old 'standardized general conditions'.

- *Reason 6: Technological developments, including innovations also have pushed the growth of ELR.*

Our last point to help explain why ELR is booming is in line with the argument presented by Miles and Sunstein (2008) that *New* Legal Realists are conducting what Legal Realists like Llewellyn and his peers only envisioned: 'large-scale quantitative studies of facts and outcome' (including explanations). *Technology* making data collection and data-analysis faster, cheaper and more in depth is a factor of prime importance here. McGinnis (2014) drew attention to the future impact of information technology on the legal profession:

> The rise of computational innovators [in the field of law] may . . . foster a more data-driven politics. A modern, law-oriented politics often is excessively rhetorical; competing ideals quickly become abstractions. We debate same-sex marriage, for instance, at the federal level in terms of claims about equality, and school funding at the state level in terms of a right to education. *The relentless march of computation, by contrast, permits a focus on the actual effects of social policies and encourages experiments to test those effects.*

In several chapters of this book we have discussed Big Data, including the disruptive technologies mentioned by Susskind (2013). For ELR these developments open new horizons (like legal predictions, evaluating with Big Data and other examples discussed in Chapters 7 and 8), while at the same time methodology, theories and statistics will prevent the legal empirical researcher ending up in a world with Big Data *Myths and Hubris* (Lazer et al, 2014).

These six (and a few other developments, like medicalization of penal law, including neuro-law and the incentives publishers and journals offer to authors doing ELR[10]) have been important in the development of ELR and make the blossoming of this branch understandable.

This brings us to the final topic: *does ELR contribute to the growth of knowledge about the functioning of legal arrangements, devices, institutions, organizations, interventions and legal policies in society?*

10.2 GROWTH OF KNOWLEDGE IN ELR: FOUR CASES SKETCHED

Growth of knowledge can be achieved through several trajectories. One is to improve the quality (validity, reliability, preciseness, coverage, replicability) of measurement instruments; medical and bio-sciences present numerous examples (like the invention of pet scans and brain imaging techniques). Growth of knowledge can also be realized by developing and using more sophisticated research designs and statistical techniques. Accumulation of knowledge can also be reached when different research methods are combined that were not combined before. And growth of knowledge can take place in the explanatory arena: some theories are capable of explaining more factors (including anomalies) than others (before).

In a paper on indicators of the growth of science, Nigel (1978) distinguished between measuring the growth of scientific manpower and the growth of scientific knowledge. He lists several indicators of the latter concept: the production of scientific papers, patent statistics, citation statistics and criteria like 'the annual increase in the number of new variables to be found in the research literature in a given field' (Nigel, 1978: 20).[11] Their pros and (many) cons are discussed, while also more substantive indicators like Popper's falsification criterion and Lakatos' (1970) 'idea of progressive and degenerative problem shifts' are mentioned. Here we follow the suggestions formulated by Lakatos, to find out if there are examples of growth of knowledge in the ELR field.

Lakatos'[12] approach is that growth (or accumulation) of knowledge in a discipline or research field (like ELR) takes place when there are *progressive problem shifts* of a *theoretical and/or empirical nature*. Theoretically progressive problem shifts are moves to new theories which enable us to explain and predict *more* than a predecessor theory allowed. A problem shift is empirically progressive if in addition to predicting new observable evidence, actual observation does indeed confirm this new prediction. A research program can be seen as a set of research activities around a certain problem where researchers (globally and often virtually) are exchanging and confronting theories and evidence, while the results of these processes are synthesized in terms of validity ('truth claims') and their relevance for practice:

> In order for a research program to be progressive, each problem shift must be at least theoretically progressive, and at least occasionally empirically progressive. In other words in a progressive program, each move from an old theory to a new one must enable us to predict more, and at least sometimes these predictions must be confirmed. If a program fails to display this characteristic, it is no longer progressive but has become degenerating.[13]

A research program, according to Lakatos, does not address an *isolated* hypothesis or *isolated* empirical findings but is related to (or part of) a *string* of theoretical and empirical activities, usually including:

> a hard core (= the explanatory center) and a 'positive heuristic', which defines problems, outlines the construction of a belt of auxiliary hypotheses, foresees anomalies and turns them victoriously into examples. This positive heuristic serves to strengthen the research program by the discovery of novel facts that the hard core can explain. These novel facts can be either new discoveries or anomalies in older research programs. . . . There is also the negative heuristic which protects the hard core of the program by deflecting criticism from it to the auxiliary (ad hoc) hypotheses stated to be the subjects of examination and test or by denying the significance of anomalies with the faithful proviso that eventually scientists will explain them. (Peterson, 1998: 24)[14]

10.2.1 Research Program on Curbing Domestic Violence: What Works and Why? (Sherman and Berk, 1984)

This is a case from a well-known research program on domestic violence in the USA that started with an experiment by Sherman and Berk (1984).[15] The purpose of the experiment (done in Minneapolis, USA) was to address the question *how police responded to misdemeanors, cases of domestic violence, and what works best to reduce this domestic violence*. The start of the program was the test of a hypothesis, deduced from deterrence theory: punishment will reduce recidivism, or the propensity to commit further crimes. From this theory, Sherman and Berk deduced the following

BOX 10.1 APPLICATIONS OF LAKATOS' METHODOLOGY OF SCIENTIFIC RESEARCH PROGRAMS (MSRP) TO DIAGNOSING GROWTH OF KNOWLEDGE IN SCIENTIFIC FIELDS

Organizational and strategy studies
Lecocq (2010) took Mintzberg et al's (2005) 'safari' of strategy studies and approaches as an overview of the field of strategy research, studied these 'ten (+1) schools in [this world], each of which constitutes a research program in itself. Each school has core ideas, makes fundamental assumptions, focuses on some empirical problems and derives some results related to strategy. Some schools may temporarily or definitively degenerate, such as the "planning school". A program that supersedes another one may generate a scientific revolution in the field. Moreover, within each school, several theories develop and complement each other, or some may disappear. For instance, although the learning school has its roots in the 60s, the school was invigorated in 1995 by the publication of Nonakaand Takeuchi's The Knowledge Creating Company'.

Economics
Caldwell (1991) analyzed Blaug's analysis of the Keynesian economic program of the first part of the twentieth century in terms of MSRP ('Methodology of Scientific Research Programs') indicators.[1]

Political science
Lustick (1997) analyzed consociatonalism[2] and Lijphart's work from this perspective.

Sociology
Ultee (1977) reviewed five sociological programs ('schools'): functionalism, the utilitarian-individualistic tradition (also known as behavioral sociology), interpretative sociology, the tradition of empirical research and Marxist sociology, to answer the question how far progress of knowledge could be diagnosed by focusing on the explanatory power of theories and their level of corroboration.

[1] However, see also Hands (1985). The article offers a re-evaluation of the applicability of Lakatos' MSRPs to analyze progress in economic theory.
[2] The two central characteristics of consociationalism are *government by grand coalition* and *segmental autonomy*. Government by grand coalition is the institutional setting in which representatives of all significant segments participate in common decision-making with regard to common concerns, whereas decision-making remains autonomous for all other issues. See http://www.britannica.com/EBchecked/topic/1920542/consociationalism, accessed 28 November 2015.

hypothesis: 'Arrest for spouse abuse reduces the risk of repeat offenses'. In this hypothesis, arrest is the independent variable, and variation in the risk of repeat offenses is the dependent variable (it is hypothesized to depend on arrest). The authors tested the hypothesis through an experiment in which the police responded to complaints of spouse abuse in one of three ways, one of which was to arrest the offender. The two others were 'attempting to counsel both parties' and 'sending assailants away from home for several hours'. When they examined the data (police records for the persons in their experiment), they found that of those arrested for assaulting their spouse, only 13% repeated the offense, compared to a 26% recidivism rate for those who were separated from their spouse by the police without any arrest. This pattern was consistent with the hypothesis deduced from deterrence theory. The theory thus received support from the experiment.

However, Sherman and Berk anticipated a possible problem: how valid was the connection they were trying to make between theory and data? Determining whether spouses were assaulted after the initial police intervention was the key measurement concern. Official records of subsequent assaults by the suspect would provide one measure. But most spousal assaults are not reported to the police, and so their research assistants also sought out the victims for interviews every two weeks during a six-month follow-up period. Although fewer than half the victims completed all the follow-up interviews, the availability of the self-report measure allowed the researchers to shed some light on the validity of the official data. In general, the two measures yielded comparable results.

Next, the problem of the external validity ('generalizibility of the findings' beyond Minneapolis) troubled the researchers. Minneapolis is no more a 'typical' US city than any other, and they could not assume that police policies that are effective in Minneapolis will be equally effective in cities with very different political histories, criminal justice agencies and population characteristics. Sherman and Berk (1984: 269) warned their readers that external validity would have to wait for replications of their investigation. In a next stage of this *research program*, Sherman, Berk and others started replications of the experiment in five other US cities. These replications used the same basic research approach, though with some improvements (we do not discuss these here except for one: data were collected about *repeat violence against other victims as well as against the original complainant*). By the time results were reported from five of the six cities, a problem was apparent: in three of the cities (Omaha, Charlotte and Milwaukee), long-term increases in domestic violence incidents among arrestees were found. In two-other locations (Colorado Springs and Dade County) the predicted deterrent effects seemed to be occurring (Sherman et al, 1992). *These new findings, instead of leading to more confidence in deterrence theory, were calling it into question.* Deterrence theory now seemed inadequate to some extent: how can it be explained that deterrence goes hand in hand with increased reoffending behavior?

So the researchers began to reanalyze the follow-up data from the cities to try to explain the discrepant results. Several new research problems were formulated: could systematic differences in the samples or in the implementation of arrest policies explain the differing outcomes or was the problem an inadequacy in the theoretical basis of the research? Was deterrence theory really the best way to explain the patterns in the data they were collecting? To answer these questions, Sherman and his colleagues turned to control theory (Toby, 1957). Control theory predicts that having a 'stake in conformity' (resulting from inclusion in social networks at work or in the community) decreases a person's likelihood of committing crimes. The implication is that people who are employed and married are more likely to be deterred by the threat of arrest than those without such stakes in conformity. And this is indeed what a re-examination of the data revealed: *Individuals who were married and employed were more likely deterred from repeat offenses by arrest, but individuals who were unmarried and unemployed were actually more likely to commit repeat offenses if they were arrested.*[16]

Summarizing

A societal problem (domestic violence) was translated into a research question (what is an effective way to reduce this problem?) and studied by deducing a hypothesis from a well–respected criminological theory. This hypothesis was tested through an experiment in a US city. Results supported the hypotheses and, through that, the general criminological theory, at least initially. Although the research design implied rigorous testing (guaranteeing internal validity, see Chapter 6), nevertheless there were worries about the generalizability (= external validity) of the findings. This made the investigators go for a follow-up, multiple city experiment. Results did contradict deterrence theory; in only two of the five cities was some confirmation of this theory found, while in three other cities the opposite was found. The investigators were thus confronted with a contradiction of a well-known theory. As adequate designs were used, the (contradictory) findings could not be neglected; the team *had* to think things through and come up with an *alternative theory* (which functioned as a positive heuristic). This challenged the Sherman group to deduce a new hypothesis from social control theory that appeared to be capable of explaining what was happening. Social control theory suggests that persons with (more) stakes in conformity and belongingness are more likely to be deterred by arrests than those without such stakes in conformity. And this is what was found.[17]

10.2.2 Research Program on Who Wins and Loses in Litigation, and Why? (Galanter, 1974)[18]

Who wins and who loses in litigation, and why? And do 'haves' fare better in courts than 'have-nots'? Some 40 years ago, Galanter (1974) tried to answer these questions in a paper that set an agenda for researchers interested in the distributive effects of law and legal procedures. It has become a well-known program within empirical legal research (although the original article 'was rejected by all the leading law reviews and a couple of political science journals as well' (Kritzer and Silbey, 2003: 3). As Niemeijer (2014) recently studied the progress made in this research program over the last 40 years, the following is largely based on his work.

Galanter's findings and theories

Galanter's essay was based on data on the relations between party characteristics and winning in litigation. He distinguished between 'one-shotters (OSs)', who use the legal system only occasionally and often involuntarily, and 'repeat players' (RPs), who use the legal system more frequently and strategically. He also differentiated between the resource-rich, well-positioned 'haves', who are often repeat players, and the resource-poor, more vulnerable 'have-nots', who are usually in the role of the OSs. RPs came out ahead in litigation compared to OSs. However, as is well-known, the article was also quite speculative, as there were, for several issues, simply no data available.

Galanter offered several explanations (= theories) for the success of 'haves' in courts. Four of these basically deal with the consequences of the distinction between RPs and OSs, while theory 5 looks the other way round and starts with some characteristics of courts. Theory 6 focuses on the role of governments.

The state of research 40 plus years later

What is the state of the evidence *40 plus years* after the Galanter paper was published? First of all, the research program has produced a 'wealth of research' inside and outside the USA that looked into the basic arguments and mechanisms outlined before (Niemeijer, 2014: 5). Here are a few examples:

- Wheeler et al (1987) provided evidence that in US State Supreme Court cases between 1870 and 1970 (financially and organizationally) stronger parties prevailed over weaker parties. These conclusions hold for different types of cases, time periods and types of legal representation.

BOX 10.2 (SMALL 'T') THEORIES ON MECHANISMS EXPLAINING WHO WINS AND LOSES IN LITIGATION, BASED ON GALANTER (1974) AND NIEMIJER (2014)

The *first theory* is that the legal system *advantages* 'haves' who regularly use the courts. RPs are involved in many similar litigations over time. 'Have-nots' are usually individual OSs. They use the courts only occasionally, for example in case of a traffic accident, a rental problem or a divorce.

The *second explanation* is that RPs have *better knowledge and experience*, are able to *develop expertise* and can *structure next transactions*. RPs have access to various sorts of *resources*. They have superior material resources and can afford best representation and legal expenses ('*better access to better lawyers*'). OSs have few resources and, in general, are likely to litigate for immediate results.

Theory 3 addresses a type of *learning* as an explanatory mechanism: RPs may develop a comprehensive litigation strategy. To RPs, each case as such is not very important. When they estimate their chances as poor and the stakes small, they may choose to settle informally; when they think they are likely to be successful they may bring a case to court. And when RPs lose a case, they can shape transactions taking into account the results of former cases.

Theory 4 basically says that RPs can *play for the rules*. They can both lobby and litigate for favourable rules. Furthermore, RPs are aware which rules are important for them and try to shape legal precedent to their favour. RPs know which rules are likely to 'penetrate' into law in action.

Theory 5 addresses two important *characteristics of courts as an auxiliary mechanism* why RPs get more out of the legal system than OSs. The first is the passive nature of courts. RPs are better equipped to navigate through the restrictive procedural requirements, to articulate their arguments and to access and present relevant information and evidence. The second is the workload of courts. It advantages parties with the ability and resources to bear the burden of delay. It often creates a pressure on OSs to opt for inferior settlements instead of a court decision.

Part of the research program is dedicated to the role governments play. *Theory 6* basically says that governments are the most successful and most capable RPs; they possess the most resources and probably have developed greater expertise in dealing with litigation in recent decades and are so commonly before the courts that judges know the actors and consider them as respected players in the game.

- Farole (1999) found similar results for the period from 1975 to 1999 with an increase of success for the government as RP.
- Dunworth and Rogers (1996) concluded that in federal court litigation the largest corporations outperformed all other parties, both as plaintiffs and as defendants. In a comparison of diversity cases they found that businesses were more successful than non-business parties.

- Hamzehzadeh (2010) showed how the development of one and the same party (Wal-Mart) from OS to RP was paralleled by an increased success in labor and employment law cases in various sorts of courts.
- Also outside the USA support for Galanter's hypothesis has been found. Dotan (1999) reported that organizations and the government had a (limited) advantage in litigation outcomes from the Israeli High Court of Justice, while others found support for the RP hypothesis for Canadian Supreme Court cases and Provincial Courts of Appeal and for the UK (Atkins, 1991).

Is the conclusion that Galanter's RP/OS theory has been backed up by new evidence and can be seen as 'confirmed'? The answer is not that simple. There is evidence that RPs seem to come out ahead in litigation and in general this appears to be internationally true, fairly constant over time, holding for most sorts of courts, at almost every stage for plaintiffs and defendants. But, the research program has also presented evidence that *criticizes* the core of this research program. Niemeijer (2014) raised the issue that the differences between what the two categories (RP/OS) get out of the legal system sometimes are quite small or not very consistent. He cites several studies to illustrate this point.

A second difficulty is whether 'haves' can be identified with RPs. Clearly not, according to Niemeijer. The drugs-dealer or the prostitute are RPs, but lose nearly always. What makes the 'haves' win: is it resources or repeat-playing?

A third difficulty concerns the relevance (and operationalization) of what 'winning in court' means. Van Koppen and Malsch (1991) suggested that plaintiffs may win in court, but that defendants and OSs may win after all, because of low compliance with court decisions. Their research showed that plaintiffs have great difficulty in implementing the decision of the court. According to some researchers, it is time to systematically take the implementation stage into consideration. Although the findings relate to a different field (judiciary sanctions and behavioral modification programs of the Dutch Justice Ministry and its Prison Agency), evaluations found major implementation problems (Nas et al, 2011: 17).

What finally has to be taken into account is that all examples by and large relate to traditional ('paper-driven') courts. What will happen to RPs and OSs when e-courts, e-justice and dispute resolution in the digital world become a natural way of doing things? It may be argued that because of the reduction of (transaction) costs and the lowering of (cultural and legal) barriers to enter the legal system, when working online, things may change (McGinnes, 2014; Susskind, 2013).

After reviewing 40 years of work within the research program, it is Niemeijer's contention that 'none of the empirical studies have really proved Galanter's hypotheses, [while] many of them identify different kinds of complications. The research has made clear that Galanter's famous assertion is *too simple*' (Niemeijer, 2014: 18).

Summarizing

'Who wins and who loses in litigation, how and why' has been the core question of a 42-year old research program developed within the confines of ELR. It started with Galanter's article in 1974. The central research questions have been studied from different perspectives, in different legal regimes, with different time horizons and by using different designs and methods. Several small 't' theories circle around, although a few new ones are developed and none have been completely discarded. The research program is also confronted with new questions. One is what happens after the court's verdict is presented. Another question is how implementation takes place during execution. These questions may lead to evidence that challenges the fundamentals of the central research topic. Progress in terms of new explanations did not take place, but that may change when the digital world continues to march into litigation and dispute resolution (Muller and Kistemaker, 2015). If not, there is a danger of a *stagnating* research program.

10.2.3 Research Program on Contracts, Behavior and Transaction Costs (MaCaulay, 1963)

More than 50 years ago MaCaulay (1963) asked 'what good is contract law?' His research suggested that it mattered a lot less than expected. Results came from a sociological study of over 40 businesses in Wisconsin (USA) showing that companies often fail to plan transactions carefully by providing for future contingencies, and seldom use legal sanctions to address problems during exchange. Written contracts were often highly standardized documents ('boiler plate contracts') that were largely confined to the drawer once drafted by the legal department and then rarely consulted to resolve disputes. 'Businessmen often prefer to rely on "a man's word" in a brief letter, a handshake or "common honesty and decency", even when the transaction involves exposure to serious risks' (MaCaulay, 1963: 58). MaCaulay's study was later called 'a pioneering work', which contributed to serious debates between schools of thought in law to explain the appropriate way to judge contract disputes before the courts ('contextualism versus formalism'). Eigen (2012: 292) suggests that his 'seminal work' spurred an interest in systematic, empirical explorations of private contracting. It 'raised an important question for contracts scholars. How should contract law respond to MaCaulay's demonstration that contract law does not seem to be used all that often in commerce?' (Gava, 2014: 411).

How did MaCaulay explain his findings? Gava (2014: 411–12) summarized the core of his theory:

> MaCaulay explained non-use of contract law by showing that reputation was the most important security for contractual performance and that the fear of losing a good reputation was, usually, far superior to costly, time-consuming recourse to law. He pointed to the institutional pressure to perform and the pride of those involved in business as strong forces operating to ensure that performance. He also noted that the companies he investigated often used contracts as bureaucratic devices to control the inner workings of complex organizations rather than primarily as tools designed to ensure performance. MaCaulay emphasized not only that contract law was infrequently used; he also highlighted the negative impact that its use could have for business dealings and business relationships.

This explanation sparked a flood of empirical and theoretical works on the use and non-use of contract law (in the market place).

Has a research program been developed and growth of knowledge realized in this 'flood of empirical and theoretical work'? Without claiming completeness, such a program exists and includes these activities:

- checking whether in other situations than the 1963 Wisconson situation (countries/types of firms/periods of time and legal regimes) the 'MaCaulay phenomenon' existed (and still exists);
- developing and testing explanations (i.e. theories on how the (new) findings can be explained).

Checking and rechecking the evidence

A number of studies have been published over the last 50 years addressing this issue (see Eigen, 2012). Here we only refer to a few.[19] Braucher et al (2013) revisited the contracts scholarship of MaCaulay, also bringing in new empirical material. Another study was done by Blegvad (1990) who did a pilot study in Denmark confronting MaCaulay with Danish material. Bozovic and Hadfield (2012: 6) studied the 'contract problem' and looked into parties engaged in innovation relationships. 'Following in MaCaulay's footsteps, we conducted semi-structured interviews with 30 businesses in California and asked them to discuss how they managed an important external relationship. Did they draft formal contracts? What role did any formal agreements play in responding to issues that arose in the relationship over time?' Rooks et al (2000: 124) acknowledged the importance of MaCaulay's work, but also noticed that 'relatively little quantitative empirical research has emerged that systematically addresses his intuitive explanations'. Weber and Mayer (2011: 53) suggest a more nuanced perspective on the actual impact of contracts:

> Work dissecting contracts indicates that some clauses play a coordination role, which does not provoke distrust between the parties, while other clauses mitigate opportunism and may well pose barriers to trust development . . . Additionally, other research has shown that some firms add more task description and process detail to their contracts without negatively impacting their relationship, as the two parties learn to write more effective contracts with one another.

Finally, Lumineau (2014: 10), who agreed with MaCaulay's point that 'introducing a contract may signal bad intentions, thereby disrupting what may otherwise be a cycle of trust and reciprocity leading to mutual trust development, developed several propositions how the controlling and the coordinating of dimensions of formal contracts influence trust and distrust in different ways by inducing specific information-processing and decision making mechanisms'.

Developing and testing explanations on the role of contracts

The first author to refer to is Williamson (2009). Though MaCaulay's work is not the only source he used in his work on how persons and organizations manage and enforce effective collaboration and coordination *without being solely dependent upon external laws, courts and contracts*, while at the same time having to deal with opportunism and other hazards, Williamson quotes MaCaulay's work as a 'significant contribution' that helped set the scene. Williamson's credible commitment theory (also known as the hostage model) is seen as a major step forward to the 1963 paper by MaCaulay. Its central mechanisms are the following. In many cases, actors have difficulty reaching cooperative solutions in their mutual relationships because they are unable to commit themselves credibly in advance to act in agreed or specified ways. There are several reasons why an actor's promise to behave cooperatively might not be believed by others. For example, the existence of cynical commitments – promises may be made by actors with no intention of living up to them. Another problem arises from time-inconsistent preferences (an actor may want to promise to behave cooperatively in the present, but in the future it may be rational to change the behavioral intention). What are the options for actors that want to enjoy the joint gains of a particular course of action? Credible commitments theory emphasizes the need to raise the cost of defection ex post and thereby reduce 'cancellation hazards'. 'Credible commitments sometimes come into place spontaneously, as where a history of good experience with a trader leads to a positive reputation effect. Often, however, credible commitments take shape as economic actors consciously agree upon mechanisms that provide added assurance. These can take the form of information disclosure and auditing mechanisms, the development of specialized dispute settling mechanisms, whereby the parties rely more on private ordering than court ordering and sometimes involve creating hostages to support exchange'.[20] Examples of hostages are a partial ownership in the collaborating organization or revenue sharing.[21]

Williamson's model has been empirically tested in different fields and has been highly influential in guiding analysis and empirical interpretation of 'non-standard' contracting arrangements. It is part of an overarching theoretical approach, known as transaction costs economics (TCE), which has also been applied in the non-legal world, as the (former) (mini-) sociological research program 'management of matches'[22] has shown (Williamson, 2009).[23]

TCE is not the only new approach related to and addressing MaCaulay's problem. MaCaulay and MacNeil developed another theory helping to explain empirical results: *relational contract theory*. It is characterized by a view of contracts as relations rather than as discrete transactions. A relational contract is a contract whose effect is based upon a relationship of trust between the parties. The explicit terms of the contract are an outline as there are implicit terms and understandings which determine the behavior of the parties. MacNeil (1980) refers to 'contract-in-law' (that is, contracts enforceable by a legal system) as an infinitesimally small fraction of the total web of contracts in the modern world, including marriage, bureaucracy and the state (Barnett, 1992: 1175).

Summarizing

MaCaulay (1963) discovered that (American) 'businessmen often prefer to rely on "a man's word" in a brief letter, a handshake or "common honesty and decency" even when the transaction involves exposure to serious risks'. This was the start of a research program finding out whether the situation outside Wisconson was more or less similar, how situations develop over time, and what caused that, even without contracts, complex (business) relationships are successfully run. Theory 1 (MaCaulay's) pointed to trust, reputation and high contract costs. Theory 2 (Williamson's credible commitments/hostage taking) was developed further to expand on theory 1 (creating excess informative content), while for a large number of fields theory 2 was tested and – often – confirmed. Though we did not discuss this point, another element of the growth of knowledge produced in this research program is that suggestions for governance models and contractual ('gap filling') arrangements have been developed (Aviram, 2003; Weber and Mayer, 2011).

10.2.4 Research Program 'Explaining (Radical Islamic) Terrorism'

A recently developed *(mini) research program* addresses the question of how to explain terrorist (radical Islamic) behavior. The program has as its starting point the 'common wisdom' that:

> terrorists tend to have 'normal' social backgrounds and are not mentally disordered. [This] has become widely accepted among terrorism researchers. Studies on Italian, German and Irish terrorists failed to provide evidence for any major psychopathology or terrorist personality; notably, many terrorists had unremarkable middle class backgrounds (Horgan, 2003: Sageman, 2004; Schmid, 2011). After 9/11, studies of jihadi terrorism seemed to confirm this image of terrorist normality. Dismissing Neo-Freudian theories that postulate terrorists to suffer from pathological narcissism, paranoia or authoritarian personality disorder, Sageman (2004: 83) concluded, 'terrorists are surprisingly normal in terms of mental health'. Silke (2008) in a review of studies into the psychology of jihadists (those by Sageman (2004) and Bakker (2006) in particular) arrived at the same conclusion. (Weenink, 2015: 17)

Weenink challenges this 'common wisdom'. 'Bakker (2006), for example, found that mental illness was overrepresented in a sample of European jihadists. Venhaus (2010: 4), in a large sample of foreign fighters, did not find 'signs of any clinical psychosis', but did note that 'antisocial behavior was clearly present in all'. Merari (2010: 268) likewise found that 'although none of the would-be suicides was diagnosed as psychotic, most of them had personality traits which made them more amenable to recruiting for suicide missions'. In the Netherlands, on the basis of files from criminal investigations into Dutch jihadist networks, De Poot and Sonnenschein (2011) found that many subjects had a criminal record, had been substance abusers, and had attained lower educational achievements. In Germany, based on interviews with 39 convicted extremists and terrorists of different ideological backgrounds (twenty-four right-wing, nine left wing, and six Islamist oriented extremists) Lützinger (2012: 60) found that they 'did not display any pathological features'; however, she did also note that 'all individuals in our group had experienced the same irregular developments and shown the same deviant behavior during the first and second socialisation instances (family and school) as other offenders who did not necessarily become extremists or terrorists'. Bouzar et al (2014) found that 40% of jihadists in a French sample had suffered from depression.

These studies diverge in design and results, but overall, suggest that the social and psychological background of terrorists tends to deviate from the average. Radical Islamists came from less privileged social strata, and although most of them were not mentally ill, many had a history of problem behavior and troubled backgrounds (Weenink, 2015: 17). Simi et al (2015: 1–2) conducting intensive 'life history interviews' with 44 former members of violent white supremacist groups who lived in 15 different states across the USA, found this:

> Though violent extremism has recently begun to receive increased scrutiny, less attention has been paid to understanding how non-ideological factors influence the process of joining an extremist group and the onset of committing violent crimes. Almost 62% of the interview subjects reported attempting suicide and/or seriously considering suicide; 57% of the sample reported experiencing mental health problems either preceding or during their extremist involvement and 59% reported a family history of mental health problems. (ibid., p. 1)

The *normalcy hypothesis of (extremist) (radical Islamic) terrorism*, which can be found in handbooks and textbooks (and in governmental reports) appears to be very much less *evident* as is currently believed. This hypothesis says that extremist (radical Islamic) terrorists are not mentally disordered and in fact quite normal. Mental health problems, aspects of psychopathology and earlier behavioral problems are believed to be of no relevance in understanding (and predicting) extremist terrorist behavior. Weenink (2015) and Simi (2015) have started to debunk these beliefs and link this behavior to the bio-criminology of violent behavior (O'Connor, 2010: 121):

> To summarize, biosocial criminology has a good deal of potential not only for an increased understanding of violence and terrorism, but for the prevention of both. Further research in this field may enhance, as well as inspire, counterterrorism solutions. To the extent that factors such as unfairness, grievance, injustice, inequity, envy, and spite are related to the causes of terrorism, there is at least moderate proof that these causes have biological connections to what are often mistaken to be solely environmental influences. No cases are likely to be driven completely by biological factors, but some terrorism problems may be driven by a combination of biological and sociological factors.

Based on work by among others Victoroff (2005), Moffitt (1993) and Nell (2006), Weenink (2015: 28–30) suggests that it is important to incorporate insights from neuroscience in the psychology of terrorism. However:

> to our knowledge his (Victoroff's) proposal found no resonance. . . . Terrorism research lags behind developments in, for example, criminology, where biosocial criminologists try to identify neurobiological risk factors for antisocial behavior and violent crime in particular. These risk factors could play some role in terrorist violence as well. Points of mutual interest between terrorism studies and

> neuroscience are not difficult to find, especially when it comes to explaining specific cases of murder and a propensity for cruelty in some individuals. Another subject of mutual interest could be the role of child abuse and neglect, of which many Islamist radicals seem to have been a victim, and which are known to affect neurological development. This is not to say that we expect neuroscience to identify biological risk factors that contribute directly to radicalization or terrorist behavior, but we do think such factors should be considered important pieces of the puzzle.

Raine (2015: 133), one if not the most prominent bio-criminologists, has found that:

> different biological, psychological, and social risk factors can interact in shaping either violence or self-sacrificing heroism. Violence and terrorism are not just low physiological arousal, yet this is certainly one of the active ingredients that, when combined with other influences, can move us toward a more complete understanding of killers . . .

Summarizing

Although the empirical evidence is still exploratory and limited, this case study 4 suggests the possibility of a progressive theoretical problem shift. To explain why some persons go for radical attacks and extreme violence and others do not, cannot be adequately explained when bio-social insights are neglected and the only theoretical line followed is to search for sociological, economic and/or religious factors. The research program opens new horizons for investigating social neuroscience and bio-psychiatry, in particular with regard to understanding terrorist psychopathology and callous-unemotional (CU) traits. These traits have often been considered key features to the broader construct of psychopathy.[24]

10.3 CONCLUDING REMARKS

Empirical legal research is blossoming, if not booming. Our sketch of four research programs (on contracts and their use, litigation and its consequences, domestic violence, and how to explain extremist (radical Islamic) terrorism) shows that these are indicators of growth of knowledge. We think that many other research programs can be found in ELR, like reoffending research, evaluating the impact of penal sanctions, experimental criminology, transnational governance and its consequences, experimental civilology, neurosciences and neurolaw, and the (LLSV) hypothesis[25] (implying that common law countries offer better investment protection than civil law countries) to name a few. Although this may look like a *feel good story*, not much can be said about the generalizability of the four cases of progress of knowledge. Given the breadth and width of ELR, only a systematic investigation will be capable of doing that, which has to include relevance, applicability and use for the legal practice and policy world. And . . . . such a systematic study should be based on systematic reviews and synthesis of existing studies, as we discussed in Chapter 5.

Luckily, the ELR researcher is not alone in doing that work: data bases and data spaces, software for content analysis and other types of data-analysis, knowledge repositories, and new specialized professions like the *empirical research law librarian* (also known as the *law library empiricist*) can help (Miguel-Stearns and Ryan, 2014). And if things may get you down, don't forget the late Eisenberg's (2011: 1737) eulogy:

> [ELR] holds great promise in several areas. [It] can provide systematic knowledge of an important aspect of society – the legal system – similar to knowledge available about other central features of society, such as the economy, crime, and health care. These other features have highly developed data gathering systems in place that dwarf the available information about legal systems. ELR can provide a common intellectual environment in which scholars from diverse disciplines communicate and collaborate.

ENDNOTES

1. 'The 60 law review volumes in the sample published 1641 articles in the years 1998 to 2008. Although only a small percentage of the articles (5.7%) presented original empirical research, nearly half (45.8%) included some empirical content. In 26.4% of the articles, the use of empirical findings was minimal, and in 13.7% it was more substantial.'
2. One of their conclusions is that 'notwithstanding increases in the amount of empirical international economic law research and advances in the quality of empirical methodologies, however, controversy remains as to whether the empirical trend is a good thing for the study of international economic law'. See Simmons and Breidenbach (2011: 220).
3. See http://en.euabc.coms/word/215) for the sources these educated guesses come from.
4. If one takes specialized legal fields and looks for trends regarding regulation, similar findings can be reported. To give one example: public health regulation. For the USA, Burris and Anderson (2013) have shown that 'legal intervention to influence individual health behavior has increased dramatically since the 1960s'. The focus has been on influencing traffic safety, gun violence, tobacco use, reproductive health and obesity, to name a few.
5. Dawson (2007) 'has examined the correlation between federal regulation and several indicators of economic performance: the level of output per unit of capital, the trend of economic growth, and total factor productivity. He examined both the effects of regulation overall, and the effects of individual areas of regulation through regression analysis . . . A one percent increase of the ratio of regulation to capital correlates with a .24 percent decrease in capital productivity' (MacKenzie, 2007: 1).
6. Thanks to Paul Smit (WODC) who collected these data (21 February 2014).
7. http://www.researchgate.net/publication/5014563_ What_is_juridification, accessed 28 November 2015.

8. Silverstein (2009) describes juridification as substituting or replacing ordinary politics with judicial decisions and legal formality.
9. This concept is deduced from 'mission creep', the expansion of a project or mission beyond its original goals, often after initial successes. Mission creep is usually considered undesirable due to the dangerous path of each success breeding more ambitious attempts, only stopping when a final failure occurs. The term was originally applied exclusively to military operations. See http://en.wikipedia.org/wiki/Mission_creep, accessed 28 November 2015.
10. Heise (2002: 827ff): 'An ever-increasing number of law reviews enables greater volume and more opportunities for legal scholars. An increasing number of outlets for legal scholarship increases the likelihood that a wider array of scholarship genres – such as empirical legal scholarship -will reach publication'.
11. See for a critique on scientometric/bibliometric indicators for legal research, van Gestel and Vranken (2011).
12. He worked in the tradition of Karl Popper and other critical rationalists (http://www.loyno.edu/~folse/Lakatos.html, accessed 28 November 2015).
13. See Pawson (2013: 102ff) who discusses theories with excess content, i.e. theories capable of explaining what an (earlier) theory 1) could and (earlier) other theories (theories 2 and 3) could not. He makes the point that 'we can never say that theory A is correct but we can say that it is better than theory B in a particular respect'.
14. He gives as an example: 'Darwin never had an adequate account of how humans inherited individual traits. It was not until the much later recognition of first Mendelian genetics and then the discovery of DNA that scientists discovered a satisfactory account of inheritance compatible with natural selection'.
15. Partly based on Schutt (2009: 44–7).
16. Later, others took this research program a step further by studying the punishment of spouse abuse from the perspective of procedural justice theory.
17. Although this is a fine example of how a research program developed, Angrist (2006: 24–6) and Angrist and Pischke (2013) address the problem of non-compliance in this experiment. Non-compliance includes treatment dilution (= when subjects or units assigned to the treatment group do not get treated) and treatment migration (when subjects or units in the control group nevertheless obtain the experimental treatment): 'In the MDVE research design three treatments were incorporated: arrest, ordering the offender off the premises for 8 hours, and some form of advice that might include mediation. The research design called for one of these three treatments to be randomly selected each time participating Minneapolis police officers encountered a situation meeting the experimental criteria. . . . In practice, officers often deviated from the responses called for . . . In some cases, suspects were arrested when random assignment called for separation or advice. Most arrests in these cases came about when a suspect attempted to assault an officer, a victim persistently demanded an arrest, or if both parties were injured. In one case where random assignment called for arrest, officers separated instead. In a few cases, advice was swapped for separation and vice versa. Although most deviations from the intended treatment reflected purposeful action on the part of the officers involved, sometimes deviations arose when officers simply forgot to bring their report forms. . . . In the MDVE, the most common deviation from random assignment was the failure to separate or advise when random assignment called for this'. Sherman and Berk (1984) presented the evidence on this problem in their cross tabulation table 1 of treatment assigned and treatment delivered (Angrist, 2006: 24–6). Angrist carried out a reanalysis of the Sherman and Berk data following a IV approach pointing to substantial selection bias in estimates using treatment delivered as the causal variable.
18. Litigation refers to the pressing of claims oriented to official legal rules, either by actually invoking official machinery or threatening to do so. This was Galanter's definition of the concept.
19. See also Eigen (2012) for an overview of contract research, and Morgan (2013).

20. Quoting American Legal Realists Llewellyn and MaCaulay.
21. Barondes (2000) gives a couple of other examples. See Williamson (2009: 470). Margaret F. Brinig identified a particularly memorable example of hostage delivery that involves the historical development of the custom of delivering engagement rings. She notes that this custom became more prevalent in the period between the two world wars at a time when states were abolishing the cause of action for breach of a contract to marry. She states that during the period, a woman was expected to remain chaste until the time of her engagement. Once she was betrothed, however, sexual intimacy with her fiancé reportedly occurred nearly half the time. All this was well and good, but if the marriage never came about, she was irretrievably barred from offering an unblemished self to a new suitor and suffered a loss in 'market value'. Thus, in her view, the delivery of the ring served as an extra-legal substitute for the disappearing contract-based cause of action. Other examples include 'earnest money' deposits, such as deposits in typical contracts for the sale of real estate; excessive liquidated damages; lower wages paid to employees in the early years of employment, accompanied by higher levels in later years; and provisions in commercial leases obligating tenants to pay for improvements.
22. Raub and Weesie (2000) who managed this Dutch National Science Foundation program, carried it out at Utrecht University, Department of Sociology.
23. Rooks et al (2000: 124) point to the problem that TCE 'largely omits the social context from the explanation of the organization of transactions' (although Williamson did not deny the relevance of the social embeddedness of transactions).
24. Hawes et al (2009: 2): 'Callous-unemotional traits, originally conceptualized as a developmental precursor to the temperament factor of psychopathy, may characterize a pathway to antisocial behavior that is distinct from a more commonly occurring one associated with an emotionally dysregulated/over-reactive temperament. . . . Importantly, emerging evidence suggests that low levels of cortisol may act as a biological marker for this callous-unemotional traits subgroup'.
25. Also known as the 'legal origin' hypothesis of LaPorta et al (see also Chapter 4).

References

Agassi, J. (1960), 'Methodological Individualism', *The British Journal of Sociology*, **11** (3), 244–70.

Agrast, M., J. Botero, J. Martinez, A. Ponce and C. Pratt (2014), *The World Justice Project, Rule of law Index 2012–2013*, Washington DC: The World Justice Project.

Aliaga, M. and B. Gunderson (2005), *Interactive statistics*, Upper Saddle River: Pearson Education Inc.

Albers, P. (2008), 'Evaluation of Courts and Judicial Systems. Improvements of Judicial Systems: European Experiences', *International Journal For Court Administration* **1** (1), 45–57.

Amodio, F. (2015), 'Crime Protection Investment Spillovers: Theory and Evidence from the City of Buenos Aires', Paper, Universitat Pompeu Fabra.

Angrist, J. (2006), 'Instrumental variables methods in experimental criminological research: what, why and how', *Journal of Experimental Criminology*, **2** (2), 23–44.

Angrist, J. and J. Pischke (2014), *Mastering Metrics: The Path from Cause to Effect*, Princeton: Princeton University Press.

Armour, J., S. Deakin, P. Sarkar, M. Siems and A. Singh (2009), 'Shareholder Protection and Stock Market Development: An Empirical Test of the Legal Origins Hypothesis', *Journal of Empirical Legal Studies*, **6** (2), 343–80.

Astbury, B. and F. Leeuw (2010), 'Unpacking black boxes: mechanisms and theory-building in evaluation', *American Journal of Evaluation* **31** (3), 363–81.

Atkins, B. (1991), 'Party capability theory as an explanation for intervention behavior in the English Court of Appeals', *American Journal of Political Science*, **35** (1), 881–903.

Aubert, V. (1963), 'Researches in the sociology of law', *American Behavioral Scientist* **7** (4), 16–20.

Aubert, V. (1969), 'Some social functions of legislation', in V. Aubert (ed.), *Sociology of law*, Harmondsworth: Penguin, pp. 99–110.

Aviram, A. (2003), 'Regulation by Networks', *Brigham Young University Law Review*, **4**, 1179–235.

Ayres, I. and J. Braithwaite (1992), *Responsive Regulation: Transcending the Deregulation Debate*, New York: Oxford University Press.

Azzam, T., S. Evergreen, A. Germuth and S. J. Kistler (2013), 'Data visualization and evaluation', *New Directions for Evaluation*, **139**, 73–84.

Bacharach, S. (1989), 'Organizational Theories: Some Criteria for Evaluation', *Academy of Management Review* **14** (4), 496–515.

Backer, C. (2007), 'Economic Globalization and the Rise of Efficient Systems of Global Private Law Making: Wal-Mart as Global Legislator', *Connecticut Law Review* **39**, 1739–1784.

Backer, T. (1991), 'Knowledge utilization: the third wave', *Science Communication*, **12**, 225–40.

Bader, M. and H. Schmeets (2014), 'Is International Election Observation Credible? Evidence from OSCE Missions', *Research & Politics*, **2**, (1), 1–6.

Bagshaw, S. and R. Bellomo (2008), 'The need to reform our assessment of evidence from clinical trials: A commentary', *Philosophy, Ethics, and Humanities in Medicine* **3** (1), 1–11.

Bail, C. (2014), 'The Cultural Environment: Measuring Culture with Big Data', *Theory and Society*, **43** (3–4), 465–82.

Bail, C. (2015), 'Taming Big Data: Using App Technology to Study Organizational Behavior on Social Media', *Sociological Methods and Research*, **43**, 1–29.

Baillargeon, N. (2007), *Intellectual Self-Defense*, New York: Seven Stories Press.

Baker, D.N., Schweitzer, E. Risko and J. Ware (2013), 'Visual Attention and the Neuroimage Bias', *Plos One*, **8** (9), e74449.

Bakker, E. (2006), 'Jihadi terrorists in Europe, their characteristics and the circumstances in which they joined the jihad: An exploratory study', The Hague: Clingendael Institute.

Ball, D. and W. Snizek (2007), 'Desk Top Graffiti: An Unobtrusive Measure of Student Culture and Campus Climate', *National Social Science Journal*, **28**, 159–64.

Ball, W. (1995), 'A Pragmatic Framework for the Evaluation of Policy Arguments', *Review of Policy Research*, **14** (1–2), 3–24.

Bamberger, M.J. and L. Mabry (2012), *Real World Evaluation*, London, Sage.

Banakar, R. and M. Travers (2005), 'Introduction', in R. Banakar and M. Travers, *Law and Social Theory*, Oxford: Hart Publishing, pp. 1–3.

Barendrecht, M., L. Kistemaker, H. J. Scholten, R. Schrader and M. Wrzesinka (2014), *Legal Aid in Europe: Nine Different Ways to Guarantee Access to Justice?*, The Hague: Hiil and WODC.

Barendrecht, M., R. Jance Raiè and S. Muller (2012), *Rule Jungling. When Lawmaking goes Private, international and Informal*, The Hague: Hiil.

Barlow, D., M. Nock and M. Hersen (2009), *Single Case Experimental Designs: Strategies for Studying Behavior*, Boston, MA: Pearson Education, Inc.

Barnett, M. and M. Finnemore (2004), *Rules for the World: International Organizations in Global Politics*, Ithaca: Cornell University Press.

Barnett-Page, E. and J. Thomas (2009), 'Methods for Research Synthesis Node', Evidence for Policy and Practice Information and Co-ordinating (EPPI-) Centre, Social Science Research Unit, Institute of Education, ESRC National Centre for Research Methods, NCRM Working Paper Series, Number (01/09), pp. 1–29.

Barondes, R. de (2000), 'The Business Lawyer as terrorist transaction cost engineer', *Fordham Law Review*, **69** (1), 31–82.

Barzelay, P. and K. Jackson (2013), *Qualitative Data Analysis with NVivo*, Thousand Oaks: Sage.

Beckers, A. (2015), *Enforcing Corporate Social Responsibility Codes. On Global Self-Regulation and National Private Law*, Oxford: Hart Publishing.

Bergh, D., R. Hanke, P. Balkundi, M. Brown and X. Chen (2004), 'An assessment of research designs in strategic management research: the frequency of threats to internal validity', *Research Methodology in Strategy and Management*, **1**, 349–71.

Berk, R. and D. Rauma (1983), 'Capitalizing on Nonrandom Assignment to Treatments: A Regression-Discontinuity Evaluation of a Crime-Control Program', *Journal of the American Statistical Association*, **78**, (381), 21–7.

Bethlehem, J., F. Cobben and B. Schouten (2011), *Handbook of Nonresponse in Household Surveys* (Wiley Handbooks in Survey Methodology), Hoboken, New Jersey: John Wiley and Sons.

Bhaskar, R. (1978), *A Realist Theory of Science*, Brighton: Harvester Press.

Bhattacherjee, A. (2012), *Social Science Research: Principles, Methods, And Practices*, Ph.D. University of South Florida Tampa, Florida.

Biemer, P. (2010), 'Total survey error: Design, implementation, and evaluation', *Public Opinion Quarterly*, **74** (5), 817–48.

Bijleveld, C. (2013), *Methoden en Technieken van Onderzoek in de Criminologie*, The Hague: Boom Legal Publishers.

Billiet, J., H. Matsuo, K. Beullens and V. Verhovar (2009), 'Non-response bias in cross-national surveys: Designs for detection and adjustment in the ESS', *Research and Methods*, **18** (1), 3–43.

Black, J. (2010), 'Financial markets', in P. Cane and H. Kritzer (eds), *Oxford Handbook of Empirical Legal Research*, Oxford: Oxford University Press, pp. 151–76.

Blegvak, D.-M. (1990), 'Commercial Relations, Contract, and Litigation in Denmark: A Discussion of Macaulay's Theories', *Law & Society Review*, **24** (2), 397–412.

Blok, A. and M. Pedersen (2014), 'Complementary social science? Quali-quantitative experiments in a Big Data world', *Big Data & Society* **1**, 1–6.

Blumer, B. (1954), 'What is Wrong with Social Theory?', *American Sociological Review* **18**, 3–10.

Boeker, M., W. Vach and E. Motschall (2013), 'Google Scholar as replacement for systematic literature searches: good relative recall and precision are not enough', *BMC Medical Research Methodology*, **13** (131), 1–12.

Boom, W. van (2011), 'Behaviour and Law – Towards Empirical Legal Studies', Speech delivered at the 98th Dies Natalis of the Erasmus University Rotterdam, 8 November.

Boom, W. van (2013), 'Empirisch privaatrecht. Enige beschouwingen over de rol van empirisch onderzoek in de hedendaagse privaatrechtswetenschap', *Tijdschrift voor Privaatrecht* **1**, 7–84.

Boom, W. van (2014/2015), 'Kritiek en methode in juridisch-dogmatisch privaatrechtelijk onderzoek – een bespreking van Asser-Vranken Algemeen Deel', *NTBR*, **4**, 124–33.

Boom, W. van and I. Giesen (eds) (2012), *Judicial Decision Making in Civil Law*, Rotterdam: Eleven International Publishing.

Boom, W. van, I. Giesen and M. Smit (eds) (2012), *Civilologie: opstellen over empirie en privaatrecht*, The Hague: BJu|Eleven.

Boom, W. van, I. Giesen and A. Verheij (2014), 'Inleiding: een handboek voor de civiloloog-privatist', in W. Van Boom, I. Giesen and A. Verheij (eds), *Capita Civilologie. Handboek empirie en privaatrecht*, The Hague: Eleven, pp. 1–24.

Boom, W. van, I. Giesen and A. Verheij (eds) (2013), *Capita Civilologie. Handboek empirie en privaatrecht*, The Hague: Boom Juridische Uitgeverij.

Booth, A., P. Meier and J. Shapland (2012), 'Alcohol pricing and criminal harm: a rapid evidence assessment of the published research literature', Paper, The University of Sheffield, School of Health and Related Research, Sheffield.

Bouckaert, B. and G. De Geest (eds) (2001), *Encyclopedia of Law and Economics*, Cheltenham: Edward Elgar.

Bouzar, D., C. Caupenne and S. Valsan (2014), *La Métamorphose opérée chez le jeune par les nouveaux discours terrorists*, France: le Centre de Prévention contre les Dérives Sectaires liées à l'Islam (CPDSI).

Bowen, G. (2006), 'Grounded Theory and Sensitizing Concepts', *International Journal of Qualitative Methods* **5** (3), 1–8.

Bozovic, I. and G. Hadfield (2012), 'Scaffolding: Using Formal Contracts to Build Informal Relations in Support of Innovation', University of Southern California Law & Economics Research Paper No. C12-3.

Braak, S. van den, S. Choenni and M. Bamberger (2015), 'Complexity in Review and Synthesis Studies', in M. Bamberger, J. Vaessen and E. Raimondo (eds), *Dealing With Complexity in Development Evaluation. A Practical Approach*, Thousand Oaks: Sage, Ch. 9.

Braak, S. van den, S. Choenni and M. Bamberger (2016), 'Emergent Technologies and Creative Use of Multiple Sources of Information', in M. Bamberger, J. Vaessan and E Raimondo (eds), *Dealing with Complexity in Development Evaluation. A Practical Approach*, Thousand Oaks: Sage, pp. 181–197.

Braak, S. van den, S. Choenni and S. Verwer (2013), 'Combining and Analyzing Judicial Databases', in B. Custers, T. Calders, B. Schermer and T. Zarsky (eds), *Discrimination and Privacy in the Information Society*. Studies in Applied Philosophy, Epistemology and Rational Ethics **3**, 191–206.

Braga, A., D. Hureau and A. Papachristos (2012), 'An Ex Post Facto Evaluation Framework for Place-Based Police Interventions', *Evaluation Review* **35** (6), 592–626.

Braithwaite, J. (2008), *Regulatory Capitalism: How it Works, Ideas for Making it Work Better*, Cheltenham: Edward Elgar.

Braucher, J., J. Kidwell and W. C. Whitford (eds) (2013), *Revisiting the Contracts Scholarship of Stewart Macaulay. On the Empirical and the Lyrical*, Oxford: Hart Publishing.

Brehm, J. (1993), *The Phantom Respondents*, Ann Arbor: University of Michigan Press.

Brems, E. (2008), 'Methods in human legal rights research', in F. Coomans, F. Grunfeld and M. Kamminga (eds), *Methods of Human Rights Research*, Maastricht: Intersentia, pp. 77–91.

Brown, C. and R. Lilford (2006), 'The stepped wedge trial design: a systematic review', *BMC Medical Research Methodology* **6**, 1–9.

Bruinsma, G. and D. Weisburd (eds) (2014), *Encyclopedia of Criminology and Criminal Justice*, New York: Springer.

Bruinsma, G. and D. Weisburd (2007), 'Experimental and quasi-experimental criminological research in the Netherlands', *Journal of Experimental Criminology*, **3**, 83–8.

Bühler-Niederberger, D. (1985), 'Analytische Induktion als Verfahren qualitativer Methodologie', *Zeitschrift Für Soziologie*, **14** (6), 475–85.

Bullis, R. (2014), 'Promoting Communications Between Social Scientists and Lawyers', *The Jury Expert*, **26** (4), 1–3.

Bunge, M. (1997), *Philosophy of Science: From Problem to Theory*, New Brunswick: Transaction Publishers.
Burca, G. de (2009), 'Developing Democracy Beyond the State', *Columbia Journal of Transnational Law*, **46**, 101–158.
Burris, S. and E. Anderson (2013), 'Legal Regulation of Health-Related Behavior: A Half-Century of Public Health Law Research', Temple University Beasley School of Law Legal Studies Research Paper No. 2013-19.
Burrows, E. and S. Walker (2013), *Developing a Critiquing Tool for Expert Opinion*, Working Papers in Health Sciences 1:3.
Caldwell, B. (1991), 'The methodology of scientific research programs in economics. Criticisms and conjectures', in G. K. Shaw, *Economics, Culture and Education*, Aldershot: Edward Elgar, pp. 95–107.
Camp Keith, L. (2010), 'Human rights instruments', in P. Cane and H. Kritzer (eds), *Oxford Handbook of Empirical Legal Research*, Oxford: Oxford University Press, pp. 353–76.
Campbell, D. and H. L. Ross (1968), The Connecticut Crackdown on speeding: time-series data in quasi-experimental analysis', *Law and Society Review*, **3** (1), 33–54.
Campbell, D. and J. Stanley (1963), *Experimental and Quasi-Experimental Designs for Research*, Boston: Houghton Mifflin Company.
Cane, P. and H. Kritzer (eds) (2010), *The Oxford Handbook of Empirical Legal Research*, Oxford: Oxford University Press.
Caracelli, J. and L. Cooksy (2013), 'Incorporating qualitative evidence in systematic reviews: strategies and challenges', *New Directions for Evaluation*, **138**, 97–108.
Caracelli, V. and J. Greene (1993), 'Data analysis strategies for mixed-method evaluation designs', *Educational Evaluation and Policy Analysis*, **15**, 195–207.
Cardozo, B. N. (1921), *The Nature of the Judicial Process*, New Haven: Yale University Press.
Carmichael, T. (2009), *How to write your research problem statement*, Wits Business School, Johannesburg, South Africa.
Castellanos-Ryan, N., J. Seguin, F. Vitaro, S. Parent and R. E. Tremblay (2013), 'Impact of a 2-year multimodal intervention for disruptive 6-year-olds on substance use in adolescence: randomised controlled trial', *British Journal of Psychiatry*, **203**, 188–95.
Centre for Reviews and Dissemination (2008), *Systematic Reviews. CRD's guidance for undertaking reviews in health care*, York: University of York.
Chambliss, D. and R. Schutt (2015), *Making Sense of the Social World. Methods of Investigation*, London: Sage.
Chassagnard-Pinet, S. and G. Delalieux (2010), 'Contractualization of the

social and environmental norms', Paper presented at the Annual Legal Research Network Conference, October, hosted by the University of Groningen.

Chilton, A. and D. Tingley (2013), 'Why the Study of International Law Needs Experiments', *Columbia Journal of Transnational Law*, **52** (1), 173–238.

Choenni, R., J. van Dijk and F. Leeuw (2010), 'Preserving privacy whilst integrating data: applied to criminal justice', *Information Polity*, **15**, 125–38.

Christen, M. and M. Alfano (2014), 'Outlining the Field – A Research Program for Empirically Informed Ethics: Morality between Facts and Norms', in M. Christen, C. van Schaik, J. Fischer, M. Huppenbauer and C. Tanner (eds), *Library of Ethics and Applied Philosophy*, **32**, 3–27.

Cobben, F. (2009), *Nonresponse in sample surveys. Methods for analysis and adjustment*, Ph.D. thesis, The Hague: Statistics Netherlands.

Cochran, W.G. (1977), *Sampling Techniques*, New York: John Wiley and Sons.

Cohen, F. (1935), 'Transcendental nonsense and the functional approach', *Columbia Law Review*, **35** (6), 809–49.

Coleman, G. (1960), 'The Scandinavian Legal Realists: A Critical Analysis', *Faculty Law Review*, **18**, 152–62.

Coleman, J. (1990), *Foundations of Social Theory*, Cambridge: Bellknap Press.

Coleman, J. S. (1986), 'Social theory, social research, and a theory of action', *American Journal of Sociology*, **91**, 1309–35.

Comes, T., M. Hiete, N. Wijngaards and F. Schultmann (2011), 'Decision maps: A framework for multi-criteria decision support under severe uncertainty', *Decision Support Systems* **52**, 108–18.

Conradie, P. and R. Choenni (2014), 'On the barriers for local government releasing open data', *Government Information Quarterly*, **31** (suppl 1), 10–17.

Cook, T. and D. Campbell (1979), *Quasi-Experimentation: Design and Analysis for Field Settings*, Chicago: Rand McNally.

Coomans, F., F. Grunfeld and M. Kamminga (eds) (2008), *Methods of Human Rights Research*, Maastricht: Intersentia.

Cormack, D. and F. Benton (1996), 'The Research Process', in D. Cormack (ed.), *The Research Process in Nursing*, Oxford: Blackwell Science, pp. 53–63.

Cornet, L. (2015), 'Using basic neurobiological measures in criminological research', *Crime* Science, **4**, 1–16.

Cornet, L. J. M., P. H. van der Laan, H. L. I. Nijman, N. Tollenaar and C. H. de Kogel (2014), 'Neurobiological Factors as Predictors of

Cognitive-Behavioral Therapy Outcome in Individuals With Antisocial Behavior: A Review of the Literature', *International Journal of Offender Therapy and Comparative Criminology*, **58** (11), 1279–96.

Costello, E. J., S. Compton, G. Keeler and A. Angold (2003), 'Relationships between poverty and psychopathology, a natural experiment', *JAMA*, **290** (15), 2023–9.

Cousins, J. B. (2003), 'Utilization effects of participatory evaluation', in T. Keleghan and D. L. Stufflebeam (eds), *International Handbook of Educational Evaluation*, Boston: Kluwer Academic Publishers, pp. 245–66.

Croes, M. and F. Leeuw (2012), 'De logos van het civiele', in W. van Boom, I. Giesen and M. Smit (eds), *Civilologie: opstellen over empirie en privaatrecht*, The Hague: Eleven, pp. 7–31.

Crona, B. and J. Parker (2011), 'Network Determinants of Knowledge Utilization: Preliminary Lessons from a Boundary Organization', *Science Communication*, **33** (4), 448–71.

Cummings, S. (2013), 'Empirical studies of law and social change: What is the field? What are the questions?', *Wisconsin Law Review*, **93** (1), 172–203.

Dalkey, N. and O. Helmer (1963), 'An experimental application of the Delphi method to the use of experts', *Management Science*, **9** (3), 458–67.

Davis, F. (1957), 'The treatment of law in American sociology', *Sociology and Social* Research, **42** (2), 99–105.

Dawson, J. (2007), 'Regulation and the Macroeconomy', *Kyklos*, **60** (1), 15–36.

Deakin, S. (2011), 'Legal evolution: integrating economic and systemic approaches', *Review of Law and Economics*, **11**, 660–83.

Deakin, S. (2014), *Law and Economics: Syllabus and Reading*, EUI, March.

Deflem, M. (2011), 'Sociology of Law', in J. Manza (ed.), *Bibliography in Oxford Bibliographies Online: Sociology*, Oxford: Oxford University Press.

DeLeeuw, E. D. (2005), 'To mix or not to mix data collection modes in surveys', *Journal of Official Statistics*, **21** (2), 233–55.

Denscombe, M. (2002), *Ground Rules for Good Research: a 10 point guide for social research*, Buckingham: Open University Press.

Derlien, H. U. (1999), 'Genesis and structure of evaluation practices in comparative perspective', in Ray C. Rist (ed.), *Program evaluation and the management of government. Patterns and Prospects across eight nations*, New Brunswick: Transaction Publishers, pp. 147–77.

Dholakia, N. and D. Zhang (2004), 'Online Qualitative Research in the Age of E-Commerce: Data Sources and Approaches', *Forum Qualitative Sozialforschung*, **5** (2), art. 29.

Diamond, S. S. and P. Mueller (2010), 'Empirical Scholarship in Law Reviews', in J. Hagan (ed.), *Annual Review of Law & Social Science*, **6**, 581–99 (Palo Alto, CA: Annual Reviews).

Dijck, G. van (2011), 'Empirical Legal Studies', *WPNR: Weekblad voor privaatrecht, notariaat en registratie*,**142** (6912), 1105–112.

Dijk, J. van, R. Choenni and F. Leeuw (2009), 'Analyzing a complaint database by means of a genetic-based data mining algorithm', *Proceedings of the 12th International Conference on Artificial Intelligence and Law*, Barcelona, pp. 226–8.

Dillman, D. (1991), 'The Design And Administration Of Mail Surveys', *Annual Review of Sociology*, **17**, 225–49.

Dillman, D. A. (2007), *Mail and internet surveys: The tailored design method*, Hoboken, New Jersey: John Wiley and Sons.

Dillman, D., G. Phelps, R. Tortora, K. Swift, J. Kohrell, J. Berck and B. Messer (2009), 'Response rate and measurement differences in mixed-mode surveys using mail, telephone, interactive voice response and the Internet', *Social Science Research*, **38** (1), 1–18.

Dixon, J. (1995), 'The Organizational Context of Criminal Sentencing', *American Journal of Sociology*, **100** (5), 1157–198.

Dotan, Y. (1999), 'Do the "Haves" still come out ahead? Resource inequalities in ideological courts', *Law & Society Review*, **33**, 1059–1080.

Draper, J. (2004), 'The relationship between research question and research design', in P.A. Crookes and S. Davies (eds), *Research into Practice: Essential Skills for Reading and Applying Research in Nursing and Health Care*, Edinburgh: Bailliere Tindall, pp. 69–84.

Dunworth, T. and J. Rogers (1996), 'Corporations in court: Big business litigation in U.S. Federal courts 1971–1991', *Law & Social Inquiry*, **21**, 497–592.

Dutch Parliamentary Electoral Studies (DPES) (2006), http://www.dpes.nl/en/data-and-results/dpes-2006, accessed 24 November 2015.

Duvendack, M. and R. Palmer-Jones (2011), *What is the evidence of the impact of microfinance on the well-being of poor people?*, EPPI-Centre, London.

Dweck, C., C. Chiu and Y. Hong (1995), 'Implicit Theories and Their Role in Judgments and Reactions: A World From Two Perspectives', *Psychological Inquiry*, **6** (4), 267–85.

Dysart, J. (2013), 'How lawyers are mining the information mother lode for pricing, practice tips and predictions', http://www.abajournal.com/magazine/article/the_dawn_of_big_data/?utm_source=feedburner&utm_medium=feed&utm_campaign=ABA+Journal+Magazine+Stories, accessed 8 July 2015.

Eberle, E. (2009), 'The method and role of Comparative law', *Washington University Global Studies Law Review*, **8** (3), 451–86.

Eekelaar, J., M. Maclean and S. Beinart (2000), *Family Lawyers: The Divorce Work of Solicitors*, London: Wiley.

Eigen, Z. (2012), 'Empirical Studies of Contract', Faculty Working Papers, http://scholarlycommons.law.northwestern.edu/facultyworkingpapers/204/, accessed 15 July 2015.

Eisenberg, T. (2011), 'The origins, nature, and promise of empirical legal studies and a response to concerns', *University of Illinois Law Review*, **20** (5), 1713–39.

Elbers, N., A. Akkermans, P. Cuijpers and D. Bruinvels (2011), 'Empowerment of personal injury victims through the internet: design of a randomized controlled trial', *Trials*, **9**, 1–9.

Elbers, N., A. Akkermans, P. Cuijpers and D. Bruinvels (2013), 'Effectiveness of a web-based intervention for injured claimants: a randomized controlled trial', *Trials*, **14** (227), 1–9.

Ellickson, R. (1991), *Order Without Law: How Neighbors Settle Disputes*, Cambridge: Harvard University Press.

Ellsberg, M. and L. Heise (2005), *Researching Violence Against Women: A Practical Guide for Researchers and Activists*, PATH, World Health Organization.

Elster, J. (2007), *Explaining Social Behavior: More Nuts and Bolts for the Social Sciences*, Cambridge: Cambridge University Press.

Elzinga, D.J. (1997), *Het Nederlands Kiesrecht*, Deventer: Tjeenk Willink.

Engel, C. (2012), 'Behavioral Law and Economics: Empirical Methods', Preprints of the Max Planck Institute for Research on Collective Goods Bonn 2013/1.

Engel, C. (2006), *The Difficult Reception of Rigorous Descriptive Social Science in the Law*, Preprints of the Max Planck Institute for Research on Collective Goods, Bonn 2006/1.

EngleMerry, S. (2012), 'Anthropology and Law', in R. Fardon, O. Harris, T. H. J. Marchand, M. Nuttall, C. Shore, V. Strang and R. A. Wilson (eds), *The Sage Handbook of Social Anthropology*, London: Sage, pp. 105–120.

Environmental Protection Agency (2006), *Data Quality Assessment: Statistical Methods for Practitioners*, EPA QA/G-9S, Washington DC.

Epstein, L. and G. King (2002), 'The Rules of Inference', *University of Chicago Law Review*, **30** (1), 1–93.

Epstein, L. and A. Martin (2010), 'Quantitative approaches to empirical legal research', in P. Cane and H. Kritzer (eds), *The Oxford Handbook of Empirical Legal Research*, Oxford: Oxford University Press, pp. 901–926.

Epstein, L. and A. Martin (2014), *An Introduction to Empirical Legal Research*, Oxford: Oxford University Press.

Erp, J. van (2010), 'Regulatory Disclosure of Offending Companies in the Dutch Financial Market: Consumer Protection or Enforcement Publicity?', *Law and Policy*, **32** (4), 407–433.

Eshuis, R., S. J. P. J. Dalm and P. O. de Jong (2014), *Evaluatie Competentiegrensverhoging 2011. Rapportage voormeting*, Cahier Den Haag: WODC.

Eshuis, R., N. L. Holvast, H. G. van de Bunt, J. G. van Erp and N. T. Pham (2012), *Het aansprakelijk stellen van bestuurders. Onderzoek naar de overwegingen die spelen bij het al dan niet intern aansprakelijk stellen van bestuurders en interne toezichthouders*, WODC/ Erasmus University: Boom Legal Publishers.

Eshuis, R. and F. Leeuw (2014), 'Over zien en toezien; de veronderstellingen achter het intern toezicht op semipublieke dienstverleners', in W. van Boom, I. Giesen and A. Verheij (eds), *Capita Civilologie; handboek empirie en privaatrecht*, The Hague, Boom Juridische Uitgeverij, pp. 955–81.

Eshuis, R. and F. van Tulder (2014), *Daling instroom civiele handelszaken onderzocht. Verslag wetenschappelijk forum, 1 mei 2014*, Den Haag: Raad voor de Rechtspraak and WODC.

Evans, D. and M. Price (2008), 'Measure for measure: utilizing legal norms and health data in measuring the right to health', in F. Coomans, F. Grunfeld and M. Kamminga (eds), *Methods of Human Rights Research*, Maastricht: Intersentia, pp. 111–31.

Faigman, D. (2002), 'Is Science Different for Lawyers?', Science, **297** (July), 339–40.

Farnsworth, W. (2007), *The Legal Analyst: A Toolkit for Thinking about the Law*, Chicago: University of Chicago Press.

Farole, D. (1999), 'Reexamining litigant success in state supreme courts', *Law & Society Review*, **33**, 1043–1085.

Farrington, D. (2003), 'Methodological Quality Standards for Evaluation Research', *The Annals of the American Academy of Political and Social Science*, **587**, 49–68.

Farrington, D. and M. Ttofi (eds) (2014), 'Criminal careers in self-reports compared with official records', *Criminal Behaviour and Mental Health*, **24**, 225–8.

Farrington, D. and B. Welsh (2005), 'Randomized experiments in criminology: what have we learned in the last two decades?' *Journal of Experimental Criminology*, **1** (1), 9–38.

Ferguson, N. (2014), *The Great Degeneration. How Institutions Decay and Economies Die*, Harmondsworth: Penguin Books.

Ferrari, V. (2015), 'Sociology of law in European civil law countries'. Some remarks and correspondent proposals, *Recht der Werkelijkheid*, **31** (1), 42–54.

Feskens, R. (2009), *Difficult Groups in Survey Research and the Development of Tailor-made Approach Strategies*, The Hague/ Utrecht: Statistics Netherlands and University Utrecht.

Festinger, L. (1957), *A Theory of Cognitive Dissonance*, Stanford: Stanford University Press.

Field, A. and R. Gillett (2010), 'How to do a meta-analysis', *British Journal of Mathematical and Statistical Psychology*, **63**, 665–94.

Fijnaut, C. (2014), *Criminologie en strafrechtsbedeling*, Antwerpen/ Cambridge: Boom Juridische Uitgeverij.

Fisher, W. III., M. Horwitz and Th. Reed (eds) (1993), *American Legal Realism*, Oxford: Oxford University Press.

Flick, U. (2009), *An introduction to qualitative research*, London: Sage.

Foot, P. (1967), 'The Problem of Abortion and the Doctrine of Double Effect', *Oxford Review* **5**, 5–15.

Freeland Judson, H. (2004), *The great betrayal, fraud in science*, New York: Harcourt.

Fuller, L. (1953), 'American legal philosophy at mid-century. A review of Edwin W. Patterson's Jurisprudence, Men and Ideas of the Law', *Journal of Legal Education*, **6**, 457–85.

Furubo, J. E., R. Rist and R. Sandahl (eds) (2002), *International Atlas of Evaluation*, New Brunswick: Transaction Publishers.

Galanter, M. (2006), 'In the winter of our discontent: law, anti-law and social science', *Annual Review of Law and Social Science*, **2** (1), 1–16.

Galanter, M. (1974), 'Why the "Haves" Come Out Ahead: Speculations on the Limits of Legal Change', *Law and Society Review*, **9** (1), 95–160.

Galligan, D. (2010), 'Legal theory and empirical research', in P. Cane and H. Kritzer (eds), *The Handbook of Empirical Legal Research*, Oxford: Oxford University Press, pp. 976–1001.

Ganann, R., D. Ciliska and H. Thomas (2010), 'Expediting systematic reviews: methods and implications of rapid reviews', *Implementation Science*, **5**, 56, 1–10.

Gao, Y., A. L. Glenn, M. Peskin, A. Rudo-Hutt, R. A. Schug, Y. Yang and A. Raine (2012), 'Neurocriminological Approaches', in D. Gadd, S. Karstedt and S. Messner (eds), *The SAGE Handbook of Criminological Research Methods*, London: SAGE, pp. 63–75.

Gardner, J. A. (1962), 'The Sociological Jurisprudence of Roscoe Pound (Part II)', *Villanova Law Review*, **7**, 165–92.

Gardner, J. A. (1961–1962), 'The Sociological Jurisprudence of Roscoe Pound (Part I)', *Villanova Law Review*, **7**, 1–26.

Gava, J. (2014), 'What we know about contract law and transacting in the marketplace – a review', *Adelaide Law Review*, **35**, 411–26.

Gawande, A. (2007), 'The Checklist. If something so simple can transform intensive care, what else can it do?', *The New Yorker, Annals of Medicine*, 10 December, http://www.newyorker.com/magazine/2007/12/10/the-checklist, accessed 14 November 2015.

Geertz, C. (1973), *The Interpretation of Culture*, New York: Basic Books.

Gerring, J. (2007), *Case Study Research. Principles and Practices*, New York: Cambridge University Press.

Gervey, B., C. Chiu, Y. Hong and C. Dweck (1999), 'Differential use of person information in decision-making about guilt vs. innocence: The role of implicit theories', *Personality and Social Psychology Bulletin*, **25**, 17–27.

Gestel, R. van and J. Vranken (2011), 'Assessing Legal Research: Sense and Nonsense of Peer Review versus Bibliometrics and the Need for a European Approach', *German Legal Journal*, **12**, 901–929.

Gibbs, J. (1966), 'The sociology of law and normative phenomena', *American Sociological* Review, **31** (3), 315–25.

Giesen, I. (2015), 'The Use and Incorporation of Extralegal Insights in Legal Reasoning', *Utrecht Law Review*, **11**, 1, 1–17.

Gill, R. (2000), 'Discourse analysis', in P. Atkinson, M. W. Bauer and G. Gaskell (eds), *Qualitative Researching with Text, Image and Sound. A Practical Handbook*, London: Sage, pp. 172–90.

Gilson, R. (1984), 'Value creation by business lawyers: legal skills and asset pricing', *Yale Law Journal*, **94**, 239–313.

Ginsburg, T. (2008), 'The Global Spread of Constitutional Review', in K. Whittington, R. Kelemen and G. Caldeira (eds), *The Oxford Handbook of Law and Politics*, Oxford: Oxford University Press, pp. 81–96.

Glaeser, E. and C. Sunstein (2014), *Moneyball for State Regulators*, http://ssrn.com/abstract=2418306, accessed 4 July 2015.

Glaser, B. and A. Strauss (1967), *The Discovery of Grounded Theory: Strategies for Qualitative Research*, Chicago: Aldin.

Golafshani, N. (2003), 'Understanding Reliability and Validity in Qualitative Research', *The Qualitative Report*, **8** (4), 597–607.

Gomm, R. (2008), *Social Research Methodology*, Houndmills: Palgrave Macmillan.

Gonzalez, E., F. Reategui and E. Naughton (2014), *Challenging the Conventional. Can Truth Commissions Strengthen Peace Processes?*, International Center for Transitional Justice and the Kofi Annan Foundation, Geneva.

Gough, D., S. Oliver and J. Thomas (2012), *An Introduction to Systematic Reviews*, London: Sage.

Granovetter, M. (1983), 'The Strength of Weak Ties: A Network Theory Revisited', *Sociological Theory*, **1**, 201–233.

Graziano, A. M. and M. L. Raulin (2004), *Research Methods: A Process of Inquiry*, Boston: Pearson.

Greenberg, R. and B. Barnow (2014), 'Flaws in Evaluations of Social Programs: Illustrations From Randomized Controlled Trials', *Evaluation Review*, **38** (5), 359–87.

Greene, J. (2005), 'Evaluation, democracy and social change', in I. Shaw, J. Greene and M. Mark (eds), *Handbook of Evaluation. Policies, programs and practices*, London: Sage, pp. 118–40.

Greene, J. D., Sommerville, R. B., Nystrom, L. E., Darley, J. M. and Cohen, J. D. (2001), 'An fMRI investigation of emotional engagement in moral judgment', *Science*, **293** (5537), 2105–108.

Greenhalgh, T., E. Kristjansson and V. Robinson (2007), 'Realist review to understand the efficacy of school feeding programmes', *BMJ*, **335**, 858–61.

Greenhalgh, T., G. Robert, P. Bate, O. Kyriakidou and R. Peacock (2004), *How to Spread Good Ideas. A systematic review of the literature on diffusion, dissemination and sustainability of innovations in health service delivery and organization*, National Coordinating Centre for NHS Service Delivery and Organization, London.

Greenhalgh, T., G. Robert, F. Macfarlane, P. Bate, O. Kyriakidou and R. Peacock (2005), 'Storylines of research in diffusion of innovation: a meta-narrative approach to systematic review', *Social Science & Medicine*, **61**, 417–30.

Greenhalgh, T., G. Wong, G. Westhorp and R. Pawson (2011), 'Protocol – realist and meta-narrative evidence synthesis: Evolving Standards (RAMESES)', *BMC Medical Research Methodology*, **11** (115), 1–10.

Greiffenhagen, C., M. Mair and W. Sharroc (2011), 'From methodology to methodography: a study of qualitative and quantitative reasoning in practice', *Methodological Innovations Online*, **6** (3), 93–107.

Grimmelikhuijsen, S. and A. Meijer (2014), 'Effects of transparency on the perceived trustworthiness of a government organization: evidence from an online experiment', *Journal of Public Administration Research and Theory*, **24** (1), 137–57.

Gosselt, J. F., J. J. van Hoof, M. D.T. de Jong, B. Dorbeck-Jung and M. F. Steehouder (2008), *Horen, zien en verkrijgen? Een onderzoek naar het functioneren van Kijkwijzer en PEGI (Pan European Game Information) ter bescherming van jongeren tegen schadelijke mediabeelden*, The Hague: WODC.

Groves, R., F. Fowler, Jr, M. Couper, J. Lepkowski, E. Singer and R. Tourangeau (2009), *Survey methodology*, Hoboken: Wiley.

Groves, R. and M. Couper (1998), *Nonresponse in household interview surveys*, Hoboken: Wiley.

Groves, R. and I. Lyberg (2010), 'Total survey error: past, present, and future', *Public Opinion Quarterly*, **74** (5), 849–79.

Guba, E. (1987), 'What have we learned about naturalistic evaluation?', *Evaluation Practice*, **8** (1), 23–43.

Guthrie, C., J. Rachlinski and A. Wistrich (2007), 'Blinking on the Bench: How Judges Decide Cases', *Cornell Law Review*, **93**, 1–44.

Haan, G. de, S. Choenni, I. Mulder, S. Kalidien and P. de Waart (2011), 'Bringing the Research lab into everyday life: exploiting sensitive environments to acquire data for social research', in: S. Nagy Hesse-Biber (ed.), *The Handbook of Emergent Technologies in Social Research*, Oxford: Oxford University Press, pp. 522–42.

Hadfield, G. K. (2001), 'Privatizing commercial law', *Regulation*, Spring, 40–46.

Hage, J. (2010), 'Comparative law and legal science', Maastricht Working Papers Faculty of Law, pp. 1–18.

Hage J. (2011), 'The Method of a Truly Normative Legal Science', in: M. van Hoecke (ed.), *Methodologies of Legal Research*, Oxford: Hart Publishing, pp. 19–44.

Hage, J. (2013), 'Juridical Acts and the Gap between Is and Ought', *Netherlands Journal of Legal Philosophy*, **42** (1), 50–66.

Hagedoorn, J. and G. Hesen (2009), 'Contractual Complexity and the Cognitive Load of R&D Alliance Contracts', *Journal of Empirical Legal Studies*, **6** (4), 818–47.

Hall, M. A. and R. F. Wright (2008), 'Systematic Content Analysis of Judicial Opinions', *California Law Review*, **96**, 63–122.

Haller, L. (2010), 'Regulating the profession', in P. Cane and H. Kritzer (eds), *Oxford Handbook of Empirical Legal Research*, Oxford: Oxford University Press, pp. 216–35.

Hammer, D., R. Kraft and D. Wheeler (2009), 'Forma: Forest Monitoring for Action – Rapid Identification of Pan-Tropical Deforestation Using Moderate-Resolution Remotely Sensed Data', Center for Global Development Working Paper No. 192.

Hamzehzadeh, B. (2010), 'Repeat-player vs. one-shotter: is victory all that obvious?', *Hastings Business Law Journal*, **6** (239), 239–59.

Hands, D. (1985), 'Second Thoughts on Lakatos', *History of Political Economy*, **17** (1), 1–16.

Hansen, H. and O. Rieper (2011), 'Institutionalization of second-order evidence-producing organizations', in O. Rieper, F. Leeuw and T. Ling (eds), *The Evidence Book: Concepts, Generation and the Use Of Evidence*, New Brunswick: Transaction Publishers, pp. 27–52.

Hansen, M. and W. Hurwitz (1943), 'On the theory of sampling from finite populations', *Annals of Mathematical Statistics*, **14**, 333–62.
Harford, T. (2014), 'Big data: are we making a big mistake?', *Significance*, 14–19.
Harré, R. (1979), *Social Being: A Theory for Social Psychology*, Oxford: Blackwell.
Hart, H. (1961), *The Concept of Law*, Oxford: Oxford University Press.
Hawes, D., J. Brennan and M. Dadds (2009), 'Cortisol, callous-unemotional traits, and pathways to antisocial behavior', *Current Opinion in Psychiatry*, **22** (4), 357–62.
Hazel Genn, D., M. Partington and S. Wheeler (2006), *Law In The Real World: Improving Our Understanding of How Law Works, Final Report And Recommendations*, London: The Nuffield Foundation.
Heath, C., J. Hindmarsh and P. Luff (2010), *Video in Qualitative Research*, London: Sage.
Hedstrom, P. (2005), *Dissecting the social: On the Principles of Analytical Sociology*, Cambridge: Cambridge University Press.
Hedstrom, P. and P. Bearman (2009), 'What is analytical sociology all about? An introductory essay', *The Oxford Handbook of Analytical Sociology*, Oxford: Oxford University Press, pp. 3–24.
Hedstrom, P. and Swedberg, R. (eds) (1998), *Social mechanisms: An analytical approach to social theory*, Cambridge: Cambridge University Press.
Heise, M. (2002), 'The past, present, and future of empirical legal scholarship: judicial decision making and the new empiricism', *University of Illinois Law Review*, **7**, 819–50.
Hempel, C. and P. Oppenheim (1948), 'Studies in the Logic of Explanation', *Philosophy of Science*, **15** (2), 135–75.
Henderson, S. and E. Segal (2013), 'Visualizing qualitative data in evaluation research', *New Directions for Evaluation*, **139**, 53–71.
Henry, G. and M. Mark (2003), 'Beyond Use: Understanding Evaluation's Influence on Attitudes and Actions', *American Journal of Evaluation*, **24** (9), 293–314.
Herlihy, J., K. Gleeson and S. Turner (2010), 'What Assumptions about Human Behaviour Underlie Asylum Judgments?', *International Journal of Refugee Law*, **22** (3), 351–66.
Hirschl, R. (2008), The Judicalization of Politics, in G. Caldeira, R. Kelemen and K. Whittington (eds), *The Oxford Handbook of Law and Politics*, Oxford: Oxford University Press, Chapter 8.
Ho, D. and L. Kramer (2013), 'Introduction: the empirical revolution in law', *Stanford Law Review*, **65**, 1195–202.
Hoecke, M. van (2011), 'Legal Doctrine: which method(s) for what kind of discipline', in M. van Hoecke (ed.), *Methodologies of legal research*.

Which Kind of Method for What Kind of Discipline?, Oxford: Hart Publishing, pp. 1–17.

Homans, G. C. (1984), *Coming to My Senses: The Autobiography of a Sociologist*, New Brunswick: Transaction Publishers.

Hood, C. and H. Margetts (2007), *The Tools of Government in the Digital Age*, London: Palgrave Macmillan.

Hood, C., O. James, G. W. Jones, C. D. Scott and T. Travers (1998), 'Regulation Inside Government: Where New Public Management Meets the Audit Explosion', *Public Money & Management*, **18** (2), 61–8.

Horgan, J. (2014), *The Psychology of Terrorism*, London and New York: Routledge.

Horst, R. van der, H. J. M. Schönberger and C. H. de Kogel (2012), *Toezicht op zedendelinquenten. Effectiviteit en veronderstelde werkzame mechanismen van vormen van toezicht*, WODC Memorandum, The Hague: WODC.

Hosemann, E. (2014), '"The New Private Law": A Historical and Comparative Perspective on the Emerging New Private Law Scholarship in the United States', *Rabels Zeitschrift fuer auslaendisches und internationales Privatrecht*, **78** (1), 37–70.

Howarth, D. (2013), *Law as Engineering. Thinking About What Lawyers Do*, Cheltenham: Edward Elgar.

Howe, K. (1988), 'Against the Quantitative-Qualitative Incompatibility Thesis or Dogmas Die Hard', *Educational Researcher*, **17** (8), 10–16.

Hsu, C. and B. Sandford (2007), 'The Delphi Technique: Making Sense Of Consensus', *Practical Assessment, Research & Evaluation*, **12** (10), 1–10.

Hutchinson, T. (2013), 'Doctrinal Research: researching the jury', in R. Watkins and M. Burton (eds), *Research Methods in Law*, London: Routledge, pp. 7–34.

Husa, J. (2007), 'About the Methodology of Comparative Law – Some Comments Concerning the Wonderland . . .', Working Paper, Faculty of Law, Maastricht University.

Impellizzeri, F. and M. Bizzini (2012), 'Systematic review and meta-analysis: a primer', *The International Journal of Sports Physical Therapy*, **7** (5), 493–502.

Jacob, S., S. Speer and J. Furubo (2015), 'The institutionalization of evaluation matters: Updating the International Atlas of Evaluation 10 years later', *Evaluation*, **21** (1), 6–31.

Jagosh, J., P. Pluye, A. Macaulay, J. Salsberg, J. Henderson, J. Sirett, P. Bush, R. Seller, G. Wong, T. Greenhalgh, M. Cargo, C. Herbert, S. Seifer and S. Green (2011), 'Assessing the outcomes of participatory research: protocol for identifying, selecting, appraising and synthesizing the literature for realist review', *Implementation Science*, **6** (24), 1–8.

Jansen, N. and R. Michaels (2007), 'Private Law and the State', *Rabels Zeitschrift fuer auslaendisches und internationales* Privatrecht, **71** (3), 345–97.

Jennissen, R. (2014), 'On the deviant age-crime curve of Afro-Caribbean populations: The case of Antilleans living in the Netherlands', *American Journal of Criminal Justice*, **39**, (2), 571–94.

Jewitt, C. (2012), 'An introduction to using video for research', National Centre for Research Methods Working Paper, 03/12 Institute of Education, London, http://eprints.ncrm.ac.uk/2259/4/NCRM_workingpaper_0312.pdf, accessed 15 May 2015.

Johnson, K., L. Greenseid, S. Toal, J. King, F. Lawrenz and B. Volkov (2009), 'Research on Evaluation Use: A Review of the Empirical Literature From 1986 to 2005', *American Journal of Evaluation*, **30**, 377–410.

Jolls, C. (2006), 'Behavioral Law and Economics', Yale Law School, New York: Public Law Working Paper No. 130.

Jones, O., A. Wagner, D. Faigman and M. Raichle (2013), 'Neuroscientists in court', *Nature*, **730** (14), http://www.nature.com/reviews/neuro, accessed 15 May 2015.

Jong, P. de and M. Herweijer (2004), *De ontwikkeling van het aantal wetten AmvB's en ministeriële regelingen in Nederland*, The Hague: WODC.

Jordana, J. and D. Levi-Faur (eds) (2004), *The Politics of Regulation in the Age of Governance*, Cheltenham: Edward Elgar.

Kalidien, S., R. Choenni and R. Meijer (2010), 'Crime statistics online: potentials and challenges', *Proceedings of the 11th Annual International Digital Government Research Conference on Public Administration Online: Challenges and Opportunities*, 131–7.

Kane, E. (1984), *Doing Your Own Research: Basic descriptive research in the social sciences and humanities*, London: Marion Boyars.

Kapardis, A. (2003), *Psychology and Law. A Critical Introduction*, Cambridge: Cambridge University Press.

Kappelhof, J. (2015), *Surveying ethnic minorities: the impact of survey design on data quality*, Ph.D., Utrecht: Utrecht University.

Katz, D. and M. Bommarito (2013), 'Measuring the Complexity of the Law: The United States Code' (1 August), http://ssrn.com/abstract=2307352, accessed 4 July 2015.

Katz, D., M. Bommarito and J. Blackman (2014), 'Predicting the Behavior of the Supreme Court of the United States: A General Approach' (21 July), http://ssrn.com/abstract=2463244, accessed 2 July 2015.

Kelsen, H. (1967), *Pure Theory of Law*, New York: The Free Press.

Kemmis, S. and R. McTaggart (2000), 'Participatory Action Research', in N. Denzin and Y. Lincoln (eds), *Handbook of Qualitative Research*, Thousand Oaks: Sage, pp. 567–605.

Khangura, S., K. Konnyu, R. Cushman, J. Grimshaw and D. Moher (2012), 'Evidence summaries: the evolution of a rapid review approach', *Systematic Reviews*, **1**, 10–19.

Kirk, R. E. (2009), 'Experimental design', in R. Millsap and A. Maydeu-Olivares (eds), *Sage Handbook of Quantitative Methods in Psychology*, London: Sage, pp. 23–45.

Kistler, S. J., S. Evergreen and T. Azzam (2013), 'Toolography', *New Directions for* Evaluation, **139**, 73–84.

Kleemans, E., C. Klein Haarhuis, F. Leeuw and M. van Ooyen (2007), 'Law enforcement interventions in the Netherlands: mapping interventions and "browsing" for evidence', *Evidence and Policy*, **3**, 487–504.

Kleemans, E. (2014), 'Organized crime research: challenging assumptions and informing policy', in E. Cockbain and J. Knutsson (eds), *Organized crime research: challenging assumptions and informing policy*, London: Routledge, pp. 57–67.

Klein Haarhuis, C. and F. Leeuw (2004), 'Fighting governmental corruption: the new World Bank programme evaluated', *Journal of International Development*, **16**, 547–61.

Klein Haarhuis, C. and B. Niemeijer (2009), 'Synthesizing Legislative Evaluations: Putting the Pieces Together', *Evaluation*, **15** (4), 403–425.

Klein Haarhuis, C., A. Weenink, R. Bokhorst and M. Smit (2015), *Governance and Safeguarding institutions in small states: The case of Aruba*, The Hague: WODC.

Klerks, M. de, C. Ketelaars and P. Robben (2013), 'Unannounced, compared with announced inspections: A systematic review and exploratory study in nursing homes', *Health Policy*, **111**, 311–19.

Klick, J. (2011), 'The empirical revolution in law and economics', Inaugural Address, Rotterdam Law School, Erasmus University Rotterdam.

Knaap, L. van der, F. Leeuw, S. Bogaerts and L. T. J. Nijssen (2008), 'Combining Campbell Standards and the Realist Evaluation Approach. The Best of two Worlds?', *American Journal of Evaluation*, **29** (1), 48–57.

Knight, J. (2009), 'Are empiricists asking the right questions about judicial decision making?', *Duke Law Journal*, **58**, 1531–56.

Kogel, C. H. de, W. Schrama and M. Smit (2014), 'Civil Law and Neuroscience', *Psychiatry, Psychology and Law*, **21** (2), 272–85.

Kogel, C. de and E. Westgeest (2015), 'Neuroscientific and behavioral genetic information in criminal cases in the Netherlands', *Journal of Law and the Biosciences*, **3**, 1–26.

Kojder, A. (2006), 'Leon Petrazycki's Socio-legal ideas and their contemporary continuation', *Journal of Classical Sociology*, **6**, 333–58.

Kolk, H. van der and K. Aarts (2001), 'Explaining Turnout Bias. Non-response and Stimulus Effects in the Dutch Parliamentary Election

Study of 1998', Paper presented at the 2001 Annual Meeting of the American Political Science Association, Hilton San Francisco and Towers, 30 August to 2 September.

Koppen, P. van and M. Malsch (1991), 'Defendants and one-shotters win after all: compliance with court decisions in civil cases', *Law & Society Review*, **25**, 803–20.

Krippendorf, K. (2013), *Content Analysis: An Introduction to its Methodology*, Thousand Oaks: Sage.

Kritzer, H. (2009), 'Empirical Legal Studies Before 1940: A Bibliographic Essay', *Journal of Empirical Legal Studies*, **6** (4), 925–68.

Kritzer, H. (2010), 'Claiming behavior as legal mobilization', in P. Cane and H. Kritzer (eds), *Oxford Handbook of Empirical Legal Research*, Oxford: Oxford University Press, pp. 260–85.

Kritzer, H. M. and S. Silbey (eds) (2003), *In Litigation. Do the 'Haves' Still Come Out Ahead?*, Stanford: Stanford University Press.

Kromhout, M. and M. van San (2003), *Schimmige werelden. Nieuwe etnische groepen en jeugdcriminaliteit*, Cahier, The Hague: WODC.

Kruisbergen, E., E. Kleemans and R. Kouwenberg (2015), 'Profitability, Power or Proximity? Organized Offenders investing their money in legal economy', *European Journal of Criminal Policy Research*, **21**, 237–56.

Kvale, S. (1996), *Interviews: An Introduction to Qualitative Research Interviewing*, London: Sage.

Laan, A. van der and M. Blom (2011), *Jeugdcriminaliteit in de periode: 1996–2010. Ontwikkelingen in zelfgerapporteerde daders, door de politie aangehouden verdachten en strafrechtelijke daders op basis van de Monitor Jeugdcriminaliteit*, Cahier, The Hague: WODC.

Lakatos, I. (1970), 'The Methodology of Scientific Research Programmes', in I. Lakatos and A. Musgrave (eds), *Criticism and the Growth of Knowledge*, Cambridge: Cambridge University Press, pp. 91–197.

Lakhani, A. (2013), 'Social network sites and the legal profession: balancing benefits and navigating minefields', *Computer Law and Security Review*, **29**, 164–74.

Landes, W. and R. Posner (1975), 'The independent judiciary in an interest-group perspective', *Journal of Law and Economics*, **18** (3), 875–901.

Langseth, P. (1997), 'EDI'S New Approach to Governance', in EDI Proceedings, Uganda Workshop for Parliamentarians. Washington, DC: World Bank.

Lanteri, A., C. Chelini and S. Rizzello (2008), 'An Experimental Investigation of Emotions and Reasoning in the Trolley Problem', *Journal of Business Ethics*, **83**, 789–804.

LaPiere, R. (1934), 'Attitudes and actions', *Social Forces*, **13**, 230–37.

La Porta, R., F. Lopez-de-Silanes and A. Shleifer (2008), 'The economic consequences of legal origins', *Journal of Economic Literature*, **46**, 285–332.

La Porta, R., F. Lopez-de-Silanes, A. Shleifer and R. W. Vishny (1998), 'Law and Finance', *Journal of Political Economy*, **106** (6), 1113–55.

Lawless, R., J. Robbennolt and T. Ulen (2010), *Empirical Methods in Law*, Aspen: Wolters Kluwer/Aspen Publishers.

Lawson, T. (1997), *Economics and Reality*, London: Routledge.

Lazega, E. (2012), 'Mapping Judicial Dialogue across National Borders: An Exploratory Network Study of Learning from Lobbying among European Intellectual Property Judges', *Utrecht Law Review*, **8** (2), 115–28.

Lazer, D., R. Kennedy, G. King and A. Vespignani (2014), 'The Parable of Google Flu: Traps in Big Data Analysis', *Science*, **343** (March), 1203–205.

Lecocq, L. and B. Damil (2010), 'Business Models as a Research Program in Strategic Management: An Appraisal based on Lakatos', *Management*, **13** (4), 214–25.

Leeuw, F. (2003), 'Reconstructing program theories: methods available and problems to be solved', *American Journal of Evaluation*, **24** (1), 5–20.

Leeuw, F. (2009a), 'Evaluation Policy in the Netherlands', *New Directions for Evaluation*, **123**, 87–103.

Leeuw, F. (2009b), 'On the Contemporary History of Experimental Evaluations and Its Relevance for Policy Making', in O. Rieper, F. Leeuw and T. Ling (eds) *The Evidence Book*, New Brunswick: Transaction Publishers.

Leeuw, F. (2011), 'Can legal research benefit from evaluation studies?', *Utrecht Law Review*, **7** (1), 52–65.

Leeuw, F. (2012), 'Linking theory-based evaluation and contribution analysis: Three problems and a few solutions', *Evaluation*, **18** (3), 348–63.

Leeuw, F. (2015), 'Empirical Legal Research: The Gap between Facts and Values and Legal Academic Training', *Utrecht Law Review*, **11** (2), 19–33.

Leeuw, F., Ger H.C. van Gils and C. Kreft (1999), 'Evaluating anti-corruption initiatives: underlying logic and mid-term impact of a World Bank Program', *Evaluation*, **5** (2), 194–219.

Leeuw, F. and S. Donaldson (2015), 'Theory in evaluation: Reducing confusion and encouraging debate', *Evaluation* **21** (4), 467–480.

Leeuw, F. and H. B. M. Leeuw (2012), 'Cyber society and digital policies: Challenges to evaluation?', *Evaluation*, **18** (1), 111–27.

Leeuw, F. and J. Vaessen (2009), *Impact Evaluations and Development.*

Nonie Guidance on Impact Evaluation, Washington DC: Nonie/ World Bank.

Leeuw, H. B. M. (in press), 'Big Data and Evaluation: A Case Study on Digital Piracy and the Graduated Response', in G. Petersson et al (eds), *Big Data and Evaluation*, Rutgers: Transaction Publishers (in press).

Leeuw, H. B. M. (2016), *Punish, seduce or persuade? An empirical assessment of anti-piracy interventions*, Ph.D., Maastricht University (in preparation).

Legrand, P. (1996), 'European Legal Systems are not Converging', *International and Comparative Law Quarterly*, **45** (1), 52–81.

Leiter, B. (2002), 'American Legal Realism', University of Texas Law, Public Law Research Paper No. 42.

Lempert, R. (2010), 'The Inevitability of Theory', *California Law Review*, **98**, 877–906.

Lenhart, A. (2009), 'Teens and Sexting: How and why minor teens are sending sexually suggestive nude or nearly nude images via text messaging', Pew Research Centre Report, http://pewresearch.org/assets/pdf/teens-and-sexting.pdf.

Leonardi, G. and S. Meyer (2014), 'Social Media as Social Lubricant: How Ambient Awareness Eases Knowledge Transfer', paper, Department of Communication Studies & Department of Industrial Engineering and Management Sciences Northwestern University, Evanston.

Lepsius, O. (2005), 'Sozialwissenschaften im Verfassungsrecht – Amerika als Vorbild?', *Juristenzeitung*, **1**, 1–13.

Lerman, J. (2013), 'Big Data and Empirical Legal Research', *Stanford Law Review*, **66**, 55–63.

Leviton, L. and E. Hughes (1981), 'Research On the Utilization of Evaluations: A Review and Synthesis', *Evaluation Review*, **5**, 525–48.

Lind, E. (1985), 'Randomized experiments in Federal Courts', *New Directions in Program Evaluation*, 28, 72–80.

Linssen, R. and H. Schmeets (2010), 'Participatie en vertrouwen in Europa', in H. Schmeets (ed.), *Sociale Samenhang: Participatie, vertrouwen en integratie*, The Hague/Heerlen: CBS, pp. 135–51.

Lint, W. (2014), 'Philosophy and policy evaluation: two worlds apart?', Thesis U Maastricht, Master of Science in Public Policy and Human Development and University of the United Nations, Maastricht.

Lipsey, M. (1995), 'What do we learn from 400 research studies on the effectiveness of treatment with juvenile delinquents?', in J. McGuire (ed.), *What Works? Reducing reoffending*, Chichester: Wiley, pp. 63–78.

Llewellyn, K. A. (1930), 'Realistic Jurisprudence, the Next Step', *Columbia Law Review*, **30** (431), 444–57.

Llewellyn, K. and E. Hoebel (1941), *The Cheyenne Way. Conflict and case law in primitive jurisprudence*, Norman: University of Oklahoma Press.
Logan, C. (1972), 'Evaluation research in crime and delinquency: a reappraisal', *Journal of Criminal Law, Criminology and Policy Studies*, **3**, 378–87.
Long, J. (2014), 'In Defence of Cornell Realism: a Reply to Elizabeth Tropman', *Theoria*, **80**, 174–83.
Luiten, A. (2013), *Improving survey fieldwork with paradata*, Ph.D. thesis, The Hague: Statistics Netherlands.
Lum, C. (2009), *Translating police research into practice. Ideas in American Policing*, Washington, DC: Police Foundation.
Lum, C., C. Telep, C. Koper and J. Grieco (2012), 'Receptivity to research in policing', *Justice Research and Policy*, **14** (1), 61–95.
Lumineau, F. (2014), 'How Contracts Influence Trust', *Journal of Management*, **20** (10), 1–25.
Lustick, J. (1997), 'Lakatos, and Consociationalism: Almond and Lijphart: Competing Research Programs in an Early-Lakatosian Mode', *World Politics*, **50** (1), 88–117.
Lützinger, S. (2012), *The Other Side of the Story. A qualitative study of the biographies of extremists and terrorists*, Wiesbaden: Bundeskriminalamt.
Lyon, F., T. Gyateng, D. Pritchard, P. Belmana, I. Vickers and N. Webb (2015), 'Opening access to administrative data for evaluating public services: The case of the Justice Data Lab', *Evaluation*, **21** (2), 232–47.
Lysy, C. (2013), 'Developments in quantitative data display and their implications for evaluation', *New Directions for Evaluation*, **139**, 33–51.
Lytton, T. (2014), 'Competitive Third-Party Regulation: How Private Certification Can Overcome Constraints That Frustrate Government Regulation', *Theoretical Inquiries in Law*, **15**, 539–71.
Macaris, C., L. Turcksin and K. Lebeau (2012), 'Multi actor multi criteria analysis as a tool to support sustainable decisions: state of use', *Decision Support Systems*, **54**, 610–20.
MaCaulay, S. (1963), 'Non-contractual relations in business: a preliminary study', *American Sociological Review*, **28** (1), 55–67.
MacCoun, R. (1998), 'Biases in the interpretation and use of research results', *Annual Review of Psychology*, **49**, 259–87.
MacDonald, G., B. Sheldon and J. Gillespie (1992), 'Contemporary studies of the effectiveness of social work', *British Journal of Social Work*, **22** (6), 615–43.
Mackenzie, D. (2007), 'The Growth Effects of Federal Regulation', *Mises Daily*, 3 August. See also https://mises.org/library/growth-effects-federal-regulation, accessed 28 November 2015.

MacNeil, I. (2000), *The New Social Contract*, New Haven: Yale University Press.

McConville, M. and W. Chui (eds) (2007), *Research Methods for Law*, Edinburgh: Edinburgh University Press.

McCrudden, C. (2006), 'Legal research and the social sciences', *Law Quarterly Review* **122**, 632–50.

McGinnis, J. (2012), *Accelerating Democracy: Transforming Governance Through Technology*, Princeton: Princeton University Press.

McGinnis, J. (2014), 'Machines v. Lawyers. As information technology advances, the legal profession faces a great disruption', *City Journal*, 28 May.

McGinnis J. and R. Pearce (2014), 'The Great Disruption: How Machine Intelligence Will Transform the Role of Lawyers in the Delivery of Legal Services', *Fordham Law Review*, **82**, 3041–66.

McMahon, F. (ed.) (2012), *Towards an Index of Human Freedom*, Vancouver and Zurich: Fraser Institute and Liberales Institut.

McManaman, L. (1958), 'Social Engineering: The Legal Philosophy of Roscoe Pound', *St. John's Law Review*, **33** (1), 1–47.

McNaughton, D. and P. Rawling (2003), 'Naturalism and Normativity', *Proceedings of the Aristotelian Society*, Supplementary Volumes, **77**, 23–45.

Mann, C. (2003), 'Observational research methods. Research design II: cohort, cross sectional, and case-control studies', *Emergency Medicine Journal*, **20**, 54–60.

Mark, M., S. Donaldson and B. Campbell (eds) (2011), *Social Psychology and Evaluation*, New York: The Guilford Press.

Mason, R. and I. Mitroff (1981), *Challenging Strategic Planning Assumptions: Theory, Cases, and Techniques*, New York: Wiley-Interscience.

Maus, I. (1986), 'Verrechtlichung, Entrechtlichung under der Funktionswandel von Institutionen', in I. Maus (ed), *Rechtstheorie und politische Theorie im Industriekapitalismus*, Munich: Wilhelm Fink Verlag, pp. 277–323.

Mayne, J. (2012), 'Contribution analysis: Coming of age?', *Evaluation*, **18** (3), 270–80.

Mayntz, R. (2004), 'Mechanisms in the analysis of social macro-phenomena', *Philosophy of the Social Sciences*, **34**, 237–58.

Meili, S. (2009), 'Perceptions of consumer class actions: the views of plaintiff's lawyers and their clients', paper at Law and Society Association annual meeting, Denver, 30 May.

Merari, A. (2010), *Driven to Death. Psychological and Social Aspects of Suicide Terrorism*, Oxford: Oxford University Press.

Merton, R. (1968), *Social Theory and Social Structure*, New York: Free Press.
Merton, R., M. Fisk and P. Kendall (1956), *The Focused Interview*, New York: Columbia University Press.
Mertz, E. (2011), 'Undervaluing Indeterminacy: Translating Social Science into Law', *DePaul Law Review*, **60** (2), 397–412.
Mertz, E. (ed.) (2008), *The Role of Social Science in Law*, Farnham: Ashgate.
Michaels, R. (2006), The Functional Method of Comparative Law, in M. Reimann and R. Zimmermann (eds), *The Oxford Handbook of Comparative Law*, Oxford: Oxford University Press, pp. 339–82.
Miguel-Stearns, T. and S. Ryan (2014), 'The Empirical Research Law Librarian. Developing the Role', *Librarian Scholarship Series*. Paper 28, http://digitalcommons.law.yale.edu/ylss/28, accessed 12 July 2015.
Miles, M. (1979), 'Qualitative data as an attractive nuisance: The problem of analysis', *Administrative Science Quarterly*, **24** (4), 590–601.
Miles, M. and A. Huberman (1994), *Qualitative Data Analysis*, London: Sage.
Miles, M., A. Huberman and J. Saldana (2014), *Qualitative Data Analysis. A Methods Sourcebook*, London: Sage.
Miles, T. and C. Sunstein (2008), *The New Legal Realism*, University of Chicago, John M. Olin Law and Economics Working Paper No. 191.
Miller, G. (2012), 'The Smartphone Manifesto', *Perspectives on Psychological Science*, **7** (3), 221–37.
Mintzberg, H., J. Lampel and B. Ahlstrand (2005), *Strategy Safari: A Guided Tour Through The Wilds of Strategic Management*, New York: Free Press.
Moffitt, T. (1993), 'Adolescence-limited and life-course persistent antisocial behavior: a developmental taxonomy', *Psychol. Rev.*, **100**, 674–701.
Moher, D., T. Klassen and A. Jones (2001), 'Assessing the quality of reports of randomized trials included in meta-analysis: attitudes, practice, evidence, and guides', in A. Stevens, K. Abrams, J. Brazier, R. Fitzpatrick and R. Lilford (eds), *The Advanced Handbook of Methods in Evidence Based Healthcare*, London: Sage: pp. 409–425.
Molnar, A., P. O'Campo, E. Ng, C. Mitchell, M. Carles, E. Renahy, A. St John and K. Shankardass (2015), 'Protocol: Realist synthesis of the impact of unemployment insurance policies on poverty and health', *Evaluation and Program Planning*, **48**, 1–9.
Monahan, I. and J. Swanson (2009), 'Lawyers at Mid-Career: A 20-Year Longitudinal Study of Job and Life Satisfaction', *Journal of Empirical Legal Studies*, **6** (3), 451–83.

Montgomery, D.C. (2005), *Design and Analysis of Experiments*, 5th edn, New York: Wiley.

Morawetz, T. (1980), *The Philosophy of Law*, New York: Macmillan.

Morawski, M., F. Leeuw and A. Ottow (2013), 'Trends in toezicht: middelen, prestaties', *Tijdschrift voor Toezicht*, **4**, 43–52.

Morgan, J. (2013), *Contract Law Minimalism: A Formalist Restatement of Commercial Contract Law*, Cambridge: Cambridge University Press.

Moynihan, D. (2013), 'Does public service motivation lead to budget maximization? Evidence from an experiment', *International Public Management Journal*, **16** (2), 179–96.

Muller, A. (2004), 'Florida's Motorcycle Helmet Law Repeal and Fatality Rates', *American Journal of Public Health*, **94** (4), 556–8.

Muller, S. and L. Kistemaker (2015), *Richting van de rechtstaat; trends naar 2025*, The Hague: Hiil.

Nachmias, D. and C. Nachmias (1976), *Research Methods in the Social Sciences*, Cheltenham: Edward Arnold.

Nagtegaal, M. (2012), *Gerapporteerde problemen van slachtoffers van seksueel misbruik in de kindertijd, een meta-review*, Cahier, The Hague: WODC.

Nas, C., M. van Ooyen-Houben and J. Wieman (2011), *Interventies in uitvoering. Wat er mis kan gaan bij de uitvoering van justitiële (gedrags) interventies en hoe dat komt*, Cahier, The Hague: WODC.

Nelen, H. (2008), 'Evidence maze; het doolhof van het evaluatieonderzoek', Inaugural address, Maastricht, Maastricht University, 18 January.

Nell, V. (2006), 'Cruelty's rewards: The gratifications of perpetrators and spectators', *Behavioral and Brain Sciences*, **29**, 211–57.

Nelson, S. and J. Simek (2013), 'Big Data: big pain or big gain for lawyers', *Law Practice Magazine*, July–August.

Neyman, J. (1934), 'On the two different aspects of the representative method: the method of stratified sampling and the method of purposive selection', *Journal of the Royal Statistical Society*, **97**, 558–606.

Nielsen, L. B. (2010), 'The need for multi-method approaches in empirical legal research', in P. Cane and H. Kritzer (eds), *The Oxford Handbook of Empirical Legal Research*, Oxford: Oxford University Press, pp. 951–76.

Niemeijer, B. (2014), 'Galanter revisited: do the "haves" (still) come out ahead?', in A. Terlouw and B. Hubeau (eds), *Legal Aid in the Low Countries*, Antwerp: Intersentia, pp. 85–102.

Nigel, G. (1978), 'Measuring the growth of science, a review of indicators of scientific growth', *Scientometrics*, **1** (1), 9–34.

Noblit, G. and R. Hare (1988), *Meta-ethnography: Synthesizing Qualitative Studies*, London: Sage.

NSF (2002), *The 2002 User Friendly Handbook for Project Evaluation*, Washington DC: NSF.

Nutley, S., A. Powell and H. Davies (2012), 'What counts as good evidence?', Provocation Paper, Research Unit for Research Utilisation (RURU), School of Management, University of St Andrews, UK.

Nuttal, C. (2003), 'The Home Office and random allocation experiments', *Evaluation Review*, **27** (3), 267–90.

Observer (2011), 'From the Lab to The Courtroom. How Psychological Scientists are Having an Impact on the Legal System', 9 November.

O'Connor, T. (2010), 'The Neurology of Crime and Violence', in L. Fenstermacher, *Protecting the Homeland from International and Domestic Terrorism Threats: Current Multi-disciplinary Perspectives on Root Causes, the Role of Ideology, and Programs for Counter-radicalization and Disengagement*, White Paper, pp.117–22 (http://www.start.umd.edu/sites/default/files/files/publications/U_Counter_Terrorism_White_Paper_Final_January_2010.pdf, accessed 29 November 2015).

Oderkerk, A. (2014), 'The Need for a Methodological Framework for Comparative Legal Research: Sense and Nonsense of "Methodological Pluralism" in Comparative Law', Centre for the Study of European Contract Law Working Paper Series No. 2014-04 Amsterdam Law School Research Paper No. 2014-31.

Office of Public Services Reform (2003), *Inspecting for improvement, Developing a customer focused approach*, London: HMSO.

O'Flynn, J. (2007), 'From New Public Management to Public Value: Paradigmatic Change and Managerial Implications', *The Australian Journal of Public Administration*, **66** (3), 353–66.

Ogloff, J. (2000), 'Two steps forward and one step backward: The law and psychology movement(s) in the 20th century', *Law and Human Behavior*, **24** (4), 457–83.

Ogloff, J. (2011), 'A Century of Psychology and Law', in P. R. Martin, F. M. Cheung, M. Kyrios, L. Littlefield, M. Knowles, J. Bruce Overmier and J. M. Prieto (eds), *IAAP Handbook of Applied Psychology*, Oxford: Wiley-Blackwell, Chapter 15.

O'Neill, M. (2015), 'Vendor Voice: Legal professionals must understand how fast-changing IoT can impact e-discovery', *Law Technology News*, 14 January.

Onwuegbuzie, A. and N. L. Leech (2007), 'A call for qualitative power analysis', *Quality and Quantity*, **41**, 105–121.

Onwuegbuzie, A., N. L. Leech and K. M. T. Collins (2012), 'Qualitative Analysis Techniques for the Review of the Literature', *The Qualitative Report*, **17**, 1–28.

Ooyen-Houben, M. van, B. Bieleman and D. Korf (2014), *Coffeeshops, toeristen en lokale markt Evaluatie van het Besloten club- en het Ingezetenencriterium voor coffeeshops*, Cahier, The Hague: WODC.

Ooyen-Houben, M. Van, B. Bieleman, D. J. Korf, A. Benschop, M. van Giessen, R. van der Nijkamp, J. M. Snippe and M. Wouters (2013), *Het Besloten club- en het Ingezetenencriterium voor coffeeshops. Evaluatie van de implementatie en de uitkomsten in de periode mei-november 2012*, Cahier, The Hague: WODC.

Ort, C., A. van Nuijs, J-D. Berset, L. Bijlsma, S. Castiglioni, A. Covaci, P. de Voogt, E. Emke, D. Fatta-Kassinos, P. Griffiths, F. Hernandez, I. Gonzalez-Marino, R. Grabic, B. Kasprzyk-Hordem, N. Mastroianni, A. Meierjohann, T. Nefau, M. Ostman, Y. Pico, I. Racamonde, M. Reid, J. Slobodnik, S. Terzic, N. Thomaidis and K. Thomas (2014), 'Spatial differences and temporal changes in illicit drug use in Europe quantified by wastewater analysis', *Addiction*, **109** (8), 1338–52.

Orücü, A. (2012), 'Methodology of comparative law', in J. Smits (ed.), *Elgar Encyclopedia of Comparative Law*, Cheltenham: Edward Elgar, pp. 560–77.

OSCE/ODIHR (2011), Republic of Belarus Presidential Election 19 December 2010, OSCE/ODIHR Election Observation Mission Final Report, Warsaw: 19 February 2011, http://www.osce.org/odihr/elections/75713, accessed 25 June 2015.

Ostrom, E. (2010), 'Beyond Markets and States: Polycentric Governance of Complex Economic Systems', *American Economic Review*, **100** (June), 1–33.

Palenberg, M. (2011), 'Tools and Methods for Evaluating the Efficiency of Development Interventions', BMZ Evaluation Division: Evaluation Working Papers, Bonn.

Palmer, V. (2004), 'From Lerotholi to Lando: Some examples of comparative law methodology', *Global Jurist Frontiers*, **4** (1), 1–31.

Pape, S. (2011), *Warnings and Product Liability. Lessons learned from cognitive psychology and ergonomics*, Ph.D., Erasmus University Rotterdam, The Hague: Eleven.

Parmentier, S. and J. Van Houtte (2007), 'Law, Justice And Social Change in the 21st Century: The Case Of Belgium', King Baudouin Foundation Brussels, Brussels.

Pawson, R. (2002), 'Does Megan's Law Work? A Theory-Driven Systematic Review', ESRC UK Centre for Evidence Based Policy and Practice: Working Paper 8: Queen Mary University of London, London.

Pawson, R. (2002a), 'Evidence-based policy: The promise of realist synthesis', *Evaluation*, **8** (3), 340–58.

Pawson, R. (2002b), 'Evidence and Policy and Naming and Shaming', *Policy Studies*, **23** (3–4), 211–30.
Pawson, R. (2006), *Evidence-based Policy: A Realist Perspective*, London: Sage.
Pawson, R. (2013), *The Science of Evaluation*, London: Sage.
Pawson, R., T. Greenhalgh, G. Harvey and K. Walshe (2004), 'Realist synthesis: an introduction', ESRC Research Methods Program Working Paper, University of Manchester.
Pawson, R. and N. Tilley (1997), *Realist Evaluation*, London: Sage.
Perry, A., D. Weisburd and C. Hewitt (2010), 'Are criminologists describing randomized controlled trials in ways that allow us to assess them? Findings from a sample of crime and justice trials', *Journal of Experimental Criminology*, **6**, 245–62.
Perry, J. E., I. Moore, B. Barry, E. Wright Clayton and A. Carrico (2009), 'The Ethical Health Lawyer: An Empirical Assessment of Moral Decision Making', *Journal of Law, Medicine and Ethics*, **37**, 461–75.
Peterson, G. (1998), 'The Scientific Status of Theology: Imre Lakatos, Method and Demarcation', *Perspectives on Science and Christian Faith*, **50** (March), 22–31.
Petrila, J. (2009), 'Finding common ground between scientific psychology and the law', in J. L. Skeem, K. S. Douglas and S. O. Lilienfeld (eds), *Psychological Science in the Courtroom. Consensus and Controversy*, London: Guilford Press, pp. 387–408.
Petrosino, A., C. Petrosino and J. Buehler (2003), 'Systematic Review of the Randomized Experimental Evidence Scared Straight and Other Juvenile Awareness Programs for Preventing Juvenile Delinquency: A Systematic Review of the Randomized Experimental Evidence', *The ANNALS of the American Academy of Political and Social Science*, **589**, 41–62.
Petrosino, A., C. Turpin-Petrosino, M. Hollis-Peel and J. Lavenberg (2013), 'Scared straight and other juvenile awareness programs for preventing juvenile delinquency: a systematic review', Campbell Collaboration, Oslo: Campbell Collaboration.
Petticrew, M. and H. Roberts (2006), *Systematic Reviews in the Social Sciences: A Practical Guide*, Malden: Blackwell Publishing.
Pirie, F. (2013), *The Anthropology of Law*, Oxford: Oxford University Press.
Plakhotnik, M. and T. Rocco (2009), 'Four components of a manuscript reporting qualitative empirical studies: A brief overview', in M. Plakhotnik, S. M. Nielsen and D. M. Pane (eds), *Proceedings of the Eighth Annual College of Education and GSN Research Conference*, Miami: Florida International University, pp. 105–111.

Poot, de C. and A. Sonnenschein (2011), *Jihadi terrorism in the Netherlands. A description based on closed criminal investigations*, The Hague: WODC & Boom Juridische Uitgevers.

Popper, K. R. (1963), *Conjectures and Refutations*, London: Routledge.

Popper, K. R. (1972), *Objective Knowledge: An Evolutionary Approach*, Oxford: Oxford University Press.

Popper, K. R. (1935; 2007), *Logik der Forschung*, Berlin: Akademie Verlag.

Posner, E. (2006), 'Contract theory', in M. Golding and W. Edmund, *The Blackwell Guide to Philosophy of Law and Legal Theory*, Malden: Blackwell, pp. 138–48.

Posner, E. and M. de Figueiredo (2004), 'Is the International Court of Justice Biased?', The University of Chicago Law & Economics, Olin Working Paper No. 234, http://ssrn.com/abstract=642581, accessed 4 July 2015.

Posner, R. (1995), 'The Sociology of the Sociology of Law: A View from Economics', *European Journal of Law and Economics*, **2**, 265–84.

Pound, R. (1910), 'Law in Books and Law in Action', *American Law Review*, **44** (12), 12–36.

Pound, R. (1911), 'The Scope and Purpose of Sociological Jurisprudence. I. Schools of Jurists and Methods of Jurisprudence', *Harvard Law Review*, **24** (8), 591–619.

Pound, R. (1911), 'The Scope and Purpose of Sociological Jurisprudence' [Continued], *Harvard Law Review*, **25** (2), 140–68.

Pound, R. (1942), *Social Control Through Law*, New Haven: Yale University Press.

Power, M. (1999), *The Audit Society. Rituals of Verification*, Oxford: Oxford University Press.

Quintanilla, V. (2012), 'Judicial Mindsets: The Social Psychology of Implicit Theories and the Law', *Nebraska Law Review*, **90**, 611–46.

Ragin, C. (2008), 'What is Qualitative Comparative Analysis (QCA)?', Department of Sociology and Department of Political Science, University of Arizona, Tucson.

Raine, A. (2013), *The Anatomy of Violence. The Biological Roots of Crime*, New York: Pantheon Books.

Ramsey, S. and R. Kelly (2006), 'Assessing social science studies: eleven tips for judges and lawyers', *Family Law Quarterly*, **40** (3), 367–80.

Raub, W. and J. Weesie (1991), 'The management of matches: decentralized mechanisms for cooperative relations with applications to organizations and households', ISCORE paper, Faculty of Social Sciences, Utrecht University.

Raub, W., V. Buskens and M. van Assen (2011), 'Micro-Macro Links

and Microfoundations in Sociology', *The Journal of Mathematical Sociology*, **35**, 1–3, 1–25.
Raz, J. (1979), *The Authority of Law*, Oxford: Oxford University Press.
Reason, P. and H. Bradbury (2001), 'Introduction: Inquiry and participation in search of a world worthy of human aspiration', in P. Reason and H. Bradbury (eds), *Handbook of Action Research: Participative Inquiry and Practice*, London: Sage, pp. 1–14.
Reeves, S., M. Albert, A. Kuper and B. D. Hodges (2008), 'Why use theories in qualitative research?', *BMJ*, **14**, 337–43.
Reimann, M. (2002), 'The Progress and Failure of Comparative Law in the Second Half of the Twentieth Century', *American Journal of Comparative Law*, **50**, (4), 671–700.
Remler, D. and G. Van Ryzin (2011), *Research Methods in Practice: Strategies for Description and Causation*, London: Sage.
Rijmenam, M. van (2015), 'How big data can improve the practice of law', https://datafloq.com/read/how-big-data-can-improve-the-practice-of-law/158, accessed 8 July 2015.
Ringrose, J., R. Gill, S. Livingstone and L. Harvey (2012), 'A qualitative study of children, young people and "sexting"', Institute of Education, London University and NSPCC.
Robbennolt, J. (2002), 'Evaluating Empirical Research Methods: Using Empirical Research in Law and Policy', 81 *Nebraska Law Review*, **81** (2), 777–804.
Rogers, E. (1983), *Diffusion of Innovations*, (1995; 2003), New York: Free Press.
Rogers, E. (1991), 'Rise of the classical diffusion model', *Current Contents*, **28**, 16.
Rooks, G., W. Raub, R. Selten and F. Tazelaar (2000), 'How Inter-firm Co-operation Depends on Social Embeddedness: A Vignette Study', *Acta Sociologica*, **43**, 2, 123–37.
Rossi, P. (1987), 'The Iron Law of Evaluation and Other Metallic Rules', *Research in Social Problems and Public Policy*, **4**, 3–20.
Rossi, P. and H. Freeman (1993), *Evaluation: A Systematic Approach*, London: Sage.
Rossi, P., M. Lipsey and H. Freeman (2003), *Evaluation: A Systematic Approach*, San Francisco: Sage.
Rossum, W. van (2010), 'Vier reflecties op empirisch onderzoek naar rechterlijke oordeelsvorming', *Nederlands Juristenblad*, **38**, 2467–71.
Rowe, G. and L. Frewer (2000), 'Public Participation Methods: A Framework for Evaluation', *Science, Technology and Human Values*, **25** (1), 3–29.
Ruiter, S. De, J. Tolsma, M. de Hoon, H. Elffers and P. van der Laan (2011),

De burger als rechter, een onderzoek naar geprefereerde sancties voor misdrijven in Nederland, The Hague/Amsterdam: WODC and NSCR.

Ryan, B. and N. Gross (1943), 'The diffusion of hybrid seed corn in two Iowa communities', *Rural Sociology*, **8** (1), 15–24.

Sageman, M. (2004), *Understanding Terror Networks*, Philadelphia: University of Pennsylvania Press.

Sandelowski, M. (2000), 'Combining Qualitative and Quantitative Sampling, Data Collection, and Analysis Techniques in Mixed-Method Studies', *Research in Nursing & Health*, **23**, 246–55.

Saunders, M. (2012), 'The use and usability of evaluation outputs: A social practice approach', *Evaluation*, **18** (4), 421–36.

Schauer, F. (2013), 'Legal Realism Untamed', *Texas Law Review*, **91**, 749–80.

Schlegel, J. (1995), *American Legal Realism and Empirical Social Science*, Chapel Hill: University of North Carolina Press.

Schluchter, W. (2003), 'The sociology of law as an empirical theory of validity', *European Sociological Review*, **19** (5), 537–49.

Schmeets, H. (2010), 'Increasing Response Rates and the Consequences in the Dutch Parliamentary Election Study 2006', *Field Methods*, **22** (4), 391–412.

Schmeets, H. (2011), 'Analysing observer report forms: an overview', in H. Schmeets (ed.), *International Election Observation and Assessment of Elections*, The Hague: Statistics Netherlands, pp. 142–63.

Schmeets, H. and M. Van den Brakel (2015), 'Selectiviteit van de respons in het Nationaal Kiezersonderzoek 2006–2012', in H. Schmeets (ed.), *Nationaal Kiezersonderzoek 2006–2012*, The Hague/Heerlen: CBS, pp. 40–50.

Schulte Nordholt, E. (2014), 'Introduction to the Dutch Census 2011', in E. Schulte Nordholt, *Dutch Census 2011, Analysis and Methodology*, The Hague: Statistics Netherlands, pp. 7–18.

Schutt, R. K. (2009), *Investigating the Social World. The Process and Practice of Research*, Los Angeles: Pine Forge Press.

Schuyt, C. (2014), 'Als je merkt dat niemand het merkt. Over fraude in de wetenschap', *Justitiële Verkenningen*, **40** (3), 73–88.

Schwarcz, S. (2002), 'Private Ordering', *North Western University Law Review*, **97** (1), 319–50.

Schwartz, R. and J. Mayne (eds) (2005), *Quality Matters: Seeking Confidence in Evaluating, Auditing And Performance Reporting*, New Brunswick: Transaction Publishers.

Scriven, M. (1976), 'Maximizing the power of causal investigations: the modus operandi method', in G. Glass (ed.), *Evaluation Studies Review Annual 1*, Beverly Hills: Sage, pp. 119–39.

Scriven, M. (1996), 'The theory behind practical evaluation', *Evaluation*, **2** (4), 393–404.

Scriven, M. (2008), 'Summative Evaluation of RCT Methodology: An Alternative Approach to Causal Research', *Journal of Multidisciplinary Evaluation*, **5** (9), 11–24.

Searle, J. (1964), 'How to Derive "Ought" from "Is"', *Philosophical Review*, **73**, 43–58.

Segal, L., R. Sara Opie and K. Dalziel (2012), 'Theory! The Missing Link in Understanding the Performance of Neonate/Infant Home-Visiting Programs to Prevent Child Maltreatment: A Systematic Review', *The Milbank Quarterly*, **90** (1), 47–106.

Shadish, W., T. D. Cook and D. Campbell (2002), *Experimental and quasi-experimental designs for generalized causal inference*, Boston: Houghton Mifflin Company.

Shadoan, G. (1968), 'Formation of contracts: a study of the common core of legal systems (by Rudolph B Schlesinger)', *Catholic University Law Review*, **18** (2), 263–8.

Shavell, S. (2002), 'Law versus morality as regulators of conduct', *American Law and Economics Review*, **4** (2), 227–57.

Shepherd, J. (2011), 'Measuring maximizing judges: empirical legal studies, public choice theory, and judicial behavior', *University of Illinois Law Review*, **5**, 104–14.

Sherman, L. W. (2010), 'An introduction to experimental criminology', in A. Piquero and D. Weisburd (eds), *Handbook of quantitative criminology*, New York: Springer, pp. 399–436.

Sherman, L. W. and R. A. Berk (1984), 'The specific deterrent effects of arrest for domestic assault', *American Sociological Review*, **49** (2), 261–72.

Sherman, L., D. Gottfredson, D. MacKenzie, J. Eck, P. Reuter and S. Bushway (eds) (1997), *Preventing crime: what works, what doesn't, what's promising?*, Washington DC: National Institute of Justice.

Sherman, L., J. Schmidt, D. Rogan, D. Smith, P. Gartin, E. Cohn, D. Collins and A. Bacich (1992), 'The variable effects of arrest on criminal careers: The Milwaukee Domestic Violence Experiment', *Journal of Criminal Law and Criminology*, **83** (1), 137–69.

Shulhal, J. and Cousins, J. (1997), 'Evaluation Use: Theory, Research, and Practice Since 1986', *American Journal of Evaluation*, **18** (2), 195–208.

Silke, A. (1998), 'Cheshire-cat logic: The recurring theme of terrorist abnormality in psychological research', *Psychology, Crime & Law*, **1** (4), 51–69.

Silverstein, G. (2009), *Law's Allure: How Law Shapes, Constrains, Saves, and Kills Politics*, New York: Cambridge University Press.

Simi, P., B. Bubolz, H. McNeel, K. Sporer and S. Windisch (2014), 'Trauma as a Precursor to Violent Extremism. How non-ideological factors can influence joining an extremist group', Research Brief, National Consortium for the Study of Terrorism and responses to terrorism (START), pp. 1–2.

Simmons, B. and A. Breidenbach (2011), 'The Empirical Turn in International Economic Law', *Minnesota Journal of International Law*, **20**, 198–222.

Singer, E. (2001), 'The use of incentives to reduce nonresponse in household surveys', in R. Groves et al, *Survey Nonresponse*, New York: John Wiley and Sons, pp. 163–77.

Sirleaf, M. (2014), 'The Truth About Truth Commissions: Why They Do Not Function Optimally In Postconflict Societies', *Cardozo Law Review*, **35**, 2263–347.

Smits, J. (2009a), *Omstreden rechtswetenschap*, The Hague: Boom Juridische Uitgeverij.

Smits, J. (2009b), Redefining Normative Legal Science: Towards an Argumentative Discipline, in F. Coomans, F. Gruenfeld and M. T. Kamminga (eds), *Methods of Human Rights Research*, Maastricht: Intersentia, pp. 45–58.

Smits, J. (2010), 'Private law 2.0. On the role of private actors in a post-national society', Inaugural lecture, Maastricht-HiiL Chair on the Internationalisation of Law, 30 November.

Smits, J. (2011), 'The Right to Change Your Mind? Rethinking the Usefulness of Mandatory Rights of Withdrawal in Consumer Contract Law', *Penn State International Law Review*, **29**, 671–84.

Smits, J. (2012), *The Mind and Method of the Legal Academic*, Cheltenham: Edward Elgar.

Smits, J. (2014), 'Law and Interdisciplinarity: On the Inevitable Normativity of Legal Studies', *Critical analysis of Law*, **1** (1), 75–86.

Snilstveit, B., S. Oliver and M. Vojtkova (2012), 'Narrative approaches to systematic review and synthesis of evidence for international development policy and practice', *Journal of Development Effectiveness*, **4** (3), 409–429.

Snow, C. P. (1959), *The Two Cultures*, London: Cambridge University Press.

Spencer, L., J. Ritchie and W. O'Connor (2003), 'Practices, Principles and Processes, in J. Ritchie and J. Lewis (eds), *Qualitative Research Practice. A Guide for Social Science Students and Researchers*, London, Sage: pp. 199–219.

Statistics Canada (2002), *Assurance Framework*, Ottawa: Statistics Canada.

Stern, E., N. Stame, J. Mayne, K. Forss, R. Davies and B. Befani (2012), *Broadening the Range of designs and Methods for Impact Evaluations*, Report of a study commissioned by the Department for International Development, Working Paper 38, London: DEFid.

Stevenson, D. and N. Wagoner (2014), 'Bargaining in the Shadow of Big Data', http://ssrn.com/abstract=2325137, accessed 5 July 2015.

Stewart, R., C. van Rooyen, K. Dickson and T. de Wet (2010), *What is the impact of microfinance on poor people? A systematic review of evidence from Sub-Saharan Africa*, London: EPPI.

Stewart R., C. van Rooyen, M. Korth, A. Chereni, N. Rebelo Da Silva and T. de Wet (2012), *Do micro-credit, micro-savings and micro-leasing serve as effective financial inclusion interventions enabling poor people, and especially women, to engage in meaningful economic opportunities in low- and middle-income countries – A systematic review of the evidence*, London: EPPI.

Stoop, I. (2005), *The hunt for the last respondent: Nonresponse in sample surveys*, The Netherlands Institute for Social Research/SCP, Den Haag: SCP.

Stoop, I. (2014), 'Representing the populations: what general social surveys can learn from surveys among specific groups', in R. Tourangeau (eds), *Hard-to-Survey Populations*, Cambridge: Cambridge University Press, pp. 225–44.

Strauss, A. and J. Corbin (1990), *Basics of Qualitative Research: Grounded Theory Procedures and Techniques*, Newbury Park: Sage.

Strawson, G. (2011), 'Thinking, Fast and Slow by Daniel Kahneman – review', *The Guardian*, 13 December.

Strevens, M. (2006), 'Scientific Explanation', in D. M. Borchert (ed.), *Encyclopedia of Philosophy*, 2nd edn, Detroit: Macmillan Reference, pp. 1–25.

Stuphorn, V. (2005), 'Neuroeconomics: The Shadow of the Future', *Current Biology*, **15** (7), 247–49.

Suchman, M. (2006), 'Empirical Legal Studies: Sociology of Law, or Something ELS Entirely?', *Amici, Newsletter of the Sociology of Law Section of the American Sociological Association*, **13** (1), 1–4.

Suchman, M. and E. Mertz (2010), 'Toward a New Legal Empiricism: empirical legal studies and new Legal Realism', *Annual Review of Law and Social Science*, **6**, 555–793.

Sunstein, C. (2013), 'Empirically Informed Regulation', Harvard Law School, Public Law and Legal Theory Working Paper Series Paper No. 13-03.

Susskind, R. (2008), *The End of Lawyers? Rethinking the Nature of Legal Services*, Oxford: Oxford University Press.

Susskind, R. (2013), *Tomorrow's Lawyers. An Introduction To Your Future*, Oxford: Oxford University Press.

Swaddle, K. and A. Health (1989), 'Official and reported turnout in British General Election of 1987', *British Journal of Political Science*, **19** (4), 527–41.

Swedberg, R. (2000), *Principles of Economic Sociology*, Princeton: Princeton University Press.

Tamanaha, B. (1997), *Realistic Socio-Legal Theory: Pragmatism and a Social Theory of Law*, Oxford: Oxford University Press.

Tamanaha, B. (2008), 'Understanding Legal Realism', Legal Studies Research Paper Series Paper #08-0133, St John's University School of Law.

Tashakkori, A. and C. Teddlie (2003), *Mixed Methodology: Combining Qualitative and Quantitative Approaches*, Thousand Oaks: Sage.

Taylor-Powell, E. and M. Renner (2003), 'Analyzing Qualitative Data', *Program Development and Evaluation*, G3658-12, 1–10.

Te Grotenhuis, M. and T. Van de Weegen (2011), *Statistical Tools. An Overview of Common Applications in Social Sciences*, Assen: Van Gorcum.

Teubner, G. (1987), 'Juridification. Concepts, aspects, limits, solutions', in G. Teubner (ed.), *Juridification of social spheres. A comparative analysis in the areas of labor, corporate, antitrust and social welfare law*, Berlin/New York: Walter de Gruyter, pp. 18–19.

Thibaut, J. and L. Walker (1975), *Procedural Justice*, Hillsdale: Erlbaum.

Thiel, S. van (2010), *Bestuurskundig onderzoek. Een methodologische inleiding*, Busse: Coutinho.

Thiem, A. (2014), 'Navigating the complexities of qualitative comparative analysis: case numbers, necessity relations, and model ambiguities', *Evaluation Review*, **38** (6), 487–513.

Thompson, V. and M. Applebaum, with James E. Allen (1974), *Population Policy Acceptance: Psychological Determinants*, Chapel Hill: Carolina Population Center.

Tijssen, H. (2009), *De juridische dissertatie onder de loep. De verantwoording van methodologische keuzes in juridische dissertaties*, Tilburg/The Hague: Boom Juridische Uitgeverij.

Timasheff, N. (1937), 'What is "Sociology of Law"?', *American Journal of Sociology*, **43**, 225–35.

Toby, J. (1957), 'Social Disorganization and Stake in Conformity: Complementary Factors in the Predatory Behavior of Hoodlums', *Journal of Criminal Law, Criminology and Police Science*, **48**, 12–17.

Tollenaar, N., A. M. van der Laan and P. G. M. van der Heijden (2014), 'Effectiveness of a prolonged incarceration and rehabilitation measure for high-frequency offenders', *Journal of Experimental Criminology*, **10**, 29–58.

Tor, A. (2011), 'Advances in the behavioral analysis of law: markets, institutions, and contracts', *Law and Contemporary Problems*, **74** (Spring), i–iv.

Traugott, M. and J. Katosh (1979), 'Response validity in surveys of voting behaviour', *Public Opinion Quarterly*, **43** (3), 359–77.

Travers, M. (2001), 'Sociology of Law in Britain', *The American Sociologist*, **32** (2), 26–40.

Trochim, W. and J. Donnelly (2007), *The Research Methods Knowledge Base*, http://www.socialresearchmethods.net/kb/resques.php, accessed 5 July 2015.

Tugendhat, T. and L. Crof (2013), 'The Fog of Law. An introduction to the legal erosion of British fighting power', Report, Policy Exchange.

Ultee, W. (1976), 'De theorie en methodologie van de problemen, toe-gelicht aan de hand van de theoretische problemen van de sociologie, *Mens en Maatschappij*, **48** (1), 1–23.

Ultee, W. (1977), *Groei van kennis en stagnatie in de sociologie. Een aantal regels van de methode en een kritische doorlichting van enkele sociologische tradities*, Ph.D. thesis, University of Utrecht, Utrecht.

Ultee, W. (2001), 'Problem selection in the social sciences: methodology', in N. Smelser and P. Baltes (eds), *International Encyclopaedia of the Social and Behavioural Sciences*, 18, Amsterdam: Elsevier, pp. 12110–17.

Underhill Moore, W. and C. Callahan (1943), 'Law and Learning Theory: A Study in Legal Control', *The Yale Law Journal*, **53** (1), 1–136.

Underhill Moore, W. and T. Hope (1929), 'An institutional approach to the law of commercial banking', *Yale Law Journal*, **38** (6), 703–719.

UN Global Pulse (2012), *Big Data for Development: Challenges and Opportunities*, White Paper, New York: United Nations.

US GAO (1986), *Teenage pregnancy: 500,000 births a year but few tested programs*, Washington, DC: GAO.

Vaessen, J., A. Rivas, M. Duvendack, R. Palmer Jones, F. Leeuw, G. van Gils, R. Lukach, N. Holvoet, J. Bastiaensen, J. C. Hombrados and H. Waddington (2014), *The Effects of Microcredit on Women's Control over Household Spending in Developing Countries: A Systematic Review and Meta-analysis*, Campbell Systematic Reviews, Oslo.

Vanberg, G. (2008), 'Establishing and maintaining judicial independence', in K. Whittington, R. Kelemen and G. Caldeira (eds), *The Oxford Handbook of Law and Politics*, Oxford: Oxford University Press, pp. 99–118.

Vanderweele, T. and N. Staudt (2011), 'Causal diagrams for empirical legal research: a methodology for identifying causation, avoiding bias and interpreting results', *Law, Probability and Risk*, **10**, 329–54.

Vaus, D. de (2001), *Research Design in Social Research*, London: Sage.

Velthoven, B. van and C. Klein Haarhuis (2010), *Geschilbeslechtingsdelta 2009. Over verloop en afloop van (potentieel) juridische problemen van burgers*, The Hague: Boom Juridische Uitgeverij.

Venhaus, J. (2010), 'Why Youth Join al-Qaeda', Washington DC: United States Institute of Peace.

Verbruggen, P. (2014), 'Regulatory governance by contract: the rise of regulatory standards in commercial contracts', *Recht der Werkelijkheid*, **28** (3), 79–100.

Victoroff, J. (2005), 'The Mind of the Terrorist. A Review and Critique of Psychological Approaches', *Journal of Conflict Resolution*, **49**, 3–42.

Voogt, R. (2004), 'I am not interested: nonresponse bias, response bias and stimulus effects in election research', Ph.D. thesis, Amsterdam: University of Amsterdam.

Vries, R. de and B. Gordijn (2009), 'Empirical Ethics and its Alleged Meta-Ethical Fallacies', *Bioethics*, **23**, 193–201.

Waddington, H., H. White, B. Snilstveit, J. G. Hombrados, M. Vojtkova, P. Davies, A. Bhavsar, J. Eyers, T. P. Koehlmoos, M. Petticrew, J. C. Valentine and P. Tugwell (2012), 'How to do a good systematic review of effects in international development: a tool kit', *Journal of Development Effectiveness*, **4** (3), 359–87.

Walle, S. van de and G. Van Ryzin (2011), 'The Order of Questions in a Survey on Citizen Satisfaction with Public Services: Lessons from a Split-ballot Experiment', *Public Administration*, **89** (4), 1436–50.

Watkins, J. (1959), 'Historical explanation in the social sciences', in P. Gardiner (ed.), *Theories of History*, Glencoe: The Free Press, pp. 503–514.

Weber, I. and K. Mayer (2011), 'Designing effective contracts: exploring the influence of framing and expectations', *Academy of Management Review*, **36** (1), 53–75.

Weber, M. (1985; 1904), 'Die "Objektivität" sozialwissenschaftlicher und sozialpolitischer Erkenntnis', in Max Weber (Hrsg.), *Gesammelte Aufsätze zur Wissenschaftslehre*, Tübingen: J.C.B. Mohr, pp. 146–214.

Webley, T. (2010), 'Qualitative approaches to empirical legal research', in P. Cane and H. Kritzer (eds), *The Oxford Handbook of Empirical Legal Research*, Oxford: Oxford University Press, pp. 926–51.

Weenink, A. (2015), 'Behavioral Problems and Disorders among Radicals in Police Files', *Perspectives on Terrorism*, **9** (2), 17–33.

Weisberg, D., F. Keil, J. Goodstein, E. Rawson and J. Gray (2008), 'The seductive allure of neuroscience explanations', *Journal of Cognitive Neuroscience*, **20**, 470–77.

Weisburd, D. (2003), 'Ethical Practice and Evaluation of Interventions

in Crime and Justice: The Moral Imperative for Randomized Trials', *Evaluation Review*, **27** (3), 336–54.
Weisburd, D., C. M. Lum and A. Petrosino (2001), 'Does research design affect study outcomes in criminal justice?', *The Annals of the American Academy of Political and Social Science*, **578**, 50–70.
Weiss, C. H. (1997), 'Theory-based evaluation: Past, present, and future', *New Directions for Evaluation*, 41–55.
Wells, G., A. Memon and S. Penrod (2006), 'Eyewitness Evidence Improving Its Probative Value', *Psychological Science in the Public Interest*, **7** (2), 45–75.
Welsh, B. C., M. E. Peel, D. P. Farrington, H. Elffers and A. A. Brag (2011), 'Research design influence on study outcomes in crime and justice: a partial replication with public area surveillance', *Journal of Experimental Criminology*, **7**, 183–98.
Westerman, P. (2011), 'Open or autonomous? The debate on legal methodology as a reflection of the debate on law', in M. van Hoecke (ed.), *Methodologies of Legal Research*, Oxford: Hart Publishing, pp. 87–108.
Wetzels, W., H. Schmeets, J. van den Brakel and R. Feskens (2008), 'The Impact of Prepaid Incentives in Face-to-Face Surveys: A Large-Scale Experiment with Postage Stamps', *International Journal of Public Opinion Research*, **20** (4), 507–16.
Wheeler, S. (2008), 'Socio-legal studies', in P. Cane and J. Conaghan, *The New Oxford Companion to Law*, Oxford: Oxford University Press.
Wheeler, S. (2010), 'Contracts and corporations', in P. Cane and H. Kritzer (eds), *Oxford Handbook of Empirical Legal Research*, Oxford: Oxford University Press, pp. 125–151.
Wheeler, S., B. Cartwright, R. Kagan and L. Friedman (1987), 'Do the haves come out ahead? Winning and losing in State Supreme Courts, 1870–1970', *Law and Society Review*, **21**, 403–445.
Whetten, D. (1989), 'What Constitutes a Theoretical Contribution?', *Academy of Management Review*, **14** (4), 490–95.
White, G. (1972), 'From Sociological Jurisprudence to Realism: Jurisprudence and Social Change in Early Twentieth-Century America', *Virginia Law Review*, **58** (6), 999–1028.
White, H. (2014), 'Ten things that can go wrong with randomised controlled trials', http://blogs.3ieimpact.org/ten-things-that-can-go-wrong-with-randomised-controlled-trials/, accessed 9 August 2015.
White, P. (2010), *Developing Research Questions: A Guide for Social Scientists*, Houndmills: Palgrave Macmillan.
Whittington, K., R. Kelemen and G. Caldeira (eds) (2008a), *The Oxford Handbook of Law and Politics*, Oxford: Oxford University Press.
Whittington, K., R. Kelemen and G. Caldeira (eds) (2008b), 'The study of

law and politics', in K. Whittington, R. Kelemen and G. Caldeira (eds), *The Oxford Handbook of Law and Politics*, Oxford: Oxford University Press, pp. 3–15.

Wijkhuijs, L., A. M. Galloway, M. H. C. Kromhout, I. C. van der Welle, M. Smit (2011), *Pardon? Evaluatie van de Regeling afwikkeling na-latenschap oude Vreemdelingenwet*, Cahier, The Hague: WODC.

Willemsen, F. and F. Leeuw, 'Big Data, Real World Events and Evaluations', in G. Petersson et al (eds), *Big Data and Evaluation*, New Brunswick: Transaction Publishers (in press).

Willemsen, F., F. Leeuw and H. B. M. Leeuw (2008), 'Toezicht en inspectie in maten en soorten', *Tijdschrift voor Criminologie*, **50**, 96–113.

Williamson, O. (1983), 'Credible Commitments: Using Hostages to Support Exchange', *The American Economic Review*, **73** (4), 519–40.

Williamson, O. (1996), *The Mechanisms of Governance*, Oxford: Oxford University Press.

Williamson, O. (2009), 'Transaction Cost Economics: The Natural Progression', Nobel Prize Lecture, Stockholm, 8 December.

Wilson, L. and A. Scarpa (2012), 'Criminal behavior: the need for an integrative approach that incorporates biological influences', *Journal of Contemporary Criminal Justice*, **28**, 366–81.

Witteveen, W. J. (2013), 'Llewellyn en het rechtsrealisme', *Regelmaat*, **28** (1), 49–58.

World Bank (2014), *Doing Business, Understanding Regulations for Small and Medium-Size Enterprises*, Washington DC: World Bank.

Wortman, P. (1983), 'Evaluation research: a methodological perspective', *Annual Review of Psychology*, **34**, 223–60.

Wubs, H., A. M. Galloway, I. Kulu–Glasgow, N. L. Holvast, M. Smit (2010), *Evaluatie van de naturalisatieceremonie*, Cahier, The Hague: WODC.

Yamamoto, T. (2007), *Tools for parliamentary oversight. A comparative study of 88 national parliaments*, Le Grand-Saconnex, Inter-Parliamentary Union.

Yeager, S. (2008), 'Where Do Research Questions Come from', in K. Yang and G. Miller (eds), *Handbook of Research Methods in Public Administration*, Boca Raton: Auerbach Publications, pp. 54–7.

Yin, R. (2003), *Case Study Research: Design and Methods*, London: Sage.

Zahorsky, R. (2015), 'Future of law includes big data, bigger competition and global jurisdictions', *ABA Journal*, http://www.abajournal.com/mobile/article/future_of_law_includes_big_data_bigger_competition_and_global_jurisdictions, accessed 8 July 2015.

Zweigert, K. and H. Kötz (1998), *An Introduction to Comparative Law*, Oxford: Oxford University Press.

Index